INSIGHT GUIDES
NEW YORK

APA PUBLICATIONS

Part of the Langenscheidt Publishing Group

HOW TO USE THIS BOOK

This book is carefully structured both to convey an understanding of the city and its culture and to guide readers through its attractions and activities:

◆ The Best Of section at the front of the book helps you to prioritize. The first spread contains all the Top Sights, while the Editor's Choice details unique experiences, the best buys or other recommendations.

◆ To understand New York City, you need to know something of its past. The city's history and culture are described in authoritative essays written by

specialists in their fields who have lived in and documented the city for many years.

◆ The Places section details all the attractions worth seeing. The main places of interest are coordinated by number with the maps.

◆ Each chapter includes lists of recommended shops, restaurants, bars and cafés.

◆ Photographs throughout the book are chosen not only to illustrate geography and buildings, but also to convey the moods of the city and the life of its people.

◆ The Travel Tips section includes all the practical information you will need, divided into five key sections: transportation, accommodations, activities (including nightlife, events, tours and sports), and an A–Z of practical tips. Information may be located quickly by using the index on the back cover flap of the book.

◆ A detailed street atlas is included at the back of the book, with all restaurants, bars, cafés and hotels plotted for your convenience.

PLACES AND SIGHTS

Chapters are **color-coded** for ease of use. Each neighborhood has a designated color corresponding to the orientation map on the inside front cover.

A locator map pinpoints the specific area covered in each chapter.

Margin tips provide extra snippets of information, whether it's a practical tip, a whimsical quote, an historical fact or advice on shopping and eating.

A four-color map shows the area covered in the chapter, with the main sights and attractions coordinated by number with the text.

PHOTO FEATURES

Photo features offer visual coverage of major sights or unusual attractions. Where relevant, there is a map showing the location and essential information on opening times, entrance charges, transport and contact details.

SHOPPING AND RESTAURANT LISTINGS

Shopping listings provide details of the best shops in each area. **Restaurant listings** give the establishment's contact details, opening times and price category, followed by a useful review. Bars and cafés are also covered here. The colored dot and grid reference refers to the atlas section at the back of the book.

SHO Shaun Hergatt
40 Broad Street (second floor of The Setai Club)
Tel: 212-809 3993
www.shoshaunhergatt.com
Open: L & D Mon–Fri D only Sat
$$$$ ⑫ [p342, A3]
Fine dining with a seasonally and locally

TRAVEL TIPS

GETTING AROUND

On Arrival

Orientation

Generally, avenues in Manhattan run north to south; streets east to west. North of Houston Street, ...ts are numbered, which ...

Travel Tips provide all the practical knowledge you'll need before and during your trip: how to get there, getting around, where to stay and what to do. The A–Z section is a handy summary of practical information, arranged alphabetically.

Contents

Maps

Inside front cover: New York.
Inside back cover: New York City Subway.

THE BEST OF NEW YORK CITY: TOP ATTRACTIONS

At a glance, everything you can't afford to miss when you visit the Big Apple, from high-energy Times Square and tall, iconic monuments to world-class museums and performance spaces

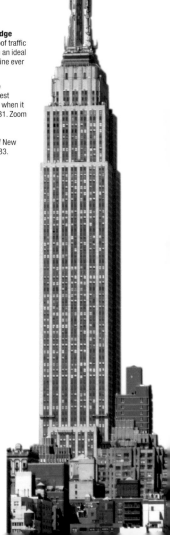

◁ The **Brooklyn Bridge** opened to foot and hoof traffic in 1883 and has been an ideal place to view the skyline ever since. See page 83.

▷ The **Empire State Building** was the tallest structure in the world when it was completed in 1931. Zoom up to the 102nd-floor observation deck for unsurpassed views of New York City. See page 183.

△ **Lincoln Center** is the cultural and intellectual hub of the city. Located on the Upper West Side, it's home to many giants of the performing arts, including the New York City Opera, the New York City Ballet, the American Ballet Theatre, and the Metropolitan Opera. See page 242.

▽ The Hayden Planetarium is just one attraction at the **American Museum of Natural History**. Others include the world's tallest dinosaur, a 34-ton (31,000kg) meteorite, a life-size fiberglass blue whale, and an IMAX theater. Don't even think about doing it all in one visit. See page 246.

◁ If you have time for only one museum, visit the **Metropolitan Museum of Art**, which has a collection of over 2 million pieces, from Native Americans to 21st-century couturiers. See page 224.

▷The **Museum of Modern Art (MoMA)** has a remarkable collection of 20th-century art. All the greats are here, displayed in a beautiful new gallery. The sculpture garden sets Rodin, Picasso, and others amid trees and reflecting pools. See page 173.

▽ If there's a classic image, then it's surely the bright lights and billboards of **Times Square**, the heart of Broadway's theater district. See page 160.

▽ The artists have long been priced out, but **Greenwich Village** still has great allure; there's a neighborhood feel to the area with its old brownstones, one-off stores, Italian bakeries, and small theaters. This is where many Manhattanites would live if they could. See page 131.

▽ In the 1850s, **Central Park** was created to provide workers with a taste of nature. Today it is the green lung of the city. See page 194.

△ The **Statue of Liberty**, which was unveiled in 1886, was a gift to the US from France, a symbol of freedom and democracy after successful revolutions in both countries. See page 90.

THE BEST OF NEW YORK CITY: EDITOR'S CHOICE

The best luxury hotels, riverside walks, unique historic sites, family attractions, and money-saving to help you discover the real New York

BEST HOTELS

The Algonquin An all-time favorite, the literary Algonquin retains an atmosphere of oak-paneled, low-key elegance and charm. See page 172.

The Carlyle On the Upper East Side, the Carlyle is one of the city's most acclaimed luxury hotels. Woody Allen plays at the Café Carlyle when he's in town. See page 315.

The Chelsea Hotel A landmark to urban decadence and the former home of beatnik poets, Warhol drag queens, and punk Sid Vicious. An affordable place for a taste of bohemia. See page 152.

Hotel Gansevoort The first luxury hotel in the Meatpacking District, with a rooftop bar and breathtaking views of the Downtown skyline. See page 309.

The Mercer Hotel In the heart of SoHo, the Mercer attracts a stylish clientele, as does its fashionable restaurant, the Mercer Kitchen. See page 309.

BELOW: lobby of the Hotel Gansevoort, Meatpacking District.

ONLY IN NEW YORK

Stroll and Spend While away the afternoon in NoLita. Uncork some Champagne while getting a pedicure in a chic salon, eat Italian food, and shop in the one-off boutiques: think cute polka dots. See page 121.

Eat and Drink Sip a $10,000 Martini at the Algonquin, or try the "haute barnyard" cuisine downtown at Peasant. See page 172.

Be Merry Join pop stars, celebrities, and jovial shoppers for the annual lighting of the Christmas tree at Rockefeller Center. See page 188.

Sail the Statue of Liberty Climb aboard a Circle Line tour or have brunch on a sleek 1929 sailboat. See page 90.

Moon over Manhattan Take a late elevator to the top of the Empire State Building and watch the moon light up Gotham. See page 183.

Cultivate Irony Mingle with models and banter with the butchers in the trend-setting Meatpacking District. See page 141.

Shop and Skate Take in the galleries, market, and small treasures of Chelsea, then don ice-skates for a spin around the Sky Rink at Chelsea Piers. See page 157.

Dine with Diplomats in the dining room of the United Nations building. See page 203.

Muse over Music Visit the home of jazz legend Louis Armstrong and find out why some called him "Dipper-mouth." See page 275.

Get Sporty Cheer on the Knicks or the Rangers at Madison Square Garden. See page 165.

Get Artsy Take the elevator to the top floor of the Guggenheim and make your way down the spiral ramp, taking in highlights of 20th-century art along the way. See page 216.

Be Bemused and Confused by History Study a lock of George Washington's hair – and his tooth – at Fraunces Tavern Museum. See page 76.

BEST PARKS

The High Line This innovative city park is located on an elevated train track once used to transport meat from the Meatpacking District to Chelsea. See page 142.

Central Park The heart (some say the lungs) of Manhattan, is where residents and visitors alike come to stroll, picnic, play ball, skate or listen to a concert. See page 194.

Prospect Park Lusher, denser, and greener than its Manhattan counterpart, this Brooklyn park occupies 585 acres (234 hectares). See page 269.

Bryant Park This pretty midtown parks offers a welcome break from the hustle and bustle of Times Square and hosts outdoor film screenings in summer and an ice rink in winter. See page 171.

ABOVE: central park.

CLASSIC NEW YORK

21 This former speakeasy is still a haunt of the powerful and the beautiful. See page 192.

The Oak Bar The Plaza Hotel may have gone part-condo, but the Oak Bar lives on. See page 193.

P.J. Clarke's Sinatra preferred the back room, along with Louis Armstrong. Johnny Depp comes now. See page 211.

White Horse Tavern Dylan Thomas drank here. And then he died. See page 138.

ABOVE: St Patrick's Cathedral.

NEW YORK FOR FREE

Culture in the Park The Metropolitan Opera, the New York Philharmonic, and the Public Theater give free performances in Central Park during the summer months. See page 194.

Native American Art is free to see at the George Gustav Heye Center of the National Museum of the American Indian in the US Custom House in Lower Manhattan. See page 75.

The Garment District The Fashion Institute of Technology (Seventh Avenue at 27th St) shows off legendary costumes, textiles, and the work of well-known photographers in its fashion museum. See page 165.

Free Travel Statue of Liberty views are still absolutely free on the Staten Island Ferry (see page 85), while Lower Manhattan has a free bus service known as the Downtown Connection. See page 85.

Free Flowers The Brooklyn Botanic Garden (see page 270) is free to the public on Tuesdays and until noon on Saturdays, also weekdays in the wintertime, while the Queens (see page 274) and Staten Island (see page 279) gardens are free all the year round.

St Patrick's Cathedral Visit one of the most spectacular Catholic churches in the United States. See page 190.

NEW YORK FOR FAMILIES

Children's Museum of Manhattan A kiddy kingdom with inventive interactive exhibits; let them touch everything. See page 237.

Carousels The entire family can ride on New York's carousels. The one in Central Park has 58 hand-carved horses and operates all year round, while the carousels in Bryant and Prospect parks are seasonal. See pages 194, 171, and 269.

Central Park From rowing in the lake and ice-skating on the rinks to swimming in the pool and exploring more than 20 playgrounds, the park is fun for everyone. See page 194.

Sony Wonder Technology Lab Wondering how to entertain those bored pre-teens? Look no more. See page 209.

South Street Seaport Sailing ships and all things nautical, in an outdoor atmosphere where kids can let off steam without embarrassing their parents. See page 82.

Intrepid Sea, Air, & Space Museum Explore an aircraft carrier, view fighter jets, and (in the future) step aboard a space shuttle. See page 171.

Fabulous Food Inexpensive snacks don't come any easier. If you only try one NY specialty, make it Nathan's Famous hot dogs on Coney Island. See page 272.

Children's Museum of the Arts Based in SoHo, this is a successful cross between a museum and a very lively community center. See page 99.

Brooklyn Children's Museum. The oldest kids' museum in the US. See page 272.

Bronx Zoo The largest urban zoo in America. What's stopping you? See page 283.

BEST WALKS

Fifth Avenue Few streets evoke the essence of the city as powerfully as Fifth Avenue, with its iconic Empire State Building, glorious Rockefeller Center, stylish shopping, and elegant St Patrick's Cathedral. See page 190.

Madison Avenue Between 42nd and 57th streets lies the spiritual home of advertising, with a skyline bristling with gleaming glass towers and streets typically jammed with taxis. See page 201.

Times Square New York's 'Crossroads of the World,' swirls with irrepressible energy from the masses of people and the eye-popping neon wattage. See page 160.

Battery Park Esplanade Perfect for a summer's day stroll, this leafy riverside path runs for over a mile, with great views of the Hudson River and the Statue of Liberty. See page 72.

Brooklyn Heights Promenade This elegant walkway has handsome townhouses on one side and views of Manhattan and the East River on the other. See page 266.

BELOW: celebrating the Christmas season at Rockefeller Center began in 1933. The most popular attraction is the Christmas tree, which is spectacularly illuminated from just after Thanksgiving until 12th Night, January 6th.

BEST VIEWS

Empire State Building
The view from the 86th-floor Observatory of this Art Deco landmark is incomparable. See page 183.

Top of the Rock Although not quite as iconic as the Empire

State Building, nonetheless the observation deck on the 70th floor of the Rockefeller Center offers terrific views of Central Park. See page 188.

Brooklyn Bridge For one of the best, and most famous, of all views of the East River and Lower Manhattan. See page 83.

Statue of Liberty The glass-ceilinged observation platform in the pedestal allows great views of New York and the harbor. See page 90.

BEST FESTIVALS AND EVENTS

TriBeCa Film Festival Mingle with the stars and see first-run films on the banks of the Hudson River. Every spring. See page 48.

Ninth Avenue International Food Festival A street fair in May when Ninth Avenue, from 37th Street to 57th Street, is lined with food stalls. See page 170.

Feast of San Gennaro A cheesy but boisterous 10-day festival in September where Little Italy shows off, and the air is heavy with garlic. See page 122.

Next Wave Festival Some of the most innovative sounds around can be heard at the

Brooklyn Academy of Music (BAM). Every fall. This is definitely a hot ticket. See page 269.

St Patrick's Day Watch the wearing o' the green on Fifth Avenue every March. See page 320.

Thanksgiving Day Parade The longest-running show on Broadway, brought to you by Macy's. See page 321.

New York City Marathon Five boroughs, 26.2 miles, tens of thousands of runners, millions of spectators. Beyond inspiring. First Sunday in November. See page 321.

For a more complete list of festivals, see page 319.

BELOW: The Rockettes perform at the opening night of the 2010 Radio City Christmas Spectacular at Radio City Music Hall.

MONEY-SAVING TIPS

Theater Tickets The **TKTS Booth**, at Broadway and 47th Street by Times Square, has discounted seats (25–50 percent off) for that night's performances. It's open Monday through Saturday 3pm to 8pm (2pm opening on Tuesdays) for evening performances, Saturday and Wednesday 10am to 2pm for matinees, and Sunday 11am to 7.30pm for both shows. Near South Street Seaport in Lower Manhattan, another booth at 186 Front Street sells discounted tickets for the following night's shows. That booth is open Monday through Saturday 11am to 6pm and Sundays 11am to 4pm. Arrive early. **Special Passes** A way to save on New York's buses and subways is to buy a **MetroCard** (save between 7–33 percent depending on how much you spend). Available for 30 days, 7 days or per ride. Go to **www.mta.nyc.ny.us**.

CityPass saves if you plan to visit attractions. Buy the pass at the first destination; then you have several days in which to visit five others. You also avoid most ticket lines. Savings of almost 50 percent; plus discounts on meals. Go to **www.citypass.com**. The **New York Pass** is a similar scheme. Go to **www.newyorkpass.com**.

Shopping All visitors can find great bargains at New York's **sample sales**, where designers sell off end-of-season clothes, or smaller sizes. See page 108.

NEW TO EVERYONE

There's a secret that New Yorkers aren't
always quick to reveal: the city can be just as
confounding to locals as visitors; that's one
of the reasons they love it

A red-tailed hawk takes a perch on a park's art installation. A line of preschoolers streams past. They're holding hands and singing a song. Someone politely asks you – you, who has been there all of 48 hours – if the trains are "running express." This is
not necessarily the boisterous, take-no-prisoners New York of the movies and television. A city so big, so iconic – so constantly in flux – is bound to defy expectations. Thomas Wolfe said, "One belongs to New York instantly, one belongs to it as much in five minutes as in five years." It's an accurate description of a city made up of immigrants from Toledo, Tokyo, and everywhere in between. It's also the perfect distillation of

a place where discoveries lie around every corner, even for lifelong residents.

Accept some things early: you won't see all the sites; you won't have time to visit all the museums; you certainly can't eat in even a fraction of the restaurants. The experience of New York is about taking to the streets and

opening up to surprises. You will return home with stories beginning, "You'll never believe what I saw on the corner of..." and "I thought it was going to be so much more..."

If this is your first visit, there's a good chance you'll be back. Discoveries can be addictive, and there's a reason why visitors buy "I NY" t-shirts by the boatload. When you return, you may have more confidence in hailing a cab, but you'll be no less "new" to the city. Just like the rest of us.

PRECEEDING PAGES: pedestrians crossing Fifth Avenue; relaxing in Brooklyn Bridge Park.
LEFT: Hudson Street, Greenwich Village. **ABOVE, FROM LEFT:** Pastis bistro in the Meatpacking District; street sign.

UFC
SILVA VS
FRANKLIN
ONE WAY
RADO
MARQUI
The DROWSY
Chaperone

NEW YORK, NEW YORKERS

New York gave us the phrase "the melting pot,"
and it's more diverse than ever, attracting those who
yearn to fade into the crowd, to see their name in
lights, or simply to find a home of like-minded souls

The first thing that strikes a visitor about New Yorkers is the talk. Well-dressed men and women fearlessly walk through traffic while barking into cell phones. Groups huddle at rooftop bars, joyfully recounting adventures while dining and drinking alfresco. Vendors holler, assuring you their handbags are genuine. Everyone has an opinion, a story to sell. All you have to do is listen.

Stock market and sculpture

In such a fast-moving, densely packed metropolis, there's a loud background to speak over, but more surprising is the range and depth of discourse. Intellectual voracity can be seen on the street at café tables with chessboards, and on the subway in the range of literature being read. You can feel the New Yorkers' lust for fact, knowledge, debate and opinion; you can barely heft it in the sheer weight of the Sunday *New York Times*.

Cerebral and cultural lives here have their rituals, temples, and haunts, like museum and gallery openings. It is not a minority thing hidden away in exclusive speakeasies, where entrance is gained by murmuring a secret password at a sliding door panel; it is the stock market and sculpture, poetry and particle physics – a polyglot landscape of lectures, plays, concerts, libraries, films, and, of course, parties. It is the casual association of great minds: Tom Wolfe stalking Brooklyn streets, Sonny Rollins practicing his sax on the Williamsburg Bridge.

LEFT: a rainy Times Square. **RIGHT:** enjoying a game of chess on the Upper West Side.

Culture and intellect transform the individual, but they also give identity to the mass, to the city as a whole. In his book *The Art of the City: Views and Versions of New York*, Peter Conrad writes, "Every city requires its own myth to justify its presumption of centrality," and he cites annotators of New York from songwriter George M. Cohan to painter Saul Steinberg, whose famous cover for the *New Yorker* was of a world shrinking to the far horizon, away from a great, spreading Manhattan.

Alexander Alland Jr, former chair of anthropology at Columbia University, said, "The intellectual life is why I am a New Yorker. It's why I stay here. I spend my summers in Europe, and

when they ask me if I'm an American, I say, 'No, I'm a New Yorker.' I don't know about everyone else, but for me that's a positive statement."

New York's rise to intellectual prominence did not begin until the 1850s. Through the Colonial era and the early 19th century, New York was at best the third city in the US, behind Boston and Philadelphia, until the publishing industry decamped here. New York had a larger population, and publishers were seeking more

Andy Warhol once said: "When reporters asked the Pope what he liked best about New York, he replied 'Tutti buoni' – everything is good. That's my philosophy exactly."

customers. As seagulls follow great ships, writers, editors, and illustrators came in the publishers' wake.

Meanwhile, at the top of the New York economic scale, captains of commerce and industry began to endow museums and to support individual artists. At the bottom of the scale, each wave of immigrants enriched and diversified the intellectual community. City College, established in 1849, acted as the great pedagogue for those without wealth, and came to be known as "the poor man's Harvard."

URBAN WOODLAND

When Henry Hudson sailed up the river that bears his name, his first mate, Robert Juett, wrote: "We found a land full of great tall oaks, with grass and flowers, as pleasant as ever has been seen." New York still has over 29,000 acres (11,700 hectares) of parks, of which 10,000 acres (4,000 hectares) are in more or less their natural state. Peregrine falcons nest on Midtown skyscraper ledges, and coyotes prowl from Westchester County down into the Bronx.

Frederick Law Olmsted, the architect who laid out Central Park, wrote that "the contemplation of natural scenes… is favorable to the health and vigor of men."

FROM LEFT: the cold winter weather encourages New Yorkers to bundle up; cooling off in the summer sun; residents of Little Italy are proud of their Italian heritage; bicycle deliveries are common in the Meatpacking District.

Immigrants

The German influx of 1848, the Irish flight from famine, migrations of Jews, Italians, Greeks, Chinese, Koreans, and Vietnamese – all brought knowledge and culture to New York, making this American city cosmopolitan. In 1933, the New School for Social Research encouraged that rich resource by founding the University in Exile (now the Graduate Faculty of Political and Social Science) as a graduate school staffed by European scholars who escaped the Nazi regime. The international dynamic continues with the Soviet Jews in Brighton Beach and the West Indians in Queens joined by the Southeast Asians of Queens' Elmhurst district. Nearly 20 percent of the Brooklyn population speaks Spanish at home, while a smaller number of people speak Russian, French or a French Creole, Chinese, Yiddish, Italian, Polish, Hebrew, or Arabic. More than 5,000 people speak Cantonese, Urdu, Bengali, Greek, Korean, and Albanian. There are more Greeks in New York than in any city but Athens, and more Dominicans than in any city but Santo Domingo.

Public schools offer bilingual instruction. In some neighborhoods, traffic signs, advertisements, and subway signs announce in two

New York taxis date from 1907, when John Hertz founded the Yellow Cab Company. He chose this color after reading a report stating that yellow was the easiest color to spot.

or three languages, most often in Spanish or Chinese, the city's unofficial second and third languages. City agencies must also provide information in Russian, Korean, Italian and French Creole. There are at least a dozen non-English newspapers published in the city itself and countless others imported. Driving tests can be taken and banking business done in other languages. Automatic cash machines offer transactions in Spanish, Chinese, and French.

The minority majority

Never in the American mainstream, New York is one of the few minority-majority cities, where the majority are from an ethnic minority. The promise for immigrants in New York is a place of opportunity. Some variation of the American dream still lives on these streets, and

> *Gone are the days of graffiti-covered subway cars and prostitutes loitering in Times Square. Of the 25 largest cities in the US, New York consistently ranks as the safest.*

immigrants come eager to share in it. Once a migrant group gets into a line of work, others follow in the same trade. In recent years Koreans have dominated the grocery business, Chinese have manned the garment industry, and Indians or Pakistanis run newsstands. Greek coffee shops and Latino bodegas have joined the New York landscape, and every nationality turns the wheel of a yellow cab.

The New York mix is defined by immigration, and also by artists. New York's bards date back to at least 1855, when Walt Whitman published *Leaves of Grass*. Singer Lou Reed, photographer Robert Mapplethorpe, novelist Jay McInerney, and filmmakers Woody Allen and Martin Scorsese, have all taken New York as their muse. These days, the works of author Jonathan Safran Foer, singer Alicia Keys, comedian Tina Fey, and many other young luminaries, continue to craft the world's image of the city.

Greenwich Village became an urban version of the artists' colony, a home to creators of all stripes, the place that gave Eugene O'Neill one of his early stages in the 1920s (at the Provincetown Playhouse) and Bob Dylan a bandstand in the 1960s (at Folk City). Miles Uptown, Harlem was home to a black intelligentsia that included the writers Langston Hughes *(see page 256)*, James Weldon Johnson, and James Baldwin, plus the political theorist W.E.B. Du Bois and the photographer James Van Der Zee, whose record of his era appeared decades later in the album *Harlem on My Mind*.

Urban pioneers

When creative people discovered SoHo in the 1970s, it was hard to get a cab to go there. Their presence led to the neighborhood's rebirth, and when it became too expensive for them, they moved to Alphabet City (avenues A, B, C, and D) on the Lower East Side of Manhattan, or across the East River to Greenpoint and Williamsburg, or to a part of Brooklyn called DUMBO, for

Down Under Manhattan Bridge Overpass. Trendy stores, bars, and restaurants followed, rents soared, and the artists scoped out new territories like Red Hook in Brooklyn and Astoria in Queens.

Pop culture and high culture are often indistinguishable. Tom Stoppard and Stephen Sondheim have regular Broadway hits, while a gospel version of *Oedipus at Colonus* sold out at the Brooklyn Academy of Music. Religion is a matter both of passion and of intellectual rigor. There are almost a dozen Roman Catholic colleges in New York City, an Islamic seminary on Queens Boulevard and *shtibels* – houses of study – where Hasidim pursue theology.

News nexus

The intellectual force of New York sends ripples far beyond the city. The principal network news in the United States originates not from the nation's capital but from New York. Two major news magazines, *Time* and *Newsweek*, and two national newspapers, *The New York Times* and the *Wall Street Journal*, are published here, and most of the leading critics of theater, film, art, dance, and music make their pronouncements from Manhattan.

Without any of those publications, important as they are, New York intellectual life would pulse just as vigorously. Outwardly expressed in individual taste and style, it has little to do with celebrity or vogue. The intellectual sweep is an eclectic striving for search and discovery. So many New Yorkers share a biographical tale that has become mythic itself. With variations, the story goes like this:

An able young man or woman feels misunderstood, unappreciated, surrounded by what playwright Eugene O'Neill called "spiritual middle-classers," and yearns to escape from small-town minds, to be among people with a broader vision. Perhaps he yearns to reinvent himself, to shake loose the trappings of his youth. Perhaps

FROM LEFT: everyone in New York is Irish on St Patrick's Day; enjoying the afternoon; taking a break from the bikes in Central Park.

Walk through Central Park in the summer and you're sure to see games of softball, basketball, volleyball, soccer, tennis – even lawn bowling, croquet, and cricket.

the fastness of language and style, craftiness, the mixing of people and crossing of borders, imagination." And cosmopolitan, in every sense, is what the Big Apple is. From the lines of sparkly clubbers and diners in SoHo and the Meatpacking District to the wild costumes in the Greenwich Village Halloween parade, New York is more than just a melting pot, it is a hothouse nursery for fantastic hybrids of talent and expression.

A great book store is a hub of imaginative activity, and in New York the Strand Book Store is arguably the best. In a former clothing store at Broadway and East 12th Street in Manhattan, the Strand carries some 2 million volumes of such variety that on a single table titles might range from *The Sonata Since Beethoven* to *Civil Aircraft of the World*.

Writers Anaïs Nin and Saul Bellow, painter David Hockney and poet/rock singer Patti Smith numbered among the Strand's regular

she has a dream, an aspiration too great or too strange to realize on hometown turf. So they come here. Whether or not dreams are realized, even in part, they come to feel the city has spoiled them for any other place. Despite, or even because of the pressure, the pace, and the grime, they discover a vigorous sense of being alive.

Rich stimulation

"New York draws the cosmopolite, the person who wants to be challenged the most, who needs the most varied and rich stimulation," said a well-known Jungian analyst, Dr James Hillman. "It is the person who is full of possibilities, but who needs New York to draw them out. You come to New York to find the ambience that will evoke your best. You do not necessarily know precisely what that might be, but you come to New York to discover it.

"If there were a god of New York it would be the Greeks' Hermes, the Romans' Mercury. He embodies New York qualities: the quick exchange,

FROM LEFT: the Strand Book Store; a lunchtime job followed by a quick break; New York has great window-shopping.

customers. Smith was on both sides of the counter, as she also worked at the store.

The complete city

So what stitches the fabric of reinvention and the rigors of intellectual life together? What draws the filmmakers, the flower vendors, and the restaurateurs to pack up and move here, and intellectuals to end their contemplations here? Back to Dr Hillman: "New York is the city of rampant creativity, of abundant imagination, whether in advertising or the theater or the stock market. Any syndrome that might characterize another city is found in New York: manic energy, depression and hopelessness, the extreme excitement of the hysteric. Psychologically, New York is the complete city."

New Yorkers *do* talk. They talk loud, and they talk a lot – enough to call it a defining characteristic. But here in New York, they also walk the walk.

FACTS THAT FIT

Biggest: Ahnighito, the biggest meteorite "in captivity," weighs 34 tons (31,000kg) and is on display at the American Museum of Natural History.

Smallest: a Morningside Heights couple claims to own the smallest apartment in the city, a 175-sq-ft (16-sq-meter) studio they bought in 2009 for $150,000.

Longest: after Broadway leaves the city, it becomes the Albany Post Road, and travels all the way to New York's state capital – a distance of 175 miles (282km).

Oldest: the oldest grave in New York is located in the back of Lower Manhattan's Trinity Churchyard, and dates from 1681.

Waterlogged: the record time for swimming the 28.5 miles (46km) around Manhattan island is 5 hours, 45 minutes.

Making the switch: Radio City's Rockettes use more than 1,300 costumes during their annual 90-minute Christmas Spectacular show.

Flipping the switch: Thomas Edison turned on New York's first public electric lights on Wall Street in 1882.

City shore: New York City has 14 miles (22.5km) of beaches. The best known is Coney Island, with its carnival rides and the original Nathan's hot-dog stand.

City core: New York City's nickname of "the Big Apple" originated in the 1920s in a series of newspaper articles about horse-racing.

DECISIVE DATES

1524
Italian explorer Giovanni da Verrazano, under Francis I of France, sights the territory that is now New York, but doesn't land his ship.

1609
Englishman Henry Hudson weighs anchor on the island, then sails the *Half Moon* up the river that now bears his name.

1624
The Dutch West India Company sets up a trading post on the southern tip of the island at what is now Battery Park.

1626
The provincial director-general of the New Amsterdam settlement, Peter Minuit, purchases Manhattan from the Algonquin tribe for 60 guilders' worth of trinkets – the equivalent of $24 in today's currency.

1630s
Dutch farmers settle land in what is now Brooklyn and the Bronx.

1643
Conflict with local Algonquin tribes leaves at least 80 Indians dead at what became known as the Panovia Massacre.

1647
Peter Stuyvesant becomes director-general and soon suppresses political opposition.

1653
Peter Stuyvesant builds a fence along what is now known as Wall Street to protect New Amsterdam from British incursion.

1660
Nearly half the population is foreign born. Irish-born Americans are the largest group in the city, then German-born Americans.

1664
In the first year of the sea war between England and Holland, Stuyvesant is forced to surrender the town to the British without a fight. New Amsterdam is renamed New York, after King Charles II's brother, James, the Duke of York.

1673
The Dutch recapture New York and rename it New Orange, again without fighting taking place.

1674
New York is returned to the British by the Anglo-Dutch Treaty of Westminster.

1690
With a population of 3,900, New York is now the third-largest town in North America.

1735
Newspaper publisher Peter Zenger is tried for slandering the British crown. He is acquitted, establishing the precedent for freedom of the press.

1765
In accordance with the Stamp Act, unfair taxes are levied against the early colonists.

1770
Skirmishes between the Sons of Liberty and the British culminate in the Battle of Golden Hill, the first blood to be shed prior to the Revolutionary War.

1776
George Washington loses the Battle of Long Island, and British troops occupy New York until 1783.

1789
New York becomes the capital of the United States of America, but only retains this status for 18 months.

1789
George Washington is inaugurated as President of the United States at the site of the Federal Hall, Wall Street.

FROM LEFT: Giovanni Da Verrazano (1485–1528); Peter Stuyvesant; 18th-century ship off Lower Manhattan; George Washington; the Great Fire of 1835; the American Civil War.

1790
A first official census reveals that the city of New York now has a population of over 33,000.

1792
A popular, open-air money market is established beneath a buttonwood tree on Wall Street.

1807
Robert Fulton, sailing along the Hudson River, establishes the first successful steamboat company in the US.

1811
An important decision is made affecting the city's future appearance: all streets are to be laid out in the form of a grid.

1820
An official Stock Exchange replaces the outdoor money market that has been held on Wall Street.

1825
The economic importance of New York increases sharply as a result of the construction of the Erie Canal, which connects the Hudson River with the Great Lakes.

1835
Manhattan, between South Broad and Wall Street, is ravaged by the "Great Fire."

1857
William M. "Boss" Tweed, elected to the County Board of Supervisors, launches a career of notorious corruption.

1858
Calvert Vaux and Frederick Law Olmsted submit plans for Central Park, which is to be the "lungs" of the city.

1860
New York becomes the largest metropolis in the United States; in the previous 30 years, Brooklyn's population increased 10 times over.

1861
The Civil War begins, and many New Yorkers are recruited for the cause.

1863
The Draft Riots rage throughout New York, and it is believed that around 100 people are killed.

1869
The American Museum of Natural History opens.

1870s
William M. "Boss" Tweed, of Tammany Hall notoriety, is arrested, tried, and taken to a jail he helped to build, before escaping to Spain.

1880
The Metropolitan Museum of Art opens.

1883
The Brooklyn Bridge opens, and there is a first gala performance by the Metropolitan Opera.

1886
The Statue of Liberty, a gift from France, is unveiled on Liberty Island.

1892
Ellis Island in New York Harbor becomes the point of entry for immigrants to the United States.

1898
New York's five boroughs are united under one municipal government.

1902
The Flatiron Building is completed.

1904
An underground subway system is established.

1911
The Triangle Fire alerts the public to the appalling living conditions of immigrants.

1913
Construction of the world's tallest skyscraper, the Woolworth Building, begins. It is superseded in 1930 by the Chrysler Building.

1929
Wall Street crashes, and with it comes the end of the Jazz Age and the start of the Great Depression.

1931
After 14 months of construction, the Empire State Building opens ahead of schedule and is heralded as a great success.

1933
Fiorello LaGuardia is elected mayor and uses Federal money to fight the devastating effects of the Great Depression.

1939
Ten years after its foundation by Abby Aldrich Rockefeller, the Museum of Modern Art moves into its new home on 53rd Street. The World's Fair opens in Flushing, Queens.

1941
The United States enters World War II.

1946
The United Nations begins meeting in New York. The permanent buildings on East 42nd–48th streets are completed six years later.

1959
The Frank Lloyd Wright-designed Guggenheim Museum opens. Work begins on Lincoln Center.

1965
A 16-hour power cut para-
lyzes the city.

1970
Economic decline sets in,
which continues until
around 1976.

1973
The World Trade Center
opens. With its 110-story
Twin Towers, it is the tallest
building in the world.

1975
Impending bankruptcy is
avoided only by obtaining a
bridging loan from the Federal government.

1977
A 27-hour power cut
occurs, with widespread
looting and vandalism.

1978
Ed Koch becomes mayor of
New York and remains in
office until 1989.

FROM LEFT: the opening of the
Brooklyn Bridge; constructing the
subway; World War II poster;
remembering the fallen on
September 11.

1982
The ibm building opens,
followed by the AT&T building in 1983.

1986
Battery Park City opens.

1987
"Black Monday" on Wall
Street. Shares suffer a 30
percent drop in value.

1990
David Dinkins becomes
the first African-American
mayor.

1993
A bomb explodes below the
World Trade Center. Six
people are killed and over
1,000 are injured.

1997
Mayor Rudolph Giuliani's
"zero tolerance" campaign
is effective, and there are
major declines in crime.

1998
The city celebrates the
Centennial of Greater New
York, marking the amalga-
mation of the five boroughs
in 1898.

2001
Terrorists crash two planes
into the World Trade Center's towers. Nearly 3,000
people are killed.

2003
Smoking is banned in bars
and restaurants. There is
another huge power cut,
but this one is met with
good spirits.

2004
The Museum of Modern Art
moves back to Manhattan.
The Time Warner Center in
Columbus Circle opens.

2008
The global financial crisis
begins on Wall Street, as
banks fail and stocks plunge.

2009
The renovation of Lincoln
Center is completed, as are
new baseball stadiums for
the Mets and the Yankees.
The Statue of Liberty's
crown reopens. The *Intrepid* returns to Manhattan.

2010
Protests surround the pro-
posed construction of the
Park51, which comes to be
known as the "Ground
Zero Mosque."

2011
When same-sex marriage is
legalized in New York State,
the city's first same-sex
wedding takes place at the
marriage bureau on Worth
Street. Ten years after the
terrorist attacks of September 11, 2001, the memorial
opens. The Occupy Wall
Street movement descends
on lower Manhattan.

THE MAKING OF NEW YORK

In its youth New York was a small outpost of trade and politics. Through the immigration of people and ideas the city matured into an international center of finance, culture, and diplomacy

It's hard to believe it all started as a small farm. For the Lenape Indians, a grouping of Algonquin tribes concentrated around the Delaware and Hudson rivers, Manahatta (island of many hills) was a wild place of streams and pine, occasionally burned and used for seasonal crops. Local legend has it that Peter Minuit, an official for the Dutch, bought the island from a tribe of Lenape known as the Canarsie (or Canarsee) for a box of trinkets worth 60 guilders, about $24, which wouldn't buy a square inch of today's Big Apple. Minuit came to govern the small village in the area approximately where Bowling Green is now situated. Foreign to the notion of land own-

The Wiechquaekeck Trail, an Algonquin trade route, ran all the way to the state capital at Albany, crossing the island of Manhattan diagonally. This is now Broadway.

ership, the Indians may not have understood the deal, but Minuit didn't understand tribal territory either, so the tribe he paid may not have had a claim to Manhattan at all.

New Amsterdam

Despite occasional skirmishes, relations between the Algonquin Indians and European

LEFT: immigrants arrive in the land of the free.
RIGHT: detail of the painting *Purchase of Manhattan* by Peter Minuit, 1626, by Alfred Friedericks.

settlers had been cordial, if not exactly friendly, but they deteriorated when the Dutch settled for good. Theft, murder, and land disputes turned into a cycle of savagery that led to the murder of a Native American woman and the Peach War of 1655.

The Dutch were not the first European arrivals. In 1524, Giovanni da Verrazano was struck by the Lower Bay's "commodiousness and beauty," but Europe paid no regard until Henry Hudson sailed under a Dutch flag into the natural harbor in 1609. Hudson traded, particularly in furs, and in 1621 the Dutch West India Company acquired exclusive trading rights to territory from Cape May (New Jersey) to New

England. Trading posts were set along the coast and rivers, and about 50 Walloon Protestants were sent to settle Nut Island (Governor's Island) off the tip of Manhattan. Soon the camp spread to the southern end of Manhattan, which settlers named New Amsterdam.

The Walloons and Dutch were joined by convicts, slaves, religious zealots, and profiteers, with tribes coming to trade occasionally. In 1647, the company sent Peter Stuyvesant to tame the wild New Amsterdam. He cracked down on smuggling and tax evasion, and kept

> Director-general Peter Stuyvesant (1646–64) was known as "Peg Leg" or "Old Silver Nails" because of his wooden leg studded with nails.

order with the whip and the branding iron. Stuyvesant got things done, but made few friends in New Amsterdam. In 17 years, he established a hospital, a prison, a school, and a post office. He also erected a barricade against the Indians and the British, from river to river

on the site of what is now Wall Street, giving the avenue its present name.

Dutch to British

The thriving Dutch town was under pressure from the British on both sides, and in 1664 King Charles II sent four warships to seize New Amsterdam. Stuyvesant was ready for war, but the townspeople were happy for a chance to be rid of him. Without a shot fired, the English raised the Union flag and renamed the town New York, in honor of the king's brother. The Dutch retook the town about 10 years later in the Second Anglo-Dutch War, but quickly negotiated a return to British hands, again without bloodshed.

The seeds of New York's independence were sown in 1765 with the Stamp Act, among a battery of legislation passed to assert King George III's authority and plump the royal coffers. The Stamp Act levied tax on everything from tobacco to playing cards and brought the cry, "No taxation without representation."

FROM LEFT: Lower Manhattan in the 1730s; Erie Canal grain barges towed down the Hudson River to New York City, 1870s.

Angry mobs stormed a government strong-hold and terrorized officials until the British repealed the act. A later tax on imported items like paper, lead, and tea followed in 1767, this time backed by the English army, the dreaded Redcoats. A battle of nerves rattled until January 1770, when the rebels and Redcoats fought the Battle of Golden Hill.

After Boston's example on April 22, 1774, New Yorkers dumped tea from an English cargo ship into the harbor. A year later, the "shot heard 'round the world" was fired at Lexington, Massachusetts, and the American Revolution began. At the Declaration of Independence's reading in New York, a mob raced to topple King George III's statue in Bowling Green. Legend has it the statue was melted into musket balls, then fired at the British troops.

General George Washington chased the British out of Boston, then came to New York, where he fared poorly. British troops beat Washington's fledgling army from Brooklyn through Manhattan, to a grim defeat at White Plains, New York. A brutal seven-year occupation followed, but in 1785, Washington returned to celebrate an American victory. Four years later he returned again, to place his hand on a Bible for the oath of office as America's first president. For the next 18 months, New York was the nation's capital.

THE GREAT FIRE OF 1835

On the night of December 16, 1835, fire tore through New York's Downtown business district and burned for over 15 hours. Raging from the East River almost as far as Broad Street, more than 600 buildings, including the Merchant's Exchange and more than half of the city's insurance companies, were destroyed with a cost of over $20 million. The blaze spread, propelled by fierce winds, in just 15 minutes to 50 timber buildings. The volunteer fire department was disorganized and ill-equipped to take on the task, handicapped by lack of wells or hoses, and the East River being frozen. Fortunately, only two people died in the blaze.

Growing pains

A small town at the turn of the 19th century, New York's population was about 35,000. A yellow fever outbreak scared some residents off to the open spaces of Greenwich Village, but most occupied the crooked lanes south of Canal Street. The public debated the new Constitution; brokers traded in the shade of a buttonwood tree on Wall Street; five people died in a riot against Columbia University doctors who robbed graves for their anatomy labs; and buffalo were brought from the western territories. Politically, the town was split between Democrats, represented by Aaron Burr, who was Thomas Jefferson's vice-president, and

Federalists, headed by Alexander Hamilton, the nation's first Secretary of the Treasury. In 1804 their years of feuding were settled in a duel when Burr shot and killed Hamilton.

The 350-mile (565km) Erie Canal from Lake Erie to Buffalo drew cargo from across the globe into the East River Harbor (now South Street Seaport). Business boomed, the population soared to 312,000 (1840), and real-estate prices rocketed. John Jacob Astor and Cornelius Vanderbilt grew rich on property and shipping.

By the 1850s, the *Evening Post* reported, "The city of New York belongs almost as much to the South as to the North," as Mayor Fernando Wood supported the "continuance of slave labor and the prosperity of the slave master." When civil war was inevitable, he proposed that the city declare itself independent to protect its business interests with the South.

In February 1860, dark-horse candidate Abraham Lincoln spoke at philanthropist Peter Cooper's free college. Lincoln's words and delivery riveted the audience, and copies of the Cooper Union address crossed the country. Lincoln won the November election without one Southern electoral vote, and five months later Confederate artillery bombarded Fort

Dark-horse presidential candidate Abraham Lincoln made an electrifying speech at a New York college in 1860. A year later, the Civil War started and tore the country apart.

Sumter. At the Plymouth Church of Brooklyn, abolitionist minister Henry Ward Beecher shrieked for "war redder than blood and fiercer than fire," and that is what he got.

In April 1861, Lincoln called for volunteers to put down the rebellious South, and New York sent 8,000 soldiers, including Irish and German regiments. Patriotism swung into vogue. Tiffany & Co. crafted military regalia and Brooks Brothers stitched uniforms.

Draft riots

The war dragged on, hopes of a speedy victory faded, New York's fighting spirit began to sag,

FROM LEFT: a woodcut illustrates the draft riots in New York, July 13–16, 1863; a consultation on the troubled, unfinished Brooklyn Bridge, 1872.

and defeatism turned to rage when Lincoln enacted conscription in 1862. When it emerged that the wealthy could buy their way out for $300, the city erupted. One July morning in 1863, a mob of several thousand stormed the Third Avenue draft office, routed police, and torched the whole block. Over several days, an orphanage on Fifth Avenue was burned, 18 black men were lynched, mutilated and left hanging from lampposts, and Union Army regiments were recalled to quell the Draft Riots. (The period of the Draft Riots was dramatically realized in Martin Scorsese's *Gangs of New York*.)

Two years later the Civil War ended, and Lincoln's body was returned to the city to lie in state at New York's City Hall.

After the Civil War, immigrants arrived from Europe. Italians crammed into Mulberry Street and Greenwich Village. Jews fled anti-Semitic pogroms in Russia, flooding the Lower East Side, and Chinese settled around Mott Street.

BOSS TWEED AND TAMMANY HALL

During the 1860s, William M. "Boss" Tweed was the most powerful politician in New York State. A man of voracious appetites, he ran the local Democratic Party as though it were his own. The root of Tammany power was the lower classes, who saw Tweed as one of them. He was a former bookkeeper and fireman who transformed into a Robin Hood figure, robbing the rich and cutting the poor in for a slice.

Tweed did some good for the poor, but most of his energy went into lining his own pockets. City contracts were padded with extra funds, and a percentage of the total – sometimes the largest percentage – fattened Tweed's wallet. On one single morning, Tweed and his cronies raked $5.5 million on a contract for the New York City Courthouse (aka the "Tweed Courthouse") in Lower Manhattan. After more than a decade as New York's uncrowned monarch and three years of litigation, Tweed was sent to Ludlow Street Prison, which, ironically, he had been responsible for building.

Hardly a typical jailbird, on one of the frequent visits to his Madison Avenue brownstone, Tweed ducked out the back and fled to Spain. He was recaptured and died in prison of pneumonia less than two years later. He was buried in the Brooklyn Green-Wood Cemetery.

A Tenement Life

A land of opportunity became a crowded corner of hardship for the immigrants who settled on New York's Lower East Side

The Lower East Side went by many names: "the typhus ward," "the suicide ward," "the crooked ward," or simply "Jewtown." The irregular rectangle of tenements and sweatshops crammed between the Bowery and the East River were the New World's ghetto.

Between 1880 and 1920, more than 2 million Eastern European Jews came to the United States, and over 500,000 settled in New York City, mostly on the Lower East Side. With 330,000 people per square mile and primitive sanitation, yellow fever and cholera were constant threats, and child labor and exploitation were facts of life. Rents were extortionate.

Families of six or seven often slept, cooked, ate, and worked in a small room – in hallways, in basements, in alleyways – anywhere they could huddle. It's baffling to imagine, and even more so to see. The Tenement Museum (see page 119) offers guided tours of apartments that replicate the look of life 100 years ago.

The "needle trade" was a keystone of the economy, and piles of half-sewn clothes cluttered the rooms. Pay was by quantity, hours were long, and the pace was relentless. Sewing machines were typically whining by 6am and droned far into the night. Sweatshop workers were charged for needles and thread, for lockers and chairs, and fined for damaged material at two or three times its regular value. Wages were minimal – maybe $8 or $10 a week for a family of five or six people, or $14 or $15 for the exceptionally productive.

Writer Michael Gold remembered, "On the East Side people buy their groceries a pinch at a time; three cents' worth of sugar, five cents' worth of butter, everything in penny fractions." Compassion for friends had a high personal cost. "In a world based on the law of competition, kindness is a form of suicide."

At the center of the neighborhood was Hester Street market, where Jews sold meat, produce, or cheap clothes from pushcarts. The area was nicknamed "the Pig Market," probably, as photo-journalist Jacob Riis said, "in derision, for pork is the one ware that is not on sale." Eastern European Jews put a high value on education and political organization, and community members were active in the labor movement. Unions were regularly organized, but strikebusters were hired by the bosses to intimidate them with threats and violence. The East Side Socialists finally saw their candidate in Congress in 1914. Organizations like the Educational Alliance sponsored lectures and demanded libraries, Yiddish theater blossomed, and religious observances continued as they had in the old country.

LEFT: an elderly woman smokes while doing handiwork in her small New York City tenement room, *c.*1890.

During the 1860s, the city was run by Tammany Hall, and Tammany Hall was run by William M. "Boss" Tweed. A larger-than-life and highly corrupt figure, Tweed ran the city as his personal piggy bank and fiefdom (see page 35). In 1898, the five boroughs formed a single government, bringing New York City's total population to 3.4 million people.

By the end of the 19th century, J.P. Morgan was on the way to creating the first billion-dollar American company (US Steel), John D. Rockefeller struck pay dirt with Standard Oil, and Andrew Carnegie established Carnegie Hall, where Tchaikovsky conducted the opening gala.

Fashion and famine

Abandoning their Downtown haunts to the immigrants, the upper crust began a 50-year march up fashionable Fifth Avenue, leaving a trail of mansions in their wake. This is when the social elite came to be known as the "Four Hundred," from the 400 guests at Mrs William Astor's annual ball. While the Four Hundred gorged themselves at lavish parties, Downtown New York was as wretched as ever. Every day 2,000 immigrants poured into the new Ellis Island immigration station, packing tenements and sweatshops ever tighter. Despite work by reformers like photo-journalist Jacob Riis, it took a tragedy to spur change.

Death trap

On March 25, 1911, as the five o'clock bell rang, fire lapped the top floors of the Triangle Shirtwaist Company near Washington Square. Around 600 workers were inside, and stairways were locked or barred by flames. Girls jumped from the eighth and ninth floors, thudding onto the sidewalk. The blaze lasted only about 10 minutes, but over 140 workers, mostly Jewish or Italian women no older than 20, were killed. The two company owners were acquitted, but the tragedy did stimulate labor reforms.

World War I had little impact on New York City. American infantrymen, known as Doughboys, returned home to find business booming, the population growing, and an era of good feelings in the city. Prohibition was a dreary note to kick off the "Roaring Twenties,"

ABOVE: the Triangle Shirtwaist Factory Fire in 1925.

GOVERNOR'S ISLAND

Local tribes called it Pagganck (Nut Island) when the Dutch purchased the tree-covered island off the southern tip of Manhattan in 1637. With 172 acres (70 hectares) of wooded land, it was a small piece of the pie in the battle between the British and the Dutch for control of the region, but when the British finally claimed victory, they reserved it for the "benefit and accommodation of His Majesty's Governors."

Defensive works were first built on the island during the American Revolution, when minute men fired on British troops from behind earthworks. After independence, the island became property of the US Army, who quickly realized its strategic importance. The Army established Fort Jay and Castle Williams, and the island became an important staging area during the War of 1812. The island was used as a prison for Confederate soldiers in the Civil War, then as a supply center for the World Wars. The US Coast Guard took over in 1966; for nearly 30 years it was a command base and home to thousands of officers and their families.

In 2001 the military decommissioned the base, and the island was proclaimed a National Monument. These days, art shows, concerts, and food festivals fill the lawns and park areas on weekends. It's a traffic-free paradise for sunbathers, bicyclists, and picnickers. Visit www.govisland.com for ferry schedules and information on events.

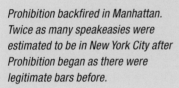

Prohibition backfired in Manhattan. Twice as many speakeasies were estimated to be in New York City after Prohibition began as there were legitimate bars before.

though the good times seemed better and the parties wilder now that drinking was taboo.

The free-spirited Twenties brought free-thinkers, too. Cheap rents and an "old quarter" atmosphere attracted writers, artists, and radicals to Greenwich Village. John Reed, Emma Goldman, Louise Bryant, and Edna St Vincent Millay advocated everything from communism to free love. Eugene O'Neill knocked 'em back at a speakeasy called the Hell Hole, and lit up the theater world at the Provincetown Playhouse.

The city may have been in a handbasket, en route to hell, but New York kept on partying – and kept on spending, too. In the 1920s, the city's stock-buying binge didn't look like it would ever slow down; it didn't matter that trades were on credit, or that the city was being bilked of millions by Tammany Hall. As long as the money kept rolling, the lights burned on Broadway, and Mayor Jimmy Walker was smiling, everything was OK. Gossip columnist and broadcaster Walter Winchell said, "In the 1920s the American people were hell-bent for prosperity and riches. And they wanted a politician who was hell-bent only for re-election… a man who would respect the national rush to get rich, who would accept greed, avarice, and the lust for quick gain as a legitimate expression of the will of the people… Walker knew what the people wanted."

Black Thursday

On October 24, 1929 – Black Thursday – the bottom fell out of the stock market, and the goodwill for Mayor Jimmy Walker went with it. The Great Depression hit New York hard; total income dropped more than half, unemployment leaped to 25 percent, and breadlines snaked along Broadway. Groucho Marx said the

FROM LEFT: effects of the Wall Street crash of 1929; the Empire State in 1930; V-E Day in Times Square May 7, 1945.

city was on the skids "when the pigeons started feeding the people in Central Park."

Before Walker could ride out a second term, his administration unraveled. Investigations into city government found a nest of corruption second only to the Tweed Ring. Governor Franklin D. Roosevelt reviewed the charges, and Walker knew he couldn't walk away without a political, and personal, skinning. He resigned his office in 1932, and took the next ship to Europe.

About a year later, the new mayor in City Hall was Fiorello LaGuardia – a small, plump man with an animated face, a line in rumpled suits, and none of Walker's finesse. He was quick-witted, savvy, and determined to whip the city into shape. Hard-nosed and almost ruthless, but by turn paternalistic and warm, the man who ordered gangster Lucky Luciano off the streets read comics over the radio every Sunday. LaGuardia had critics, but for a city ravaged by the Depression, he was their closest thing to a savior. After his 1933 election, LaGuardia joined Franklin Roosevelt's New Deal, launching programs to revive the economy. His government built bridges, highways, and housing, and found work for artists and writers in the Federally funded Works Progress Administration.

At the same time, big projects begun in the 1920s came to completion. Art Deco changed the skyline of the city with the Chrysler Building in 1930, the Empire State Building and the Waldorf-Astoria Hotel in 1931, and Rockefeller Center in 1933. The 1939–40 New York World's Fair attracted more than 44 million people to Queens for the "Worlds of Tomorrow," at Flushing Meadows-Corona Park, where the Xerox copier, the electronic computer, and television premiered to the American public.

JIMMY AND THE JAZZ AGE

Presiding over Jazz Age New York was Mayor James Walker. In the 1920s, a blossoming of art and culture throughout the city but especially in Harlem (known as the first Harlem Renaissance) filled the streets. Duke Ellington and Count Basie played the Cotton Club, Small's Paradise, and other ritzy after-hours clubs. Alcohol flowed, despite Prohibition. A gambler, lady's man, and former Tin Pan Alley songwriter, Walker left the running of the city to Tammany Hall hacks. Meanwhile, he played craps with reporters and flaunted his affair with a Broadway actress. When he raised his own salary by $10,000, Walker told critics, "Think what it would cost if I worked full time."

In 1941, the US entered World War II, and the city was swept into the war effort. Actual and supposed German spies were arrested, Japanese families were incarcerated on Ellis Island, and blackouts were ordered – even the torch of the Statue of Liberty was turned off. In the basement of a Columbia University physics lab, Enrico Fermi and Leo Szilard experimented with atomic fission, groundwork for what was later called the Manhattan Project: the atomic bomb.

Postwar boom and bust

The postwar United Nations came to the city in 1947 and Idlewild (now Kennedy) Airport opened in 1948. New York had peace, a healthy economy, and the riches of technology. The glass-walled UN Secretariat Building brought a new sleek look to Midtown and kicked off the 1950s modernity. Glass-box skyscrapers lined Park and Madison avenues, then spread to the West Side and the Financial District. Birdland, the bebop nightclub named for saxophonist Charlie Parker, opened on Broadway, and Franklin National Bank issued the world's first credit card.

Then, as in many northeastern cities, came a postwar decline. The middle class moved to the suburbs, corporations relocated, and poor blacks and Hispanics flocked into a run-down city. Tensions were dramatized in the 1957 version of *Romeo and Juliet*, the musical *West Side Story*.

In the summer of 1964, a young black man was shot by police under questionable circumstances, and rioters in Harlem raged for six days. Gender and sexual politics also caught light in the '60s. In 1969, gay rights gained momentum from a police raid on the Stonewall Inn in Greenwich Village. The next year, legendary McSorley's Old Ale House was forced to admit women.

The Harlem riots passed, but the bitterness was unresolved. By 1975, the city was on the verge of bankruptcy, and was forced to go cap in hand to the Federal government. President Gerald Ford's response was summarized in the *Daily News*: "Ford to City: Drop Dead."

Ed Koch

In 1976, feisty mayor Edward Koch attempted another financial rescue – this time backed by a Federal government loan guarantee of $1.65 billion. A resurgence of corporate development fed capital into the economy, and the city climbed back onto its feet. Half-empty

FROM LEFT: NY's tallest building from 1973 to 2001; former mayor Ed Koch; the destruction of the World Trade Center site.

since their 1973 opening, the twin towers of the 110-story World Trade Center sparkled into life; in 1974, Philippe Petit tightrope-walked between the towers. Three years later, George Willig climbed the South Tower, and was fined one penny per story. Battery Park City and the South Street Seaport were developed in Lower Manhattan, and the 1977 Citicorp Building led to the growth of a forest of new skyscrapers. One UN Plaza, the 37-story AT&T (now Sony) building, and the dark-glass IBM building personified the era.

New York acquired an international reputation for excess. In 1977, Studio 54 exemplified a sybaritic, cocaine-driven culture. A power failure that year led to widespread looting – in contrast to the community spirit around a major blackout in 1965, and the later massive Northeastern blackout in 2003. In December 1980, John Lennon, the former Beatle, was murdered outside his home, the Dakota building.

Broadway theatres began their shows an hour earlier to give tourists and out-of-towners a chance to get clear before the late-night mugging shift punched in. The gap between rich and poor widened and the legacy of homelessness was on almost every street corner. Aids and drug abuse pushed the health-care systems beyond their capacity, and racial

200 ticker-tape parades have taken place in Lower Manhattan, along what is known as the "Canyon of Heroes." The Yankees, the Mets, and Nelson Mandela have all been honored.

conflicts erupted. Manhattan businesses and middle-class workers fled to the suburbs or New Jersey, further weakening the New York tax base.

Good times, bad times

Moguls like Donald Trump snatched up New York real estate like squares on a Monopoly board, and the glitz of conspicuous consumption was lionized on the pages of *Vanity Fair*, a long-defunct magazine revived by Condé Nast in 1983. But by 1987, the good times had turned sour even for the tycoons, with two of Wall Street's biggest share dealers heading for jail and the market taking a record one-day dive of 508 points. On the streets, the annual murder rate peaked at 2,245 and the number of citizens on welfare reached a new high. International terrorism arrived in 1993, when a car bomb in the World Trade Center killed six people.

NEW YORK WORLD'S FAIRS

The American Institute Fair was held every year in New York City from 1829 until the end of the 19th century. This is frequently considered to be the first World's Fair, although it was quite small compared to later events. In 1829, 30,000 people attended first at Niblo's Garden and then later at the Crystal Palace. The Exhibition of the Industry of All Nations in 1853 was a World's Fair held in the wake of the highly successful 1851 Great Exhibition in London. It showcased industrial achievements and national pride.

The 1939–40 New York World's Fair, on the current site of Flushing Meadows-Corona Park, allowed visitors to take a look at "the world of tomorrow." More than 40 million people attended its exhibits in two seasons. It was the first exhibition with a futuristic theme, and one of the main purposes was to lift the spirits of the American people in the midst of the Great Depression.

The 1964–5 New York World's Fair, again in Flushing Meadows-Corona Park, was held without the approval of the Bureau of International Expositions, the only fair to do so. The Space Age was one of the major themes of this popular event, and more than 51 million people visited. General Motors updated their *Futurama* show for what proved to be the fair's most popular attraction. Many of the pavilions from 1964 have been renovated or reused, to the improvement of the area.

In the 1993 mayoral election, an abrasive New York district attorney, former Department of Justice prosecutor Rudolph ("Rudy") Giuliani promised to get tough on crime. The first Republican mayor for two decades, he more than kept his promise, extending "zero tolerance" on lawbreaking and police corruption, jaywalking, begging, graffiti, and non-recyclers. The policy didn't endear him to all, but it did win respect, and the crime rate fell, to make New York one of the safer big cities in the US. By 1997, the murder rate had fallen two-thirds from its 1990 high.

Business Improvement Districts (BIDS) sprang up across the city, construction boomed, and seedy areas like Times Square were cleaned up. The economy rebounded from the 1987–92 slump, and unemployment fell. Giuliani was returned for a second term in 1997 and his ambitions turned towards the US Senate, but in 2000 his luck ran out. Prostate cancer and a messy separation from his second wife forced him out of the contest, which was won by a Democratic candidate, Hillary Rodham Clinton.

Terrorism

On the morning of September 11, 2001, four passenger planes were hijacked by terrorists. Two of them were crashed into the World Trade Center's towers. New Yorkers and viewers around the world watched the towers collapse, killing 2,606 people, including 343 of the firefighters and 60 members of the police force who raced to the scene.

Smoke at "Ground Zero" hung in the air for three weeks, and the wreckage smoldered for weeks after. More than 20,000 New Yorkers were displaced from their homes near the 16-acre (6.5-hectare) disaster area. Even criminals were subdued; the week following the attack, crime in Manhattan fell 59 percent.

Mayor Giuliani personified New York's resilience. His trademark abrasiveness turned to a straight-talking compassion and earned the town's trust. These qualities were called on again just nine weeks later when an American

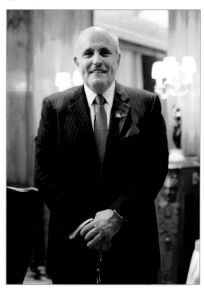

Airlines morning flight for Santo Domingo crashed in the Rockaway district of Queens. Terrorists were not blamed but, in a bitter twist, the crash site was home to many emergency workers who bore such a toll on 9/11.

Giuliani's popularity was such that he had only to endorse Michael Bloomberg as his successor to win the election for the Republican, self-made media mogul. Bloomberg, a political novice, put $41 million of his own money into the campaign. Known on Wall Street for his financial data empire, and in the gossip columns for glamorous female companions after his 1993 divorce, Bloomberg inherited daunting tasks. As well as the massive rebuilding program in Lower Manhattan, the city had an $8.7 billion budget shortfall, and New York's social services had already been ruthlessly pruned. Fears of a recession and the effects of the terror attack spiked unemployment numbers. Bloomberg enjoyed a high approval rating and, in 2009, he was re-elected for an unprecedented third term.

FROM LEFT: former mayor Rudy Giuliani; baseball game at the new Citi Field.

Back to the future

But, as always in New York, energy came and rejuvenation began. The Hudson River waterfront was revitalized, Governor's Island reopened as a retreat for visitors, the spectacularly reorganized Museum of Modern Art returned from Queens and opened its new building to great acclaim. The gleaming Time Warner complex rose over Columbus Circle, with the distinctive triangular facades of the green Hearst Tower climbing nearby to join it in 2006.

On the fifth anniversary of the 2001 attack, a memorial visitor center was opened at the south side of the World Trade Center site. Architect Daniel Libeskind's plans to erect Freedom Tower on the site have progressed, controversially of course, but the building, renamed One World Trade Center, is still on track to open in 2013. The city took a blow with the 2008 financial crisis, but the construction goes on: new baseball stadiums opened for both the Mets and the Yankees in 2009; the Lincoln Center renovation was completed; and the Museum of African Art is scheduled to open in 2012 on Museum Mile.

KANDINSKY

CULTURE AND THE CITY

New York is both a breeding ground and an international showcase for art and artists of every kind. If you can make it here, they say, you can make it anywhere

New York bristles with world-class performing arts venues, in Lincoln Center, Carnegie Hall, and Madison Square Garden, as well as the big-ticket theaters that cluster around Broadway. The Off-Broadway scene has become so big that it has spawned a thriving and energetic Off-Off-Broadway family.

Parks across the city offer free, fresh-air culture with outdoor performances of the New York Philharmonic, the Metropolitan Opera, and the Public Theater's Shakespeare in the Park. On every New York corner and subway platform, a dreamer or a talented student works the "if I can make it here, I can make it anywhere" refrain. The "if" being key to that kick-step off the city streets.

One-third of all American independent movies are made here, and great jazz was crafted in clubs like Birdland. Artists of all kinds have thrived in the Big Apple, from Edward Hopper in his Washington Square studio and Andy Warhol's Factory divas, to Bob Dylan and Jimi Hendrix, who was "discovered" in a Village bar by British bass player Chas Chandler.

Live music

New York is famous for great jazz clubs, like the Blue Note and the Village Vanguard in Greenwich Village. Excellent up-and-coming bands of all kinds play at BAM (Brooklyn Academy of Music), home since 1982 to the innovative Next Wave Festival.

CBGB's on the Lower East Side, birthplace of Talking Heads and The Ramones, slammed its doors in 2006, and the Knitting Factory moved from TriBeCa to Brooklyn, but Sounds of Brazil (SOB) in SoHo is a lively world-music venue, the Mercury Lounge showcases cutting-edge bands, and Le Poisson Rouge in the Village books an eclectic mix of all of the above.

Cultural centers

The Upper West Side's cultural heart is the Lincoln Center for the Performing Arts (see page 242), the largest cultural center in the US. The Metropolitan Opera and New York City Opera, and the Philharmonic reside here, with

---

PRECEDING PAGES: visitors at the Guggenheim Museum.
LEFT: detail from *Twenty Marilyns*, Andy Warhol, 1962.
RIGHT: Central Park musician.

concerts and recitals in Avery Fisher Hall and Alice Tully Hall. The Vivian Beaumont and Mitzi E. Newhouse theaters put on productions and, each September, the New York Film Festival opens at the Lincoln. Jazz at Lincoln Center, a few blocks downtown at the Time Warner complex, thrives under the artistic direction of Wynton Marsalis.

World-famous Carnegie Hall was opened to the public with Tchaikovsky's American debut in 1891, and later hosted Albert Einstein, Amelia Earhart, Winston Churchill, Frank Sinatra, The Beatles, and Elton John. Charles Dana Gibson drew the Gibson Girls and established *Life* magazine in a studio on the premises, and dancer Isadora Duncan lived at the hall. In the late 1950s, developers wanted the plot for office space, but violinist Isaac Stern led a group of citizens to save the site from the wrecker's ball.

In Studio 1011–12, Baroness Hilla von Rebay convinced Solomon Guggenheim to fund promising artists, and established the Guggenheim

TRIBECA FILM FESTIVAL

First established in 2002 by Robert De Niro and producer Jane Rosenthal, the TriBeCa Film Festival has rapidly become a major fixture in the moviemakers' calendar. The impetus of the project was originally intended to lead a Downtown regeneration in response to the 2001 terrorist attacks, but just five years later (in an event that had climate change as a major theme and was opened by the former vice-president Al Gore), more than 200 titles were screened to an enraptured and ready audience.

The first festival drew crowds of more than 150,000 people, and at least $10.4 million was raised in charity for local TriBeCa merchants. The next year, the crowds doubled, donations grew almost fivefold, and screenings featured outdoor drive-in (or sit-in) shows along the banks of the Hudson River.

Many well-known films have gotten their start at the TriBeCa Film Festival. Paul Greengrass's acclaimed *United 93* premiered at the festival, as did *Mission Impossible III*. In 2011, the festival achieved another first, hosting the premiere of a video game, the decidedly cinematic LA Noire. The TriBeCa Film Festival is so successful that *New York* magazine began to wonder if the festival isn't getting too big, and that isn't something New Yorkers often wonder.

In the summer, movies and music aren't confined to theaters and clubs. Free outdoor film screenings and concerts take over in Madison Square Park, Bryant Park, and other parks.

Foundation, with Alexander Calder and Wassily Kandinsky among the beneficiaries. The baroness's acquisitions formed the core of the Guggenheim collection, housed in the Frank Lloyd Wright building on Fifth Avenue.

Visual arts

Art auctions came to public attention in the 1990s when a Van Gogh sold for $82.5 million at Christie's (Van Gogh once wrote that he wished his paintings were worth what he had spent on the paint). Experts said the auction frenzy was a blip, but in 2004 Picasso's *Garçon à la Pipe* fetched $104 million at Sotheby's. And in one dizzying week in 2007, Andy Warhol's *Green Car Crash* fetched $71.7 million at Christie's, while Mark Rothko's *White Center* sold for $72.8 million at Sotheby's.

The Metropolitan, the Guggenheim, and others line "Museum Mile" *(see photo feature on page 228)* along Fifth Avenue. The Metropolitan, along with the Museum of Modern Art on West 53rd Street, are the biggest and best. The Frick, once a private Fifth Avenue mansion, shows fine Rembrandts and Vermeers. The New York Public Library on 42nd Street exhibits art in a grand setting, its Reading Room providing an office for many writers.

Moving pictures

Once upon a time in New York, Radio City Music Hall was to movies what Lincoln Center is to ballet and opera. Now it's an Art Deco treasure, and even the ladies' powder room is worth visiting. Designed by a showman who was known for lavish silent-film theaters, S.L. "Roxy" Rothafel's Radio City opened for vaudeville shows in 1932 as a "palace for the people." Radio City is still an exciting place to see a special screening or catch a gig.

FROM LEFT: the 64th Annual Tony Awards at Radio City Music Hall on June 13, 2010; Carnegie Hall; the TriBeCa Film Festival is a highlight of New York's spring events.

Movie lines often wind around the block in Manhattan, providing eavesdropping and people-watching opportunities. (And, no, the skinny, nervy guy waiting ahead of you isn't Woody Allen.) Space is precious in the city, and multiplex theaters can make movie-going seem like standing in line to watch a TV screen. The Angelika Film Center on West Houston Street in Soho, though, has six screens, an espresso bar, and an atmosphere as good as the coffee. The Film Forum on West Houston Street features revivals, obscurities, and director series, as do the Museum of Modern Art, Anthology Film Archives, and the Museum of the Moving Image, aptly located by the Kaufman Astoria film studio complex in Queens.

Lincoln Center's Walter Reade Theater, home of the New York Film Festival, screens foreign and independent films, as do Brooklyn Academy of Music's BAM Rose Cinemas. Downtown, the IFC Center opened in 2005 in the Village's historic Waverly Theater, while every spring, the TriBeCa Film Festival, co-launched by actor Robert De Niro, is the high-profile, hot-ticket event at which to be seen and to attend the latest screenings.

Dance

New York's dance boom began in the 1960s, with an infusion of funding and the defection

Off-Broadway theater dates back to the Greenwich Village production of four one-act plays by Eugene O'Neill in 1916.

of Russian superstars Rudolf Nureyev, Mikhail Baryshnikov, and Natalia Makarova. The legendary George Balanchine hand-picked the New York City Ballet company, putting them through almost superhuman training. "Mr B" said, "Dancers are like racehorses; they need a jockey on their backs." Balanchine, who designed much of the performance space at the Lincoln Center's New York State Theater, died in 1983. The American Ballet Theater occupies the Lincoln Center's Metropolitan Opera House when the opera is out of season. ABT began with a more classical repertory than the New York City Ballet but, under Mikhail Baryshnikov's artistic direction, welcomed contemporary choreographers like Twyla Tharp.

The Dance Theater of Harlem, founded in 1969, performs both classical and contemporary repertories. Other venues for dance, particularly modern dance, range from the Joyce Theater in Chelsea to the Ailey Center and the City Center, both in Midtown West.

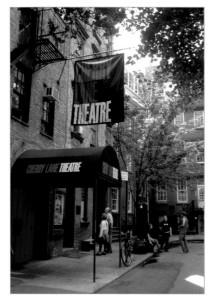

Theatrical stories

In 1901, the glare of electric signs earned the theater district of Broadway the name of the Great White Way. Taking in Seventh Avenue and several side streets, its heyday was before talking pictures and long before television. By the 1970s and '80s, the streets were dirty with drugs, pornography, and prostitution, but Times Square today is a twinkly tourist mecca of theaters, hotels, megastores, and restaurants.

The Shubert Theatre (1913) and Shubert Alley are named for the Shubert brothers, who built dozens of venues. The Palace on West 47th Street was a vaudeville theater until the 1930s, whose boards were trodden by Sarah Bernhardt. Now it's a prime venue for lavish musicals like *Beauty and the Beast* and one-off gigs. The Belasco Theatre, founded in 1907 by flamboyant playwright-actor-director David Belasco, was famously haunted by his ghost until the 1970s production of *Oh! Calcutta.* Perhaps the nudity spooked the spook.

Today, Broadway is in exuberant health. Excellent drama draws crowds, but the big noise is the musicals. Successful musicals often have longer runs, to make back their bigger investments. The original *A Chorus Line* opened in the 1970s and ran for 6,137 performances, before being overtaken by *Cats,* which yowled for more than 20 years. Recent hits like *The Book of Mormon* should fill seats for years to come.

Off-Broadway venues are a feeding ground for the bigger theaters and a cultural force in themselves. The Lucille Lortel, the Cherry Lane, and the Public Theater: time to take a bow.

BUYING BROADWAY TICKETS

The TKTS booth in Times Square has discounted seats (25–50 percent off) for that night's performances. It's open Monday through Saturday 3pm to 8pm for evening performances (opens at 2pm on Tuesdays), Saturday and Wednesday 10am to 2pm for matinees, and Sunday 11am to 7.30pm. A booth at 186 Front Street near South Street Seaport opens daily at 11am and sells tickets for the following night's shows. Lines form early and are long. Unsold tickets can often be bought at theater box offices an hour or so before show time. The Times Square Visitor Center in the Embassy Theater, Broadway between 46th and 47th streets, also sells theater tickets.

FROM LEFT: enjoying an evening at the Lincoln Center; the Cherry Lane Theatre; the Shubert Theatre near Broadway.

HOLLYWOOD ON THE HUDSON

Plenty of celebrities call New York home, but in movies set in the urban jungle, the glittering stars are the skyscrapers, brownstones, streets and parks

Ever since *The Lights of New York* was released in 1927, the city and its landmarks have been illuminating the big screens of the world's celluloid consciousness. King Kong atop the Empire State Building is an enduring image – although the 1976 remake was a disaster. Peter Jackson's 2005 resurrection of the title with Naomi Watts fared better.

The Empire struck back when New York writer-director Nora Ephron made *Sleepless in Seattle*, itself a pastiche of the 1957 three-hankie weepie *An Affair to Remember*. Director Spike Lee portrayed life uptown in *Mo' Better Blues* and across the East River in *Crooklyn*. The city was turned into a maze of paranoia and hallucination in Darren Aronofsky's *Black Swan*.

Fonda and Redford went *Barefoot in the Park*, and Scorsese's *Raging Bull* rampaged around Greenwich Village, too. *How to Marry a Millionaire* was set in the apartment of sassy dames Monroe, Grable, and Bacall at 36 Sutton Place South. Oliver Stone has visited *World Trade Center*, as well as *Wall Street* not once, but twice. And Woody Allen may be filming in London and Paris these days, but his decades of celebrating the Upper East Side are a vital part of cinematic history.

Over 200 films are made here each year, and the number continues to rise, so there's no *Escape from New York* to Hollywood just yet.

BELOW: Will Smith in *I Am Legend*.

ABOVE: Naomi Watts atop the Empire State Building in the 2005 remake of *King Kong*.

ABOVE, FROM LEFT: *Sex and the City*; the Big Piano scene in *Big*; *Night at the Museum*.

THE WORLD'S BIGGEST BACKLOT

First-time visitors taking a stroll through Madison Square Park may recognize the Flatiron Building at the park's south end, but not necessarily because of its iconic architecture. "That's the *Daily Bugle* building from *Spider Man*," they might point and say. It seems every block of the city been immortalized on celluloid (or, these days, in pixels). Forget booking a walking tour, just take to the streets and you'll be transported to the world's biggest backlot. Grab a pastrami sandwich at Katz's, the deli from *When Harry Met Sally*. Shop at FAO Swartz, where Tom Hanks and Robert Loggia did their jumping piano duet in *Big*. Hop over to Brooklyn Heights and take in the storefronts and brownstones from *Moonstruck*. Kids will demand a visit to the American Museum of Natural History to see if they can harness the magic of *Night at the Museum*. Out-of-towners won't find Grand Central Terminal and Central Park to be the dens of filth and crime depicted in Neil Simon's *The Out-of-Towners*, but they'll recognize the clock atop the information booth, the Bethesda Fountain, and countless other symbols of the city. When budgets are tight, Toronto sometimes stands in for the Big Apple, but if Hollywood is making a true New York film, there's no substitute for the real thing.

ABOVE: *When Harry Met Sally*. **RIGHT:** under attack in *Cloverfield*.

DINERS, DELIS, AND DEGUSTATION

You can get a hot dog for around a dollar, or a double-truffle hamburger for 100 times that price. This is New York, where the only culinary dilemma is too much choice

New York is, and always was, a great place to eat. From bagels to corned-beef sandwiches, Italian fine dining to curbside fast food, and from sashimi to sauerkraut, the breadth of cuisines is matched only by the range of prices. It's easy to feast well for a few dollars on a hot dog or banquet at Per Se for – if not a king's, then at least a royal sommelier's – ransom.

Food and fashion

Fashion and trends are vital in all that is New York, and celebrity chefs have left the town peppered with famous-name kitchens (some now leftovers as their famous founders cook up franchises and offshoots elsewhere, like Miami and Las Vegas). Meanwhile, the appetites for star-chef servings are increasingly fed by restaurateurs from out of town, and from as far afield as London, Paris, and Italy.

The styles and chefs may be international but the ingredients may not be. The local and sustainable food movements have become so entrenched in the city that seasonal menus detailing where the ingredients were sourced are a regular occurrence. Cookshop, Blue Hill, and Telepan are just a few outlets leading the charge among what have come to be known as "farm-to-table" or "greenmarket" restaurants. Vegetarian dishes have graduated from a regular option to a mainstay, with vegan diets increasingly available, while the prefix "free" – as in "lactose-free" and "gluten-free" – is sprinkled over many menus.

LEFT: pancakes in Midtown. RIGHT: dining out on the Lower East Side.

To guarantee you're eating local, visit one of the city's greenmarkets. None is more important than the Union Square Greenmarket. Every Monday, Wednesday, Friday, and Saturday, sidewalks fill up with stands hawking local foods. In the winter, start the day with cider and cinnamon donuts; during the summer, there's lemonade and fruit-filled pastries. Or come for a lunchtime picnic, and pick up bread, wine, locally cured meats, and cheese.

The first visible signs of food are often at street corners, on silver carts. In the morning, many New Yorkers grab their breakfasts here on the way to the office, so don't be afraid to give these vendors a go. The coffee is good and the

bagels make a quick and tasty meal. For a snack or lunch on-the-go, skip the soggy pretzels, charcoal-burned ears of corn, and over-boiled hot dogs. There are better options. *Empanadas* (South American savory pastries), chow fun noodles, wholegrain pancakes, chocolate-truffle cookies, or mango ices are also right there at the curb, often prepared quite well.

You'll find convenient sandwich shops, corner bodegas, and soup stands selling to people who try to eat without messing up their shirts, but you'll also see tiny storefronts catering to the latest food fad. Competition and rent can be ruthless – Vietnamese *bánh mì* sandwiches might be all the rage one moment, then all of a sudden it's meatballs or dumplings that everybody craves. Some trends die quicker than others. Southern barbecue and gourmet hamburgers are here to stay, while the cupcake and fried chicken crazes are a fading memory.

Fast and slow

Pizzas range from street-corner slices, often made with a crunchy semolina flour, to the Sullivan Street Bakery, where the slice is about the only thing they have in common. Jim Lahey is a passionate campaigner of "slow food" and applies the principles he learned in Tuscany (using only high-grade flour and wild yeast, plus fresh, all-natural ingredients) to the no-frills pizzas sold in his bakeries. His signature slice is the seductively simple pizza *pomodoro*, with a thin tomato puree.

Some of the world's finest and most expensive restaurants – Per Se, Le Bernadin, and Adour Alain Ducasse at the St Regis to name but a few – are in Midtown. Many Manhattan mainstays are here too, with the longevity prize going to the excellent nonagenarian Oyster Bar at Grand Central Terminal. For Midtown dining, it pays to do some homework (that's where this guide comes in handy). While spontaneity is fun farther downtown, in Midtown it's best

---

CULINARY CELEBRATIONS

No one could possibly sample every pork rib, chocolate truffle, and slice of sashimi in the city. That doesn't mean people don't give it a shot at the food festivals that are held nearly every week. Conglomerations of stands, sometimes offshoots of major restaurants, take over streets, parks, and convention centers.

Some festivals are à la carte, while some offer tickets that grant all-you-can-eat (and drink) privileges. The major ones include the Ninth Avenue International Food Festival in the spring, the Barbecue Block Party in summer, and the New York Wine and Food Festival in the fall.

FROM LEFT: Sardi's is an old-school, theatrical experience; Chelsea Market.

to make reservations, especially to dine before or after the theater.

Restaurants here, especially the more expensive ones, sometimes have formal dress codes. Men are suited (or at least jacketed) and women are groomed for a glamorous night on the town. Many Midtown restaurants are closed Sundays, and for lunch on Saturdays, as their corporate customers have gone.

The Meatpacking District is good for both dining and posing, even if the patrons are often wafer-thin models who don't look as if they eat, ever. Prepare to eat late, and stay up even later. The nearby Chelsea Market, at Ninth Avenue and 15th Street, is a dreamland for food fetishists – a dozen or so bakeries, meat markets, kitchen suppliers, and other stores of a gastronomic bent, all based in former warehouses.

Once SoHo gained recognition as an artistic center, people began streaming here in search of "the scene." The prices often reflect SoHo's chicness, but there's no need to go hungry, or to pay through the nose. You can shell out $35+ for a steak at Balthazar, but you can also eat for plenty less at Snack.

Famous diners

Robert De Niro is one of TriBeCa's most famous diners. The actor moved here in 1976, and began investing in restaurants: Nobu,

> *Tiny restaurants like Degustation and Momofuku Ko offer a front-row view of the action. Diners sit at a bar and chat up the chefs as they prepare intricate dishes directly behind it.*

Locanda Verde, and the Tribeca Grill. To avoid these movie-star prices, head for the reasonably priced neighborhood bistro Landmarc, finishing off with frozen yogurt from Emack & Bolio. De Niro promoted his 'hood as a cool area in which to hang out, and it still is.

The once-mean streets of the Lower East Side are now very much the domain of hipsters. Get a taste of the area's heritage as an enclave of immigration with a visit to Katz's Delicatessen. To watch Uptown elegance moving to young and hip Downtown and loving it, head for the Chinatown Brasserie, or try Morimoto or Buddakan in the Meatpacking District.

Around the world and back

Ethnic food can often be found in pockets around the city. The stretch of 9th Avenue north of the Port Authority is awash with Thai eateries. 32nd street between 5th Avenue and Broadway — otherwise known as Korea Way — boasts over a dozen specialists in *bibimbap* and *kimchi*. Near 28th Street and Lexington, just south of Murray Hill, is "Curry Hill," a collection of reasonably priced Indian restaurants. This is to say nothing of Little Italy and Chinatown.

It's no surprise that immigrants pack their recipes when they depart for New York, and even if there isn't a particular block, they always find at least one storefront to share their delicacies. Eats from around the world are easily found in this part of town. Utensils are not required when you sit down for an Ethiopian feast at Meskerem. Jacketed waiters hover at your table, slicing from huge cuts of meat at the rodizio-style Brazilian behemoth Churrascaria Plataforma. Tsampa will give you a Himalayan take on noodles and dumplings, there's always ilili for Lebanese, and Peruvian delights are on offer at Lima's Taste. Name a country and New York just may offer a local purveyor of its signature dish.

A list of restaurants appears at the end of each Places chapter, with a map grid reference.

FOOD ON THE MOVE

In a more cosmopolitan world, it is less likely New York has a monopoly on any one thing, but the city can still claim dominance in some quintessential dishes

The variety of food on offer is one of the reasons why dining in New York is so appealing. Sure, the peanuts and kabobs (kebabs) you may see being sold from carts aren't masterpieces, but there's nothing like eating them while walking down Fifth Avenue. The legendary H&H Bagels may have closed up its storefront, but Murrays has taken up the mantle and makes some of the world's finest bagels. When it comes to pizza, contentious would be a mild word to describe the debate over who tosses the best, but classics like Di Fara, Grimaldi's, Lombardi's, John's, and Patsy's usually get a vote, while new places like Artichoke Basilles and Kesté are entering the contest.

For an egg cream (a mixture of chocolate, milk and sparkling water), few do it better than Gem Spa in the East Village. Grab a dozen oysters and a bowl of Manhattan clam chowder at the Grand Central Oyster Bar. For years, Junior's was the place to get a New York cheesecake, but these days many swear by Artisinal. People make pilgrimages for the hot dog at Nathan's Famous in Coney Island and stand in line for burgers at Corner Bistro in Greenwich Village. Are they the best around? Taste them and decide.

ABOVE: you can buy classic hot dogs from carts all over Midtown. The most coveted dogs are seared on cart-top flat grills.

RIGHT: cupcakes are a popular treat in New York, especially when they are from small, locally owned bakeries.

KEEP ON TRUCKING

In recent years, a fleet of food trucks has sprung up, moving daily to feed food-loving office workers in largely un-foodie neighborhoods. Other major American cities have their own food-truck scenes, but few can compete with the variety in New York.

So just what can you eat from a truck? Many serve sweets, including Cupcake Stop (www. cupcakestop.com), which offers miniature and full-size versions of its cakelettes, and Treats Truck (www.treatstruck. com), a cart that sells the all-American classics: chocolate chip cookies, brownies, and Rice Krispie squares. Wafels & Dinges (www.wafelsand dinges.com) serves – you guessed it – Belgian waffles. There are fancy ice-cream trucks, including The Big Gay Ice Cream Truck (www.biggayice creamtruck.com) and Van Leeuwen (www.van leeuwenicecream.com).

There are also plenty of savory foods – look for dumplings (www.rickshawdumplings.com), Tai-wanese chicken (www.nyccravings.com), schnitzel (www.schnitzelandthings.com), and burgers (www.lacensebeef.com). Since there are no seats at which to eat these purchases, most people stake out space on public park benches.

To track down a particular food truck, check out the info on the Midtown Lunch website (www. midtownlunch. com), or follow your individual favorites on their websites, Twitter, or Facebook.

RIGHT: the dumplings at the Rickshaw Dumpling Truck come in a variety of flavors, including pork and chicken. Sometimes they offer duck dumplings as a popular special.

ABOVE: join the crowds at Bryant Park on 42nd Street, a lovely place to eat street-vendor food thanks to its proliferation of tables and chairs.

ABOVE: the Wafels & Dinges truck serves sweet Belgian-style waffles all around the city.

PLACES

A detailed guide to the entire city, with principal
sites clearly cross-referenced by number to the maps

Manhattan is divided into three areas: Midtown, Uptown, and Downtown. Midtown and Uptown are crisscrossed by a street grid system where avenues travel north and south, and streets travel east and west.

Midtown East is best known for the Grand Central Terminal, the United Nations headquarters, and the Chrysler Building, while Midtown West is home to Times Square, Rockefeller Center, and the Museum of Modern Art. Cool, elegant Uptown is epitomized by the Upper East Side – between 82nd and 104th streets are cultural treasures so lavish that they have earned this stretch the name Museum Mile.

The Upper West Side is both more towering and more family-oriented, evidenced by the taller buildings and baby carriages. At the top end of Manhattan are Harlem and Washington Heights, which have been undergoing a cultural renaissance.

Downtown is more of a challenge to navigate, as its smaller streets do not follow a pattern and it uses names instead of numbers. At the northern edge are Gramercy Park and Chelsea. Further south it's Greenwich Village, Chinatown, and the Lower East Side. To the east is Alphabet City, with avenues A, B, C, and D, plus NoHo (North of Houston) and NoLita (North of Little Italy), making a large-scale map of this area look like a bowl of alphabet soup.

The southern part of Downtown is the center of financial New York, where Wall Street banks keep tabs on the money before the Meatpacking District soaks it up again in its high-end restaurants and boutiques. Don't forget the outer boroughs, which are covered near the end of the book.

All together, the city covers a whopping 300 square miles (776 square km). With a little time, a sturdy pair of shoes, and a MetroCard, you are sure to see enough to convince you this is more than a place. It's a pulsing and evolving masterpiece.

PRECEDING PAGES: summertime in Central Park; view over Midtown. **LEFT:** Manhattan at night. **ABOVE, FROM LEFT:** Statue of Liberty; New York's famous taxis.

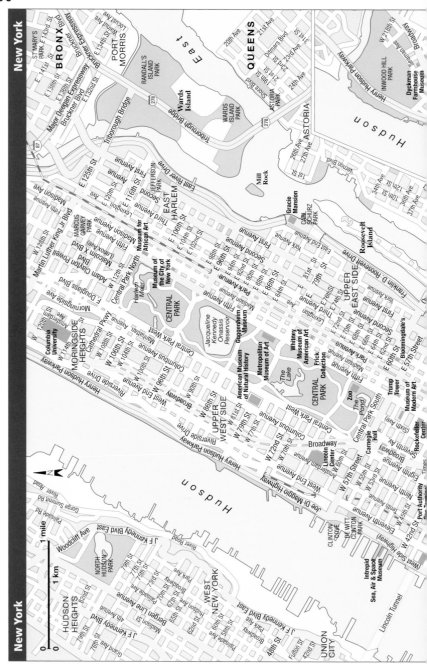

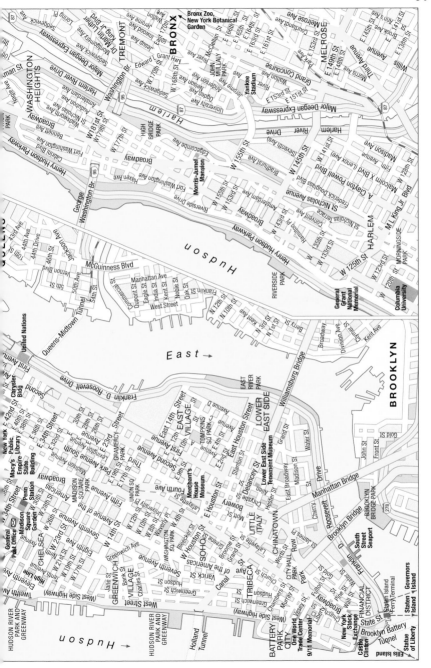

Bronx Zoo,
New York Botanical
Garden

BRONX

TREMONT

WASHINGTON
HEIGHTS

MELROSE

Harlem

HARLEM

MORNINGSIDE
PARK

Morris-Jumel
Mansion

HIGH
BRIDGE
PARK

Yankee
Stadium

Major Deegan Expressway

General
Grant
National
Memorial

RIVERSIDE
PARK

Columbia
University

Hudson

McGuinness Blvd

West Street

QUEENS

Queens-Midtown Tunnel

United Nations

Chrysler
Bldg

East →

New York
Public
Library

Macy's

Empire
State
Building

Penn
Station

Madison
Square
Garden

General
Post Office

CHELSEA

High Line

MADISON
SQUARE
PARK

GRAMERCY
PARK

UNION SQ
PARK

Merchant's
House
Museum

STUYVESANT
SQ PARK

EAST
VILLAGE

TOMPKINS
SQ PARK

EAST RIVER
PARK

Williamsburg Bridge

BROOKLYN

Lower East Side
Tenement Museum

LOWER
EAST
SIDE

East Houston St

GREENWICH
VILLAGE

SOHO

LITTLE
ITALY

CHINATOWN

TRIBECA

Manhattan Bridge

Brooklyn Bridge

BROOKLYN
BRIDGE PARK

South
Street
Seaport

CITY HALL
PARK

FINANCIAL
DISTRICT

New York
Stock
Exchange

Brooklyn Battery
Tunnel

BATTERY
PARK

One World
Trade Center

9/11 Memorial

HUDSON RIVER
PARK AND
GREENWAY

Holland
Tunnel

Hudson →

Castle
Clinton

Staten Island
Ferry Terminal

Statue
of Liberty

Ellis Island

Governors
Island

LOWER MANHATTAN

Lower Manhattan is where New York began.
Now it's an area of high finance and poignant
memories, brand new parks and the
revitalized South Street Seaport

Below Chambers Street and the Brooklyn Bridge is the original New York, where the Dutch and the English first settled, the country's first hotel was built, the first president was sworn in, and the city's first theatrical opening night took place. Clipper ships bound for the California Gold Rush sailed from Lower Manhattan's piers in the 1850s, and by 1895 the first skyscraper stood 20 stories above lower Broadway.

Financial powerhouses

Over a century later, New York's financial powerhouses and city government areas are bracketed by outdoor havens like the South Street Seaport and Battery Park. Some of the landmark office buildings on or near Wall Street have been converted to high-tech business-use and residential apartments.

But Manhattan's oldest neighborhood also has some of its most moving history, being the site of two memorials to modern tragedies. Just as events in the 20th century shifted the area from a maritime economy to one of financial commerce, so, too, have events early in the 21st century changed the face of Lower

Manhattan once again. The changes have been absorbed with typical New York energy – adapting and reconstructing, facing the future, without missing a beat.

PLACES OF PILGRIMAGE

Between West Street and Trinity Place is the site of the former World Trade Center. Rising an impressive 110 stories into the sky, the Twin Towers were the most prominent structures in a 16-acre (6.5-hectare), seven-building complex that took 17 years

Main Attractions
9/11 MEMORIAL
BATTERY PARK CITY
CASTLE CLINTON
WALL STREET
CITY HALL
BROOKLYN BRIDGE
SOUTH STREET SEAPORT

Maps and Listings

LEFT: the view over Lower Manhattan.
RIGHT: on the Brooklyn Bridge.

ABOVE: *An Icon of Hope*, in Battery Park, is a memorial to the victims of the World Trade Center atrocity.

to complete. It was a classic piece of 1970s architecture, and the view from the South Tower's 107th-floor Observation Deck was one of the best in the city.

On September 11, 2001, a day few will forget, 2,606 New Yorkers died as the result of suicide terrorist attacks. Nearby St Paul's Chapel (see page 79) offered aid in the crisis, and acted as an unofficial spot where grief-stricken families could mourn their loss.

The grounds of the World Trade Center have changed dramatically in the last couple years, as work concludes on its redevelopment and the centerpiece **One World Trade Center**, a 1,776ft (541-meter) skyscraper which is due to open in 2013. At the southern end of the site, a tribute center now provides a space for all to share memories and to remember. And at the base is the stunning new memorial to the victims.

Tribute WTC Visitor Center ❶

Address: 120 Liberty Street (between Greenwich and Church sts), www.tributewtc.org
Telephone: 866-737 1184

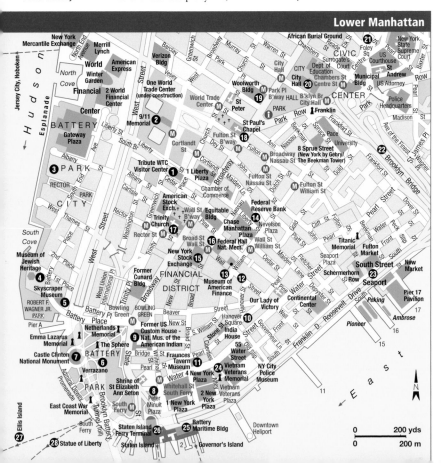

Lower Manhattan

Opening Hours: Mon and Wed–Sat 10am–6pm, Tue noon–6pm, Sun noon–5pm
Entrance Fee: charge
Subway: World Trade Center/Rector St

Opened in late 2006, the WTC Tribute Visitor Center is a project of the September 11th Families' Association, a non-profit organization set up in the aftermath of the tragedy to allow those most affected to stay in touch. The purpose-built center is comprised of five themed galleries: a running documentary on life before the attack has testimonies from former employees and local residents describing life as part of the WTC community, while other galleries focus on the day's events as they unfolded, and the subsequent rescue and clean-up operation.

Understandably, the center is very moving, and no matter how many documentaries are aired on television, little can prepare visitors for the stark reality of salvaged items, including a battered but instantly recognizable airplane window, or the variety of faces that peer out from the wall of "missing people" posters. A rolling list of names provides an intense reminder of the scale of the loss, while a collage of personal photos and mementoes ensures that we remember the victims' lives and not just their deaths.

Ultimately, the center is a tribute not only to the lives lost, but to those coping with being left behind. A wall in the final gallery allows visitors to add their thoughts and wishes for the future.

9/11 Memorial ➋

Address: One Liberty Plaza (entrance at Greenwich and Albany sts), www.911memorial.org
Telephone: 212-266 5211
Opening Hours: daily 10am–9pm, until 6pm in January and February
Entrance Fee: optional donation
Subway: World Trade Center/Rector St

After years of designs, speculation, and unfortunate delays, the **9/11 Memorial** finally opened exactly 10 years after the attacks. It is free to the public, but all visitors must make reservations to visit. Do not wait until

ABOVE: 9/11 mourners at St Paul's Chapel.
BELOW LEFT: the Firefighters' Monument at the Tribute WTC Visitor Center.
BELOW RIGHT: towers of light: a haunting tribute at Ground Zero.

the last minute, as slots fill up weeks or months in advance.

The **World Financial Center**, with its towers and elegant waterfront **Winter Garden**, was repaired after structural damage during the attacks, and high-profile occupants such as Dow Jones and the *Wall Street Journal* were soon able to move back in. It features stores, restaurants, and regular arts events held in the Winter Garden.

Battery Park City ③ is a huge, 92-acre (37-hectare) development stretching along the Hudson River, and is highly desirable residential property. A third of the area around Battery Park City is public space, and linked to Manhattan's riverfront expansion by scenic walkways that meander north to TriBeCa and beyond. Running alongside the Hudson River is the pretty, green, and leafy **Battery Park Esplanade**, which stretches for more than a mile. It's a fine place to stroll and reflect (look out for the skateboarders). There are also benches that offer relaxing vantage points for enjoying the splendid views over the Hudson River and across to the Statue of Liberty.

ABOVE: banker on a break.
BELOW: strolling along Battery Park Esplanade.

Another tribute to the past lies on the southwestern tip of Manhattan Island.

The Museum of Jewish Heritage ④

Address: 36 Battery Place (at 1st Place), www.mjhnyc.org
Telephone: 646-437 4202
Opening Hours: Sun–Tue and Thur 10am–5.45pm, Wed 10am–8pm, Fri 10am–3pm (until 5pm during Eastern Standard Time)
Entrance Fee: charge
Subway: Bowling Green/Rector St

With more than 2,000 photographs, artifacts, and original documentaries, the museum provides an insight into the experiences of Jewish people through the Holocaust and into the present day. In 2003, the building was extended by a new wing with a digitally equipped performance center which runs a program of film, theater, music, and the spoken word. Steven Spielberg contributed video testimonies from Holocaust victims compiled while directing *Schindler's List*.

Beyond the museum, pathways wind through **Robert F. Wagner Jr Park**, which has attractive landscaped

gardens, deck-topped brick pavilions, and places to sit with fine views of New York Harbor. Here are opportunities to meditate on the Jewish Museum's aim, which is to provide a thoughtful and moving chronicle of history, keeping the memory of the past alive and offering hope for the future.

Skyscraper Museum ❺

Address: 39 Battery Place (at West St), www.skyscraper.org
Telephone: 212-968 1961
Opening Hours: Wed–Sun noon–6pm
Entrance Fee: charge
Subway: Bowling Green/Rector St

Visitors with an interest in modern architecture may enjoy this celebration of tall buildings in this, the most vertical of modern cities. Through exhibitions, programs, and publications, the small museum explores skyscrapers as objects of design, products of technology, sites of construction, investments in real estate, and places of work and residence. The interior itself is a dazzling example of the form, with mirrored floor and ceiling offering a bewildering perspective.

Above: inside the Museum of Jewish Heritage.
Below Left: the Museum of Jewish Heritage.
Below: worker in the Financial District.

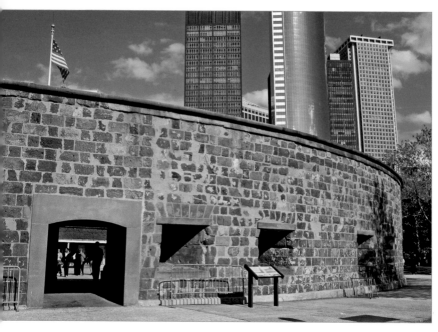

ABOVE: Castle Clinton, built as a defensive fort, is the place to buy tickets for the ferry to the Statue of Liberty.

TIP

Romantics should look at Shearwater Sailing, www.shearwatersailing. com, tel: 212-619 0885, which offers a variety of trips on a 1929 double-masted schooner, including harbor cruises that sail close to the Statue of Liberty and Ellis Island. There's a bar on board, or you can book for the excellent brunch cruise.

EARLIEST NEW YORK

At the island's tip, **Battery Park ❻** is where New Amsterdam was first settled by Europeans, and New York's history began. Named for the battery of protective cannons that once stood here, this is famously where Manhattan begins, or ends – as the song goes, "...the Battery's down." The park, as well as having wonderful views and many memorials, now contains a lovely natural garden, the **Bosque**. Fritz Koenig's huge bronze sculpture *The Sphere* had stood for more than 30 years in the World Trade Center Plaza, and withstood the tons of metal and concrete crashing down on top of it on 9/11. In 2002, the battered globe was moved to Battery Park. There is constant talk of plans to move it closer to the 9/11 Memorial, but for now it sits at the foot of a rosebed called Hope Garden. An eternal flame burns in memory, and it is a fine spot for contemplation.

Castle Clinton ❼

Address: Battery Park, www.nps.gov/cacl
Telephone: 212-344 7220
Opening Hours: daily 8.30am–5pm
Entrance Fee: free
Subway: Bowling Green/South Ferry

Built as a fort to defend against the British in the War of 1812, Castle Clinton was renamed Castle Garden in 1823 and became the city's premier place of amusement, where Samuel Morse gave his first public telegraph demonstration and Swedish singer Jenny Lind made her American debut in a tumultuously acclaimed concert in 1850 (for which some wealthy New Yorkers paid a then-unheard-of $30 a ticket). Not long after, the area was joined to the mainland by landfill and served as the New York State Immigration Station, where more than 8 million immigrants were processed between 1855 and 1890.

For two years, potential settlers were processed on a barge moored in the Hudson, but when the new headquarters opened on Ellis Island in 1892, the tide of immigration shifted. Home to the New York Aquarium until 1941, Castle Clinton was made a national monument in 1950 and opened to the public in 1975.

Saints and Sails

Peter Minuit Plaza ❽, east of Battery Park, is named for the first governor (director general) of New Amsterdam. In a tiny park nearby, a plaque commemorates some of the city's lesser-known arrivals: 23 Sephardic Jews, dropped off by a French ship in 1654, who founded New Amsterdam's first Jewish congregation, Shearith Israel.

Turn left on State Street, once lined by wealthy merchants' houses, to come to the **Shrine of St Elizabeth Ann Seton** (7 State Street), in the only 1790s Federal-style mansion still standing here, now surrounded by giant glass towers. The chapel by the shrine is dedicated to the first American-born saint, who founded the Sisters of Charity in 1809 and was canonized in 1975 by Pope Paul VI.

Herman Melville, author of *Moby Dick*, was born in a house near 17 State Street, where today **Seaport Museum New York** (www.seany. org, tel: 212-748 8600; Thur–Sun 10am–5pm, weather permitting; charge) offers a glimpse into the nautical heritage of the city. Indoor exhibits have been closed due to budgetary issues, but visitors can still tour the country's largest collection of privately maintained historic vessels, including the 125-year-old 279ft (85-meter) wrought-iron sailing ship *Wavetree*, the four-masted wooden-decked 377ft (115-meter) *Peking*, and the tugboat *W.O. Decker*, which is available for private charters.

On the other side of State Street from Battery Park, the former **US Custom House** was designed by Cass Gilbert and built in 1907. A magnificent example of Beaux Arts architecture, with a facade embellished by ornate limestone sculptures that represent four of the world's continents and "eight races" of mankind, this grand edifice also has striking Reginald Marsh murals on the rotunda ceiling inside.

And, in what could seem an ironic twist, this spot, where Peter Minuit is believed to have given goods to the value of $24 to local Indians for the purchase of Manhattan Island, is now a major museum to tribal culture.

National Museum of the American Indian ❾

Address: George Gustav Heye Center, 1 Bowling Green, www.nmai.si.edu
Telephone: 212-514 3700
Opening Hours: Fri–Wed 10am–5pm, Thur 10am–8pm
Entrance Fee: free
Subway: Bowling Green

Operated by the Smithsonian Institution, the museum details

ABOVE: a costume from the National Museum of the American Indian.
BELOW: the Shrine of St Elizabeth Ann Seton.

the history and cultural legacy of America's native peoples through artifacts, costume, artworks, and online resources. The glass-cased exhibits seem dwarfed by the grand surroundings of the Custom House, but the museum is a worthy achievement nevertheless, and often presents music and dance performances in addition to its permanent displays.

Bowling Green and Hanover Square

Give a pat to Di Modica's *Charging Bull*, a statue forever linked to bullish Wall Street. He digs in his hooves at the northern end of **Bowling Green Park**, New York's first public park. Then wander up Beaver Street to Broad Street, or take a quick detour back to State Street before following Pearl Street to **Hanover Square** ❿.

The square burned to ashes in the Great Fire of 1835, one of many fires that destroyed virtually all remnants of Dutch New Amsterdam. According to one eyewitness who was watching from Brooklyn, "The sparks from that fire came over the river so thick that the neighbors...

ABOVE: a display at the National Museum of the American Indian.
BELOW: Bowling Green was New York's first public park.

were obliged to keep their roofs wet all night." The square recovered to become a thriving commercial center, and includes **India House** (1 Hanover Square), an 1850s Italianate brownstone that's been home to a private club (at lunchtime) for maritime movers and shakers since 1914. You don't have to be a member, however, to drop in for a drink at the **Blue Bar at Bayard's** upstairs (Tue–Fri 4pm–11pm).

Captains of industry have dined at **Delmonico's**, at the corner of Beaver and William streets, since the 1830s, when two Swiss brothers established the city's first formal French-style restaurant. Stop and admire the impressive marble columns at the entrance, reputedly shipped over from Pompeii, or venture inside for a drink and a bit of market eavesdropping at The Grill.

Fraunces Tavern Museum ⓫
Address: 54 Pearl Street (at Broad St), www.frauncestavernmuseum.org
Telephone: 212-425 1778
Opening Hours: Mon–Sat 10am–5pm, Sun 10am–5pm from Jun–Aug

Entrance Fee: charge
Subway: Wall St/Broad St

Farther south, at the corner of Pearl and Broad streets, is one of Old New York's oldest buildings. Built in 1719 for a French Huguenot merchant, the house was extended and made into a tavern by Samuel Fraunces in the 1760s. The New York Chamber of Commerce got its start over a few mugs of ale here, and George Washington gave an emotional farewell address to his officers in 1783 in the Long Room. The tavern was restored to its 18th-century appearance and opened again in 1907.

The wood-paneled tavern is still an atmospheric bar-restaurant, with dining rooms for private rental. On the two floors above is the intriguing **Fraunces Tavern Museum**, where exhibits include a lock of Washington's hair, the Long Room complete with period furniture, a fragment of one of Washington's teeth (not, contrary to legend, wooden), and a shoe that belonged to his wife, Martha. The cases housing the exhibits were built by Tiffany & Co. in 1907.

East Meets West

Waterfront development has transformed the banks of Manhattan along the Hudson River and East River from a parade of rotting piers into miles of recreation and relaxation. The work began downtown, funded by the Lower Manhattan Development Corporation. New public spaces full of greenery have been established at the revitalized Coenties Slip, Old Slip, Peck Slip, and Burling Slip. It is all contributing to a 2-mile (3km) long promenade where you can walk, jog, bike, or just sit and look out toward Brooklyn. And the work goes on, making room for retail spaces, pavilions, and an archipelago that will connect Battery Park to Old Slip.

WALL STREET

Walk north on William Street (its twists and turns a reminder of when it was known as Horse and Cart Street) to **Wall Street ⑫**, traditional hub of the financial world, where the narrow stone canyons are lined by towering banks, brokerage houses, and law offices.

A worldwide symbol of wealth, power, and deal-making, remembered for traumatic scenes during the 1929 stock market crash, the street took its name from the 17th-century wall – or, more accurately, a wooden blockade built by the Dutch as protection against the threat of Indian and English attacks. The country's first stock exchange began just in front of **60 Wall Street** in 1792, when 24 brokers gathered beneath a buttonwood tree. The building at **55 Wall Street** is a massive columned landmark that dates to 1841 and served as the original Merchants' Exchange, and later as

ABOVE: Battery Park Espanade.
BELOW: the Fraunces Tavern.

ABOVE: Wall Street was named for the wooden barrier that was erected by the Dutch against the English in the mid 1600's.
RIGHT: stock broker.
BELOW: at the New York Stock Exchange.

headquarters for the influential First National City Bank.

Financial history

A few buildings south at the corner of William Street is the former Bank of New York, founded by Alexander Hamilton in 1784 and the new home of the **Museum of American Finance** (48 Wall Street, www.maof.org, tel: 212-908 4110; Tue–Sat 10am–4pm; charge). Affiliated with the Smithsonian, the museum is dedicated to the trading and financial industries, with a collection of antique stocks and bonds, ticker tape from the 1929 crash, and memorabilia from the era of the robber barons, a group that included Messrs Carnegie, Frick, and Rockefeller. A new exhibit details the credit crisis that led to the financial disasters of 2008.

Following William Street to Maiden Lane will lead to **Nevelson Plaza**, with seven tall abstract sculptures by the late Louise Nevelson, a longtime New York resident.

Money may not be art, but there's a lot of it at the **Federal Reserve Bank**

(33 Liberty Street, www.newyork fed.org, tel: 212-720 6130), west of Nevelson Plaza. Constructed in 1924, this imposing edifice is said to house nearly a quarter of the world's gold reserves (as well as wheelbarrows-full of old and counterfeit cash). Tours are available, but security is tight and visits must be booked ahead.

Easy Street

Double back to Wall Street and the corner of Broad Street, where the **New York Stock Exchange** was constructed in 1903, its building fronted by an impressive facade of Corinthian columns. Since 9/11, though, the Stock Exchange's Visitors' Gallery is no longer open for spectators to observe the speculators. The exchange has an annual trading volume of over $5 trillion.

The Greek temple-style **Federal Hall National Memorial** (26 Wall Street, www.nps.gov/feha, tel: 212-825 6990; Mon–Sat 9am–5pm) is, however, open to the public. It's on the site of the original Federal Hall, where on April 30, 1789, George Washington was sworn in as the first President of the

United States (there's an impressive statue of him on the steps); it later became a branch of the US Treasury Department. Today it's run by the National Park Service and includes historical memorabilia, plus the suit that George Washington wore at his inauguration.

Trinity Church ⓱

Address: 89 Broadway (at Wall St), www.trinitywallstreet.org
Telephone: 212-602 0800
Opening Hours: Mon–Fri 7am–6pm, Sat 8am–**4pm**, Sun 7am–4pm
Entrance Fee: free
Subway: Wall St/Rector St

At the very top of Wall Street where it meets Broadway, pretty Trinity Church is a serene survivor of early New York. First established in 1698, the present 1846 church is the third one built on the same site. **Trinity Church graveyard** contains some of the oldest graves in the city – including that of Alexander Hamilton, the US's first Secretary of the Treasury, who owned a house at 33 Wall Street and was killed in a duel with Aaron Burr. A small **museum** offers a look

at the original charter, among other historic artifacts.

St Paul's Chapel ⓲

Address: 209 Broadway (between Fulton and Vesey sts), www.trinitywall-street.org
Telephone: 212-233 4164
Opening Hours: Mon–Fri 10am–6pm, Sat 10am–3pm, Sun 7am–9pm
Entrance Fee: free
Subway: Fulton St/Broadway

St Paul's Chapel, part of the Trinity Church Parish, is situated five blocks north on Broadway, between Fulton and Vesey streets. Built in 1766, this Georgian-style landmark is the only church left from the Colonial era, when luminaries like Prince William (later King William IV) and Lord Cornwallis worshipped here. George Washington's personal church pew is also preserved.

Although it is located just one block east of the World Trade Center, remarkably, the building was not damaged on September 11, 2001, and was used as a shelter for many of the volunteers and workers who helped in the aftermath. The chapel

EAT

For a choice of cafes and restaurants, head for cobblestoned Stone Street, said to have been the first paved street in New York City. This tiny alley, tucked away in the concrete canyons of Lower Manhattan, is situated off Hanover Square, between South William and Pearl streets.

BELOW: Trinity Church is a slice of Old New York.

BELOW: protesters at Occupy 2.0 in Duarte Square.

is now the site of a permanent 9/11 exhibit: *Unwavering Spirit: Hope and Healing at Ground Zero*, honoring the eight-month-long volunteer effort of its parishoners during and after the tragedy.

CITY HALL AREA

The handsome, gargoyle-topped **Woolworth Building** N (233 Broadway) was known in its heyday as the "cathedral of commerce." Designed by architect Cass Gilbert, from 1913 until 1930, when the Chrysler Building was completed, its 60 stories and soaring height of almost 800ft (245 meters) made it the tallest building in the world. The Gothic Revival tower cost five-and-dime baron Frank W. Woolworth $13 million, and was officially opened by President Woodrow Wilson, who pushed a button in Washington that successfully lit up all of the floors.

Turning around, you will get a close up view of one of the skyline's newest stars, **8 Spruce Street** (aka New York by Gehry or The Beekman). A creation of the inimitable Frank Gehry, this skinny 76-story

curiosity undulates as if it were made of water. It's a singular and spectacular addition to the evolving Downtown landscape.

Since 1910, New York has honored everyone from Teddy Roosevelt to Nelson Mandela (and, of course, the New York Yankees) with ticker-tape parades that conclude at handsome **City Hall** N. At the junction of Broadway and Park Row, this French Renaissance/Federal-style edifice has been the seat of city government since DeWitt Clinton was mayor in 1812, and was co-designed by French architect Joseph-François Mangin, responsible for the Place de la Concorde in Paris.

Protests and politicking

City Hall Park, a triangular, tree-shaded former common in front of City Hall, has played an important role throughout the city's history: as the site of public executions, alms-houses for the poor, and a British prison for captured Revolutionary soldiers. It's also where Alexander Hamilton led a protest against the tea tax in 1774, and where, two

Occupy Wall Street

On weekends and evenings Lower Manhattan has a reputation as a quiet and empty place. Certain streets can seem utterly deserted for blocks. In the last few years, the volume of people and voices has increased, due in large part to a growing sense of discontentment.

In 2010, protestors filled Park Place in opposition to the construction of the Cordoba House (now known as Park51). Proposed as a community center for Muslims, it was quickly dubbed the "Ground Zero Mosque." What started as a small movement became a national debate, with politicians and pundits of all types contributing their opinions. The main issue: should a Muslim organization build so close to the World Trade Center site? It is yet to be resolved, but latest word has Park51 leaning towards commercial tenants, rather than religious ones.

When disillusioned young people began camping out in Zuccotti Park in September 2011, no one could have predicted that in a matter of weeks their protest of corporate greed known as "Occupy Wall Street" would catch on worldwide. The message is clear. As a crucible for political movements and discussions, New York is still as essential as anywhere else in the country.

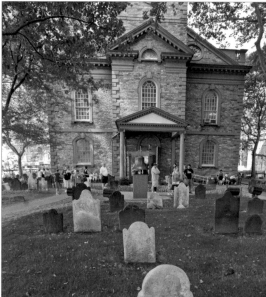

years later, George Washington and his troops heard the Declaration of Independence for the very first time.

Behind City Hall stands the former New York County Courthouse, dubbed on its completion in 1878 the **Tweed Courthouse**. This was after the revelation that "Boss" Tweed and his Tammany Hall cronies (see page 35) had pocketed some $9 million of the final $14 million construction costs.

After extensive refurbishment, the courthouse is now the home of the New York City Department of Education. Tours can be arranged by appointment (tel: 212-788 2656).

Past sumptuous **Surrogate's Court** (31 Chambers Street), with its eight Corinthian columns, **Foley Square ㉑** is named for another Tammany Hall politician. It's also the site of worthy civic structures like the 1936 Cass Gilbert-designed **United States Courthouse** (1 Foley Square), and the **New York State Supreme Court** (60 Centre Street), built in 1913, where New Yorkers are summoned for jury duty.

When workers were excavating the foundations of a new Federal courthouse building, the skeletons of African slaves were discovered. Now a city, state, and Federal landmark, the **African Burial Ground** is commemorated by a memorial at the corner of Duane and Elk streets.

The **Municipal Building** (1 Centre Street), slightly to the south, is an enormous, ornate 1914 McKim, Mead, & White confection. In the second-floor civil wedding chapel you can tie the knot in about five minutes (after the proper preliminaries, of course).

In the lobby of the Municipal Building, **City Store** (www.nyc.gov/citystore; Mon–Fri 10am–6pm) is a place for unusual gifts (manhole cover cufflinks or genuine New York taxi medallion, anyone?) and can provide a wealth of information on the city.

ABOVE LEFT: City Hall.
ABOVE: the churchyard at St Paul's.
BELOW: romance in the churchyard.

ABOVE: people stroll along the many shops on Fulton Street at South Street Seaport
BELOW: the Brooklyn Bridge: the "new eighth wonder of the world."

BRIDGE AND HARBOR

For one of the best of all views of the **East River** and Lower Manhattan, walk down Frankfort Street or along Park Row. Both lead to the pedestrian walkway that leads onto the **Brooklyn Bridge** ㉒, one of the world's first suspension bridges83. As the pointed arches of the bridge's great Gothic towers come into view, recognition is immediate, for this is another icon of New York that has etched itself into the world's visual vocabulary.

Alternatively, walk toward the East River along **Fulton Street**, to the place from where (until the Brooklyn Bridge was built) ferries carried New Yorkers to Brooklyn, from the Fulton Street pier. In the 1800s, this part of town was the center of New York's maritime commerce, where spices from China, rum from the West Indies, and whale oil from the Atlantic were bought and sold, where ships were built, and where sailors thronged to enjoy a seedy red-light district. All that ended after the Civil War, when the old East River port fell into a decline, and big ships no longer sailed here.

South Street Seaport ㉓

Address: Fulton Street (at South St), www.southstreetseaport.com

Telephone: 212-732 7678
Opening Hours: Mon–Sat 10am–9pm, **Sun** 11am–8pm
Entrance Fee: free, charge for some attractions
Subway: Fulton St/Broadway-Nassau

South Street Seaport bills itself as a 12-block "museum without walls." Near the **Titanic Memorial Lighthouse**, at the corner of Fulton and Water streets, **Schermerhorn Row** is lined by the last surviving Federal-style commercial buildings in the city, part of a block of early 19th-century warehouses.

Cannon's Walk is another block of restored buildings, between Fulton and Beekman streets. Around the corner on Water Street, the **Herman Melville Gallery** and **Whitman Gallery** are on either side of **Bowne and Co.** (211 Water Street), a 19th-century printing shop.

Pier 17 is a three-story pavilion that juts over the East River at the end of Fulton Street. In addition to the third-floor food court's ethnic delicacies, there are dozens of stores.

In summertime, on the north side of Pier 17, is **Water Taxi Beach**, one of the city's newly developed man-made beaches. From May through October, it's a family-friendly environment during the day with food stands and plenty of sand (trucked in from New Jersey) on which to sun. At night, DJs spin tunes for an adult-only crowd. Check the website (www.watertaxibeach.com) for opening and closing dates as they change each season.

In summer, catch free evening concerts on **Pier 16**. The adjacent booth sells tickets for one-hour **Downtown Liberty Harbor Cruises**, operated by Circle Line (www.circlelinedowntown.com, tel: 866-782 8834).

The Seaport Museum's impressive collection of **historic vessels** occasionally cast off to conduct elegant cruises around Manhattan.

Back toward Battery Park

The last few sites extend around the tip of the island, offering wonderful views along the way. South of South Street Seaport – past Pier 11, and just beyond **Old Slip**, a landfilled inlet

TIP

Stockbrokers and other wired types can be seen surfing the net in City Hall Park and seven other places, taking advantage of Lower Manhattan's free wireless internet hotspots. For a map, log on to www.downtowny.com/wifi.

BELOW: cyclists on the Brooklyn Bridge.

The Brooklyn Bridge

The Brooklyn Bridge was the inspiration of engineer John Augustus Roebling. The span of almost 1,600ft (488 meters), from City Hall across the East River to Brooklyn's Cadman Plaza, was the world's longest ever conceived. Steel-cable suspension gave unmatched stability and strength, as well as a striking image.

Construction began in 1867 and took 16 years to complete. Building was marred by tragedy. Two years into the project, Roebling was killed by a ferryboat. His son, Washington Roebling, took over, but fell victim to the bends during riverbed excavation. An invalid the rest of his life, Roebling Jr monitored the works by telescope as his wife, Emily, supervised the project. When the bridge opened in 1883, 12 people were trampled to death in a panic, fearing a collapse.

Despite its beginnings, the Brooklyn Bridge was dubbed the "new eighth wonder of the world," and has inspired artists ever since. The walk across the bridge is indeed a wonder, and residents of Brooklyn employed downtown often prefer it to the subway, even if it means leaving a little early for work.

SHOPPING

The financial district may not be renowned as a shopping district, but where people work, they buy. Designer clothing, jewelry, gourmet delicacies and gifts can all be found in the Wall Street vicinity, catering to those who prefer to spend their lunch hours perusing the racks and shelves.

Books

The Mysterious Bookshop
58 Warren Street (at W. Broadway and Church St)
Tel: 212-587 1011
www.mysteriousbookshop.com
A tiny enclave dedicated to whodunits, including out-of-print, signed, and first editions, just a couple blocks from City Hall on the border of TriBeCa.

Clothing

Canali
25 Broad Street
(at Beaver St and Exchange Place)
Tel: 212-842 8700
www.canali.it
The New York storefront for the legendary Italian masters of men's formal wear. Suits are made in Milan and tailored on site.

Century 21
22 Cortlandt Street (at Trinity Place)
Tel: 212-227 9092
www.c21stores.com
A bustling temple to discount designer-clothes, dubbed 'New York's Best Kept Secret'. What it lacks in organization it makes up for in selection, with several floors of designer gear at knock-down prices. Check

your patience at the door.

Department Stores

J&R Music & Computer World
23 Park Row (SW end of City Hall Park)
Tel: 212-238 9000
www.jr.com
The city's most famous electronics store has expanded in recent years to include housewares and office supplies. It's still the place to go for anything with a circuit board.

Gifts

Bowne & Co. Stationers
211 Water Street (South Street Seaport)
www.southstreetseaportmuseum.org
Part museum and part letterpress office, this recreation of a 19th-century shop is worth the visit just to see the vintage printing equipment.

Home

Korin
57 Warren Street (at W. Broadway)
Tel: 212-587 7021
www.korin.com
You may not have the precision skills of a professional chef, but you can at least have the tools. Any home cook will be astounded by the selection of knives and cutlery available at this Japanese specialist. It

goes well beyond just sushi knives.

Jewelry

Kenjo
40 Wall Street (at Nassau and William sts)
Tel: 800-548 8463
www.kenjo.net
For those who still wear wristwatches they would be hard pressed to find a better selection of designer watch brands (sorry, no Rolexes) or service than at this paean to gears and bands.

Tiffany & Co.
37 Wall Street
(at William St)
Tel: 212-514 8015
www.tiffany.com
On a pedestrian-only stretch of Wall Street, across from the former Bank of Manhattan Trust Building (now a Trump property), bankers buy gifts for their loved ones in unmistakable blue boxes.

Markets

The Greenmarket at Bowling Green
Broadway at Battery Place
www.grownyc.org
One of the smallest greenmarkets in one of the city's smallest parks is a welcome edition amid the skyscrapers. Open Tuesdays and Thursdays, 8am–5pm. There are also greenmarkets at City Hall, Zuccotti Park, and Battery Park City.

LEFT: Century 21.

where 18th-century ships berthed to unload their cargo – is a park where stranded sailors used to congregate. Today, at the foot of a brick amphitheater near the corner of Coenties Slip and Water Street, is a monument to other young men.

A 14ft (4-meter) monument erected by the city in 1985, the **Vietnam Veterans Memorial** ㉔ is made of green glass etched with excerpts of letters written to and from soldiers in Vietnam. It is movingly illuminated at night. Nearby is the **New York City Police Museum** (100 Old Slip, www.nycpolicemuseum.org, tel: 212-480 3100), with exhibits on the many aspects of policing New York.

A few blocks away, the rusting **Battery Maritime Building** ㉕ (11 South Street), a steel landmark Beaux Arts structure built in Whitehall Street in 1909, is the boarding point for ferries to **Governor's Island** (www.govisland.com) each spring and summer. The island is also the site of corporate parties and special events that the public can join.

On the next pier down from the Maritime Building is the refurbished **Staten Island Ferry Terminal** ㉖ (1 Whitehall Street, www.nyc.gov for schedule). The 25-minute cruise to Staten Island not only offers close-up views of the Statue of Liberty but is also free, making it the best bargain in town. There are rumors the ferry will be forced to charge in future because of its huge costs. In the meantime, however, the shiny new terminal and a new fleet of ferries make this a trip you really should make.

Another essential cruise departs a little farther around the waterfront. **Ferries** leave for Ellis Island and the Statue of Liberty a few steps from the East Coast War Memorial in Battery Park. Tickets and schedule information are available from **Statue Cruises** (http://statuecruises.

ABOVE: taking in the view of Manhattan from the Staten Island ferry.

TIP

There are dozens of stops on the free, seven-days-a-week Downtown Connection bus service in Lower Manhattan. Buses run from near South Street Seaport to Battery Park City, via Battery Park, from 10am to 7.30pm, roughly every 10 minutes on weekdays and 15 minutes on weekends (www. downtownny.com).

TIP

Driving to Brooklyn? It's a prettier ride over the bridges, but consider taking the Brooklyn Battery Tunnel. Access is easy from the West Side Highway near Battery Park, and you avoid the oft-congested interior of Downtown.

com, tel: 877-523 9849), or at Castle Clinton.

Ellis Island ㉗

Address: Ellis Island, www.ellisisland. org
Telephone: 212-561 4588
Opening Hours: Ferries daily approx. 9am–5pm
Entrance Fee: free, **charge** for ferry
Subway: South Ferry/Whitehall St

Ellis Island (see page 92) was known as the "Island of Tears" because of the medical, mental, and literacy tests applicants had to undergo in the 32 years that it served as gateway to the United States. Today, it is a national monument and one of the city's most popular tourist destinations. Outside the museum, a promenade offers wonderful views of the Statue of Liberty and the Manhattan skyline.

Statue of Liberty ㉘

Address: Liberty Island, www.nps. gov/stli
Telephone: 212-363 3200
Opening Hours: Ferries daily approx. 9am–5pm
Entrance Fee: free, charge for ferry

RIGHT: "Give me your tired, your poor..."
BELOW: fun in the sun on Water Taxi Beach.

Subway: South Ferry/Whitehall St

The Statue of Liberty (see page 90) was completed in France in July 1884, and arrived in New York Harbor in June of 1885 on board the French frigate *Isère*. In transit, Lady Liberty and her crown, torch, tablet, and other accessories were reduced to 350 pieces and packed in 214 crates, but it took only four months to reassemble the statue in its entirety. On October 28, 1886, the dedication took place in front of thousands of spectators. Extensive renovations are underway on the interior, which is scheduled to reopen in late 2012.

BEST RESTAURANTS, BARS AND CAFES

Restaurants

Adrienne's Pizzabar
54 Stone Street (at William Street)
Tel: 212-248 3838
www.adriennespizzabar.com
Open: L & D daily $$ ① [p342, B4]
Many consider this to be the best pizza below Canal Street.

Battery Gardens
Battery Park (opposite 17 State St)
Tel: 212-809 5508
www.batterygardens.com
Open: L & D Mon–Sat, L only Sun $$$ ② [p342, A4]
Multi-leveled dining rooms facing the Statue of Liberty. Touristy, but still worth stopping by.

Bennie's
88 Fulton St (at Gold St)
Tel: 212-587 8930
www.benniesthaicafenyc.com
Open: L & D daily $ ③ [p342, B3]
It's nothing to look at, but this Downtown Thai cafe is the best-tasting bargain in the South Street Seaport neighborhood.

Bridge Café
279 Water St (at Dover St)
Tel: 212-227 3344
www.bridgecafenyc.com
Open: L & D daily $$$ ④ [p342, B3]
Located "under" the Brooklyn Bridge, this hideaway has been here since the 1790s.

Carl's Steaks
79 Chambers St (at Church St and Broadway)
Tel: 212-566 2828
www.carlssteaks.com
Open: L & D daily $ ⑤ [p342, B2]
This Philadelphia-style cheesesteak sandwich shop may not compete with Pat's in Philly, but for Downtown New York it will do just fine.

Delmonico's
56 Beaver St (at William St)
Tel: 212-509 1144
www.delmonicosny.com
Open: L & D Mon–Fri, D only Sat $$$$ ⑥ [p342, B3]
The place for power lunches; a club-like steakhouse that closes at weekends.

Fraunces Tavern
54 Pearl St (at Broad St)
Tel: 212-968 1776
www.frauncestavern.com
Open: L & D daily $$$ ⑦ [p342, A4]
Historic, welcoming dining rooms and a good museum too. Great for lunch or a drink.

Gigino at Wagner Park
20 Battery Place (at West St)
Tel: 212-528 2228
www.gigino-wagnerpark.com
Open: L & D daily $$ ⑧ [p342, A4]
Gorgeous sunsets with a view of Lady Liberty at this moderately priced Italian spot – the terrace is ideal in summer.

Harry's Café
1 Hanover Sq
Tel: 212-785 9200
www.harrysnyc.com
Open: L & D Mon–Sat $$ ⑨ [p342, B3]
Folks refused to accept that the original Harry's closed, so the owners reopened it, offering great steaks and seafood.

Ise
56 Pine St
Tel: 212-785 1600
www.iserestaurant.com
Open: L & D Mon–Fri $$ ⑩ [p342, B3]
Follow the Japanese expats for authentic gyoza, yakitori, and katsu.

Merchants River House
1 Esplanade Plaza (at Albany St)
Tel: 212-432 1451
www.merchantsriverhouse.com
Open: L & D daily $$ ⑪ [p342, A2]
Eat facing the Hudson, as cruise ships set sail.

SHO Shaun Hergatt
40 Broad Street (second floor of The Setai Club)
Tel: 212-809 3993
www.shoshaunhergatt.com
Open: L & D Mon–Fri D only Sat $$$$ ⑫ [p342, A3]
Fine dining with a seasonally and locally inspired menu, and an award-winning wine list.

Bars and Cafes

The Bar
1 West St ① [p342, A3]

Prices for a three-course dinner per person with half a bottle of wine:
$ = under $20
$$ = $20–$45
$$$ = $45–$60
$$$$ = over $60

In the lobby of the Ritz-Carlton Battery Park – expensive, but the comfy setting is worth it.

Jeremy's Ale House
28 Front Street (at Peck Slip) ② [p342, B3]
For happy hours, check out this rowdy South Street Seaport bar popular with firefighters.

Paris Café
19 South St (at Peck Slip) ③ [p342, C3]
A longtime seaport hangout.

SouthWest NY
25 Liberty St ④ [p342, A2]
Good terrace food in warm weather; great year-round for cocktails.

Looking up at the World Trade Center

It was once a monument to commerce and a symbol of bravado. It became the site of the worst terrorist attack on American soil. Now it is a place of remembrance and hope

On the morning of August 7, 1974, New Yorkers gathered in the streets of Lower Manhattan and did something that only tourists are inclined to do. They looked up at the skyscrapers in awe. A diminutive Frenchman, aptly named Philippe Petit, had strung a cable between the two tallest buildings in the world, and he was "dancing" his way across the tightrope at a height of over 1,300ft (396 meters). The World Trade Center, barely a year old at the time, was now not only a center of international commerce, but the site of the world's most audacious stunt.

Thirty-seven years later, New Yorkers looked up again. Only the audacity they witnessed was even more unbelievable and far more sinister. The two towers were on fire, ignited by jet fuel from two terrorist-piloted planes that crashed into them. In a matter of hours, they would be piles of rubble. The rubble would bury more than 2,600 people. It was impossible to know what might come next.

On September 11, 2011, exactly ten years after the devastating attacks, families of the victims gathered for the dedication of a memorial. They ran their fingers over names inscribed in bronze panels. They stood in the shade of white oak trees and watched water cascade into the reflecting pools that sit in the deep footprints of the two towers. They had heard about this for years, but actually seeing it was different. Somber, powerful, cathartic, it was so many things. The next day, the memorial opened to the public and the first of what is sure to be millions of visitors took in the haunting and beautiful tribute to the fallen.

With an accompanying museum scheduled to open in late 2012, the memorial will be complete. The design, however, reminds of the void, not just in the skyline, but in the lives of everyone affected by the attacks. To limit the crowds and give each visitor ample time to explore, the memorial distributes passes via an online reservation system. They also recommend multiple visits to see the changing reflections in the water at different times of day. Because that's what the site is ultimately about: reflection.

One World Trade Center

Even as they reflect on the past, New Yorkers are looking up once more. Standing a patriotic 1776ft (541 meters) tall, the building that during its initial construction was known as The Freedom Tower has finally joined the family of skyscrapers that make up the world's most recognizable skyline. The road to completion was longer than many might have hoped, but for a structure of such stature – in height, but

LEFT: a visitor to the 9/11 Memorial Preview Site in New York. **RIGHT:** names of the victims from the September 11, 2001 terrorist attacks.

also in historical importance – the job had to be done right.

Designed by David M. Childs, the glimmering tower consists of 2.6 million square feet (234,000 square meters) of space, 55,000 of which have been designated as lower-level retail space. The grand lobby will soon house art exhibits, bathed in natural light that will pass through the 2,000 pieces of prismatic glass. A 1,000-seat performing arts center from the mind of Frank Gehry will stage dance programmed by the Joyce Theater. There will be two world-class restaurants and two floors dedicated to television broadcasting. At the top, visitors will be afforded the finest, and highest, view of the city from the observation deck, while the soaring spire will double as a communications antenna.

Back on the ground, at the northeast corner, subways and the PATH train will arrive and depart from the World Trade Center Port Authority Trans-Hudson Transportation Hub, a stunning white structure with a glass ceiling and a ribbed exterior. Its creator, Santiago Calatrava, was inspired by the image of a child releasing a dove from a pair of hands. The hub will mirror this action every September 11th, when the glass ceiling will retract and expose the grand pavilion to the open air.

And the transportation hub is not the only new neighbor. Four other new skyscrapers are under construction: 1,329ft (405-meter) 2 World Trade Center, with its four diamond shaped peaks, will be home to four trading floors, each encompassing 65,000 sq ft (6,038 square meters); 3 World Trade Center will welcome retailers and trading firms into its 2.8 million square feet (241,547 square meters) of office space; 4 World Trade Center has set aside a third of its square footage for the new offices of the Port Authority, the agency that is also overseeing the construction of 5 World Trade Center, which will sit on the former site of the Deutsche Bank building that was irreparably damaged in the attack.

All the buildings have been built with safety and sustainability as a top priority, far exceeding building codes and employing state-of-the-art technology and materials to achieve LEED certification. Opening dates vary, but some unveilings should occur as early as 2012 or 2013, 40 years after the original World Trade Center first had people putting their hands to their brows and looking skyward.

THE STATUE OF LIBERTY

A potent icon in the United States for more than 120 years, the Statue of Liberty is still the most evocative sight in New York City

Like millions of other immigrants, Italian-born writer Edward Corsi's first glimpse of America was the heroic figure of Lady Liberty, her hand thrust skyward with a torch to light the way. He wrote: "Looming shadowy through the mist, it brought silence to the decks of the *Florida*. This symbol of America – this enormous expression of what we had all been taught was the inner meaning of this new country – inspired awe in the hopeful immigrants."

Partly because of the statue's significance as a symbol of freedom and democracy, security measures have been implemented since 9/11. Visitors are screened before boarding the ferry, and backpacks and large bags are not permitted. Renovations on the interior of the crown and pedestal are planned through the end of 2012, during which time both will be closed. However, Liberty Island will remain open throughout the project. When the interior reopens, a limited amount of tickets to visit the crown will be available per day, so make reservations far in advance.

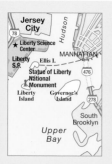

The Essentials

Address: www.nps.gov/stli
Tel: 212-363 3200
Opening Hours: daily 9am–5pm; seasonal variations.
Entrance Fee: free, but fee for ferry and extra charge for crown access
Transportation: Statue Cruises, Battery Park

ABOVE: the tablet that Liberty holds in her left hand reads (in Roman numerals) "July 4, 1776," the date of America's independence from Britain.

RIGHT: there are 25 windows in Liberty's crown which symbolize gemstones found on earth. The seven rays of the crown represent the seven seas and continents of the world.

A Gift from France

The Statue of Liberty was a gift from the people of France to the United States to symbolize the spirit of successful revolutions in both of their countries.

In 1865, Edouard-René Lefèvre de Laboulaye, an intellectual, politician, and admirer of America, suggested to a young sculptor named Auguste Bartholdi that he make a large monument in honor of French and American brotherhood. By 1874, enough money had been raised by the French – through lotteries, subscriptions, and entertainment – to construct the statue. Funding for the pedestal was slower to materialize in the United States, however, and it took a concerted campaign from Joseph Pulitzer through his newspaper, *The World*, to raise the necessary finance.

Gustave Eiffel, who later built the Eiffel Tower, designed the ingenious framework that supports the thin copper skin. In 1885 Bartholdi's statue, called *Liberty Enlightening the World*, was shipped to the US, and was formally dedicated in a ceremony on October 28, 1886.

ABOVE: the statue is situated on 12-acre (5-hectare) Liberty Island, which is owned by the Federal government. The observation platform in the pedestal allows great views of New York and the harbor.

ELLIS ISLAND

More than 100 million Americans trace the history of their families' US citizenship back to the Grand Hall of Ellis Island

Visitors arrive by boat in front of the Ellis Island Immigration Center's main building, exactly as thousands of hopeful migrants did during the center's operation from 1892 to 1954. The grand red-brick exterior and the high, vaulted ceiling of the Great Hall were meticulously restored and reopened in 1990, after nearly four decades of decay since the facility's closure. The daunting reconstruction effort was driven mainly by public subscription, to which more than 20 million Americans donated. In addition to historic exhibits, Ellis Island houses an archive of records of the millions of immigrants who were processed through its halls as well, as the Wall of Honor, where the names of all the people who passed through are displayed (note that sections of the Wall of Honor are periodically closed for repairs to the island's seawall).

Free ranger guided tours depart at the top of every hour and detail the history of the island. For an even more in-depth and harrowing look at the immigrant experience, book a spot on the Ferry Building Tour (Tue, Thur, Fri 11.30am and 2.30pm; free). Visitors are led through recently restored structures that were run by the United States Public Health Service and served as the island's hospitals.

The Essentials

Address: www.nps. gov/elis
Tel: 212-363 3200
Opening Hours: daily 9am–5pm, seasonal variations
Entrance Fee: free, but fee for ferry
Transportation: Statue Cruises from the pier at Battery Park

Top: the Ellis Island Immigration Museum is operated by the National Park Service. The immigration archive, compiled from passenger manifests of ships docking at the island during its operation, is also available online at www.ellisisland.org.

Above: reliving history: on January 1, 1892, the first immigrant processed at Ellis Island was Annie Moore. Annie arrived from Ireland on the SS *Nevada*, on her 15th birthday.

A New Life in the New World

The promise of a new life called to more than 22 million people from all over the world. Among these were Irving Berlin, Bob Hope, and the singing von Trapp family, all of whom entered the United States via the immigration center on Ellis Island. Applicants were taken through a selection process intended to sift out the physically and mentally infirm and the criminal, who were returned to the ships on which they came. These unfortunates gave the island its nickname: the Island of Tears.

Families wishing to research their genealogical history need only consult www.nps.gov/elis, pick up the How to Trace Your Immigrant Ancestor booklet available at the Ellis Island information desk, or visit the American Family Immigration History Center on the island. You will be shown how access to manifest records and documents from the National Archives and Records Administration and other foundations, offices and web sites.

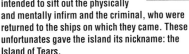

RIGHT: young visitors to the island are catered for with a self-guided tour and a Junior Ranger program, run by the National Park Service.

BELOW: the tiling of the Great Hall is a legacy of Rafael Guastavino (1842–1908), himself an immigrant from Catalonia in northern Spain. Already a successful builder when he came to the US, his specialty was Catalan vaulting. His work can also be seen over the Oyster Bar at Grand Central Terminal.

ABOVE: the restoration of Ellis Island, backed by public generosity, was inspired by the energetic work of Lee Iacocca, the chairman of the Chrysler corporation.

SoHo and TriBeCa

Stylish boutiques, good food, landmark buildings, and an independent film scene contribute to Manhattan's lively and constantly evolving hubs of style

SoHo, an acronym for **So**uth of **Ho**uston, is bordered by Canal Street to the south, Lafayette Street to the east, and Sixth Avenue (Avenue of the Americas) to the west. When Abraham Lincoln made his first campaign speech at nearby Cooper Union, the area was the center of the city's most fashionable shopping and hotel district. By the end of the 19th century, however, the narrow streets were filled by factories, their imaginative cast-iron facades masking sweatshop conditions so horrific that the City Fire Department dubbed the entire region "Hell's Hundred Acres."

Temples of industry

The neighborhood could have been razed to the ground in the 1960s if local artists hadn't started moving into the old lofts, and the city hadn't changed zoning laws to allow them to do so legitimately.

Around the same time, determined conservationists established the **SoHo Cast Iron Historic District** to protect the appearance of these elaborate "temples of industry." As a result, apartments are now too expensive for all but the most successful (or those who got in when prices were low), and most of SoHo's remaining art galleries have relocated above street level to avoid the exorbitant rents. Others have absconded completely – to Chelsea or Brooklyn. If SoHo is no longer the artists' neighborhood of old, it does maintain a New York combination of grit and blatant commercialism, where burly men unload trucks right by outrageous window displays, and double-decker tour buses lumber and wind slowly through the cobblestoned streets.

LEFT: sunshine and shopping on SoHo's Prince Street. **RIGHT:** young diners at the Tribeca Grill.

Soho and Tribeca, East Village and the Lower East Side

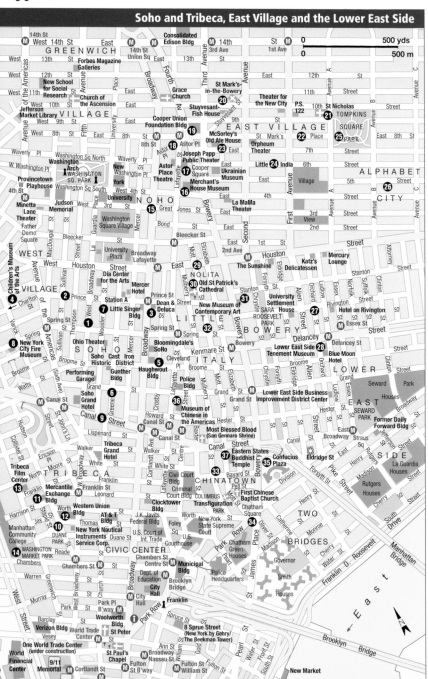

Rising 15 stories above the neighborhood, the Soho Grand manages to fit in with the "temples of industry," thanks to its industrial-chic decor and cozy bar and lounge, a meeting place for fashion and entertainment-industry types. It's also one of the few hotels where pets are not only welcome but are as pampered as their owners (witness the dog statues in the foyer). If you check in without an animal, you can request a complimentary bowl of goldfish.

Prince Street ❷

Cutting across the top of West Broadway, Prince Street has all but forsaken galleries and turned into prime shopping territory, and the surrounding streets have been swift to follow suit. It now carries a mix of familiar designer brands – including Calvin Klein Underwear at No. 104 – as well as more unusual stores such as Kid Robot at No. 126, selling a selection of Japanese toys and gadgets aimed equally at kids and graphic-designer adults.

Housed in an attractive former post-office building at the corner of

THE STREETS OF SOHO

The main drag is **West Broadway ❶**, lined by stores offering everything from jewelry to quirky household wares. On Saturdays in particular, it's packed with crowds of tourists loaded down with shopping bags. From Houston to Canal is a generous selection of designer and top-end boutiques including US giants Tommy Hilfiger, Ralph Lauren, and DKNY, interspersed with European designers such as Missoni and Prada, which is housed in a Rem Koolhaas design.

At the end of a hard day's credit-card abuse, the best-dressed shoppers head to the **Soho Grand Hotel** (310 West Broadway, at Grand and Canal streets, *see page* 309). When it opened in 1996, this was the first new hotel in this part of town since the mid-1800s, when the fashionable American House Hotel stood at the corner of Spring Street, and the white-marble St Nicholas on Broadway and Broome held gala polka parties.

LEFT: vintage shops are plentiful.
BELOW: SoHo is a shopper's paradise.

ABOVE: Bloomingdale's Department Store.
BELOW: something for everyone at Dean & Deluca.

TIP

TOAST stands for the TriBeCa Open Artist Studio Tour, when over 100 artists throw open their doors. This four-day event is usually held in spring. Details can be found at www.toastart walk.com.

Prince and Greene streets, **Station A** (103 Prince) is Apple's suitably stylish retail temple. Fight your way through the crowd to iPods, iPads, iMacs, or whatever is the latest product. Check your email on one of the display models while you're there or check out the upstairs theater, where free seminars are held on how to get the best from your tech toy.

The Romanesque Revival-style building on the opposite corner dates from the same period, but a century or so later has been transformed into the small, luxurious **Mercer Hotel** (see page 309). Beneath it is a highly acclaimed basement-level restaurant, the **Mercer Kitchen**.

Broadway and beyond

Once home to the city's most elegant stores, and later to textile outlets, discount stores, and delis, the stately cast-iron buildings on Broadway below Canal Street reacquired cachet in the 1980s, first as museums, then as galleries, and then as stores like Crate & Barrel and Banana Republic. A Downtown **Bloomingdale's** (504 Broadway) has added more shopper traffic to the busy sidewalks.

Despite the presence of Bloomies and a handful of upscale stores, the SoHo stretch of Broadway is best seen as West Broadway's younger, more mainstream cousin. Here you can find stores selling the latest jeans, sneakers, and casual daywear. Recent imports H&M, Topshop, and Uniqlo are proving particularly popular with SoHo's young trendsetters looking for style on a budget.

A 1904 cast-iron confection called the **Little Singer Building**, designed by Ernest Flagg (and now home to swank, multimillion-dollar apartments), stands across Broadway from **Dean & Deluca** ❸ (560 Broadway), at the opposite corner of Prince Street. Dean & Deluca has been described by the *Washington Post* as "a combination of Paris's Fauchon, London's Harrod's Food Halls, and Milan's Peck all rolled into one," and presents food as art: a cornucopia of fruits, vegetables, and imported gourmet grocery specialties. This has proved to be so successful a formula that Dean & Deluca stores have branched out. The stand-up coffee bar is stocked with delectable

pastries, and is a perfect place for a quick snack – although if you arrive before 10am, expect a long line of pre-work coffee drinkers.

If the Harry Potter novels made J.K. Rowling a billionaire, evidence that it did just as much for her US publisher **Scholastic Books** is their huge and colorful book store at 555 Broadway. Aisles of kids' books, arts and crafts, and free Saturday events make this a good family stop.

Walking east on Prince leads to Lafayette Street, where urbanites can pick up hip-hop-influenced streetwear from stores such as Wesc or Brooklyn Industries.

Children's Museum of the Arts ❶

Address: 103 Charlton Street (between Greenwich and Hudson sts), www.cmany.org
Telephone: 212-274 0986
Opening Hours: Wed, Fri–Sun noon–5pm, Thur noon–6pm
Entrance Fee: charge
Subway: Spring St/Canal St

A successful cross between a museum and a particularly lively day-care center, the Children's Museum aims to encourage tiny artists through inspiration – it has a collection of 2,000 works of children's art from around the world – and through interactive exhibits and artist-led classes for kids. Group activities are tailor-made for specific age groups – for example, the "WEE Arts" program allows children aged 10 months to five years to explore art (or make a mess) using playdough, paints, and a variety of other child-friendly materials, while for older kids, a highlight are classes that teach the basics of puppetry, podcasting, and filmmaking.

Flora and Miss Lizzie

Back on Broadway, the **Haughwout Building** ❺ is the palazzo-style structure near Broome Street. The Haughwout is one of SoHo's oldest – and most striking – cast-iron edifices. Designed by John Gaynor, it was constructed in 1857 as one of the country's first retail stores, complete with its first elevator.

Named after a Revolutionary War general, **Greene Street** ❻, like Mercer and Wooster streets, runs parallel to

ABOVE: the Children's Museum of the Arts.
BELOW: Prada is housed on the premises of the former Guggenheim Museum.

ABOVE: the New York Fire Museum.

TIP

It seems obvious, but it can confuse even the most seasoned SoHo pilgrim. West Broadway and Broadway are two different streets that run parallel to each other. Always double check your destination's address or you might end up on a corner, scratching your head.

West Broadway and Broadway. In the late 19th century this was the center of New York's most notorious red-light district, where brothels with names like Flora's and Miss Lizzie's flourished behind shuttered windows. Now the same windows attract a very different sort of browser – gazing longingly over summer dresses in bright, '80s-influenced colors at Anna Sui (No. 113).

As befits one of the SoHo Cast Iron Historic District's prime thoroughfares, Greene Street also offers a rich concentration of this uniquely American architecture at its best, including (at the Canal Street end) the city's longest continuous row of cast-iron buildings.

At the corner of Broome Street, the 1872 **Gunther Building** is particularly worthy of notice. Before continuing, stop and admire the cream-colored architectural "king" of cast-iron splendor at **72–76 Greene Street**, just opposite. This impressively ornate structure was designed and built by Isaac Duckworth in 1873.

Wooster Street arts scene

For more shopping and a selection of SoHo's few remaining galleries (which seem to hop from street to street on a regular basis), walk across to stone-cobbled **Wooster Street ❼**. The long-established **Dia Center for the Arts** has managed to stay anchored to the second-floor space at 141 Wooster Street with the *New York Earth Room*, a room interior filled with real earth, by Walter De Maria (Wed–Sun noon–6pm, closed 3–3.30pm). The Dia Center also has a major gallery space at Beacon in the Hudson Valley.

In addition to galleries, this end of Wooster also has the **New Ohio Theater** (66 Wooster, www.sohothink tank.org), where the Soho Think Tank presents independent theater productions, and, near the corner of Grand Street, the ever-popular and experimental **Performing Garage** (33 Wooster, www.thewoostergroup. org, tel: 212-966 9796), which has presented the Wooster Group's unique brand of theater, dance, and performance art since 1967.

Food for thought

John Broome was a successful merchant who imported tea and silk from China at the end of the Revolutionary War, so he might have appreciated the fresh produce and other goods sold at the **Gourmet Garage** (453 Broome, at Mercer Street, www.gourmetgarage.com), an indoor market serving the restaurant trade and SoHo locals.

In general, Broome Street is one of SoHo's least jazzed-up thoroughfares, unless you count the ornate Calvert Vaux-designed edifice at No. 448, built in 1872. A lunch treat awaits a little farther on at the corner of West Broadway in the characterful **Broome Street Bar**. Situated in a pretty 18th-century house, the Broome Street Bar with its friendly staff has been serving sandwiches, soups, and burgers at its wooden tables since SoHo was involved in the arts scene.

Crossing West Broadway, you're on the fringe of the South Village, where chic little shoe salons and boutiques nestle among places like the **Birdbath Bakery** on Prince between West Broadway and Thompson Street, which, until very recently, had been run as the Vesuvio Bakery by the same family since the 1920s. Vesuvio had locals lining up for its freshly baked bread, and now Birdbath follows in its footsteps with a focus on organic and sustainable baked goods.

Milady's, another neighborhood bar and restaurant (162 Prince Street), has been around for close to half a century, and is one of a dwindling number of SoHo eateries left from less fashionable times.

One of these refreshment stops should provide the stamina for a detour down Thompson to Spring Street, then west across Sixth Avenue to the New York Fire Department's museum, on one of Spring Street's last blocks before it meets the river.

New York City Fire Museum ❽

Address: 278 Spring Street (at Varick and Hudson sts), www.nycfire museum.org
Telephone: 212-691 1303
Opening Hours: Mon–Sat 10am–

Below: stalls on Canal Street.

5pm, Sun 10am–4pm
Entrance Fee: charge
Subway: Spring St

It's worth the walk to Engine Company No. 30's former headquarters to visit this charming museum. The restored fire house's original features include the brass sliding pole and apparatus doors, providing a perfect setting for one of the country's largest collections of firefighting apparatus and memorabilia. Highlights include the shiny red antique hand- and horse-pulled wagons – especially popular with children. A special extension houses a permanent 9/11 exhibit, with powerful images from that sad day.

ABOVE: The New York City Fire Museum exhibits historic artifacts of firefighting history.
RIGHT: TriBeCa looking toward City Hall.
BELOW: a NY minute at the Tribeca Grand.

Canalside

Back on West Broadway, SoHo comes to a halt at **Canal Street ❾**, where stores sell plastic odds and ends, rubber tubing, neon signs, household appliances, and barrels of peculiar industrial leftovers. It's all mixed together in a bedlam of hot-dog carts and street vendors displaying old books, bootleg CDs and DVDs,

handbags, and, from time to time, a few bona fide treasures.

TRIBECA

In the late 1970s, artists in search of lower rents migrated south from SoHo to TriBeCa – the **Tri**angle **Be**low **Ca**nal – which runs south of Canal Street to Chambers Street, and west from Broadway to the Hudson River. Called Washington Market in the days when the city's major produce businesses operated here (before they moved to Hunt's Point in the Bronx), this part of the Lower West Side is one of Manhattan's most pleasant neighborhoods.

Now an eclectic blend of renovated commercial warehouses, Corinthian columns, condo towers, and celebrity restaurants, TriBeCa was where artists like David Cale or Laurie Anderson showed their early works, at venues like the Alternative Museum and Franklin Furnace (both now closed).

Change of pace

Today's TriBeCa scene has more to show in the culinary than in the fine arts, but its largely residential atmosphere makes a pleasant change of pace from SoHo's tourist-packed streets. A block south of Canal, the Tribeca Grand Hotel, rising from the triangle bordered by Sixth Avenue, Walker and White streets, looms over one of the area's oldest survivors: an 1809 brick house at **2 White Street**, just off West Broadway, which dates back to an earlier era when this was one of the city's original residential enclaves.

Grand designs

The **Tribeca Grand** Hotel (see page 309), younger sister to the Soho Grand, keeps the residential tradition alive with its hip, trendy hospitality. Features for glamorous guests include an atrium lounge and 203 ergonomically designed rooms, with extra-large windows and great amenities.

The handsome **Clocktower Building** at 108 Leonard Street (also 346 Broadway) – named for its ornate tower – is the former New York Life Insurance Building, which was remodeled by Stanford White in 1898.

The building now houses the studio for **AIR, Art International Radio**, the internet-based radio station that showcases music, interviews with artists, and "audio art." Its 13th-floor Clocktower Gallery features installations and a residency program for up-and-coming artists.

On the corner of Thomas Street and West Broadway, two blocks below Leonard Street, a red neon sign spells out "Cafeteria," but don't be fooled. This 1930s mock-stone building has housed **The Odeon**, one of Downtown's hippest restaurants, since it opened in 1980 (see page 107). Unlike many trendy spots, it shows no signs of fading away and is still a favorite with the cognoscenti, especially late into the night.

Duane and Staple

Below Thomas is **Duane Street**. Named for New York's first post-Revolution mayor, it meets Hudson Street at tiny triangular **Duane Park** ❿ – all that's left of a farm that the city bought for $5 in 1795.

Staple Street, a narrow strip of cobblestone where "staple" produce was once unloaded, connects the park with the ornate, brick former **Mercantile Exchange Building** ⓫, on the corner of Harrison and Hudson streets.

The neighboring 1920s **Western Union Building** ⓬ at 60 Hudson Street soars 24 stories above the rest of the neighborhood like a layered missile, and is made of 19 different shades of brick. Its lobby, where even the letterboxes are marvels of Art Deco artistry, is also stunning. Unfortunately you can no longer walk through it to West Broadway, but you can still get a good glimpse through the gate by the main doors.

Old and new

Greenwich Street is where much of TriBeCa's new development is centered, but you can still find authentic early remnants – like the

BELOW: actor Morgan Freeman at the TriBeCa Film Festival.

TIP

Need to recharge? Slope into Bliss spa at its flagship SoHo location (568 Broadway at Prince Street, www.blissworld. com, tel: 877-862 5477) for premium pampering. There are other locations around town, too.

19th-century lantern factory between Laight and Vestry streets, which now houses million-dollar lofts.

The corner of Greenwich and Franklin streets is the place where actor Robert De Niro transformed the old Martinson Coffee Factory into the **Tribeca Film Center** . On the first floor is the **Tribeca Grill** (see page 107). Many come here in the hope of seeing De Niro or film-biz luminaries from the upstairs offices. Chances are, the closest you'll get to a sighting is one of De Niro's dad's paintings on the walls, and while you do occasionally see people talking "back-end" and reading scripts, most of the clientele are regular business types and star-struck tourists. The food, however, rarely disappoints.

The late 18th- and early 19th-century brick houses on **Harrison Street** look incongruous, like a stage set in the shadow of **Independence Plaza**'s gargantuan 1970s apartment towers, but like the house on White Street, they're evocative survivors of TriBeCa's residential beginnings.

Just off Harrison, **Bazzini's** at 339 Greenwich Street is a hardy remnant of the area's old commercial incarnation; it has been a fruit and nut wholesaler since 1886. While Bazzini's has since branched into standard deli fare, it's still the most authentic place to buy huge bags of pistachios.

Grass and a gazebo

Opposite the big line of condo dwellings stretching between Duane and Chambers streets, **Washington Market Park** has a thick grassy meadow to stretch out on, and even a fanciful gazebo to daydream in. P.S. 234, The Independence School – its wrought-iron fence embossed with Spanish galleons in full sail – is across from the park, and worth noting.

From Chambers and West Street, you can reach **Hudson River Park** via a pedestrian bridge that stretches across the West Side Highway. Walkways and bike paths extend north along the river beyond Pier 25, and south to connect to Battery Park City. If you continue south, there's a scenic riverside walk, complete with views of the Statue of Liberty.

BELOW: the exterior of the Angelica Theater.

It's Pronounced How-stun

The border between SoHo and the West Village is Houston Street. Pronounced "*how-stun*," it was named for William Houstoun, a delegate from Georgia who married the daughter of Nicholas Bayard III, a prominent New Yorker and grandson of an original mayor. The city's three major arthouse cinemas – Film Forum, The Angelica, and Landmark Sunshine – are situated on the street (the Anthology Film Archives is one block north). Also marking the point where numbered streets begin, it is a heavily trafficked, and not particularly attractive, thoroughfare. Still, years of construction have made it safer and easier to negotiate, and the stores, bars, and restaurants keep opening.

SHOPPING

Whether you're willing to spend a couple thousand on a designer dress, or just a few 10-dollar bills on some new cutlery, SoHo is the place to go. And the quality is bleeding over into TriBeCa. While it's hard to do the neighborhoods justice with a handful of choices, here are some more of the best.

Accessories

Edon Manor
391 Greenwich Street (at N. Moore and Beach sts)
Tel: 212-431 3890
www.edonmanor.com
The shoes are the main draw at this TriBeCa accessory shop, but there are handbags and sunglasses too. Be warned. It's ridiculously expensive.

Kate Spade
454 Broome Street (at Mercer St)
Tel: 212-274 1991
www.katespade.com
The flagship store of the reigning queen of handbags. There's clothing too, but the bags steal the show. Around the corner, Kate's husband Jack has his own eponymous storefront dedicated to men's fashion.

Books

Scholastic Store
557 Broadway (between Prince and Spring sts)
Tel: 212-343 6166
www.scholastic.com/sohostore
This enormous retail space sells thousands of high-quality and educational children's books and toys.

Clothing

Kirna Zabête
96 Greene Street (at Spring St)
Tel: 212-946 9656
www.kirnazabete.com
For more than 10 years two former fashion-industry professionals have run this temple to designer clothes, shoes, and handbags and have touted it as one-stop shopping in a neighborhood bursting with boutiques.

Uniqlo
546 Broadway (at Spring and Prince sts)
Tel: 877-486 4756
www.uniqlo.com
The ever-expanding Japanese chain is an alternative to stores like The Gap, Banana Republic, and Old Navy. Also at 34th Street and 5th Avenue.

Vera Wang
158 Mercer Street (at Prince St)
Tel: 212-382 2184
www.verawang.com
It's surprising that it took until 2008 for the legendar designer to open a SoHo store bearing her name. There's bridal wear, of course, but also her complete ready-to-wear collection.

What Goes Around Comes Around
351 W. Broadway (at Grand and Broome sts)
Tel: 212-343 1225
www.whatgoesaroundnyc.com

The selection of jeans alone is worth the trip to this TriBeCa gem that sell vintage clothing that complements today's fashions.

Gifts

Pylones
69 Spring Street (at Crosby and Centre sts)
Tel: 212-431 3244
www.pylones-usa.com
A little bit ridiculous, but also ridiculously well priced, this French import is the perfect place to find colorful and whimsical (and sometimes even useful) gifts.

Home

Moss
150 Greene Street (at W. Houston St)
Tel: 212-204 7100
www.mossonline.com

An unabashedly strange and wonderful collection of modern furniture, lighting, housewares, and decorative items, this could be a store at a design museum, but it is its own unique creation.

Sur La Table
75 Spring Street (at Crosby St)
Tel: 212-966 3375
www.surlatable.com
This national chain has just about anything any serious home cook would need.

Stationery

Kate's Paperie
435 Broome Street (between Broadway and Crosby St)
Tel: 212-941-9816
www.katespaperie.com
A great selection of gorgeous paper, stationery, cards and writing supplies, from calligraphy pens to calendars.

RIGHT: colorful clothing at Uniqlo.

RESTAURANTS, BARS AND CAFES

Restaurants

Balthazar
80 Spring St (at Broadway and Crosby sts)
Tel: 212-965 1414
www.balthazarny.com
B, L, & D daily **$$$** ⓭ [p340, B4]
Parisian-style brasserie; hard to imagine SoHo without it.

Blaue Gans
139 Duane St (at W. Broadway and Church St)
Tel: 212-571 8880
http://kg-ny.com/blaue-gans
L & D daily **$$$** ⓮ [p342, B2]
Locals love the neighborhood feel of this Viennese-style restaurant, as well as the European fare, including schnitzel,

goulash, and bratwurst.

Blue Ribbon
97 Sullivan St (at Prince and Spring sts)
Tel: 212-274 0404
www.blueribbonrestaurants.com
D daily, until 4am **$$$** ⓯ [p340, B3]
The first in a mini-empire of Downtown "Blue Ribbons." At all the outlets (Blue Ribbon Sushi a few doors north, Blue Ribbon Bakery, 33 Downing St, and Blue Ribbon Downing St Bar next door), there's exceptional quality food and service for a price. All are open late.

Bouley
163 Duane St (at W. Broadway and Hudson St)
Tel: 212-964 2525
http://davidbouley.com

L & D Mon–Sat **$$$$** ⓰ [p342, B2]
David Bouley's "new French" food experience transcends price, and his flagship restaurant is undoubtedly one of New York's Top Ten. Bouley moved into this new space in 2008, and the restaurant is better than ever.

Bread
20 Spring St (at Elizabeth and Mott sts)
Tel: 212-334 1015
B, L & D daily **$** ⓱ [p340, C4]
Follow Spring Street due east for a snack that doesn't smack of SoHo prices. Hot sandwiches come with pesto, chicken and avocado, goat's cheese and shiitakes, or fresh sardines and tomatoes. There's pasta and a very good antipasti plate, too.

Bubby's
120 Hudson St (at N. Moore St)
Tel: 212-219 0666
http://bubbys.com
B, L, & D daily **$$** ⓲ [p340, A4]
Funky joint, kid-friendly but also a celeb-spot from time to time. Comfort food is top of the menu. Open 24 hours a day, except for Monday when they close at midnight.

Capsouto Frères
451 Washington St (at Desbrosses and Watts sts)
Tel: 212-966 4900
www.capsoutofreres.com
L & D Tue–Sun, D only Mon **$$$** ⓳ p340, A4)

French in the most traditional sense, this far-West Side bistro serves *escargots*, onion soup gratinée, and duck confit.

Centrico
211 W. Broadway (at Franklin St)
Tel: 212-431 0700
www.myriadrestaurantgroup.com/centrico
D daily, L Sun **$$$** ⓴ [p342, B1]
Zarela Martínez (of Zarela's, at 2nd Ave and 50th St) brought the true regional cuisines of Mexico to NYC. Her son succeeds her in this stylish Downtown location.

Corton
239 W. Broadway (at White and North Main sts)
Tel: 212-219 2777
www.cortonnyc.com
D Mon–Sat **$$$$** ㉑ [p342, B1]
Some of the city's most refined French cuisine in a decidedly modern dining room. Justly celebrated as one of the best new restaurants.

The Harrison
355 Greenwich St (at Harrison and North Moore sts)
Tel: 212-274 9310
www.theharrison.com
D Mon-Fri, **$$$** ㉒ [p342, B1]
The creative menu continues to impress hard-to-impress New Yorkers. If they're still on the menu, try the lamb milanese, or local skate wing with sauce *gribiche*. Dessert might be a brown butter fig tart or corn custard with stewed peaches.

LEFT: David Bouley, king of Tribeca cuisine.
RIGHT: long cocktails for a cool crowd.

www.megurestaurants.com
D daily $$$$ [p342, B2]
Extravagant Japanese.
Megu's menu is over-
whelming and maybe
overpriced, but it's much
talked about around
town.

Nobu
105 Hudson St (at Franklin and
N. Moore sts)
Tel: 212-219 0500
www.noburestaurants.com
L & D Mon–Fri, D only Sat–Sun
$$$$ [p342, B1]
TriBeCa celeb-spot,
unique for its Japanese-
Peruvian cuisine and
near-impossibility of getting a booking. Nobu
Next Door is a second-
best, and does not
accept reservations.

The Odeon
145 W. Broadway (at Duane
and Thomas sts)
Tel: 212-233 0507
http://theodeonrestaurant.com
L & D Mon–Fri, Br & D Sat–Sun
$$$ [p342, B2]
Great bar atmosphere,
and a tasty French-
American menu: a
strong point of the
TriBeCa scene.

Raoul's
180 Prince St (at Sullivan and
Thompson sts)
Tel: 212-966 3518
http://raouls.com
D daily $$$ [p340, B3]
French bistro with 25
years of serving the
international chic set.

Tribeca Grill
375 Greenwich St (at Franklin
St)
Tel: 212-941 3900
www.myriadrestaurantgroup.com/
tribecagrill
L & D Mon–Fri & Sun, D only
Sat [p342, B1]
Co-owned by actor Rob-
ert De Niro and chef
Drew Nieporent, the
Grill is still packing
them in almost 20
years later.

Kittichai
60 Thompson St (at Spring and
Broome sts)
Tel: 212-219 2000
www.kittichairestaurant.com
B, L, & D Mon–Fri, Br & D Sat–
Sun $$$ [p340, B4]
Elegant Thai food, in a
refined dining room on
the ground floor of the
Thompson Hotel.
Brunches are packed
with those taking advan-
tage of the "Unlimited
Cocktail" deal.

Landmarc
179 W. Broadway (at Leonard
and Worth sts)
Tel: 212-343 3883
www.landmarc-restaurant.com
L & D Mon–Fri, B, L, & D Sat–
Sun $$ [p342, B1]
This chic bistro has
become a restaurant
"landmark" in NY's Gold
Coast territory: it's got
both style and unpreten-
tious prices. Food is
mostly Italian, but with
French influences too.
Reservations only taken
for parties of six or more.

Locanda Verde
377 Greenwich St (at Franklin
and North Moore sts)
Tel: 212-941 8900
http://locandaverdenyc.com
B, L, & D daily $$$
[p342, B1]
An Italian media darling,
it's as good for breakfast
as it is for lunch and din-
ner.

Lucky Strike
59 Grand St (at W. Broadway
and Wooster St)
Tel: 212-942 0772
www.luckystrikeny.com
L & D daily $$ [p342, B1]
Hip and seasoned bistro
fare, always a good bet.
Affordable and late-nite.

Megu
62 Thomas St
(at W. Broadway)
Tel: 212-964 7777

Prices for a three-course
dinner per person with
half a bottle of wine:
$ = under $20
$$ = $20–$45
$$$ = $45–$60
$$$$ = over $60

Bars and Cafes

The Bubble Lounge
228 W. Broadway
(at N. Moore St)
[p340, A4]
Bubble Lounge always
finds a reason to cele-
brate with its selection
of more than 300 cham-
pagnes and sparkling
wines.

Cupping Room Café
359 W. Broadway (between
Broome and Grand sts)
[p340, B4]
A cozy place for
brunch.

Emack & Bolio
W. Houston and W. Broadway
[p340, B3]
For high-end ice cream
and frozen yogurt in as
many flavors as
Crayola crayons, this
place can't be beaten.
Locations on the
Upper East and West
sides, too.

Fanelli's
94 Prince St at Mercer
[p340, B4]
This is where trendy
SoHo grew up, around
this down-to-earth cor-
ner hangout.

Kitchenette
156 Chambers Street
(at Greenwich St and W.
Broadway) [p342, A2]
A family-friendly bakery
and breakfast spot.

Puffy's Tavern
81 Hudson St
(at Harrison and Jay sts)
[p342, B1]
Open until 4am, this is
one of TriBeCa's most
laidback bars.

SHOPPING

Sinatra might not have approved of these alternate lyrics, but they certainly ring true: If you can't buy it here, you can't buy it anywhere

For anyone who rates shopping as one of life's greater imperatives, New York is the place to be. Manhattan has every kind of shop imaginable. In terms of orientation, a general rule of thumb is that the big department stores are in Midtown. Many of these are opulent – including Barneys and Bergdorf Goodman. Uptown and in Midtown you'll also find stores with world-famous names, like the popular Apple boutique and the powerhouse toy store FAO Schwartz, on Fifth Avenue.

The more quirky stores are downtown. Greenwich Village, SoHo, NoHo and the Meatpacking District are places where stylish shoppers go to find the latest fashions from up-and-coming designers, as well as vintage pieces. And the style goes beyond clothing: ABC Carpet and Home offers a mix of luxurious home decor, and more unusual finds. Even the bath goods – like those at Kiehl's – are coveted.

Some purchases don't always have a long shelf life, but are worth every cent. World-class chocolate shops like Kee's, legendary cheesemongers like Murray's, and oenologists like Astor Wine & Spirits can offer expert advice on consumable gifts for friends, family, or yourself. So go ahead, take the plunge – just don't forget that sales tax of around 8 percent.

LEFT: the iconic Macy's sign in Herald Square, at the intersection of Broadway and Sixth Avenue at 34th Street. There are now Macy's stores all over the US, but this is the original, built in 1902. The visitor center on the second floor has staff to help people find their way around the store, and also provides tourist information.

ABOVE: New York institution Bloomingdale's takes up an entire block on Third Avenue in the Upper East Side (there's also a branch in SoHo). Bloomies is full of everything you could ever need, and a lot you don't but want to buy anyway. Most of the top designers are here.

ABOVE: SoHo's Dean & Deluca stocks gourmet food and fine wine, wonderful cheeses, charcuterie, chocolate, and freshly ground coffee. The goods aren't cheap, but neither is the quality.

THE PRICE IS RIGHT

You can buy anything in New York, but smart shoppers know how to get the best for less. New York City's biggest shopping period starts the day after Thanksgiving (known as "Black Friday") through to New Year's Day. During this time, you may find sales (particularly early on the morning of Black Friday) along with festive holiday decorations and, at the department stores, magnificently decorated windows that draw crowds so big they need to put up velvet ropes.

Other than that, the best months for sales are February and August, as the stores clean out their inventory to make way for the next season's wares.

Savvy shoppers who don't like to wait for sales often frequent New York's bargain houses, which include Century 21 and Loehmann's. Here, the clothing won't be well lit and lined up on elegant displays – in fact, you may have to dig through bins, and often you won't find items in a variety of colors or sizes. For some shoppers, it's a frustrating prospect – but for diehard deal hunters, it's great to know there's a bargain waiting if they are willing to look.

BELOW: the shop at the Cooper Hewitt Design Museum has all the latest to grace your home.

ABOVE: if the prices of the high-end stores are too intimidating, don't be afraid to window-shop.

RIGHT: Century 21 is a shopping destination for much of the under-30 crowd.

THE EAST VILLAGE AND THE LOWER EAST SIDE

From historic synagogues on the Lower East Side to the trendy shops in NoLita; from dim sum in Chinatown to cutting-edge clubs in Alphabet City – this is Manhattan's melting pot

B ordered by 14th Street to the north and Houston Street to the south, and roughly centered between Third Avenue and Avenue B, the **East Village** is a place that stays up late, where fashion and politics have always been more radical than elsewhere in the city, and whose residents have included Beat icons like Allen Ginsberg and William Burroughs, as well as Yippies, Hell's Angels, and punk rock pioneers.

Beneath its scruffy avant-garde surface, the East Village is also a neighborhood of immigrants, with Ukrainian and Puerto Rican social clubs next to cutting-edge boutiques, and free health clinics not far from expensive co-op buildings. Like other Downtown neighborhoods, old and new are juxtaposed here in an ever-changing mosaic.

EAST VILLAGE

At the beginning of the 20th century, lower Broadway around 9th Street was part of the "Ladies' Mile" of fashionable retailing that extended north to 23rd Street. Later, it was just a dingy pause away from SoHo (when that area was still known as SoHo), but all that changed when Tower Records and other consumer meccas moved in. Unofficially known as **NoHo** ⑮ (**North of Houston**), this stretch of the East Village includes Broadway from Astor Place down to Houston Street, a place crowded with fashion, art, and design stores.

Some interesting home-furnishing emporia also tempt along Lafayette Street, where the huge **Chinatown Brasserie** (380 Lafayette, at Great Jones Street) serves up Asian food with a helping of trendy, Downtown attitude (see page 128).

Main Attractions
MERCHANT'S HOUSE MUSEUM
ASTOR PLACE
ST MARK'S PLACE
TOMPKINS SQUARE PARK
ALPHABET CITY
LES TENEMENT MUSEUM
NEW MUSEUM
LITTLE ITALY
CHINATOWN

LEFT: Lower East Side folk.
RIGHT: NoHo knitwear.

Merchant's House Museum
16

Address: 29 E. 4th St (at Lafayette St and the Bowery), www.merchantshouse.com
Telephone: 212-777 1089
Operating Hours: Thur–Mon noon–5pm
Entrance Fee: charge
Subway: Astor Place

A block up from Great Jones Street on West 4th Street (just above Lafayette), drop in and see the city as it used to be at the "Merchant's House," a compact Greek Revival-style brick townhouse built in 1832. The same family, the Tredwells, lived here for generations until Gertrude Tredwell died in 1933, in the house where she was born. Their furnishings and personal effects have been preserved as they would have looked in the 19th century.

This is a good opportunity to see how wealthy New Yorkers lived – a nice companion to the slightly later Theodore Roosevelt Birthplace near Gramercy Park (see page 147). Visitors are free to walk around the house, and a booklet provides information on its history and the Tredwell family; groups requiring a tour guide need to book in advance.

NoHo arts

A detour east along 4th Street will take you to the slightly shabby **La MaMa** experimental theater (74A E. 4th St, www.lamama.org, tel: 212-475 7710). A pioneer of the avant-garde

ABOVE: NoHo residents catch up over a drink.
RIGHT: the exterior of the Merchant's House Museum.
BELOW: Merchant's House Museum interior.

since 1961, the theater has three performance spaces and an art gallery.

Continuing north on Lafayette Street, **Colonnade Row** was originally a group of nine columned homes, built in 1833 when this was one of the city's most elegant neighborhoods. Only four of the houses still stand: current occupants include the perennially stylish **Indochine** restaurant at No. 430 (see page 128) and the **Astor Place Theatre** (No. 434), where the Blue Man Group is currently resident.

Across the street is the **Joseph Papp Public Theater**  (www. publictheater.org, tel: 212-539 8500), a red-brick, five-theater complex that originally housed the Astor Library. Since 1967, the theater has been the host of the city's Shakespeare Festival (with free performances in Central Park during the summer), as well as more contemporary productions – from the world premiere of *Hair* to *A Chorus Line* to *Bring in 'Da Noise, Bring in 'Da Funk* – that have gone on to be bit hits on Broadway.

For great live music, spend an evening in **Joe's Pub** (425 Lafayette Street, www.joespub.com, tel: 212-967 7555), an innovative small venue, bar, and satellite of the Joseph Papp Public Theater. You can have dinner here, too.

Around Astor Place

Lafayette ends at **Astor Place** ⓲, where a large Kmart reflects a departure from the Village's countercultural roots. The area's most notable landmark, besides the handsome **Astor Place subway kiosk** and the glassy condo building by Gwathmey Siegel, is the giant black cube by Tony Rosenthal called *The Alamo*. One of the first abstract sculptures installed on city property, it stands at the intersection of Astor Place, St Mark's Place, and Lafayette Street. Tourists like to give it a spin (push it and see), but it goes largely unnoticed by local workers as they hurry by.

The imposing brown Italianate **Cooper Union Foundation Building** ⓳, between Third and Fourth avenues, opened in 1859 as one of the country's earliest centers of free education. Now well known as an art school (varied exhibitions, www.cooper.edu, tel: 212-353 4100), this is also where Abraham Lincoln gave the popular speech said to have launched his presidential campaign.

A statue of the schools' founder-philanthropist Peter Cooper by Augustus St-Gaudens, who was a student here, stands behind Cooper Union at **Cooper Square**, where Third and Fourth avenues converge at the top of the Bowery. **41 Cooper Square** is the address and name of the school's newest center for classrooms, studios, and labs. Designed by Thom Mayne, it's a remarkable piece of modern architecture, full of slanted steel planes, creases, grids, and twists.

Historic Fish

Walking from the Cooper Union to Third Avenue, you'll come across Stuyvesant Street, which veers off at an angle toward Second Avenue. St

KIDS

It's only 8 acres (3 hectares), but Sara Roosevelt Park – bordered by Canal, Chrystie, Houston, and Forsyth streets – is a hidden sanctuary with basketball, volleyball, and handball courts, soccer fields, five playgrounds, and a community garden.

BELOW: the cast-iron Astor Place subway kiosk is one of New York's finest.

ABOVE: Loisaida Festival.
BELOW: St Mark's-in-theBowery.

The second-oldest church building in Manhattan (after St Paul's Chapel), St Mark's was nearly destroyed by fire in 1978, and was restored with the help of local residents. It has suffered a little again in the intervening years and is in need of attention, but when you consider its age this is hardly surprising. St Mark's has a long history of liberal religious thought – a reflection of the neighborhood that manifests itself in such longstanding community programs as the Poetry Project – and holds art shows in the parish hall.

East Village North

Continuing on 10th Street into the East Village, toward First Avenue, the **Theater for the New City** (www. theaterforthenewcity.net, tel: 212-254 1109,) on First Avenue was founded in 1971 as a venue for experimental Off-Broadway productions. Today it continues to put on new plays, as well as providing a performance space for theater groups that don't have their own.

If you feel the need for an energy rush, there's espresso and pastries at **Veniero** on 11th Street near First

Mark's Bookshop (www.stmarks bookshop.com, tel: 212-260 7853), at the corner of Third and Stuyvesant, is a long-established store stocked with obscure new fiction, art books, and political tomes – its peaceful aisles provide a refreshing break.

The red-brick Anglo-Italianate houses on Stuyvesant Street and on East 10th Street form the heart of the **St Mark's Historic District**. The handsome home at 21 Stuyvesant is the **Stuyvesant-Fish House**, a national historic landmark built by former Dutch governor Peter Stuyvesant's great-grandson by marriage, Hamilton Fish, which is now owned by the Cooper Union.

St Mark's-in-the-Bowery ㉀

Address: 131 E. 10th St (at Second Ave), http://stmarksbowery.org
Telephone: 212-674 6377
Opening Hours: daily, times vary
Entrance Fee: free
Subway: Astor Place/Third Ave

Loisaida

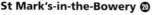

Puerto Rican poet Bittman "Bimbo" Rivas wrote, "I dig the way you talk, I dig the way you look." The object of his affection was the Lower East Side, or as he referred to it, *Loisaida*. It was a Splanglish appropriation of the geography and the name stuck. When an influx of Puerto Ricans arrived in New York in the 1940s–60s, this is where they came. They called themselves Nuyoricans and by the 1970s they had established the Nuyorican Poets Cafe, where Rivas read his poetry, and Loisaida Inc, which aimed to combat poverty, drugs, and violence in the community. Nuyoricans are now scattered throughout the boroughs, but the spirit remains in Alphabet City, where the Loisaida Festival is held every Memorial Day weekend.

Avenue, testimony to an Italian enclave that flourished here in the early 1900s. You can't miss the red neon sign (even though a few of the letters have ceased working); once inside choose from a toothache-inducing array of tiny Italian pastries to take out, or sit down and enjoy one in the high-ceilinged cafe.

Not far away, **St Nicholas** ㉑ Carpatho-Russian Orthodox Greek Catholic Church is a reminder of this ethnic and religious melting pot. Originally built for a predominantly Episcopal parish as St Mark's Chapel, inside it has tiled walls and a beamed ceiling dating from 1894.

Over on 9th Street, Performance Space 122, better known as **P.S.122** (First Avenue at 9th Street, www. ps122.org, tel: 212-477 5289), is a multi-arts organization set up to nurture young and mid-career artists. The East Village has been a center for live performances ever since Second Avenue was lined by Yiddish theaters in the 1890s; a reminder of those times is the venerable **Orpheum Theater** situated at 126 Second Avenue.

Velvet Underground

St Mark's Place ㉒, a continuation of 8th Street between Third Avenue and Avenue A, is the East Village version of Main Street. In the 1960s, this was the counterculture center of the East Coast, where Andy Warhol presented Velvet Underground "happenings" and, later, barefoot freaks tripped out at the Electric Circus. It's now a gentrified condo/retail center of stores and residences.

The Fillmore East, which presented the East Coast's most psychedelic concerts, is also gone, but St Mark's Place is still one of the city's liveliest thoroughfares. Sidewalk cafes and restaurants heave with customers, and the bazaar-like atmosphere is augmented by street vendors selling T-shirts, leatherwear, jewelry, and bootleg CDs and DVDs.

Shop for retro, punk, or retro-punk gear here, then pause for refreshment around the corner – down Third Avenue to East 7th Street – at a true drinking-man's pub.

McSorley's Old Ale House ㉓

Address: 15 E. 7th St (between Second and Third aves), www.mcsorley-snewyork.com
Telephone: 212-474 9148
Opening Hours: Mon–Sat 11am–1am, Sun 1pm–1am
Subway: Astor Place/8th St

McSorley's has been in business since the 1850s, although women weren't allowed inside until more than a century later. This was a favorite New York hangout of the Irish writer Brendan Behan, among other luminaries. The decor hasn't changed much over the past 150 years – there's still sawdust on the floor and standing-room only at the bar – but space *has* been made for a ladies' bathroom.

ABOVE: St Mark's Book Store in the East Village.

DRINK

An enjoyable drinking spot in the smartened-up Lower East Side is 'inoteca at 98 Rivington Street, a stylish wine bar with over 300 quality Italian wines. Plates of tasty Italian nibbles keep hunger at bay while you pop another cork.

A short time ago, Vietnamese *bánh mì* sandwiches were all the rage. Savory concoctions of meat, pate, pickled veggies, and cilantro, they could be found in almost every neighborhood. Nicky's Vietnamese Sandwiches, at 150 East 2nd Street, pre-dates the craze and survived it. Rightfully so: they're fantastic.

Every last patch of wall is covered with photos, posters, cartoons, and other curios; eagle-eyed patrons might spot an original wanted poster for Abraham Lincoln's assassin. As with New York's other remaining 19th-century saloons, McSorley's can be a bit of a tourist trap, but it's so much a part of the area's history that it still has its regulars – all of whom must abide by the McSorley motto: *Be Good, Or Be Gone*.

Music legends

Back on St Mark's, the block between Second and Third is lined by a motley array of music stores, tattoo parlors, and places to get piercings in a variety of body parts. cbgb-omfug, previously at 315 The Bowery, was the city's coolest live-music venue and the birthplace of the New York punk scene. The club was forced to close at the end of 2006 – joining the roll-call of local businesses forced out by rising property prices. In 2008, the space reopened as a John Varvatos clothing boutique. The poster- and sticker-covered walls were left intact, and are behind glass.

Down the block, Daniel Boulud's sausage-and-beer restaurant, DBGB, opened to rave reviews in 2009.

Cheap and spicy

Once upon a time you could find just about any cuisine in the East Village for next to nothing. Many of the neighborhood's old stalwarts have been forced on, making way for new (more expensive) restaurants. However, if cheap and spicy is your preference, you can't do much better than head for "**Little India**" ㉔, a strip of Indian restaurants on 6th Street between First and Second avenues. In the evening the air is filled with enticing smells, and visitors drift from menu to menu in the attempt to make a decision. All the restaurants here are inexpensive, most stay open pretty late, and some have live Indian music on weekend evenings.

Farther east on 6th Street is Avenue A, and a cafe-lined stretch that continues to **Tompkins Square Park** ㉕. Formerly reclaimed swamp that was used as a drill ground and recruiting camp during the Civil War, it was later the center of the *Kleine Deutschland*

BELOW: McSorley's Old Ale House dates from 1854.

(Little Germany) community that thrived here 100 years ago. The park was an infamous gathering place for hippies and runaways in the 1960s, and became a focal point for conflicts between homeless activists and police in the 1980s. Today, however, it's a generally peaceful place, frequented by young mothers with kids and neighborhood folk exercising their pets in the specially enclosed dog-friendly area. Many of the homes have been renovated (the 19th-century row houses on 10th Street are a good example), fueling a hike in rents as in other "reclaimed" parts of the city, and creating resentment from the locals fighting to stay in the area.

Alphabet City

Nowhere is this urban reclamation more evident than in the area known as **Alphabet City** 🏵 (Avenues A, B, C, and D). For decades the very name was synonymous with crime and little punishment, but now slums and barbed wire have been supplanted by bars and restaurants with a young, hip clientele.

Tiny community parks have been divested of drug dealers and twinkle at night with fairy lights, while former bodegas have metamorphosed into fashion boutiques with SoHo prices. Avenue A in particular is on the up, and although still a little rough around the edges, now wears its graffiti like a badge of honor.

As in other cutting-edge neighborhoods, though, it's wise to exercise a degree of caution, and here it's easy – just follow the alphabet. Avenues A, B, and C are fine anytime. Avenue D is fairly safe until midnight, but just for now it's an idea to avoid it after that.

Dining possibilities in the area are seemingly limitless, but an inexpensive stalwart has always been **Odessa** (119 Avenue A at 7th Street, open 24 hours), a survivor of the neighborhood's Eastern European past, where specialties include home-cooked *pierogies*, *blintzes*, and *borscht*.

ABOVE: Tompkins Square Park.

LOWER EAST SIDE

Technically, this area starts east of Tompkins Square Park, where Avenue C unofficially becomes Losaida Avenue (*Losaida* is Puerto Rican Spanglish for "Lower East Side"). But the traditional Lower East Side, with its Jewish-immigrant roots still in place, is south of East Houston Street, bordered by the Bowery and the East River. This is where the narrow streets are lined by tenements that date back 150 years.

The ABCs of Punk Road

The West Village had established itself as the cool and mellow testing grounds for folk troubadours and masters of jazz. At the other end of the island, an opposite movement was taking place. Stressing attitude over musicianship, the pioneers of punk claimed the East as their own in the 1970s and 80s, congregating around the Bowery, St Mark's Place and Tompkins Square Park. Many trace the origins back to the Velvet Underground's "happenings" and the high-energy rock of the New York Dolls, and Iggy Pop and The Stooges, but punk didn't really take off until 1976, when The Ramones came barreling into the limelight with a style that was like a revved up version of the Beach Boys. Legendary club CBGB anchored the scene, showcasing Patti Smith, The Misfits, and the Cramps. The Sex Pistols, The Clash, and other imports from London joined in, giving the aggressive style an international flavor.

By the 80s the tide began turning toward New Wave acts like Blondie, Talking Heads, and Devo. Some say the Tompkins Square Park Riot of 1988, where police clashed with young "punks," marked the end of the punk era, but even today you can catch some descendants of punk music in clubs like the Mercury Lounge.

ABOVE: Katz's Delicatessen.
BELOW: Bowery Subway.

These days you'll see stores with Jewish names and Chinese or Hispanic owners, a reminder that this neighborhood has always welcomed new arrivals. Modern newcomers are the bohemian-minded bars, clubs, and shops thriving along Ludlow, Orchard, and other streets, a trend that was kicked off in 1993 when **Mercury Lounge** – one of the city's best small music venues – kicked open its doors at 217 East Houston Street (check out listings in *Time Out New York* or the *Village Voice*).

Today, you can shop for exotic foods from family stores that have been here for decades, then stroll along next door for a cutting-edge outfit – evidence of the gentrification of an immigrant neighborhood, but also of the vibrancy of change.

Delis and designers

Walk along East Houston to the top of **Orchard Street** ㉗ to reach a favorite Lower East Side retail destination.

Serious shoppers may want to stop first at **Katz's Delicatessen** (205 East Houston, near Ludlow Street, http://katzsdelicatessen.com) for a little sustenance. The menu here has hardly changed since opening day in 1898 – and their pastrami sandwich has long been a New York culinary landmark.

New customers include the many construction workers currently working on the apartment blocks and fashionable hotels that are springing up in the area.

Once crowded with peddlers selling old clothes and cracked eggs, today the top of Orchard from East Houston to Rivington is being heavily redeveloped, with stylish new stores selling an intriguing mix of marked-up second-hand clothing, bespoke jewelry, street-smart sneakers, and designer clothes.

In the company of cool

The crowning glory of this upscale takeover is **The Hotel on Rivington**, by Ludlow Street (see page 310) – a 21-story glass tower with unrivaled views over the Lower East Side. Bouncer-like doormen guard the entrance to the über-designed interior, and sharply dressed urbanites toy with French-fusion cuisine at **Thor**. The arrival of this hotel loudly proclaimed the Lower East Side's new status of cool, and more hotels are planned for the future.

Three blocks west of The Hotel, proof of the area's continuing role as a center for immigrants is the 19th-century **University Settlement House** on Eldridge Street (at Rivington). The first settlement house in the US, the organization continues to provide advice and assistance to local immigrants and low-income residents today.

Farther south along Orchard Street, the lifestyle stores and boutiques give way to the Lower East Side's famous discount premises, selling bargain fashions, fabrics, linens, and shoes. The scene is frenetic at times, and bargaining is encouraged, but make sure you know what you want beforehand to ensure you get a good price.

Old favorites

Old favorites include Giselle at 143 Orchard, with four floors of discounted women's fashion (labels include Escada, Laurel, and Valentino), Ben Freedman at 137 Orchard, for 75 years the purveyor of bargain men's apparel, and Sam's Knitwear at 93 Orchard, where Polish immigrant Sam Goldstein has provided vintage and modern suits to snappily dressed men since 1969.

Head west on Delancey Street for some old-world comfort food at **Sammy's Roumanian Steak House** (175 Chrystie Street, just north of Delancey), a memorable, if not inexpensive, place to feast, and where a traditional pitcher of chicken fat comes with every meal. On a corner

of Delancey is a well-known tribute to the area's first immigrant families.

Lower East Side Tenement Museum ㉘

Address: 108 Orchard St (at Delancey and Broome sts), www.tenement.org
Telephone: 212-982 8420
Opening Hours: tours 10.30am–5pm daily
Entrance Fee: charge
Subway: Delancey St/Essex St

This museum is dedicated to the story of what life was like for poor immigrants in New York at the end of the 19th century. The address at 108 Orchard is the visitors' center and the starting point for tours of the tenements, which can only be visited with a guide.

Tours cover different themes, but all last one hour, during which visitors explore the recreated apartments of families who lived in the cramped quarters at 97 Orchard Street – each arranged to provide insight into the

ABOVE: the all-glass and uber cool Hotel on Rivington.
BELOW: a sign of the Lower East Side's Jewish heritage.

families' ethnic backgrounds and daily lives. What is remarkable is the imagination and resilience with which they sought to combat poverty and assimilate into New York society. The museum's tours are very popular, so be sure to book in advance. From April to December the museum also conducts weekend walking tours of the Lower East Side.

Designer tenement

The **Blue Moon Hotel** on Orchard (see page 310) has tried to bridge the gap between the tenement experience and the area's modern-day desirability by converting a traditional tenement building, empty since the 1930s, into a fashionable hotel. Many of the building's original features have been restored, and items recovered during the renovation – including newspapers and Yiddish sheet music – have been put on display. Room prices are *very* contemporary, though.

Farther down Orchard Street you'll find Il Laboratorio del Gelato, an artisanal maker of Italian-style *gelati*, with surprising flavors like wasabi and rose petal. Around the corner,

on Broome, you'll see the trendy Babycakes vegan bakery. Sadly, as in other parts of the city, soaring rent prices are forcing many of the traditional stores and eateries to close; the Tenement Museum publishes a list of all surviving specialty food shops in the area. Unfortunately a local fave, Guss' Pickles, closed in 2009 (though The Pickle Guys at 46 Essex Street are trying to fill the void).

Living history

The Lower East Side's Jewish population produced an extraordinary number of famous actors and comedians. Oscar-nominated actor Sam Jaffe was born in an apartment at 97 Orchard Street – the 1863 tenement now run by the Tenement Museum – while a couple of blocks south, Grand Street's Seward Park High School (at Ludlow Street) counted Tony Curtis and Walter Matthau among its graduates. The high school closed in 2006, and has been divided up into five different schools, offering courses in a variety of fields.

In the 19th century, the area's sub-standard working and living conditions (ably chronicled by Jacob Riis) were instrumental in spawning anarchist and socialist movements. Emma Goldman preached her gentle anarchism on the Lower East Side, radical newspapers such as the *Jewish Daily Forward* flourished, and settlement houses offering immigrants health and education assistance were established.

Landmark buildings

The faces of Karl Marx and Friedrich Engels peer from a frieze above the entrance to the landmark building at **173 East Broadway** (between Pike and Rutgers) where the old *Daily Forward* was published, which has been converted into condos. A block south, the glorious red-brick **Henry Street Settlement** (265 Henry Street), founded in 1893 as

the country's first volunteer nursing and social-service center, continues to serve the immigrant community and offers classes, health clinics, and after-school clubs.

Religion played an important role in the lives of immigrants. Although many of the synagogues in the area are no longer used, the **Eldridge Street Synagogue**, an 1887 Moorish-style landmark close to Division Street, has been the recipient of a 20-year restoration. Guided tours are available Sun–Fri, www.eldridgestreet.org, tel: 212-219 0888; charge.

NoLita ㉙

Dubbed **NoLita**, for **No**rth of **Li**ttle **Ita**ly, the retail heart of this area, with its good-looking, arty residents and one-off (but pricey) fashion boutiques, is Mulberry Street, particularly between Houston and Kenmare. The best way to enjoy NoLita is simply to stroll around and drink in its exuberant atmosphere – a laid-back mix of the traditional and the trendy – before stopping off for a drink and a tasty tidbit in one of the watering holes on Elizabeth or Mott streets, now also with their share of fashionable stores.

Old St Patrick's Cathedral ㉚, on the corner of Mott and Prince streets, was the seat of New York's Catholic archdiocese until 1879, when the "new" St Patrick's Cathedral on Fifth Avenue was completed. Construction of the cathedral began in 1809, was interrupted by the War of 1812, and was eventually finished three years later. It was rebuilt in 1868 after being destroyed by fire, and remains a unique landmark.

Across Mott Street from the cathedral graveyard, a plaque on the wall of a red-brick Victorian building explains that this was the School of the Children's Aid Society, created for the care and education of immigrant children. Designed in 1888 by Calvert Vaux, the English architect who also designed Jefferson Market Library and helped create Central Park, it's now one of NoLita's most coveted apartment blocks.

Farther south on Centre Street are more desirable apartments; one in particular is the **Police Building**.

LEFT: vintage fashion at Marmalade on Ludlow Street.
ABOVE: a sewing machine on display at the Lower East Side Tenement Museum.
BELOW: East Side watering hole.

ABOVE: the New Museum of Contemporary Art.

TIP

To save a few dollars while enjoying some lager or cabernet, seek out restaurants without liquor licenses. Most will let you bring your own, and there are over 20 in the East Village and Lower East Side alone. Filter your restaurant search results with "BYOB" at http://ny mag.com.

This Beaux Arts edifice served as a police headquarters until 1973 (the current doormen do not look unlike the building's former employees).

New Museum of Contemporary Art ❸

Address: 235 the Bowery (at Prince St), www.newmuseum.org
Telephone: 212-219 1222
Opening Hours: Wed, Sat, Sun 11am–6pm, Thur, Fri 11am–9pm
Entrance Fee: charge
Subway: Bowery/Broadway-Lafayette St

In contrast to the Beaux Arts beauties around it, the New Museum of Contemporary Art is designed to make an emphatic statement in this historic neighborhood. Consisting of a series of cubes and rectangles, like a giant stack of boxes, the building provides a spectacular purpose-built home for the museum, which highlights the latest contemporary art and design.

Art timeline

The location of the New Museum is a timeline of New York artistic trends. From its beginnings in 1977 on Fifth Avenue, it moved to SoHo during the 1980s, then followed SoHo's artists to Chelsea. The museum's arrival on the Lower East Side seals the status of the neighborhood as a center of innovative creativity.

LITTLE ITALY ❷

Crowds – led along by tantalizing food stands and raucous games of chance – are an integral part of the festivals that draw visitors to the streets of Little Italy. The **Feast of St Anthony** takes place on Mott Street between Grand and Canal streets in late May, while Mulberry Street from Canal to East Houston becomes a lively pedestrian mall during the 10-day **Feast of San Gennaro**, held in September.

This area has been an Italian neighborhood since the 1880s, when large numbers of immigrants arrived in New York, mainly from southern Italy. The most pleasant part is along **Mulberry Street**, north of Canal, where the atmosphere abruptly changes from boisterous to almost mellow, and the sidewalks are lined by cafes and social clubs.

Buon appetito!

Little Italy used to be about the food, but now it is mostly a touristy spot and shrinking by the day. Good Italian restaurants are hard to find, but **Umberto's Clam House**, now back on Mulberry Street after a short stint on Broome, is a classic. The restaurant's first Mulberry Street location was where gangster Joey Gallo met an abrupt and bloody end over dinner in 1972.

Walking north on Mulberry past the headquarters of the Society of San Gennaro, you come to one of the oldest houses in Little Italy, a small white Federal-style building erected in 1816 for Stephen Van Renssellaer, a member of one of New York's oldest families. Originally at 153 Mulberry Street, the entire house was moved to its present site at No. 149 in 1841.

At the corner of Grand and Mulberry, **E. Rossi and Co.** has gifts, novelties, and religious relics to browse through, before it's time to sample the delicacies at **Ferrara**, a pastry shop and cafe since 1892.

CHINATOWN ㉝

One of the largest Chinese-American settlements in America, Chinatown got its start in the 1870s, when Chinese railroad workers drifted east from California in the wake of anti-Asian sentiment. Once squeezed into a three-block area bordered by Mott, Pell, and the Bowery, today's Chinatown encompasses around 40 blocks, swinging around Little Italy to Houston Street. Although Chinatown is now a little faded in some areas, half of

its appeal is in negotiating the vendors, tourists, and residents that fill its busy streets.

Chinatown's heart lies south of Canal, where Worth Street, East Broadway, and the Bowery meet at **Chatham Square ㉞**. Though the square is named after William Pitt – the Earl of Chatham – the **Kim Lau Memorial Arch** was built in honor of a Chinese-American pilot who died in World War II.

Nearby **Confucius Plaza ㉟** is a lightly dilapidated concrete high-rise with apartments, stores, and a school. A bronze statue of the philosopher Confucius stands in front, facing the square.

Tucked in among all the Chinese banks lining the Bowery is a remnant of old New York: built in 1785, **No. 18 Bowery** or the Edward Mooney house, after its first owner, a prosperous meat wholesaler – is a Federal-style house and the oldest surviving row house in Manhattan. It's now

ABOVE: celebrating Chinese New Year.
LEFT: dining out in Little Italy.

TIP

A walking tour isn't exactly "rock-and-roll" but the East Village Rock Tour is undeniably fun, with visits to the former homes of Joey Ramone, Iggy Pop, and Madonna. Visit www. rockjunket.com or call 212-209 3370.

City of Immigrants

Getting started may be tough, but Lady Liberty's legendary call still beckons far across the globe

The US Census Bureau estimated in 2010 that there were 8,175,133 people in New York. Of these, more than 35 percent were born outside the United States, and more than 30 different regions of the globe were represented in the population. The common term "melting pot" was first used by Israel Zangwill, an immigrant himself, to describe the masses huddled on the Lower East Side.

The New York migrant groups challenge city planners: the standard four-part categories – white, black, Hispanic, Asian – are hopelessly inadequate for the kaleidoscope of culture, race, and nationality of the people who live in the city. There's as much diversity within ethnic groups as there is between them, and the social and political splits within a group are often the most divisive.

A sample of Asians, for example, is as likely to include Koreans or Indians as it is Chinese immigrants, and they are just as likely to come from vastly different socio-economic backgrounds. Foreign-born blacks may resemble African-Americans, but black immigrants include French-speaking Haitians, plus English-speaking Barbadians, Trinidadians, and Jamaicans, Senegalese and Ghanians.

Among Latino groups, bound together by a common language, are deep-rooted cultural differences. Mexicans and Chileans, Cubans and Puerto Ricans keep their cultural distinctions in the city's neighborhoods, just as they did back home. Little wonder, then, that the 2 million Latinos, easily the city's largest ethnic group, have yet to consolidate a unified political voice.

Syncretism

In the end, it doesn't matter where people come from: they are here, and more arrive every day. New York's immigrants don't boil into a homogeneous cultural stew; they keep their identities and languages, and build new institutions and alliances. Nor is New York an example of pluralism – a multiethnic society where everyone has an equal say.

That tag is too static, and doesn't account for the dynamism, or for the possibilities of confrontation and conflict. The right term for New York's cultural mix is probably syncretism; a continuous state of cultural collision, blending, and overlapping, where groups and individuals influence each other to create something new.

New York is a city of immigrants, and has been since the Dutch shared the town with English, French, and Scandinavian settlers as well as with free Africans, black slaves, and Native Americans. The give-and-take – and often the push-and-shove – between cultures is what gave the city its vitality and a rough-cut worldliness.

Although immigrants come from farther away and speak languages never heard by New Yorkers 300 years ago, the same explosive energy runs through the city today.

LEFT: dancers perform in the Cinco de Mayo Parade.

occupied by offices. There is, of course, a McDonald's with a pagoda-style entrance and Chinese signage. Another striking Bowery landmark is the domed building at 58 Bowery that has housed banks since it was built in 1924.

Long-ago gangland

Walk west to **Columbus Park** – a pleasant space with basketball courts, benches, and a children's play area – to reach the bottom of busy **Mulberry Street**, one of Chinatown's two main thoroughfares, the other being **Mott Street**. In the mid-19th century, this was part of the notorious Five Points slum district, evoked at length in Martin Scorsese's 2002 epic, *Gangs of New York*, where street gangs ran rampant and squatters' huts formed an equally notorious shantytown (later cleared to make way for Columbus Park).

The best place to learn about the neighborhood is at an old (1900s) school building on the corner of Mulberry and Bayard, now the Chinese community museum.

Museum of Chinese in the Americas ㊱

Address: 215 Centre St (between Howard and Grand sts), www.mocanyc.org
Telephone: 212-619 4785
Opening Hours: Mon and Fri 11am–5pm, Thur 11am–9pm, Sat and Sun 10am–5pm
Entrance Fee: charge, free on Thursdays
Subway: Canal St
Founded in 1970, when the area's population began to explode, this tiny museum features a permanent exhibit on the Chinese-American experience, with many items donated by residents or salvaged from demolitions. It also has a research library and a gift shop, and organizes regular walking tours and lectures. The

exhibitions are located in a brand-new museum as of 2009.

Shiny restaurants

From the museum, walk south to Canal Street and turn left. As you enter Chinatown, you'll pass stands selling fruit, vegetables, and snacks, including leaf-wrapped packets of sticky rice. Crowded with vendors hawking Taiwanese dvds and stores stocked with designer "knock-offs," this is a scene that feels far removed from the rest of Manhattan. From Canal Street, turn south down Mott Street to find shiny Singapore-style restaurants with marble facades and plastic signs. These are part of the "new" Chinatown built by recent, wealthier immigrants from Hong Kong and Shanghai; some are excellent, and surprisingly cheap.

Signs of the "old" Chinatown are still visible, however, especially at the **Chinese Community Center**, which first opened on Mott Street in 1883. Next door, in the **Eastern States Buddhist Temple** ㊲, there's a multi-armed statue of the Goddess Kuan-Yui. The air is thick with the scent of sweet incense.

EAT

Although it's possible to find good Chinese food anywhere in New York, one of the best places is the Nom Wah Tea Parlor, 1 Doyers Street at Chatham Square, http://nomwah.com, tel: 212-962 6047. Serving dim sum in a tiny space, this is the oldest teahouse in Chinatown.

BELOW: shop for flowers and food in Chinatown.

TIP

Here we go 'round Mulberry Street... If you head for Little Italy and walk north looking for NoLita (North of Little Italy), you'll end up in NoHo. NoLita is a misnomer: the neighborhood is really "NoSLita", the Northern Section of Little Italy, but this doesn't sound nearly as cool.

Farther along, the **Church of the Transfiguration** was built for a Lutheran congregation in 1801 and was sold to the Roman Catholic Church in 1853. Today it offers Catholic services in Cantonese and runs a school for local children.

Turn right down **Pell Street** and you'll see the shopfront facade of the **First Chinese Baptist Church**. Ting's Gift Shop on the corner of Doyers Street and Pell is the perfect place to pick up trinkets and knick-nacks. Nearby is the headquarters of the Hip Sing Association, one of Chinatown's many *tongs*, or fraternal organizations. From the 1870s until the 1930s, these groups were involved in often violent disputes that were sensationalized as "*tong* wars" by the non-Chinese press.

The Chinatown grapevine

The narrow lane off to the right is the most crooked street in Manhattan; in the 1600s it was a cart track leading to one of the first breweries. Later, **Doyers Street** became an important communications center, where men gathered to get the latest news from China and to drop off letters and money for home with the small shopkeepers whose premises served as combination banks and post offices.

In keeping with this tradition, the current Chinatown post office was built on the site of the old brewery. Nearby is the **Nom Wah Tea Parlor**, the neighborhood's oldest restaurant. Unlike many places in the area, it generally closes early (around 9pm), but has some of the best dim sum in Chinatown. The interior is much as it was in 1921 when it opened, with sagging red-leather banquettes, linoleum floor, and ceiling fans. Prices are as old-fashioned as the decor.

Food and festivals

Food is one of the main attractions of Chinatown and, with hundreds of restaurants to choose from, the hardest part is picking where to eat. Options range from the extremely cozy New Malaysia Restaurant on Bowery to the Golden Unicorn on East Broadway, where house specialties are served in luxurious surroundings, or the Peking Duck House on Mott Street, a favorite of former New York mayor Ed Koch.

For a deeper taste and sense of Chinese culture, drop in at one of the movie theaters that show films from Taiwan and China, or visit the **Asian-American Arts Centre** (111 Norfolk Street), which features ongoing exhibits. For many years, the **Asian-American Dance Theatre** presented traditional and contemporary dance productions here, too.

Chinese New Year combines feasts, dance, and music, and begins with fanciful parades. The festivities start around the end of January, and go on for several days, usually into February, but the street decorations tend to hang around a little bit longer.

BELOW: an exhibit at the Museum of Chinese in the Americas.

SHOPPING

The stores on the east side of Manhattan below 14th Street are an eclectic mix of old and new. Vintage clothes and traditional Jewish and Chinese items are hawked alongside the latest fashion, music, and wonderfully fresh produce.

Clothing

Calypso
426 Broome Street (at Crosby and Lafayette sts) and 280 Mott Street (at East Houston St)
Tel: 212-941 9700 and 212-965 0990
www.calypsostbarth.com
What started as a small line of resort-wear has expanded into a mini-empire of luxury fashion with two stores in NoLita (and others in SoHo, TriBeCa and Midtown).

Foley & Corinna
114 Stanton Street (at Ludlow and Essex sts)
Tel: 212-529 2338
http://foleyandcorinna.com
A well-chosen collection of new and vintage clothes, shoes, jewelry, and handbags.

Crafts

Pearl Paint
308 Canal Street
(at Mercer St)
Tel: 800-451 7327
www.pearlpaint.com
Where artists come for paints, canvases, and just about every other supply they need.

Department Stores

Pearl River Mart
477 Broadway (at Broome and Grand sts)
Tel: 800-878 2446
http://pearlriver.com
Located on the border of SoHo and Little Italy, this is one-stop shopping for Chinese gifts, fashion, and groceries.

Food

Russ and Daughters
179 East Houston Street (at Allen and Orchard sts)
Tel: 212-475 4880
http://russanddaughters.com
The great purveyor of smoked fish, caviar, bagels, and cream cheese – an East Village mainstay for nearly 100 years.

Market

Essex Street Market
120 Essex Street (at Delancey St)
www.essexstreetmarket.com
This excellent indoor market features more than 20 independent merchants of fresh meat, fish, produce, gourmet cheeses, and other culinary items. Most are open Mon–Sat.

Hester Street Fair
Corner of Hester and Essex sts
www.hesterstreetfair.com
Grab food, clothes, and accessories every Saturday from 10am–6pm on the site of New York's oldest and biggest push-cart market.

Movies

Kims Video & Music
124 First Avenue (at 7th and 8th sts)
Tel: 212-533 7390
www.mondokims.com
A treasure trove for collectors of obscure cinema you can't find streaming online, with many films organized by director. Open until midnight.

Music

Other Music
15 E. 4th Street (at Astor Place and Broadway)
Tel: 212-477 8150
www.othermusic.com
One of the last great places to buy CDs or vinyl, where the staff are perhaps the city's most dedicated music geeks.

ABOVE: Chinatown's bustling Mott Street.
RIGHT: Essex Street Market.

BEST RESTAURANTS, BARS AND CAFÉS

Restaurants

Angelica Kitchen
300 E. 12th St (at 1st and 2nd aves)
Tel: 212-228 2909
www.angelicakitchen.com
L & D daily $$ ㉜
[p340, D2/3]
Veg out on organic vegetarian cuisine, run by people with a retro mindset.

Angon
320 E. 6th St (at 1st and 2nd aves)
Tel: 212-260 8229
L & D Tue–Sun $ ㉝
[p340, D3]
One of the better places on this bargain strip known as "Curry Row."

Caracas Arepa Bar
91 E. 7th St (at 1st Ave and Ave A)
Tel: 212-228 5062
http://caracasarepabar.com
L & D daily $ ㉞
[p340, D3]

Locals flock to this casual Venezuelan restaurant for: warm cornmeal pancakes topped with savory meat and vegetable options, and served with hot sauce.

Chinatown Brasserie
380 Lafayette St (at Great Jones St)
Tel: 212-533 7000
www.chinatownbrasserie.com
L & D daily $$ ㉟
[p340, C3]
One of the big new Downtown "in" spots for Asian cuisine. Big and brassy, with a noisy scene.

I Coppi
432 E. 9th St (at 1st Ave and Ave A)
Tel: 212-254 2263
www.icoppinyc.com
D daily $$$ ㊱ [p340, D3]
This Tuscan restaurant oozes authenticity thanks to its brick

walls, terracotta floors, wood-burning oven, and pretty garden. Dishes are rustic but sophisticated. It's pricey for the casual neighborhood, but highly romantic and very enjoyable.

Da Nico
164 Mulberry St (at Broome and Grand sts)
Tel: 212-343 1212
http://danicoristorante.com
L & D daily $$ ㊲ [p342, C1]
Old-style Little Italy restaurant that former mayor Rudy Giuliani counted as a favorite.

DBGB Kitchen and Bar
299 Bowery (at 1st and 2nd sts)
Tel: 212-933 5300
www.danielnyc.com/dbgb.html
L & D daily $$$ ㊳
[p340, C3]
This sleek restaurant elevates the humble – hot dogs, sausages, and burgers – to the elegant, with smooth service and prices to match.

Degustation
239 E. 5th St (at 2nd and 3rd aves)
Tel: 212-979 1012
http://degustationnyc.com
D Mon–Sat $$–$$$ ㊴
[p340, C3]
The room is tiny but the flavors are big at this Franco-Spanish tapas and wine bar, which has a fantastic tasting menu.

Indochine
430 Lafayette St (at Astor Pl and 4th St)
Tel: 212-505 5111
www.indochinenyc.com

D daily $$$ ㊵ [p340, C3]
Trendy, tropical decor, French-Vietnamese food, still sexy after all these years. It's located across from the Public Theater, and offers a decently priced pretheater deal.

Ippudo
65 4th Ave (between 9th and 10th sts)
Tel: 212-388 0088
www.ippudony.com
L & D daily $$ ㊶ [p340, C2]
The ramen at this Japanese import is nowhere near the cheap packaged noodles favored by penniless students. This is savory and artistic soup.

Itzocan
438 E. 9th St (between 1st Ave and Ave A)
Tel: 212-677 5856
www.itzocanrestaurant.com
L & D daily $ ㊷ [p340, D3]
Cheap and chic Mexican with French-accented preparations in a tiny intimate spot on the edge of Alphabet City.

Jewel Bako
239 E. 5th St (at 2nd and 3rd aves)
Tel: 212-979 1012
D Mon–Sat $$$$ ㊸
[p340, C3]
A tiny "Tiffany" of sushi, where you don't need to cash in diamonds to eat.

Katz's Delicatessen
205 E. Houston St (at Ludlow St)
Tel: 212-254 2246
http://katzsdelicatessen.com
B, L, & D daily $$ ㊹
[p340, C/D4]
This old-style Jewish deli is a New York institution.

LEFT: the kitchen at WD-50.

The huge space is often packed, especially on Sunday mornings. Portions are huge, and the service is friendly. A must for any first-time NY visitor.

Lombardi's Pizza
32 Spring St (at Mulberry and Mott sts)
Tel: 212-941 7994
www.firstpizza.com
L & D daily $$ ⑮ [p340, C4]
Descended from the first pizzeria in the USA (opened in 1897), this is a Little Italy classic. It's open late: join the crowds, line up for a table (no reservations are taken), and be ready to pay cash.

Momofuku Noodle Bar
171 1st Ave (at 10th and 11th sts)
Tel: 212-475 7899
www.momofuku.com
L & D daily $$
⑯ [p340, D3]
This shrine to Korean haute cuisine also has a few sophisticated siblings in the neighborhood, including Momofuku Ssam a few blocks north and nearby, reservation-only Momofuku Ko.

Peasant
194 Elizabeth St (at Prince and Spring)
Tel: 212-965 9511
http://peasantnyc.com
D only Tue–Sun $$$ ⑰ [p340, C4]
Like eating in a sophisticated Italian country home, with hearty flavors matched only by the wine list. A romantic setting.

Peking Duck House
28 Mott St (at Pell and Mosco sts)
Tel: 212-777 1810
www.pekingduckhousenyc.com

L & D daily $$$ ⑱ [p342, C2]
The crisp-skinned duck is served tableside with scallions, hoi sin sauce and rice-flour pancakes.

Prune
54 E. 1st St (at 1st and 2nd aves)
Tel: 212-677 6221
www.prunerestaurant.com
L & D daily $$$ ⑲ [p340, C4]
Uptowners venture here for a foodie's dream. Chef Gabrielle Hamilton always makes culinary news with her tasty dishes.

The Redhead
349 E. 13th St (at 1st and 2nd aves)
Tel: 212-533 6212
www.theredheadnyc.com
D Mon–Sat, Br Sat–Sun $$ ㊿ [p340, D2]
A bar serving gastropub cuisine. Try the fried chicken with cornbread or bacon peanut brittle.

Schiller's Liquor Bar
131 Rivington Street (at Norfolk St)
www.schillersny.com
Tel: 212-260 4555
B, L, & D daily $$ ㊶ [p342, D1]
A hipster scene at affordable prices, and good grub to boot. Open late.

WD-50
50 Clinton St (at Rivington and Stanton)
Tel: 212-477 2900
www.wd-50.com
D daily $$$$ ㊷ [p342, D1]
WD stands for Wally Dufresne, who presides over a brilliant American-eclectic menu. A place (and prices) appreciated by all New York foodies.

Bars and Cafes

Back Room
102 Norfolk St (between Delancey and Rivington sts) ⑫ [p340, D4]
One of New York's favorite speakeasy style bars, this is a cozy place for an after-dinner cocktail. But, be warned, it gets crowded in the evenings.

ChickaLicious
203 E. 10th St (at 1st and 2nd aves) ⑬ [p340, D3]
ChickaLicious is a tiny dessert bar serving yummy sweets with sweet wines.

De Robertis
176 1st Ave (at 10th and 11th sts) ⑭ [p340, D3]
This local favorite is an Italian pasticceria and cafe established over a century ago.

Max Fish
178 Ludlow St (at E. Houston and Stanton sts) ⑮ [p340, D4]
A rowdy rocker-art bar with its own gang of regular hipsters.

Prices for a three-course dinner per person with half a bottle of wine:

$ = under $20
$$ = $20–$45
$$$ = $45–$60
$$$$ = over $60

Momofuku Milk Bar
251 E 13th Street (across from Momofuku Ssam) ⑯ [p340, D2]
Serving cakes and pies filled with candy bars, and milk and shakes sweetened with cereal (yes, really).

Pianos
158 Ludlow St (at Stanton) ⑰ [p340, C/D4]
Catch up-and-coming bands, get out on the dance floor, or just hang out at this Lower East Side institution.

Veniero
342 E. 11th St (between 1st and 2nd aves) ⑱ [p340, D3]
A lovely spot for an espresso, but we dare you not to order the cannoli, too.

RIGHT: fresh dumplings.

GREENWICH VILLAGE

Greenwich Village was once a true bohemian neighbourhood; now is the domain of the rich and fashionable, with quiet streets lined with multimillion-dollar homes and glitzy nightlife in the Meatpacking District

Writers and poets, artists and radicals, runaway socialites, and others seeking freedom from conventional lifestyles have long flocked to Greenwich Village, spotlit in recent history by poets and musicians of the 1950s and '60s.

Today, as other neighborhoods set the trends, New Yorkers often think of "the Village" as one big tourist attraction. Untrue. A commercial element exists, serviced by double-decker tour buses, but many streets are as quietly residential as they were in the 18th and early 19th centuries, when the village of Greenwich was first settled by pioneers fleeing illness and epidemics at the tip of the island.

Success and the city

Spiraling real-estate prices have forced out all but the most successful, but the Village (both Greenwich and the West Village) is still where many people would choose to live: witness the "Gold Coast" on West 9th Street or the buildings facing the Hudson River, which are home to celebrities and financiers.

Bordered by 14th Street to the north, the Hudson River to the west, and Broadway to the east (where the

East Village begins), this is where the offbeat and the fashionable mingle with ease, and where the annual Halloween Parade is a riotous spectacle attended by both.

AROUND WASHINGTON SQUARE

Walking south on Fifth Avenue, **Washington Arch** rises in the distance. Designed in wood by Stanford White to commemorate the 1889 centennial of the first president's inauguration, the imposing marble arch from 1918 is the entrance to

LEFT: summertime in Washington Square.
RIGHT: a bakery in West Village.

ABOVE: thousands of toy soldiers are on display at the Forbes Galleries.

delightful, the Strand was started in 1927 and is the perfect place to track down that elusive edition.

Grace Church ❷, just to the south, is one of New York's loveliest ecclesiastical structures. Built in 1846, its exterior white marble, now a muted gray, was mined by convicts from the infamous Sing Sing prison in upstate New York.

Turn right at 10th, and walk toward Fifth Avenue crossing **University Place**, which runs parallel to Fifth for several blocks, to West 12th Street, where a block-shaped building houses the **New School for Social Research**, which offers classes in everything from Arabic to screenwriting.

At Fifth Avenue and 12th Street, the **Forbes Galleries ❸** (www.forbes galleries.com, tel: 212-206 5548; Tue–Sat 10am–4pm, Thur groups only; free) hold the late Malcolm Forbes's collections of tin soldiers and other collectibles. The toys are organized in

Washington Square ❶, the symbolic heart of Greenwich Village.

Booksellers and collectors

A walk east from the square and then north up Broadway will lead you to the **Strand Book Store** (www.strand books.com, tel: 212-473 1452; until 10.30pm every night; rare books room closes at 6.20pm). Dusty and

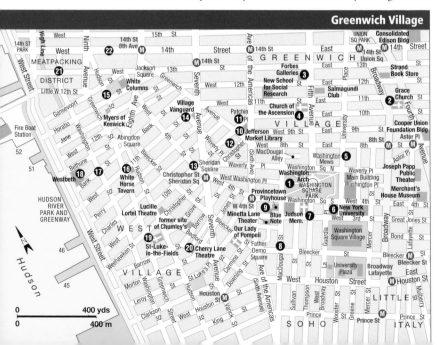

entertaining displays across themed rooms, while the air is filled with appropriate sound effects, from military marches to war cries. The galleries also host art shows.

The nearby **Salmagundi Club**, at 47 Fifth Avenue, is the country's oldest artists' club, founded in 1870. Its facilities are for members only, but there are walk-in classes (www.salmagundi.org, tel: 212-255 7740) should you fancy joining the artistic fraternity for a few hours.

Washington Square sites

Take a stroll along 9th and 10th streets, two of the most picturesque in the city. Lined by stately brick and brownstone houses, they have been home to numerous artists and writers (Mark Twain lived at 14 West 10th). The **Church of the Ascension** ❹ on the corner of Fifth and 10th was designed by Richard Upjohn in 1840, and features a marble altar relief by sculptor Augustus St-Gaudens.

Pretty **Washington Mews** ❺ runs between Fifth and University Place, just above Washington

Square. Originally built as stables for the townhouses along Washington Square North, the pretty row houses here and along nearby **MacDougal Alley** were converted to artists' studios after the arrival of the motor car put stables out of business. The painter Edward Hopper lived and worked at 3 Washington Square North for 54 years, from 1913 until his death in 1967. Washington Mews has retained much brickwork cobbling, and on a winter's day when the snow settles between

ABOVE: the Strand Book Store has 18 miles of used books.
BELOW: all that jazz in Washington Square.

TIP

Note the Playwrights Sidewalk in front of the Lucille Lortel Theater, replete with names like Eugene O'Neill and Sam Shepard, whose celebrated work has been performed here.

ABOVE LEFT: Village café.
ABOVE RIGHT: Bob Dylan in the Village.

the bricks in the road, the setting is particularly lovely.

All this eventually leads to **Washington Square** itself. Originally a potter's field, where the poor and unknown were buried, it later became a parade ground, and still later a residential park.

Though it's lost the cachet it had in the days of Henry James – who grew up nearby and based his novel *Washington Square* on his childhood memories – on weekend afternoons the park fills with musicians and street performers playing to appreciative crowds of Japanese camera crews, out-of-town students, tourists, chess hustlers, and pot dealers. During the school term, NYU students congregate on the grass,

Village Voices: Bob Dylan

In the 1950s and '60s, the cafe scene of Greenwich Village drew poetic, artistic, and politically inquisitive newcomers to New York. Low rents may well have been a factor, together with a boho-artistic aura that had been gaining strength since the 1920s. Deep in the Village, major musical moments of the mid-20th century took place in MacDougal Street, many at an unpromising little coffee bar called the Cafe Wha? David Barry, a musician who frequented and played at the cafe, once said, "It was a grubby, awful scene there."

In spite of this, a number of careers in the American folk revival began and grew. On first reaching New York on January 24, 1961, Bob Dylan took a subway straight to Greenwich Village and blew into the Café Wha? in a flurry of snowflakes. Barry remembered those times well. "Although Dylan could neither sing or play the guitar, he clearly had something on stage that none of the rest of us did."

Up-and-coming folk singers such as Joan Baez and Dave Van Ronk (later nicknamed the Mayor of MacDougal Street on account of his avuncular status in the area) were among "the rest of us" in the exploding Village folk scene. The media also took notice of Dylan, with a laudatory review of one of his performances appearing in *The New York Times*. He signed with an agent and changed his last name (it was originally Zimmerman). Shortly after he was signed to Columbia Records and released his eponymous debut album.

The famous cover of Dylan's second album, *The Freewheelin' Bob Dylan*, was shot along Jones Street (between West 4th and Bleecker), as Dylan and his girlfriend Suze Rotolo walked along huddled together. Shortly after the record came out, Dylan's popularity reached a new high and he and Rotolo broke up. He left the Village, but forever left his mark on it.

and the atmosphere is generally less frantic.

With two blocks of Greek Revival townhouses, **Washington Square North** retains a 19th-century elegance, at odds with the monolithic **New York University ⑥** buildings across the park. Past nyu's busy Kimmel Student Center, Bobst Library, and Catholic Center (all on Washington Square South), is **Judson Memorial Church ⑦**. Designed in 1890 by Stanford White in Romanesque Revival style, the church has been a cultural and religious center in the Greenwich community for decades.

Beat streets

Turn off Washington Square South onto **MacDougal Street ⑧**, into the heart of what was once a beatnik haven, where world-weary poets wore black, sipped coffee, and discoursed on the meaning of life late into the night. These days, the area is a magnet for out-of-towners, drawn by ersatz craft shops and "authentic" ethnic restaurants. Only a handful of Beatera establishments remain, however, including **Café Wha?** on MacDougal between Bleecker and West 3rd, once a hangout of Allen Ginsberg.

Nevertheless, a stroll around these streets offers the pleasure of a pilgrimage down passageways of past grooviness and cloisters of cool. Some nights echoes of the young Bob Dylan or Jimi Hendrix seem to drift around the intersection of Bleecker and MacDougal streets. And there's still plenty of entertainment, from performances by jazz greats to contemporary drama at the **Minetta Lane Theatre**, toward Sixth Avenue.

Blue Note ⑨

Address: 131 W. 3rd St (between MacDougal St and Sixth Ave), www. bluenote.net
Telephone: 212-475 8592
Opening Hours: music nightly 8pm and 10.30pm with an occasional extra set at 12.30am, also jazz brunch Sun 12.30pm
Entrance Fee: charge
Subway: W. 4th St

This club has been drawing jazz fans to Greenwich Village for over 25 years. It's comforting to think that

ABOVE: the Village's very own Italian-Gothic fantasy, Jefferson Market Library.
LEFT AND BELOW: fans will happily queue up at the Blue Note for the chance to see jazz stars.

no matter what transformations take place on the surrounding streets, inside the Blue Note the beat goes on.

THE WEST VILLAGE

The area west of the Avenue of the Americas (Sixth Avenue) and a few blocks north is where the Village hosts the annual Halloween Parade; witnessed the gay-rights riots at the Stonewall Inn in the late 1960s; and where attractive, quiet knots of streets wind around confusingly between the major avenues.

A good place to start is the striking **Jefferson Market Library** ⓾ at 10th Street and Sixth Avenue. Part of a complex that included the old Women's House of Detention, it was built as a courthouse in 1877. This is where Harry Thaw went on trial for shooting America's then most famous architect, Stanford White, in 1906, after White had an affair with Thaw's wife, in one of New York's most celebrated scandals. The upstairs rooms still have a court-like feel, with dark wood and stained-glass windows. Next door is a pretty community garden, open to all.

ABOVE: the Village Vanguard helped to launch the careers of jazz greats Miles Davis and John Coltrane.
RIGHT: shops along Christopher Street.
BELOW: a cafe in the West Village.

Walk west on 10th Street to **Patchin Place** ⓫ – a mews where Eugene O'Neill, journalist John Reed, and poet e.e. cummings all lived. Continue on **Christopher Street** ⓬, symbolic center of the gay community and a main cross-street that slants across the West Village to a renovated pier, walkway, and bike path that, on a sunny day, make New York seem like a brand-new city. (At night, however, it's still the haunt of hustlers, so be alert.)

Just past **Waverly Place**, with its curved row of small Federal-style houses, is the **Northern Dispensary**. A non-profit health clinic from 1831 until fairly recently, it's one of the oldest public buildings in the city. A few doors up, and nearly four decades ago, the modern gay-rights movement got its spontaneous start one night in 1969 at the **Stonewall Inn** (53 Christopher Street, www.thestone wallinnnyc.com), a gay bar whose

habitués got tired of being rousted by police. Today, there's a bar with the same name operating next door, with a gay-pride flag.

Just across the street, tiny fenced-in **Christopher Park** has a statue of Civil War general Philip Sheridan. **Sheridan Square** ⓭ itself isn't a square at all, it's actually at the triangular junction where Grove, Christopher, and West 4th streets meet.

At 121 Christopher Street is the **Lucille Lortel Theatre** (tel: 212-924 2817, www.lortel.org), a theater that for many years has been the friend and supporter of new writers.

Village Vanguard ⓮

Address: 178 Seventh Ave S. (at W. 11th St), www.villagevanguard.com
Telephone: 212-255 4037
Opening Hours: music nightly at 9pm and 11pm, occasional extra set Sat 12.30am
Entrance Fee: charge
Subway: 14th St

If it's music that gives a cultural *frisson*, this is the right neighborhood: the tiny Vanguard has been in business over 70 years, and pictures of its musical alumni line its walls. With a capacity of just 123, the historic basement venue has kept the sort of intimacy most jazz clubs – and musicians – only dream of. If you are lucky enough to get tickets, be warned that it's meant for jazz and jazz alone – conversation or, heaven forbid, cell ringtones during a performance are a throw-out-able offence. On Mondays, the house jazz orchestra plays.

West of 4th Street

The nearer to the river you head, the deeper you go into the oldest part of Greenwich Village, which makes up for any lack of the chic and glitz found in nearby districts with a nicely low-key neighborliness.

Flowing north–south is **Hudson Street** ⓯, its main artery. Over the past few years, this area has acquired

ABOVE AND BELOW: dogwalkers in all weathers.

ABOVE: the Cherry Lane Theatre. **BELOW:** the Meatpacking District. **RIGHT:** White Horse Tavern.

curious British connections, with a clutch of British businesses on Greenwich Avenue.

A favorite is **Myers of Keswick** (634 Hudson St, www.myersofkeswick.com, tel: 212-691 4194), a British specialty shop where Keith Richards and Elton John have stocked up on pork pies and bags of Walkers crisps. Their sausage rolls are spectacular and, although there isn't any seating, they'll heat them up for you.

White Horse Tavern 16

Address: 567 Hudson St (at W. 11th St)
Telephone: 212-989 3956
Opening Hours: daily 11am–3am
Subway: Christopher St

The White Horse has been serving drinks at the corner of 11th Street since 1880, and is one of the last remaining wood-paneled bars in New York. The Horse was a haunt of Dylan Thomas, where he had several too many (some say 18) whiskies,

before dragging himself back to the Chelsea Hotel. The next day, he died. Although on the tourist route, the White Horse retains much charm. Weekends are manic, so try to visit during the week.

Pretty thoroughfares

Near the White Horse, cute little **Abingdon Square** leads to the start

of **Bleecker Street**. This end of the street has fallen hard to the onslaught of high-fashion stores (Marc Jacobs, Prada, luxury leather specialists Mulberry), and many locally owned businesses have been forced out by escalating rents.

Nevertheless, Bleecker is bisected by some of the Village's prettiest thoroughfares. **Bank Street** ⓱ is particularly scenic, with its cobblestones and pastel houses, and lies in the center of the **Greenwich Village Historic District**'s finest 19th-century architecture.

Toward the west end of Bank Street, **Westbeth** ⓲ is a sprawling, government-funded artists' enclave (sometimes open for performances), that looks out over the Hudson. It's only a short walk from the church of **St-Luke-in-the-Fields** ⓳, built in 1821. **17 Grove Street**, built in 1822, is a wooden home that brims with character, as does **Grove Court**, a gated alleyway with a cluster of attractive brick houses. Grove Street intersects **Bedford Street**, one of the oldest Village byways. At No. 102 is the original "Twin Peaks," built in 1830 as an artists' residence, with two peaks in its gabled roof.

Byways and speakeasies

A left turn leads to the former site of **Chumley's**, a speakeasy turned bar and restaurant, where novelist John Steinbeck and playwright Eugene O'Neill were regulars. A leftover from Prohibition, it had an unmarked entrance around the corner on Barrow Street – until it closed in 2008.

Tiny poet Edna St Vincent Millay was a tenant at **75 Bedford Street**, Manhattan's narrowest house at just over 9ft (3 meters) wide. A bigger tenant was John Barrymore, of the theatrical dynasty. And before her break into stardom, Barbra Streisand worked as an usher at the **Cherry Lane Theatre** ⓴ (38 Commerce Street, www.cherrylanetheatre.org, tel: 212-989 2020), a nurturing space for American playwrights since 1924.

St Luke's Place is lined by gracious Italianate row houses. New York's Jazz Age mayor Jimmy Walker lived at No. 6, and two lamps – a sign of mayoral honor – are at the foot of the steps.

TIP

The basketball court on the corner of West 3rd Street and 6th Avenue used to be home to some of the city's best pick-up games. It's now primarily reserved for league play, but spectators still come to see the high-flying talent.

BELOW: dining in the Meatpacking District.

Washington Square Park

Some parks have playgrounds or ponds, art installations or annual festivals and events. More than any other park in New York, Washington Square has personality

Walking down Fifth Avenue, you spot the Washington Arch from blocks away. Inspired by the Arc de Triomphe, it is a truly grand entrance to Downtown's liveliest patch of green. In Henry James's day, the park contained "a considerable quantity of inexpensive vegetation, enclosed by a wooden paling, which increased its rural and accessible appearance..." Vegetation remains in the form of trees and flowerbeds, but step through the gate on a weekend afternoon and any thoughts of the rural will be dispelled by the pulsing energy of the place.

Skateboarders zip past as a student from New York University's Tisch School of Arts secures a movie camera to a tripod with dreams of being the next Spike Lee or Martin Scorsese. A breakdance troop sets up shop near the fountain, turns on a boombox, and tries to entice a crowd of sightseers to drop dollars into their hat. A hungry barista grabs a crepe from one of the city's only vegan pushcarts, while in a shaded corner on the south end, fierce matches rage on concrete chessboards. Bobby Fischer played here as teenager and eyes are still peeled for the next prodigy.

A colorful history is buried beneath the layers of concrete – at one time it served as a graveyard for the indigent and unknown. In 1888, Mark Twain took a train from Connecticut to meet Robert Louis Stevenson and they sat on the park benches discussing the writerly life, a moment immortalized by artist Francis Luis Mora. On the same benches is where, according to his autobiography, Marlon Brando first got drunk and passed out. A group of concerned citizens including Eleanor Roosevelt, who lived on Washington Square West, successfully campaigned to have car traffic removed from the park.

These days, the place has never looked better. The Arch received a facelift in the late 1990s, while the entire park has been under renovation since 2006, a daunting and controversial project that involved realigning the fountain that has been the centerpiece for more than 150 years. With work nearing completion, there is an extra sheen on the soul of Greenwich Village that is, among other things, a campus quad for NYU students, a stage for buskers, and a shady place to rest and play.

LEFT: playing in the fountain of Washington Square Park. **ABOVE:** the famous Arch.

MEATPACKING DISTRICT ㉑

Until a decade or so ago, the Meatpacking District was just what it sounded like – a warehousing, wholesale meat market, and distribution area for butchered goods making their way into the city's restaurants and grocery stores. Located on Manhattan's west side, to the west of the West Village and just south of Chelsea, it's bordered to the north by **West 14th Street** ㉒ (or even a couple blocks further north, depending on who you ask), to the south by **Gansevoort Street**, and from Hudson Street to the east to the Hudson River at the west. In fact, it is so well located (with decent subway and bus access) that it should have seemed inevitable that such prime real estate would eventually be developed for more fashionable pursuits. But, back when this was a red-light district (and the streets were literally stained red from the cow carcasses in the slaughterhouses) there was nothing cool about this stretch of Manhattan.

First came the lounge-style nightclubs, in the late 1990s, lured by the promise of large warehouse spaces

– then came the crowds of Manolo- and Jimmy Choo-clad fashionistas, making their way to Pastis restaurant at night and high-end boutiques by day. At its peak, the neighborhood became a symbol of *Sex and the City*-style trendiness, with late-night crowds of fabulous people posing on the cobblestone street – right next to the last remaining meatpacking plants.

Over the next few years, the Meatpacking District went mainstream, trading in the "insider's

ABOVE: the High Line.
LEFT: the glamorous Hotel Gansevoort.
BELOW: wild grasses on the High Line.

secret" pedigree for a more broad popularity. You're as likely to see bachelorette parties and bridge-and-tunnel (Manhattan speak for those from New Jersey and the outer boroughs) club kids in for a night of dancing as you are to glimpse the Manhattan elite at night.

That said, during the day the exclusive boutiques remain a draw for everyone who loves to be current and fashionable. These include storefronts for Alexander McQueen (417 W. 14th St, www.alexandermcqueen.com), Diane von Furstenberg (874 Washington St, www.dvf.com), and Stella McCartney (429 W. 14th St, www.stellamccartney.com), not to mention a gorgeous glass-encased Apple store (401 W. 14th St, www.apple.com/retail/west14thstreet).

Sleeping and eating

Two major hotels – the **Hotel Gansevoort** (see page 309), with its rooftop pool, and **The Standard** hotel – bring crowds of visitors, and the exclusive Soho House (a private club of British origins, with an even harder-to-access rooftop pool)

ABOVE: a meatpacker on the job.
BELOW: West 14th Street and 9th Avenue.
RIGHT: fashionistas negotiate the cobble streets of the Meatpacking District.

continues to add cachet to the district (see page 309).

And the restaurant scene here continues to grow. Celebrity chefs like Jean-Georges Vongerichten, who opened **Spice Market** in 2004, and Mario Batali, who launched **Del Posto** in 2006, have outposts here. And, because of the club scene, many restaurants keep their kitchens open late into the night.

The **High Line**, a major new park built on an elevated railroad track, has brought a lot of attention to the area. Now, you can sit on this path-in-the-sky and watch the sunset over the river, without having to buy a loft space – something unimaginable before.

Things change quickly around the Meatpacking District, so there's little point in picking out more specific highlights. (The closing of popular Florent restaurant taught everyone that.) However, a growing number of galleries signal the movement of Chelsea's art scene further south, as will the Whitney Museum of Art branch, when it opens in a few years – heralding the Meatpacking District's next act.

SHOPPING

Shopping

While the Meatpacking District is attracting McQueen, McCartney, and other major designers, down in the Village tiny storefronts try to hold their own in a land of soaring rents.

Antiques

The End of History
548½ Hudson Street (at Perry Street)
Tel: 212-647 7598
www.theendofhistoryshop.blogspot.com
With perhaps the neighborhood's most stunning window display, this specialist in glasswork and ceramics is as much a museum as it is a store.

Clothing

Ludivine
172 W. 4th Street (at Jones St)
Tel: 646-336 6576
www.boutiqueludivine.com
One store that helped bring Parisian fashion to the streets of New York with price tags as high as the fashion.
Marc Jacobs
382 and 403 Bleecker Street (at W. 11th and Perry sts)
Tel: 212-206 6644
www.marcjacobs.com
Jacobs has all but claimed ownership of the Village, with the two stores on Bleecker dedicated to men's and women's wear, as well as ones specializing in children's wear, accessories, and stationery. He also has a store just over Houston in SoHo.

Food

Li-Lac Chocolates
40 Eighth Avenue (at Jane St)
Tel: 212-924 2280
www.li-lacchocolates.com
One of the city's lesser-known chocolate shops is also one of its best. During the Christmas period lines go into the street.
Murray's Cheese
254 Bleecker Street (between 6th and 7th aves)
Tel: 212-243 5001
www.murrayscheese.com
There are few cheese stores in the country as renowned as Murray's.

Gifts

Monocle
535 Hudson Street (at Charles St)
Tel: 212-229 1120
http://shop.monocle.com
A new and hip place to buy a carefully selected line of clothing, accessories, and miscellany. Think of it as a curated department store.

Home

Mxyplyzyk
125 Greenwich Avenue (at W. 13th st)
Tel: 800-243 9810
http://mxyplyzyk.com
Don't worry about pronouncing the name. Just enjoy perusing their shelves of well-made, attractive, and affordable houseware.

Jewelry

Ten Thousand Things
423 W. 14th Street (between 9th and 10th aves)
Tel: 212-352 1333
http://tenthousandthingsnyc.com
Much of the gorgeous handcrafted jewelry here goes for thousands of dollars, but you can find some lovely and unique items in the $100 range.

Shoes

Christain Louboutin
59 Horatio Street (at Greenwich St)
Tel: 212-255 1910
www.christianlouboutin.com
A temple to outrageous shoes at outrageous prices.

BEST RESTAURANTS, BARS, AND CAFES

Restaurants

AOC
314 Bleecker St
(at Grove St)
Tel: 212-675 9463
www.aocnyc.com
B, L, & D daily $$ ➌ [p340, B2]

The dishes are served here as simply and perfectly as in a Paris bistro. Unlike other hurried New York spots, here *le savoir-vivre* reigns, and you can linger and talk all night if no one needs your table. There's a little garden patio for summer, too.

Babbo
110 Waverly Pl (at MacDougal St and 6th Ave)
Tel: 212-777 0303
http://babbonyc.com
D only daily $$$$ ➎ [p340, B2]

Make a reservation quite a few days in advance for Mario Batali's top-of-the-line Italian gem. Some say it now has the best, most elegant Italian cuisine in New York City.

Barbuto
775 Washington St (at W. 12th St)
http://barbutonyc.com
212-924 9700
L & D daily $$ ➎ [p340, A1]

Another great restaurateur, Jonathan Waxman, forges into the Meatpacking District at – what's this? – reasonable prices. He presents imaginative American cuisine using seasonal ingredients.

Blue Hill
75 Washington Pl
(at 6th Ave and Washington Sq W.)
Tel: 212-539 1776
www.bluehillfarm.com
D only daily $$$$ ➎ [p340, B2]

A mellow, sophisticated spot with rave reviews for its finely conceived American dishes created with fresh produce from the proprietors' own farm in upstate New York.

Café Asean
117 W. 10th St (at Greenwich and 6th aves)
Tel: 212-633 0348
www.cafeasean.com
L & D daily $ ➎ [p340, B2]

Cash only, but worth it when the priciest item on the Southeast Asian menu is little over $20. A local secret.

Camaje
85 MacDougal St (at Bleecker and Houston sts)
Tel: 212-673 8184
http://camaje.com
L & D daily $–$$ ➎ p340, B3]

Chef Abigail Hitchcock prepares top-notch French bistro dishes with imagination and heart. The casual atmosphere and reasonable prices make this a real find.

Da Silvano
260 6th Ave (at Bleecker and Houston sts)
Tel: 212-982 2343
http://dasilvano.com
L & D daily $$$ ➎ [p340, B3]

You're pretty much guaranteed a celebrity sighting at this Tuscan hotspot, which is always in the gossip columns.

Do Hwa
55 Carmine St (at Bedford St)
Tel: 212-414 1224
http://dohwanyc.com
L & D Tue–Fri, D only Sat–Mon

$$ ➏ [p340, B3]

It's hard to find good Korean outside of the West 30s. But you will find it here.

Fatty Crab West Village
643 Hudson St (at Horatio and Gansevoort sts)
Tel: 212-352 3592
www.fattycrab.com
L & D daily $$ ➏ [p340, A1]

This trendy Malaysian-fusion restaurant serves up whole, shell-on crabs swimming in an addictive red chilli sauce. Also consider ordering the pork-belly tea sandwiches and pork-filled steamed buns. In the summer, its watermelon juice hits the spot.

Kesté Pizza & Vino
271 Bleecker St
(at Morton St)
Tel: 212-243 1500
http://kestepizzeria.com
L & D daily $$ ➏
[p340, B2]

Gourmet pizza done in an authentic Neapolitan style with a chewy, bubbly crust and incredibly fresh toppings.

The Little Owl
90 Bedford St (at Grove St)
Tel: 212-741 4695
www.thelittleowlnyc.com
L & D daily $$$ ➏
[p340, B2]

A memorable name for a small Village hotspot known to serve a spectacular burger and the best pork chops around.

Macelleria
48 Gansevoort St (at 9th Ave)
Tel: 212-741 2555
www.macelleria.com
L & D daily $$$ ➏ [p340, A1]

LEFT: Pastis is an iconic Meatpacking District haunt.

The name is Italian for "butcher's shop," as befits this chic dining room in a former meat warehouse. Reservations essential at weekends.

Mercadito
100 7th Avenue S. (at Grove St)
Tel: 212-647 0830
www.mercaditorestaurants.com
D daily, L Sat–Sun **$$** ⑥⑤ [p340, B2]
This Mexican hotspot has plenty of taco options, but it's hard to resist the allure of ancho-rubbed pork topped with pineapple.

Minetta Tavern
113 MacDougal St (at Bleecker and W. 3rd sts)
Tel: 212-475 3850
www.minettatavernny.com
D daily, L Sat–Sun **$$$** ⑥⑥ [p340, B3]
Old-time, comfy landmark. Recently relaunched with much buzz and an upscale brasserie menu.

Il Mulino
86 W. 3rd St (at Sullivan and Thompson sts)
Tel: 212-673 3783
www.ilmulino.com
L & D Mon–Fri, D only Sat–Sun **$$$$** ⑥⑦ [p340, B3]
A loyal clientele has made this Italian Village classic almost like a club. Endless courses justify the expensive tab, and, after decades of excellent service, no one complains.

Paradou
8 Little W. 12th St (at 9th Ave)
Tel: 212-463 8345
www.paradounyc.com
D only Mon–Thur, L & D Fri–Sun **$–$$** ⑥③ [p340, A1]
What might seem like just another Meatpacking District bistro is a real gem – although the

small, bright room and lovely garden are no longer a secret.

Pastis
9 9th Ave (at Little W. 12th St)
Tel: 212-929 4844
www.pastisny.com
B, L, & D daily **$$$** ⑥⑨ [p340, A1]
There's food for most tastes most hours at this ultra-fashionable Meatpacking District brasserie, as tempting as the pretty people who come here. Open late.

Pearl Oyster Bar
18 Cornelia St (at Bleecker and W. 4th sts)
Tel: 212-691 8211
http://pearloysterbar.com
L & D Mon–Fri, D only Sat **$$** ⑦⓪ [p340, B2]
Raw-bar discovery in a Village side street full of tiny restaurants. Chowder is served perfectly, as is the lobster roll.

Risotteria
270 Bleecker St (at Morton St)
Tel: 212-924 6664
http://risotteria.com/
L & D daily **$** ⑦① [p340, B2]
Nestled in the Italian heart of Bleecker Street, this casual restaurant knows its arborio from its canaroli; this is the place to come for risotto.

Spice Market
403 W. 13th St (at 9th Ave)
Tel: 212-675 2322
www.spicemarketnewyork.com
L & D daily **$$$** ⑦② [p340, A1]
Exotic Meatpacking District duplex that really does feel like a Southeast Asian bazaar, serving four-star Malay cuisine. Part of the Jean-Georges Vongerichten stable.

The Spotted Pig
314 W. 11th St (at Greenwich St)
Tel: 212-620 0393
www.thespottedpig.com
L & D daily **$$** ⑦③ [p340, A2]
A trendy gastropub, open late and always full. Great sandwiches, then New Wave Italian for dinner. Get the sheep's milk ricotta gnudi.

The Standard Grill
848 Washington St (at W. 13th St)
Tel: 212-675 2322
http://thestandardgrill.com
L & D daily **$$$** ⑦④ [p340, A1]
The food is better than "standard" and the crowd is fashionable at the new Meatpacking District destination to see and be seen. Come late, or if you're staying in the Standard Hotel.

Bars and Cafes

Buddha Bar
25 Little W. 12th St (at 9th Ave)
⑲ [p340, A1]
The Meatpacking District bar scene on a Las

Vegas level.

Blind Tiger Ale House
281 Bleecker St (at Jones St)
⑳ [p340, B2]
Blind Tiger has one of the city's best selections of beer, including elusive cask ales.

Grom
233 Bleecker St (at Carmine St)
㉑ [p340, B3]
Grom has some of the best gelato in New York.

Peanut Butter & Co.
240 Sullivan St (at Bleecker and W. 3rd sts) ㉒ [p340, B3]
Anything and everything ever imagined with this staple of the American diet, from milkshakes to peanut butter/fluffernutter sandwiches, and much, much more.

Prices for a three-course dinner per person with half a bottle of wine:

$ = under $20
$$ = $20–$45
$$$ = $45–$60
$$$$ = over $60

RIGHT: trusty condiments.

UNION SQUARE AND CHELSEA

The blocks between 14th and 34th streets are
buzzing with flowers and fresh produce, art
galleries, and the latest restaurants

The area from Madison Park to
Union Square – loosely referred
to as the Flatiron District – is
home to writers, photographers, ad
agencies, publishers, new restaurants,
and new media firms. Chelsea has a
thriving art gallery scene, a thriving
gay scene, and a riverside sports and
entertainment development that
attracts an estimated 8,000 visitors a
day. Even Gramercy Park has shed its
usual well-heeled reserve and become
the destination *du jour*.

GRAMERCY PARK ❶

On the East Side between 20th
and 21st streets, Gramercy Park is
a genteel square that punctuates
Lexington Avenue and Irving Place
with welcome leafy greenery. This is
Manhattan's sole private park, established in the 1830s, a place where
immaculately kept beds and gravel
paths sit just out of reach behind an
ornate fence. Only residents of the
surrounding townhouses have keys,
although there are a limited number for guests of the Ian Schrager-led
Gramercy Park Hotel (see page 310).
Once a faded relic from the Jazz
Age, the building has been gutted
and redesigned as a lavish, idiosyn-
cratic hotel draped in rich velvets,

deep reds and azures, and decorated with antique-framed modern
art and glittering chandeliers. The
Gramercy's "21st-century bohemia"
has scored well with the reviewers
that matter, and if celebrity-spotting
is your thing, head for the resident
Rose or Jade bars. Part of the previous building has been put aside as
condos, the popularity of which will
soon bring a new generation of mon-
ied residents to Gramercy Park.
   On the park's southern perimeter,
look at the elaborate 19th-century

LEFT: the High Line Elevated Park in Chelsea.
RIGHT: the lobby of the Gramercy Park Hotel.

facades of the **National Arts Club**, home to the Poetry Society of America, and the **Players Club** next door, where members have included leading American theater actors, as well as Mark Twain, Winston Churchill, and Frank Sinatra.

Change is afoot on the other side of the Arts Club, at the former Parkside Evangeline Residence for Young Women. Until recently this attractive corner building provided inexpensive, dorm-style accommodation to women attempting to find their feet in New York. Unfortunately its owners, the Salvation Army, put it up for sale at the end of 2006, prompting a clamor to own one of the last developable properties on the park.

Irving Place, which Samuel Ruggles named for his friend Washington Irving, runs south from Gramercy Park to 14th Street, and is lined by pretty brownstones that continue with particular charm along East 19th Street.

At 18th Street, **Pete's Tavern** (www. petestavern.com) is a dark, historic bar where the atmosphere reeks of speakeasies and spilled beer. Its interior has featured in several beer commercials, as well as in episodes of *Seinfeld* and *Sex and the City*. Short-story scribe O. Henry is said to have written *The Gift of the Magi* here. Down at 15th Street, **Irving Plaza** (tel: 212-777 6800, www.irvingplaza.com) is one of the city's best small rock music venues. Drifting northward, the often overlooked green space between Madison Avenue and Broadway from 23rd to 26th streets is **Madison Square Park ❷**. In summer, Shake Shack sells arguably the city's best burgers and hot dogs. A block south, the **Metropolitan Life Insurance Tower ❸**, completed in 1909, was briefly considered the world's tallest building at 54 stories. Until its recent incarnation as a place to meet and greet like-minded fashion and media types in a number of watering holes,

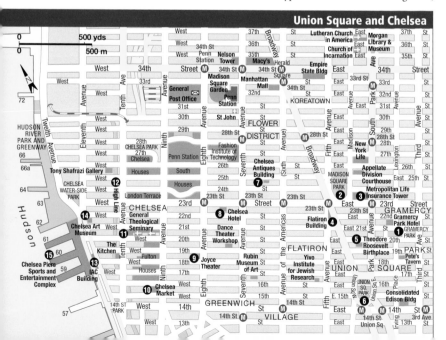

future when it was erected in 1902. It soon became known as the **Flatiron Building** ❹ because of its distinctive shape, and is considered by most to be the oldest skyscraper in New York City. Rising 285ft (87 meters) into the air, the Fuller was immortalized in 1903 with a classic black-and-white shot by photographer Alfred Stieglitz, who described the building as "looking like a monster steamer." The architect was Daniel Burnham, of the influential Chicago firm of the same name that specialized in early skyscrapers.

Word got around the offices and bars of New York that the building produced particular eddies in the wind that caused women's skirts to fly around as they walked along 23rd Street. Large groups of young men were interested enough to gather in the area to find out. To disperse them, the story goes, cops would chase them away with the words "23, skidoo."

The neighborhood immediately south has been dubbed **SoFi** by realtors, which stands, not surprisingly, for **So**uth of **Fi**latiron, but the nickname hasn't caught on with many others. From here, Broadway follows the

however, the Madison Park area was noted mainly for its proximity to one of Manhattan's favorite architectural whimsies, which rises from the corner where Broadway crosses Fifth Avenue below 23rd Street.

FLATIRON DISTRICT

The triangular Fuller Building raised eyebrows and hopes for a bright

The land that makes up the Chelsea Historic District was inherited in 1813 by Clement Clarke Moore. He sold the land but imposed restrictions that kept its elegance intact.

LEFT: the Flatiron Building was once described as "looking like a monster steamer."
BELOW: a statue in Madison Square Park.

old "Ladies' Mile," a shopping route that, during the latter part of the 19th century, ranged along Broadway and Sixth Avenue, from 23rd Street down to 9th Street. Lord & Taylor, which began as a small shop downtown on Catherine Street and opened on the southwest corner of Broadway and 20th Street in 1872, moved uptown to 38th and Fifth in 1914, where it is still open for business.

Roosevelt Birthplace ❺

Address: 28 E. 20th Street (at Park Ave South and Broadway), www.nps. gov/thrb
Telephone: 212-260 1616
Opening Hours: Tue–Sat 9am–5pm
Entrance Fee: charge
Subway: 23rd St

Just east of Broadway is the place where Theodore Roosevelt, 26th President of the United States (from 1901–9) was born in 1858. Theodore Roosevelt came from one of the East Coast's wealthiest families, and in the 1850s the house at 28 East 20th Street was a fashionable residence. The current building is actually a 1920s replica of the house in which "Teddy"

spent his childhood: the original was knocked down in 1916, but after his death in 1919 it was faithfully recreated as a memorial. About 40 percent of the furnishings come from the original home; the rest was either donated by family members or are authentic period pieces. The living quarters are only accessible as part of the tour, which is worth taking simply to see how a rich family like the Roosevelts would have lived in the mid-19th century, when this part of New York was considered the wealthy suburbs.

UNION SQUARE ❻

Named for the busy convergence of Broadway and Fourth Avenue, Union Square sits comfortably between 17th and 14th streets. A stylish prospect in the mid-1850s, later it was more or less deserted by genteel residents and became a thriving theater center. Eventually the theaters moved to Midtown, and the square became known for political meetings – in the years before World War I, anarchists and socialists regularly addressed sympathizers here.

BELOW: flowers for sale at the Greenmarket.

Green and Fresh

If you were to ask celebrity chefs with restaurants near Union Square Park where they buy their ingredients, many could simply point out the window to the patches of concrete and the farmstands that are set up every Monday, Wednesday, Friday, and Saturday. The Union Square Greenmarket is more than a place to find apples in the fall and peaches in the summer. It is a community meeting place and essential source of produce for many New Yorkers, including those who make a living out of making meals.

Organic, and often exotic, meats are available alongside hand-tied pretzels and pungent goat's cheese. The Lower East Side Ecology Center runs a composting program, where locals can dispose of food scraps, while GrowNYC offers a textile recycling drop-off service. At peak seasons, as many as 140 vendors will be offering their products, and the variety is astounding. In summer, you can easily find supplies for a gourmet picnic, including wine, artisan bread and homemade jams. You may even catch one of the cooking demonstrations hosted by the same celebrity chefs who shop there. For more information visit www.grownyc.org.

ABOVE: Union Square's Greenmarket.

Rallies continued to draw crowds throughout the 1930s, but finally even radicalism dwindled, and the area went into a decline that lasted until the 1980s.

Today, Union Square brims with life, a resurgence that might be attributed to the **Greenmarket**, which brings farmers and their produce to the northern edge of the square on Mondays, Wednesdays, Fridays, and Saturdays. While there are other fruit and vegetable markets in other parts of the city, this is the biggest and the best. *Syfy* television network sponsors free Wi-Fi in the park, and Manhattanites with portable computers can be seen leisurely surfing the web near the market porters.

Food for the soul can be found at the **Union Square Theatre**, 100 East 17th Street, a historically appropriate locale in light of Union Square's 19th-century theatrical past.

A huge Barnes & Noble and Whole Foods dominate the outer edges of Union Square. In the evening, young tourists and skateboarders congregate around their doors.

CHELSEA

West of Fifth Avenue to the Hudson River, from 14th up to about 30th Street, Chelsea borders the Midtown Garment District and includes the **Flower District**. In the spring and summer, these blocks are crowded with leafy vegetation and bathed in a sweet loamy odor.

Fifth Avenue between 14th and 23rd streets has stores like Coach and Paul Smith, while the Avenue of the Americas (**Sixth Avenue**) is lined by modern chains that have continued the fashion tradition by moving into the historic Ladies' Mile buildings.

If you have a big yen for vintage accessories and goods, head for the **Chelsea Antiques Building ❼** at 110 West 25th between Sixth and Seventh avenues. There are fine scavenging opportunities here, with an enticing jumble of items like gilded chairs, metal lamps, and bathtubs.

Theodore Roosevelt was the first US president to own a car, fly in an airplane, go underwater in a submarine, and entertain an African-American in the White House (Booker T. Washington, in 1901).

Many of the stores in the Chelsea Market have glass walls that back onto a walkway. Too tempting to resist is Amy's Bakery. Watch as the bread is kneaded, shaped, and then placed in an oven, and chances are you'll leave with a loaf under your arm.

RIGHT: on the streets of Chelsea.
BELOW: the entrance to the Chelsea Hotel.

Chelsea Hotel

Walking west on long, busy 23rd Street (or better yet, a ride on the M23 crosstown bus) will take you past the **Chelsea Hotel 8** (see page 152). One of the city's most famous residential hotels, this 12-story, red-brick building is where Dylan Thomas died in 1953, Andy Warhol filmed *Chelsea Girls* in 1967, and punk rocker Sid Vicious allegedly murdered his girlfriend Nancy Spungen (he died of a drug overdose before he could be convicted).

The time has passed when you could join the hotel's eclectic collection of residents in the lobby, and have a look at the unusual artwork (done by guests and changed at a whim). A recent sale of the hotel has many worried it will be converted into condos. As Chelsea itself becomes more and more gentrified and property prices and desirability soar, the unique character of the hotel is increasingly under threat. At the ground level is the El Quijote Spanish restaurant, a relic of the days when waiters wore red jackets and paella was served in enormous

portions. Grab a bite before it too disappears.

Art Deco and dance

The Art Deco sign to the **Joyce Theater 9** (175 Eighth Avenue at 19th Street, www.joyce.org) is easily spotted from the street. The Joyce presents some of the city's most innovative dance performances, from Spanish Gypsy flamenco to classical ballet, and Native American troupes.

Other original work is staged at the **Dance Theater Workshop** (219 West 19th Street, www.newyorklive arts.org). The lobby has a welcoming coffee shop where you can kick back with specialty hot chocolate and a big cookie.

Before or after indulging, stop by the **Rubin Museum of Art** (150 West 17th Street, www.rmanyc.org). The Rubin is the first museum in the Western world dedicated to the art of the Himalayas and surrounding regions. The emphasis is on educating visitors about the region, and there are wall notes and interactive displays.

Continue on to the striking architecture of the **Chelsea Market** , at 75 Ninth Avenue between 15th and 16th streets, where an ambitious renovation transformed what were once 18 buildings erected between 1883 and 1930 into a hugely popular indoor food market. Much of the original brickwork and steel has been left bare, giving the food court an artsy, industrial feel.

The interior of the Chelsea Market has a waterfall and sculptured seating, around which are scattered more than 20 locally owned stores selling specialty foods and home design items, as well as plenty of tempting places to eat.

The area is trendy and stylish, so much so that this neighborhood is almost indistinguishable from the cool and gritty Meatpacking District, which stretches west along 14th Street to the Hudson in the West Village.

Fans of architecture will also love the blocks between Eighth and Tenth avenues, from 19th to 23rd streets. This is the **Chelsea Historic District**.

General Theological Seminary ⓫

Address: Entrance is at 440 21st St (between Ninth and Tenth aves), www.gts.edu
Telephone: 212-243 5150
Opening Hours: Mon–Sat noon–3pm
Entrance Fee: free
Subway: 23rd St/Eighth Ave

This lovely seminary was established in 1817, and prepares students for ordination into the Episcopal Church. Among its best buildings are the Chapel of the Good Shepherd and St Mark's Library; among its most important buildings is the **Desmond Tutu Center**, which emphasizes peace and reconciliation. The seminary's tree-lined quadrangle is one of New York's best-kept secrets: a calm oasis amid the busy urban streets all around, where visitors can sit under a tree and listen to the sound of birds.

Walking east on 20th and 21st streets from Tenth Avenue brings you to one of the Chelsea Historic District's most scenic stretches of Greek Revival and Anglo-Italianate townhouses, the tree-lined streets a reminder of Chelsea's desirability as a residential area. A block farther south, between Tenth and Eleventh avenues, **The Kitchen** (512 West 19th Street, http://thekitchen.org) is a longstanding center where video, dance, and performance art are staple fare.

Parallel to Tenth Avenue and stretching to the West Village is the **High Line** ⓬, a disused railroad line that has been transformed into a sky-high green promenade for walkers. In 2009, the sections between Chelsea and the Meatpacking District opened. In time, the High Line will extend all the way to 34th Street (see page 156).

Dominating the space between West 18th and 19th streets at Eleventh Avenue is the Frank Gehry-designed **IAC Building** ⓭. This is the acclaimed architect's first NYC office building. Not everyone is

ABOVE: detail from a mandala painted on cotton at the Rubin Museum.
BELOW: Chelsea Market.

TIP

The Chelsea Art Museum is just one of many galleries in the area. Most are closed on Mondays.

pleased with the enormity of the edifice, which is way out of scale for low-key Chelsea, but few can fault its impressive facade.

Galleries galore

Once SoHo became overrun with boutiques and restaurants, gallery owners moved north to Chelsea. One of the best is the **Tony Shafrazi Gallery** (544 West 26th Street, www.tonyshafrazigallery.com, tel: 212-274 9300). The gallery may hold only two or three exhibitions each year, but they are always worth seeing. Past exhibits have focused on names as famous as Andy Warhol, Picasso, and Keith Haring.

Although galleries are scattered throughout the neighborhood, **22nd Street** between Tenth and Eleventh avenues is particularly packed with light, converted warehouse-style galleries, spearheaded by the Chelsea Art Museum at the end of the street.

Chelsea Art Museum ⑭

Address: 556 W. 22nd Street (at Tenth and Eleventh aves), http://chelseaartmuseum.org

Telephone: 212-255 0719
Opening Hours: Tue, Wed, Fri, Sat 11am–6pm, Thur 11am–8pm
Entrance Fee: charge
Subway: 23rd St/Eighth Ave

One of the larger spaces in the area, the museum showcases international and abstract art that might not otherwise be exhibited in New York. Depending on the exhibition, at any time the gallery could be showing a mixture of film, photography, painting, and interactive installations. A rooftop sculpture garden makes a welcome respite for summertime relaxation, and the museum also has an excellent gallery store, with a large selection of artist-produced fanzines and literature.

Gallery-hopping

This activity is particularly popular on Thursday nights, when most venues keep later hours, but note that all galleries tend to close on Mondays. Despite the avant-garde nature of some of the work, the galleries themselves are mainly unintimidating places, and inquiries are met with friendly, informed responses.

The **Pace Gallery** (545 West 22nd Street, http://thepacegallery.com) is

RIGHT: Frank Gehry's IAC Building.
BELOW: relaxing on the High Line.

SHOPPING

It's easy to find popular chains like The Gap, Old Navy, H&M, Container Store, Home Depot or Bed, Bath and Beyond along the major thoroughfares, but a more eclectic mix of specialists are hidden on the side streets.

Antiques

Antiques Garage
112 W. 25th Street (at 6th and 7th aves)
www.hellskitchenfleamarket.com.
Part of the Hell's Kitchen Flea Market group, this indoor collection of antiques draws over 100 vendors every Saturday and Sunday from 9am–5pm.

Art Galleries

Matthew Marks Gallery
523 W. 24th Street (at 10th Ave)
Tel: 212-243 0200
www.matthewmarks.com
One of the first dealers to make the move to Chelsea (back in the early 90s), Marks has mounted consistently beloved exhibitions at his four exhibition spaces on 22nd and 24th. If you can't afford the art, there are always books and posters.

Books

Forbidden Planet
840 Broadway (at 13th St)
Tel: 212-473 1576
www.fpnyc.com
Just south of Union Square you'll find an emporium of comic books, action figures, and manga art.

Books of Wonder
18 W. 18th Street (at 5th and 6th aves)
Tel: 212-989 3270
www.booksofwonder.com
Dedicated to youth literature, this wonderful store contains everything from classic board books to the latest paranormal romance (or whatever is the current craze). Local authors visit for frequent signings.

Clothing

Intermix
125 5th Avenue (at 20th St)
Tel: 212-533 9720
www.intermixonline.com
The Flatiron outpost of a popular group of boutiques that sell a mixed selection of items from dozens of the world's top designers.

Electronics

Tekserve
199 W. 23rd Street (at 6th Ave)
Tel: 212-929 3645
www.tekserve.com
Outside of the official (and rather sterile) Apple stors, this is the best place for Apple products, accessories, and expert advice. A jumbled and wonderful place for enthusiasts.

Food

Eataly
200 5th Avenue (at 23rd St)
Tel: 212-229 2560
http://eatalyny.com
Another hit from Mario Batali, this gourmet food court sells cured meats, cheese, pasta, espresso, and just about anything to cook up an authentic Italian meal. There are also restaurants, bakeries, and sandwich shops on the premises for fancy dinners or a quick lunch.

Gifts

Abracadabra
19 W. 21st Street (at 5th and 6th aves)
Tel: 212-627 5194 http://abracadabrasuperstore.com
Kids will be entranced by the thousands of costumes, masks, and novelties on display in a place where every day is Halloween. It has an extensive collection of rental costumes, perfect for parties and parades.

Home

ABC Carpet & Home
881 and 888 Broadway (at 19th St)
Tel: 212-473 3000
www.abchome.com
This company offers a lovely collection of produts for the home and is also dedicated to sustainability.

Sports

Paragon Sports
867 Broadway (at 18th St)
Tel: 212-255 8889
www.paragonsports.com
It doesn't look that big from the outside, but this mazelike building of sporting equipment has everything from running sneakers and tents to snowboards and scuba gear.

LEFT: ABC Carpet and Home.

The High Line

It's only fitting in a city where most new development is of the vertical variety that one of its newest parks is an elevated one – and it's as lovely as it is unique

The city's most famous green space is easily Central Park – but its coolest is the High Line. Opened in 2009, this innovative city park is located on an elevated train track that was used between the 1930s and 1980 to ship meat from the Meatpacking District to Chelsea's refrigerated warehouses.

Climb up to the High Line and you will be instantly transported away from the taxis and buses to a walking path that has been landscaped and lined with the type of plant life that grew here naturally after the rail was abandoned – tall grasses, wild flowers, and low bushes. Space can be tight in summer and on weekends, so bikes and dogs are not allowed up, but in the winter the High Line feels eerily hushed and removed from the noise of the city.

The first section of the park to open runs from Gansevoort Street, in the West Village, to 20th Street in Chelsea; the second stretch, which covers 20th to 30th strees, opened a little over a year later; development has begun on the final leg, taking the path almost to the Hudson River, all the way to the Jacob Javits Center.

No matter where you start, your walk will offer an entirely new vantage point on the metropolis. You may come so close to some condos that you can almost reach out and knock on a living room window (although it is best to resist the temptation). You can quite literally pass under the Standard Hotel. As Robert Hammond, cofounder of the Friends of the High Line, said, "There's a spot around 17th Street where you can stand and see buildings by Frank Gehry, Jean Nouvel, and Shigeru Ban." Gentle fountains and small gardens are scattered throughout, not to mention vendors tempting with ice cream. This is one spot in the city where you are encouraged to linger.

You'll become very aware of the fact that the High Line is, in fact, not a straight line – it is a meandering, winding path. In some areas where it widens, there are benches, and an amphitheater has been set up for lectures, discussions, and to be used as outdoor classroom for the High Line's programs for schoolchildren.

For more information, go to www.thehighline.org or tel: 212-500 6035. There is no charge, and park hours change seasonally.

LEFT: the High Line and the Standard Hotel.
ABOVE: High Line amphitheater.

worth seeing, the size of the space allowing for some impressive works. The main room has an attractive wood-beamed ceiling. There are two more Pace galleries on 25th Street and another on 57th Street. The appearance of Comme des Garçons and Balenciaga on 22nd Street hint that change might be afoot as art turns into retail, but for now galleries still dominate.

In the early days of moving pictures, the Famous Players Film Studio was located on West 26th Street; today, the **Silver Screen Studios** at Chelsea Piers are where such popular TV shows as *Law and Order* have been in post-production.

Chelsea Piers ⓑ

Address: W. 23rd Street (at Twelfth Ave and Hudson River), www.chelseapiers.com
Telephone: 212-336 6666
Opening Hours: daily, various opening hours
Entrance Fee: charge
Subway: 23rd St/Eighth Ave

The last stop on the crosstown M23 bus is **Pier 62**, the hub of this huge sports and entertainment complex, which sprawls south along the

Hudson from 23rd to 17th streets, and which has brought such a wealth of leisure opportunities to the city.

A Fitness Club is open to members only, but there are other facilities the public can use for a fee. The development includes **Pier 61**, with the double Sky Rink, **Pier 60**, which has a fabulous spa with a range of treatments including facials and massages, and **Pier 59**, which offers a golf-driving range. Other activities include bowling, indoor soccer, dance classes, and basketball.

The Chelsea cruise

The transformation of Chelsea's dilapidated piers has given new access to the Hudson River. Passenger yachts and schooners (Classic Harbor Line, tel: 646-336 5270, www.sail-nyc.com; and Spirit Cruises, tel: 866-483 3866, www.spiritcitycruises.com) offer day and evening cruises, with wine tastings, music, and dinner often included. For non-passengers, the walkway by the piers weaves around for more than a mile, providing great riverside views and fine sunsets.

TIP

When visiting Chelsea Piers, ask someone to tell you about the site's history. One fascinating fact is that the *Titanic* was scheduled to dock at the piers on April 16, 1912. Of the 2,000 passengers onboard, only 675 were rescued. The survivors arrived at Chelsea Piers four days later.

LEFT: the view over Chelsea Piers.
BELOW: hailing a taxi.

BEST RESTAURANTS, BARS AND CAFÉS

Restaurants

Bar Jamón
125 E. 17th St (at Irving Pl)
Tel: 212-253 2773
www.casamononyc.com
D daily, L Sat–Sun $$$ **75**
[p340, D2]
Lusty Spanish tapas and snacks served up by Mario Batali. Its sister restaurant, Casa Mono, is next door.

Blossom
187 9th Ave (at 21st and 22nd sts)
Tel: 212-627 1144
http://blossomnyc.com
D daily, L Fri–Sun $$ **76**
[p338, A4]
The best in mock pastas and spicy starters. Dishes perfect for vegans who want to indulge in guilty pleasures.

Blue Water Grill
31 Union Sq W (at 16th St)
Tel: 212-675 9500
www.bluewatergrillnyc.com
L & D daily $$$ **77** [p340, C1]
Big, beautiful fish house; excellent seafood in a converted bank building.

Boquería
53 W. 19th St (at 5th and 6th aves)
Tel: 212-255 4160
www.boquerianyc.com
L & D daily $$ **78** [p340, C1]
Flavors of Spain from tiny tapas to midweek suckling pig platter specials to share. Small space and always crowded Flatiron hotspot.

Buddakan
75 9th Ave (at 16th St)
Tel: 212-989 6699
www.buddakannyc.com
D daily $$$ **79** [p340, B1]
On the border between Chelsea and the Meatpacking District, Buddakan is hugely popular for the food and its vast, chandeliered dining room.

Chat 'n Chew
10 E. 16th St (at 5th Ave and Union Sq)
Tel: 212-243 1616
http://chatchewnewyorkcity.com
L & D daily, Br Sat–Sun $ **80** [p340, C1]
American comfort food and prices to match in a room with a nice, funky line in retro decor.

Co.
230 9th Ave (at 24th and 25th sts)
Tel: 212-243 1105
http://co-pane.com
L & D Tue–Sun, D only Mon $$ **81** [p338, A3]
This Chelsea place is one of a new wave of Neapolitan pizza hotspots.

Cookshop
156 10th Ave (at 20th St)
Tel: 212-924 4440
http://cookshopny.com
B, L, & D daily $ **82** [p338, A4]
Marc Meyer's experimental menu changes daily and serves up fashionably sustainable treats. Fine dining without ethical sacrifices.

Craft
43 E. 19th St (at Broadway and Park Ave S)
Tel: 212-780 0880
www.craftrestaurant.com
D daily $$$$ **83** [p340, C1]
The menu is split into sections (vegetable, sides, meat, and fish), and you concoct your own meal – a nightmare for the indecisive, but wildly popular otherwise. Part of Tom Colicchio's mini-empire, which includes Craftbar around the corner and Colicchio & Sons in the Meatpacking District.

Del Posto
85 10th Ave (at 16th St)
Tel: 212-497 8090
http://delposto.com
D daily, L Mon–Fri $$$$ **84** [p338, A4]
Haute modern Italian on a grand scale with matching prices. Glitzy Roosevelt-era decor and big meaty dishes served with largesse. Extravagance at its best.

Eleven Madison Park
11 Madison Ave (at 24th St)
Tel: 212-889 0905
www.elevenmadisonpark.com
L & D Mon–Fri, D only Sat $$$$ **85** [p338, C4]
There's a vaulted ceiling, an elegant atmosphere, expensive and excellent New American food on the menu here, including the ever-popular suckling pig.

Gramercy Tavern
42 E. 20th St (at Broadway and Park Ave)
Tel: 212-477 0777
www.gramercytavern.com
L & D Mon–Fri, D only Sat–Sun $$$$ **86** [p340, C1]
A fave for its food, service, great New American cuisine, and the high-ceilinged dining room.

Hill Country
30 W. 26th St (at 6th Ave and Broadway)
Tel: 212-255 4544 www.hillcountryny.com L & D daily $$ **87** [p338, C4]
If you're looking for some live honky-tonk music, brisket like they do it in Texas, and barbecue bought by the pound, there is nowhere else but

here.
Les Halles
411 Park Ave S. (at 28th and 29th sts)
Tel: 212-679 4111
http://leshalles.net
B, L, & D daily $$$ **88** [p338, C4]
This steakhouse/bistro packs in the crowds, who come to soak up the French atmosphere. It's where Anthony Bourdain got his start.

Mesa Grill
102 5th Ave (at 15th and 16th sts)
Tel: 212-807 7400
www.mesagrill.com
L & D Mon–Fri, Br & D Sat–Sun $$$ **89** [p340, C1]

ABOVE: the Gramercy Tavern bar.

Sophisticated Southwestern fare that put energetic Bobby Flay on the culinary map. Still hot after all these years.

Morimoto

88 10th Ave (at 15th and 16th sts)
Tel: 212-989 8883
www.morimotonyc.com
L & D Mon–Fri, D only Sat–Sun
$$$$ 90 [p338, A4]
Excellent sushi, maki, and modern Japanese dishes like braised black cod.

Naka Naka

458 W. 17th St (at 9th and 10th aves)
Tel: 212-929 8544
D Tue–Sun **$$** 91 [p338, A4]
Tatami mats greet you at this shoebox-sized Japanese restaurant. A quiet spot in a busy neighborhood; the modest menu serves sushi and soba dishes.

Old Homestead

56 9th Ave (at 14th and 15th sts)
Tel: 212-242 9040
www.theoldhomesteadsteakhouse.com
L & D daily **$$$$** 92 [p338, A4]
A classic, old-school steakhouse if ever there were one. Watch out for the "colossal" crab cakes.

Pongal

110 Lexington Ave (at 27th and 28th sts)
Tel: 212-696 9458
www.pongalnyc.com
L & D daily **$$** 93 [p338, C4]
This kosher vegetarian restaurant, specializing in the food of Gujarat, Punjab, and southern India, is a very good choice on a block filled with many Indian eateries.

Red Cat

227 10th Ave (at 23rd and 24th sts)
Tel: 212-242 1122
www.theredcat.com
L & D Tue–Sat, D only Sun–Mon
$$$ 94 [p338, A3]
Hipsters love the Red Cat. Great room, excellent food, cool clientele – a stylish place before or after gallery-hopping.

Rickshaw Dumpling Bar

61 W. 23rd St (at 5th and 6th aves)
Tel: 212-924 9220
http://rickshawdumplings.com
L & D daily **$** 95 [p338, B4]
Chinatown comes to Chelsea at a delicious spot that serves up tasty little packets of dumplings. Order them steamed or fried; they're extremely affordable.

Scarpetta

355 W. 14th St (at 9th Ave)
Tel: 212-691 0555
www.scottconant.com
D daily **$$$$** 96 [p340, B1]
Just northwest of the Meatpacking District is ambitious and rich modern Italian fare in an airy dining room.

Shake Shack

Madison Square Park
Tel: 212-889 6600
http://shakeshack.com
L & D daily **$** 97 [p338, C4]
The first in the empire remains as popular as ever. Some say the spectacular burgers, dogs, shakes, and fries are the best in America. Be prepared to wait in line, regardless of the weather.

Tocqueville

1 E. 15th St (at 5th Ave)
Tel: 212-647 1515
http://tocquevillerestaurant.com
L & D Mon–Sat **$$$** 98 [p340, C1]

Fans swear by this trendy French-American just around the corner from Union Square. Particularly noted are the seared sirloin and roast chicken.

Bars and Cafes

71 Irving Place Coffee and Tea Bar

71 Irving Place, at 18th and 19th sts 23 [p340, C/D2]
This is a great alternative to the ever-present Starbucks. Order the signature Irving Farm Blend.

City Bakery

3 W. 18th St (at 5th and 6th aves) 24 [p340, C1]
A popular Flatiron hangout with pastries, soups, sandwiches, and more.

Flatiron Lounge

37 W. 19th St (at 5th and 6th aves) 25 [p340, C1]
Serves up excellent Martinis and other cocktails in swank surroundings.

Lady Mendl's

Inn at Irving Place, 56 Irving Pl (at 17th and 18th sts) 26 [p340, D2]

Prices for a three-course dinner per person with half a bottle of wine:

$ = under $20
$$ = $20–$45
$$$ = $45–$60
$$$$ = over $60

Lady Mendl's is an elegant tea salon in a Gramercy Park townhouse.

Old Town Bar and Restaurant

45 E. 18th St (at Broadway and Park Ave S.) 27 [p340, C1]
Old Town has a wonderful long bar and great hamburgers, and was an inspiration for the television comedy Mad About You, starring Paul Reiser and Helen Hunt.

Pete's Tavern

129 E. 18th St (at Irving Pl) 28 [p340, D2]
Pete's is a long-running establishment that's better for drinks than dinner, but there's loads of atmosphere.

RIGHT: Chelsea dining alfresco.

Times Square

Revitalization marches on at the Crossroads of the World, where these days the traffic is either on foot or by bike

Times Square named for the former *New York Times* offices, has a history as lively as its street life. Theaters, hotels, and restaurants sprang up in the 1920s, when impresarios like the Shubert Brothers staged 250 shows a year. Prohibition brought speakeasies, gangsters, and the characters of Damon Runyon's earthy tales. At the end of World War II, more than 2 million people crowded into

the area to celebrate V-J Day. But by the 1960s, Times Square was known mainly for its sleaze, crime, and pornography. In the 1990s, the square was transformed back into a tourist magnet for the more than 20 million visitors who come here each

year. Of course, with the tourists came traffic jams and the less-than-gracious crowds. In recent years, the renovation of Father Duffy Square and the conversion of Broadway from 42nd to 47th streets into a pedestrian-only zone have done wonders to alleviate these problems. The square is far from a calm harbor, but it has been a long time since it has been this inviting.

Above: the Great White Way: free walking tours begin at the Times Square Information Center in the historic Embassy Theater on Broadway between 46th and 47th streets.

Left: musical theater has a long tradition on Broadway. Shows, beginning in the 17th century. Theaters were originally located in Lower Manhattan, but over time moved farther north to Midtown.

Below: Lauren Bacall, a former Miss Greenwich Village, seen here 21 years later at Loew's State Theatre for the world premiere of the movie *How to Marry a Millionaire*.

The Essentials

Address: Broadway between 42nd & 48th sts; www.timessquarenyc.org
Opening Hours: Times Square Information Center, daily 8am–8pm. Walking tours every Friday at noon
Subway: 42nd St/ Times Square

THE NEW YORK TIMES

Times Square took its name from the *New York Times*, formerly headquartered at the Times Tower, where 42nd Street intersects Seventh Avenue, and now called One Times Square. The *New York Daily Times*, founded in 1851 (the *Daily* was dropped in 1857), was bought in 1896 by ambitious Tennessee newspaperman Adolph S. Ochs.

The paper moved to 229 West 43rd Street in 1913, where Ochs's great-grandson, chairman Arthur Sulzberger Jr, continued the mission to produce "an independent newspaper… devoted to the public welfare" under the well-known slogan: "All the News That's Fit to Print."

In a decision that has delighted Manhattanites, the company commissioned architect Renzo Piano to create a new addition to the New York skyline at Eighth Avenue between 40th and 41st streets. This landmark *Times* building changes color with the light.

The *New York Times* has won 95 Pulitzer Prizes, and has a circulation of over 1 million readers.

ABOVE: a mosaic tile advertisement for the newspaper which gave the square its name.

BELOW: breadlines on Broadway: during the Great Depression in the 1930s, a city newspaper opened a relief kitchen in Times Square to feed the poor.

ABOVE: Times Square's renovations have restored its status as a family-friendly destination. Toys "R" Us has a Ferris wheel inside its flagship store.

LEFT: Times Square may have been cleaned up, but tricky pickpockets and con-artists are still drawn to the big crowds. Police are always present and willing to offer advice or directions.

MIDTOWN WEST

The lights of Broadway shine most brightly here, glittering off tourist-friendly Times Square, the Museum of Modern Art, and the dancing queens of Radio City

The West Side shines more brightly than the East, at least in terms of sheer neon wattage, and what Midtown West lacks in finesse it makes up for in tenacity. This is where billboards vie with world-class art, and where, as the old saying goes, there's a broken heart for every light on Broadway.

At the center of it all, Times Square has donned new neon baubles like an aging beauty queen with a facelift. Flash and frenzy dazzle the eye. The nasdaq headquarters in the Condé Nast building dominates with a huge led display teeming with the latest stock-market quotes. And Broadway – the glamorous Great White Way – has been rejuvenated.

But then, that's the story of Midtown West. It's been bruised, but it's never gone down for the count. The lights that burn on Broadway, and a bevy of new hotels, restaurants, stores, and other businesses, make sure the West Side is alive and booming.

AROUND HERALD SQUARE

Starting at 34th Street, the transition from East to West Midtown begins at **Herald Square ❶**, where Broadway intersects Sixth Avenue. Named for the *New York Herald* newspaper, whose headquarters once stood here, today this chaotic intersection is best known for its retail temples.

Just south of Herald Square is the slightly faded **Manhattan Mall**, where four of the building's nine floors are occupied by nearly a dozen eateries and a variety of retailers aimed at teenage tastes and corresponding, slimline wallets. The big draw in this area, however, is New York's very definition of a "big store" – Macy's.

LEFT: Broadway, looking towards Times Square. **RIGHT:** a food cart in Herald Square.

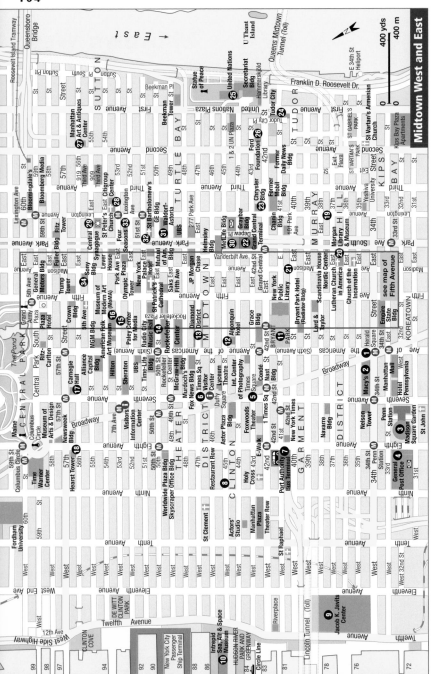

Midtown West and East

Macy's ❷

Address: 151 W. 34th St (at Broad-way), www.macys.com
Telephone: 212-695 4400
Opening Hours: Mon–Sat 10am–9.30pm, Sun 11am–8.30pm
Subway: 34th St/Herald Sq

A New York institution for more than a century, Macy's is, like the sign says, the biggest department store in the world, and worth seeing for its size alone. The giant building is divided into a men's and a women's store, which can be a little confusing if you get stuck in one but want the other, but staff are always on hand to point you in the right direction. Don't leave without visiting the "Cellar," a gourmet kitchenware emporium with gadgets and accessories that even the most creative chef would covet.

The Garment District

Exiting Macy's on Seventh Avenue puts you right in the middle of the Garment District, a jangly, soot-covered workhorse that still turns out a lot of America's fashion. There's not much to do or see here, except take in the ambience, but dedicated bargain-hunters have been known to walk away with first-class deals from the factory floor or sample sales.

Showrooms, too, dot the area, where you can find the latest, if not always the greatest, fashions, although you may have to shop around a little, both for the bargains and the showrooms themselves. That said, you are much less likely to see young men pushing clothing racks through the streets as you would in the past. These days high-rise condos and hotels are going up and small offices are taking over the buildings that used to house manufacturers.

The structure at Seventh Avenue and 33rd Street is Madison Square Garden, disliked by purists not only for its functional, clumsy design but also for replacing McKim, Mead, & White's magnificent Pennsylvania Station, demolished in 1963. The "new" **Penn Station** is now 50ft (15 meters) beneath it, where it shuttles a quarter-million commuters daily to Long Island and elsewhere.

Madison Square Garden ❸

Address: Seventh Ave (at 31st and 33rd sts), www.thegarden.com
Telephone: 212-465 6741
Opening Hours: schedule of events change daily
Entrance Fee: charge
Subway: 34th St/Penn Station

ABOVE: Macy's Thanksgiving Day Parade.
BELOW: the Isaac Singer statue on the corner of Seventh Avenue.

ABOVE: the New York Knicks vs. the Charlotte Bobcats at Madison Square Garden.
BELOW: Madison Square Garden.

Once located between Madison and Fifth avenues – that is, in Madison Square itself – this is one of America's biggest entertainment arenas, where rock and pop shows, ice hockey, basketball games, tennis matches, and even circuses are held. Whatever your feelings about the building, there's no denying it fulfills its function. The popular all-access tour has been temporarily discontinued due to construction but will hopefully be up and running in 2012 or 2013.

The best way to appreciate this building is to attend one of the Garden's events. Last-minute tickets for sports events are often available on the day (don't expect to sit together if there's more than one of you), or you can book ahead online or through Ticketmaster (www.ticketmaster.com) or StubHub (www.stubhub.com).

There are few New York experiences more authentic than watching a home team play at home. Just don't expect a quiet game.

If you're a Glenn Miller fan, you may want to check out the venerable **Hotel Pennsylvania** (see page 313), across Seventh Avenue at 33rd Street. This used to be the Big Band era's hottest ticket, immortalized by Miller's hit *Pennsylvania 6-5000* – still the hotel's phone number. Sadly, the busy terminus-style lobby has replaced glamor with function, but at least it's easy for guests to purchase theater tickets and newspapers from the various stands in reception.

Behind Madison Square Garden, the **General Post Office** ❹ is hardly an attraction, but it *is* impressive, with a monumental Corinthian design that makes your average Greek temple look like a tiki hut. There's also the oft-quoted slogan on the frieze: "Neither snow nor rain nor heat nor gloom of night stays these couriers from the swift completion of their appointed rounds." The motto was stolen from Herodotus, who obviously never mailed a letter in Manhattan.

Heading back to Herald Square, Broadway slices through the Midtown grid up to 42nd Street. This is the Downtown end of Times Square, the garish heart of Midtown West, and one of the city's most dramatic success stories.

TIMES SQUARE ⑤

Address: Broadway (at 42nd to 48th sts), www.timessquarenyc.org
Subway: 42nd St/Times Square

Stretching along **Broadway** to 48th Street, with the **Theatre District** sprawled loosely on either side, Times Square has had long-awaited renovations that have once again made it the "Crossroads of the World." The most exciting development is the conversion of Broadway from 42nd to 47th Street into a pedestrian only mall (see page 167).

Whether you're here for a show or not, be sure to take a stroll down **Shubert Alley**, a busy walkway that runs behind the Booth and Shubert theaters, from 45th to 44th Street. **Sardi's** restaurant, at 234 West 44th Street (see page 177), is a venerable Broadway landmark. In addition to its fabled dining rooms with star caricatures galore, there's a great bar, abuzz with show talk before or after the theater. Sadly, Vincent Sardi Jr, son of the founder, died in 2007, but the show, as they say, goes on.

Theatrical nostalgia buffs should head for the **Lyceum Theatre**, a block east on 45th Street. Open since 1903, it is the oldest continually operating theater on Broadway and – with its elaborate Baroque facade and dramatic mansard roof – probably the most beautiful.

The information hub

The **Times Square Visitor Center** ⑥ (daily 8am–8pm) is a walk-in facility

TIP

For those arriving in Penn Station, skip the cabstand at 32nd Street and Seventh Avenue. The wait there can be interminable. Go to the lesser-used exits onto Eighth Avenue and flag down a cab yourself. It's more work, but it's much quicker.

LEFT: the masses in Times Square.
BELOW: the busy intersection of Times Square is now closed to traffic.

Foxwoods Theatre, a relatively new theater with wide aisles and good views of the stage from most seats. Formerly known as both the Hilton Theatre and the Ford Center for Performing Arts, it was built on the site of the old Lyric Theater (1903), and has retained some of its elegant facade.

The Foxwoods also occupies the site next door, the former premises of the Apollo Theater (1920), and the design has incorporated into its internal decor some of the Apollo Theater's embellishments. Appropriately, for several years the Foxwoods was the Broadway home of the most recent revival of that perennial musical, *42nd Street*. Its latest production is also Broadway's most expensive: *Spider-Man Turn off the Dark*.

Also on 42nd Street are New York's outlet of the world-famous **Madame Tussauds** wax museum, the **E-Walk** entertainment complex (with 13 movie theaters) and the AMC Empire which has 25 movie theaters. Most of the dining choices are from chain restaurants.

I want my MTV

At the corner of 44th Street is the **Viacom** building, where the **Times Square Studio** and headquarters of **MTV** are located. Joining the retail roster on the square and keeping with the MTV vibe are **Quicksilver**, the skate and surf clothing chain, and **Aeropostale**, a low-cost fashion brand.

Despite the square's transformation, there's still a perceptible sleaze factor seeping over from the few remaining sex shops that are peppered between the discount clothing and cheap food joints on Eighth Avenue, where the **Port Authority Bus Terminal ❼** (between 40th and 42nd and now cleaned up) is a major commuter hub.

This sleazy atmosphere continues to change, however, with the opening of the new **New York Times Building**, opposite the bus terminal on Eighth Avenue, between 40th and

in the landmark **Embassy Theater**, on Seventh Avenue between 46th and 47th streets. There are stands offering information and tickets for Broadway shows, sightseeing tours, and many other activities around the city, not just in Times Square. A brand new set of exhibits detail the seedy and celebratory history of the square, including a replica of the New Year's Eve ball that drops every 20 minutes for those not lucky enough to be around on December 31. Free leaflets are available in multiple languages, and there are computer kiosks and public lavatories.

There are advisers on hand to deal with questions, but they often seem so harassed it might be better to grab a handful of leaflets to flip through in the center's theater-style seats. Free walking tours leave from the center every Friday at noon.

Times Square is changing all the time, and over the past few years or so has started to attract the sort of big-name businesses that first put it on the map: Condé Nast, Reuters, and Ernst & Young all have office space here (though Condé Nast may soon be relocating to One World Trade Center). One cultural attraction is the

The Show Goes On

Even in the darkest days of financial crisis, the Broadway lights have continued to shine and make visitors forget their troubles

Broadway's 40 theaters sell more than 12 million tickets annually, earning upward of $1 billion. Andrew Lloyd Webber's imported musical megahits – *Phantom of the Opera*, *Cats* – dominated the box office for a decade, but American dramas and comedies (often lumped together as "straight plays") are also produced with reassuring regularity. In an average season of 35 new productions, roughly half will be new plays. Recent hits like *The Book of Mormon* have been selling tickets over a year in advance of performance, and mainstays like *The Lion King* and *Wicked* continue to play to packed houses. Even the critically dismissed *Spider-Man* musical pulls in more than $1 million a week.

In the early 20th century over 100 new plays were staged each season. Playwrights and composers like Eugene O'Neill, Lillian Hellman, Cole Porter, Irving Berlin, Rodgers and Hart, Arthur Miller, and Tennessee Williams all made their names in New York, and their work is often revived. Contemporary American playwrights such as David Mamet, Wendy Wasserstein, Sam Shepard, and John Guare have also seen revivals in recent years.

Of the 40 theaters known as "Broadway," only a handful are on the Great White Way itself, including the Broadway Theatre, the Palace, and the Winter Garden. The rest are on side streets from 41st to 54th Street, not counting the Vivian Beaumont Theater at Lincoln Center, home to a recent celebrated run of War Horse.

One of the oldest and most splendid theaters, the Lyceum (1903), is a neo-Baroque beauty on West 45th Street, just east of Times Square. The New Victory on 42nd Street is even older, but has had a more troublesome history. Built by Oscar Hammerstein in 1900 as the theater Republic, its name was given a patriotic boost during the 1940s. Thirty years later it was reduced to showing porno movies, but now the New Victory presents colorful, fresh productions, often aimed at children.

Broadway may make the headlines, but Off-Broadway is considered by many to be the true soul of New York theater. Some playwrights bypass Broadway altogether in favor of smaller venues. Off-Broadway is also where plays are staged that are unsuitable for the mainstream, whether for their content or for cost reasons. A hit in an Off-Broadway theater like Playwrights Horizons or the Public Theater provides the confidence backers need to move uptown. *Rent*, *Bring In 'Da Noise, Bring In 'Da Funk* and *A Chorus Line* started this way.

With limited time on a New York visit, it can be better not to fixate on a particular show, but to have a number of options, and choose the one that offers the best ticket deal. It can also be rewarding to play a hunch and try something relatively unheard of. This may offer the most memorable kind of New York theater experience, as well as giving the chance to see something spectacular before the critics make ticket prices soar.

RIGHT: Rebecca Faulkenberry debuts as Mary Jane Watson in 'Spider-Man Turn Off the Dark'

41st. This gleaming new addition to the NY skyline has been designed by Renzo Piano using ceramic tubes to create a curtain-wall effect that acts as a sunscreen, and changes color throughout the day.

WEST OF TIMES SQUARE

Heading west and a little to the north on Eighth or Ninth avenues, things get interesting in the old **Hell's Kitchen** neighborhood, now known as **Clinton ❽**. At the start of the 20th century, Hell's Kitchen was one of the most notorious slums in the country. Immigrants were crammed into unsafe and unsanitary tenements, and Irish gangs governed the streets like petty overlords. The police were afraid to venture into the neighborhood alone.

There's still a certain gut-level edginess to the area, and a new generation of immigrants, but there are also artists and actors, as well as culinary discoveries to be made. Ninth Avenue from 57th Street to 42nd Street is a globetrot for diners, with reasonably priced restaurants offering an atlas of international cuisines.

A stretch of West 46th Street from Eighth to Ninth avenues – known as

Restaurant Row – is a solid block of brightly colored eateries popular among the pre-theater crowd. During the annual **Ninth Avenue Food Festival** (May), thousands of New Yorkers flock to gorge themselves on a huge variety of delicacies available from street vendors and the restaurants themselves. If you love to eat, this is an event that you should go out of your way to attend.

Off-Broadway

There's also an active Off-Broadway theater scene on 42nd Street between Ninth and Tenth avenues, where the block of small, experimental, or low-budget venues here are known collectively as **Theater Row**. This makes an attractive pairing with Restaurant Row for an evening out.

On the way between Restaurant Row and Theater Row, theater-lovers might consider a quick detour down West 44th Street. Between Ninth and Tenth avenues is the headquarters of New York's most famous acting school – the legendary **Actors' Studio**.

Though there's not much to look at, this small building on an otherwise residential street spawned such greats as Marlon Brando, James Dean, Paul Newman, and Robert De Niro – all practitioners of the school's "Method" style of acting.

Harborside

There's little of note to see west of here, except for the Jacob K. **Javits Center ❾**, at Twelfth Avenue and 34th Street. This is one of the country's largest convention and exhibition spaces – home to the National Boat Show and other events – and it keeps getting larger. In 2010 a new hall, Javits Center North, was completed, and renovations on the main hall will continue through 2013. Conventioneers love being here, but unless you have an interest in one of the visiting exhibitions, it's not worth going out of your way to the Javits.

Non-delegates might like to consider a little sightseeing. A bit farther uptown, at Pier 83 on 42nd Street, **Circle Line** boats depart for delightful cruises around Manhattan.

Intrepid Sea, Air, and Space Museum ⑩

Address: Pier 86 (at W. 46th St and 12th Ave), www.intrepidmuseum.org
Telephone: 212-245 0072
Opening Hours: Apr–Sept daily 10am–5pm, Sat–Sun until 6pm, Nov–Mar Tue–Sun 10am–5pm
Entrance Fee: charge
Subway: 42nd St/Port Authority

The museum is centered on one giant exhibit, the USS *Intrepid*, a decommissioned World War II aircraft carrier with a deck the size of a few football fields. It's strewn with aircraft, from fighter jets to Concorde, and a retired submarine, the USS *Growler*. The *Intrepid* reopened in 2009 after a two-year, $58 million refurbishment, and an even bigger project lies on the horizon. Having acquired the decommissioned Space Shuttle *Enterprise*, the museum plans to build a complex on the other side of the West Side Highway that will house it and other space-themed attractions. This will be at least a few years.

STROLLING SIXTH AVENUE

For an alternative route, walk east instead of west from Times Square to **Sixth Avenue**. Signs announce the **Avenue of the Americas**, but don't be fooled: to New Yorkers, Sixth Avenue is Sixth Avenue, no matter how many flags hang from the lampposts. At the corner of 42nd Street is pretty **Bryant Park ⑪**, where fashion shows, summer concerts, and sometimes outdoor movies occur. In winter there's skating on the pond, a pretty sight, especially when the snow is piled high around the **Bryant Park Grill** (see page 176), which looks out over the park from behind the New York Public Library. The Art Deco **Radiator Building** at 40th Street is now the fashionable **Bryant Park Hotel** and bar, and is helping to perk up the square around the park.

At the next corner is the **International Center of Photography** (1133 Sixth Avenue at 43rd Street, www.icp.org, tel: 212-857 0000; closed Mon; charge), which has a permanent collection of over

ABOVE: Bryant Park.

EAT

For Korean food, head over to West 32nd Street between Broadway and Fifth Avenue, aka Koreatown. There are a few other notable Korean eateries in the blocks north and south of here, but this is the heart of the Seoulful action. There's karaoke to boot.

EAT

For a touch of elegance after the neon wattage of Times Square, head north to 57th Street, and the opulent, recently reopened Russian Tea Room (see page 177).

100,000 photographs – including the archives of *Life* magazine. Visiting exhibitions can include real gems, so if you're interested in photography, make sure to find out what's on while you're in New York.

Clubs and diamonds

Turning right at 44th Street leads to the neighborhood of the **Algonquin Hotel** ⑫ (see page 312), where Dorothy Parker, Robert Benchley, and other distinguished literati traded wit at the famous Round Table. Much has been done to preserve the appearance and atmosphere of this historic hotel.

If you are rich or well connected, West 44th Street has several opportunities for genteel rest and relaxation. No. 27 is the premises of the **Harvard Club**, whose interior can more easily be observed by peering into a back window, rather than shelling out for four years' education; No. 37 houses the distinguished **New York Yacht Club**, with an 1899 nautically themed Beaux Arts facade.

Another right turn off Sixth Avenue leads to the **Diamond District** ⑬, a block-long enclave along 47th Street where close to $500 million's worth in gems is traded every day. Most of the diamond merchants are Hasidic Jews, distinguished by black suits, wide-brimmed hats, and long beards. From 47th Street north, corporate monoliths march up Sixth Avenue. Names change, but the structures stay the same. This stretch

RIGHT: the exterior of Radio City Music Hall.
BELOW: The Rockettes perform at the opening night of the Radio City Christmas Spectacular at Radio City Music Hall.

Radio City Rockettes

For more than 75 years, the Radio City Rockettes have performed in their Art Deco palace in Rockefeller Center. They began in St Louis as the "Missouri Rockets," and were brought to New York by S.L. (Roxy) Rothafel, who changed their name to the "Roxyettes" and debuted their high-precision, all-American show at his own Roxy theater. They danced at the opening of Radio City Music Hall on December 27, 1932, and have been resident ever since. The Christmas show at Radio City is an American institution on a par with the Barnum & Bailey Circus, and draws an annual audience of over 1 million. Proficiency in jazz and tap dancing, and a height between 5'6" and 5'11" (1.68–1.80 meters) are requirements for ensemble dancers.

ABOVE: MoMA is home to Andy Warhol's *Campbell's Soup* series.

of Sixth is really the backyard of the Rockefeller Center and its famous performance space.

Radio City Music Hall ⑭

Address: 1260 Sixth Ave (at 50th and 51st sts), www.radiocity.com
Telephone: 212-247 4777
Opening Hours: box office Mon–Sat 11.30am–6pm (until 8pm Oct–Dec); tours daily 11am–3pm
Entrance Fee: charge
Subway: 47th–50th St/Rockefeller Center

The world's largest indoor theater graces the west side of the Rockefeller Center. Built in 1932 as a palace for the people, both the exterior and interior are magnificent, and a guided tour is highly recommended. From the massive chandeliers in the Grand Lobby to the plush, scalloped auditorium, Radio City was built to impress; it's the last word in Art Deco extravagance. The acoustics are excellent, and even the restrooms were custom-designed. The Stuart Davis mural that graced the men's smoking lounge was thought so important it was acquired by the Museum of Modern Art.

The **Paley Center for Media** ⑮ (25 West 52nd Street, www.paley center.org, tel: 212-621 6800; Wed–Sun noon–6pm, Thur until 8pm; charge), formerly the Museum of Television and Radio, is a feast for committed couch potatoes. The vast archive of vintage radio and TV shows can be rented for an hour at a time, and is the perfect rainy-day activity. There are daily screenings, too.

Museum of Modern Art ⑯

Address: 11 W. 53rd St (at Fifth and Sixth aves), www.moma.org
Telephone: 212-708 9400
Opening Hours: Mon, Wed, Thur, Sat, & Sun 10.30am–5.30pm (until 8.30pm first Thur each month Sept–June), Fri 10.30am–8pm
Entrance Fee: charge, free on Friday evenings
Subway: 53rd St/Fifth Avenue

The Museum of Modern Art, known to culture vultures as MoMA, offers one of the world's most exciting and provocative art collections (see page 178). Even if the thought of modern art leaves you cold, the building alone is worth visiting. The ingenious use of light and space means you can be walking along a corridor and suddenly find yourself looking out over a sculpture, or through to the city outside.

ABOVE: the Mariinsky Orchestra, conducted by Valery Gergiev, performs in Carnegie Hall.

Perhaps the most accessible section is the Architecture and Design floor, with groundbreaking designs. It is these imaginative inclusions that, combined with some of modern art's most famous paintings, give MoMA the edge. Be prepared for crowds of fellow art-lovers.

Carnegie Hall

Address: 57th St and Seventh Ave, www.carnegiehall.org
Telephone: 212-247 7800
Opening Hours: box office Mon–Sat 11am–6pm, Sun noon–6pm (box office closed Sat–Sun from June–mid-Aug); tours Mon–Fri 11.30am, 12.30pm, 2pm and 3pm, Sat 11.30am and 12.30pm, Sun 12.30pm
Entrance Fee: charge
Subway: 57th St

As every American knows, there's only one way to get to Carnegie Hall – practice, practice. The joke is about as old as the hall itself, which was built in 1891 by super-industrialist Andrew Carnegie. Ever since Tchaikovsky conducted at the opening gala, Carnegie Hall has attracted the world's finest performers, including Rachmaninov, Toscanini, and Sinatra. It would be pleasant if the

hall's exterior were as inspiring as its history or acoustics.

Carnegie Hall is, in fact, the umbrella title for three separate halls. The Issac Stearn Auditorium/Ronald O. Perelman Stage is the hall's original space. The auditorium seats nearly 3,000 people and was described by Isaac Stearn as "larger than life." Two smaller stages complete the complex, one with 600 seats, and one half that size.

Midtown goes green

Two blocks west is another of the city's spectacular new constructions, the **Hearst Tower** , soaring up like a giant, glass origami-model, with walls of glass facets that catch the light in ever-changing colors. This is also New York's first recognized "green" skyscraper, low-impact technologies and recyclable materials having been used throughout.

Midtown West wraps up with a flourish on **Central Park South**, famed for luxury hotels and lines of limousines. It's a good place to catch a **horse-drawn carriage** and clip-clop around the park – especially in December, when Midtown glistens with holiday lights.

SHOPPING

Some might refer to Midtown West as a desert when it comes to interesting stores. After all, one of its biggest draws seems to be the Kmart next to Penn Station. Look closer and you will find oases of retail scattered throughout the area.

Bargains

Jack's 99 Cent Store
100 W. 32nd Street (at 6th Ave)
Tel: 212-268 9962
http://jacks99world.com
A lot more interesting than a Dollar General, Jack's is a multi-floored discount store – upstairs is Jack's World, where things are more than a dollar, but still a bargain. Part of the fun is seeing what surprising items you can find.

Books

The Drama Book Shop
250 W. 40th Street (at 7th and 8th aves)
Tel: 212-944 0595
http://dramabookshop.com
An embarrassment of riches for the theater fan, this is where you go to buy the scripts of plays that are both famous and not so famous.

Clothing

Yeohlee
25 W. 38th Street (at 5th and 6th aves)
Tel: 212-631 8099
http://yeohlee.com
A brand-new boutique

from an exciting new designer who is staking her claim in the Garment District.

Department Stores

Muji
620 8th Avenue (at 40th St)
Tel: 212-382 2300
www.muji.us
It's fitting that you would find this eclectic mix of sleek and modern Japanese apparel, furniture, housewares, and beauty products in the sleek new New York Times Building.

Electronics

B & H Photo & Video
420 9th Avenue (at 33rd and 34th sts)
Tel: 212-444 6615
www.bhphotovideo.com
Owned and run by Hasidic Jews, this is perhaps the country's best store for cameras and audiovisual equipment. There's a fascinating and efficient system of conveyer belts that bring products from the sales people to the register. Closed Saturdays and Jewish holidays.

Food

H & H Bagels
639 W. 46th Street (at West Side Highway)
Tel: 212-765 7200
http://hhbagels.com
After closing its legendary 80th Street store-

front, this bakery and warehouse are all that remain of the bagel masters. It is way out on the West Side Highway (near the Intrepid), but for bagels this good, the trip should be worth it.

Gifts

Delphinium Card & Gift
353 W. 47th Street (at 9th Ave)
Tel: 212-333 7732
http://delphiniumhome.com
Quirky greeting cards and gifts, including elections just for kids.

Home

MacKenzie Childs
14 W. 57th (at 5th and 6th aves)
Tel: 212-570 6050
www.mackenzie-childs.com
Depending on your tastes, this colorful and whimsical collection of

striped and checked tableware, furniture, kitchen and bath products is gaudy or gorgeous.

Souvenirs

One Shubert Alley
346 W. 44th Street (at 8th and 9th aves)
Tel: 212-944 4133
A jam-packed little shop dedicated to Broadway memorabilia.

Toys

Toys "R" Us
1514 Broadway (at 44th St)
Tel: 646-366 8800
www.toysrus.com
It may be part of a giant chain, but there are no others like this one in Times Square, where a Ferris wheel spins in the middle of a multi-story wonderland of toys.

LEFT: H&H Bagels are a New York icon.

BEST RESTAURANTS, BARS AND CAFÉS

Restaurants

Algonquin Hotel, Blue Bar, & Lobby
59 W. 44th St (at 5th and 6th aves)
Tel: 212-840 6800
www.algonquinhotel.com
B, L, T, & D daily $$$ 99 [p338, C2]
Whether it's Martinis at the Blue Bar or afternoon tea in the wood-paneled lobby, there's a sense of literary history in the air once shared by Dorothy Parker and other members of the Round Table. The people behind a recent renovation worked hard to change nothing.

Angus McIndoe
258 W. 44th St (at Broadway and 8th Ave)
Tel: 212-221 9222
http://angusmcindoe.com
L & D Mon–Sat, Br & D Sun $$ 100 [p338, C1]
Newer than Joe Allen's and Sardi's, the latest drop-in place provides three levels for various theater stars to unwind after a show.

Aureole
One Bryant Park (at Broadway and 6th Ave)
Tel: 212-319 1660
www.charliepalmer.com
L & D daily $$$$ 101 [p338, C2]
This is arguably the finest restaurant in the Times Square neighborhood. It's certainly the most expensive, but the lunch prix-fixe is a nice deal.

Barbetta
321 W. 46th St (at 8th and 9th aves)
Tel: 212-246 9171
www.barbettarestaurant.com
L & D Tue–Sat $$$ 102 [p338, C1]
The grande dame of "Restaurant Row" has been doing uninterrupted business since 1906. An elegant townhouse plus dreamy garden make for a grand experience of delicious Italian food.

Becco
355 W. 46th St (at 8th and 9th aves)
Tel: 212-397 7597
http://becco-nyc.com
L & D daily $$ 103 [p338, C1]
A fixed price, all-you-can-eat pasta paradise. Moderate in price with wine, very cheap without it.

Le Bernardin
155 W. 51st St (at 6th and 7th aves)
Tel: 212-554 1515
www.le-bernardin.com
L & D Mon–Fri, D only Sat $$$$ 104 [p336, B4]
Top-of-the-line for fish- and seafood-lovers. One of the best restaurants in the country.

Bryant Park Grill
25 W. 40th St (at 5th and 6th aves)
Tel: 212-840 6500
www.arkrestaurants.com
L & D daily $$$$ 105 [p338, C2]
There's a busy lunch scene at this terraced eatery behind the New York Public Library; it's a great place for a drink and a meeting spot in the early evening too, hosting an attractive after-work crowd.

Café Un Deux Trois
123 W. 44th St (at Broadway and 6th aves)
Tel: 212-354 4148
http://cafeundeuxtrois.biz
B, L, & D daily $$ 106 [p338, C2]
Midtown madness, but with a pre-theater or lunchtime brasserie menu. The *pommes frites* are perfect.

Carnegie Deli
854 7th Ave (at 54th and 55th sts)
Tel: 212-757 2245
www.carnegiedeli.com
B, L, & D daily $ 107 [p336, B4]
This New York institution provides a tourist-filled version of the authentic deli experience. The lines are long, and the enormous pastrami sandwiches come with an extra charge for sharing.

China Grill
CBS Building, 60 W. 53rd St (at 6th Ave)
Tel: 212-333 7788
www.chinagrillmgt.com
L & D Mon–Sat, D only Sun $$–$$$ 108 [p338, D1]

Fabulous nouvelle Asian restaurant which can be reasonably priced with some careful study of the creative menu.

Daisy May's bbq usa
623 11th Ave (at 46th St)
Tel: 212-977 1500
www.daisymaysbbq.com
L & D daily $ ⑩ [p338, B1]
Finger-lickin' barbecue. Serious eaters can order ahead for a whole barbecued hog. It'll cost ya! But everything else is cheap.

Gallagher's Steakhouse
228 W. 52nd St (at Broadway and 8th Ave)
Tel: 212-245 5336
www.gallaghersnysteakhouse.com
L & D daily $$$ ⑩ [p338, C1]
A one-time celeb hangout and a New York tradition since 1927. It's easy to spot; look for beef in the windows.

Il Gattopardo
33 W. 54th St (at 5th and 6th aves)
Tel: 212-246 0412
www.ilgattopardonyc.com
L & D daily $$$ ⑪ [p338, D1]
Tiny restaurant with attractive ivy-covered garden serving authentic Neapolitan dishes. Try the meatballs.

Hourglass Tavern
373 W. 46th St (at 9th Ave)
Tel: 212-265 2060
www.hourglasstavern.com
D Tue–Sun $$ ⑫ [p338, C1]
The gimmick here (a formula that has been popular for years) is that diners must be in and out in 60 minutes.

Joe Allen
326 W. 46th St (at 8th and 9th aves)
Tel: 212-581 6464
http://joeallenrestaurant.com
L & D daily $$ ⑬ [p338, C1]
Long-time theater hangout serves basic

American food with the added bonus of possible celebrity sightings.

John's Pizzeria
260 W. 44th St (at Broadway and 8th Ave)
Tel: 212-391 7560
www.johnspizzerianyc.com
L & D daily $ ⑭ [p338, C1]
Quality thin-crust pizza, plus much more on the menu, in a former church. What's better, the stained glass or the pie?

The Modern
Museum of Modern Art, 9 W. 53rd St (at 5th and 6th aves)
Tel: 212-333 1220
www.themodernnyc.com
L & D Mon–Fri, D only Sat $$$$ ⑮ [p338, D1]
Food really is an art, as is the setting overlooking MoMA's Sculpture Garden. Celebrate a special occasion here. The Bar Room is open for lunch and dinner on Saturday and Sunday.

Oceana
120 W. 49th St (at 6th and 7th aves)
Tel: 212-759 5941
http://oceanarestaurant.com
L & D Mon–Fri, D only Sat–Sun $$$$ ⑯ [p338, C1]
Spectacular seafood and one of the city's best raw bars served in the ground floor of the McGraw Hill Building. If tables aren't available, the 50ft (15-meter) marble bar is gorgeous and a good alternative.

Russian Tea Room
150 W. 57th St (at 6th and 7th aves)
Tel: 212-581 7100
www.russiantearoomnyc.com
L & D Mon–Fri, Br & D Sat–Sun $$$ ⑰ [p336, B4]
The menu will never be the same, but the place is back, right where it

always was, just left of Carnegie Hall in a space that is pretty in pink, red, and green all over.

Tony's Di Napoli
147 W. 43rd St (at Casablanca Hotel between 6th and 7th aves)
Tel: 212-221 0100
www.tonysnyc.com
L & D daily $$ ⑱ [p338, C2]
Family-size portions of tasty Italian fare. Fresh food draws huge crowds for pre-theater feasts.

Trattoria Dell'Arte
900 7th Ave (at 56th and 57th sts)
Tel: 212-245 9800
www.trattoriadellarte.com
L & D daily $$$ ⑲ [p336, B4]
The fabulous antipasti double as a popular main course. This trattoria is always buzzing with culinary cognoscenti.

The View
1535 Broadway (at 45th and 46th sts)
Tel: 212-704 8900
www.nymarriottmarquis.com
D Mon–Sat, Br, & D Sun $$$ ⑳ [p338, C1]
High atop the Marquis Hotel in Times Square is New York's only revolving restaurant, with a wonderful panoramic view of the skyline. Sunday brunch and early dinner (great for sunsets) are particular favorites.

Wondee Siam and Wondee Siam II
792 9th Ave (at 53rd St) and 813 9th Ave (at 54th St)
Tel: 212-459 9057 and 917-286-1726
http://wondeesiam2.com
L & D daily $–$$ ㉑ [p336, B4]
In a neighborhood of Thai restaurants, the tiny Wondee Siams are among the most affordable and authentic. The original can barely fit a dozen people, but will

Prices for a three-course dinner per person with half a bottle of wine:

$ = under $20
$$ = $20–$45
$$$ = $45–$60
$$$$ = over $60

save you money (it's also a BYOB).

Burger Joint
119 W. 56th St (at 6th and 7th aves) ㉙ [p336, B4]
A humble little bar hidden on the ground floor of Le Parker Meridien Hotel that serves one of the city's best burgers.

Café 2 at MoMA
11 W. 53rd St (at 5th and 6th aves) ㉚ [p338, D1]
The canteen-style eatery at the museum offering tasty tapas-style snacks as well as soups, salads, and desserts. Alternatively try to squeeze into Terrace 5, the museum's full-service café, for views of the Sculpture Garden.

Heartland Brewery
W. 43rd St (at Broadway and 6th aves) ㉛ [p338, C2]
Although they do a brisk bar biz with the microbrew, there's a little something for everyone on the menu, from crab cakes to basic pub grub.

Sardi's
44th St (at Broadway and 8th Ave) ㉜ [p338, C1]
Of course, lunch and dinner are served at this legendary Theater District mainstay, but a drink at the bar is a must. Sip a cocktail surrounded by the trademark caricatures of every Broadway name. Friendly barmen.

LEFT: the Algonquin Hotel restaurant.

MUSEUM OF MODERN ART

Attention and praise is lavished on MoMA's building almost as much as on its world-class collection

"One of the most exquisite works of architecture to rise in this city in at least a generation" was the *New York Times'* welcome to MoMA's Midtown home, when it reopened at the end of 2004 after an extensive refit.

Yoshio Taniguchi, the Japanese architect chosen for the project, said his aim was "the imaginative and disciplined use of light, materials, and space." The new facility offers almost twice the floor space of the former building, with airy galleries on the second floor and more intimate exhibition areas on the levels above. The top floor provides expansive, skylit space for temporary exhibitions.

The much-admired Sculpture Garden follows the original 1953 design, setting Rodin, Picasso and Tony Smith pieces among trees and calm reflecting pools. In 2010, Yoko Ono gifted a Wish Tree for the garden. It is a small tree to which visitors can attach short notes detailing their wishes.

ABOVE: *The Starry Night,* 1889, Vincent Van Gogh. "Looking at the stars," he said, "always makes me dream."

RIGHT: *The Couple,* 1955. Gilberto Giacometti's bronzes took inspiration from African tribal art.

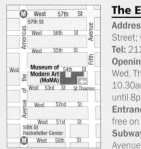

The Essentials

Address: 11 West 53rd Street; www.moma.org
Tel: 212-708 9400
Opening Hours: Mon, Wed, Thur, Sat, and Sun 10.30am–5.30pm, Fri until 8pm
Entrance Fee: charge, free on Friday evenings
Subway: 53rd St/Fifth Avenue

MoMA in the Making

The Museum of Modern Art's collection was started by Abby Aldrich Rockefeller, Mary Quinn Sullivan, and Lillie P. Bliss in 1929 with just eight prints and a single drawing. Abby's enthusiasm for the works of modern artists like Matisse, Van Gogh, and Chagall was not shared by her husband, John D. Rockefeller, who decried the work as "unintelligible," and unfit for public viewing. The opening show of works by Cézanne, Gauguin, Van Gogh, and Serrat was held on the 12th floor of a building on 57th Street and Fifth Avenue. After three transfers to larger premises, MoMA moved to its present location in 1939.

The museum's collection, which began so modestly, now includes more than 150,000 works, among them paintings, sculptures, drawings, prints, photographs, architectural models and drawings, furniture, and design objects. MoMA also has around 22,000 films and 4 million film stills. The library and archives are among the premier facilities of their kind in the world.

Above: *Paimio Chair* 1931–2, Alvar Aalto. The Paimio Chair is a bentwood virtuoso piece that pushed the limits of plywood furniture making.

Right: *Woman with Her Throat Cut*, 1932, by Gilberto Giacometti.

Top: *The False Mirror*, 1928, René Magritte.

Right: *Side 2*, 1970, by Shiro Kuramata: innovative storage from MoMA's architecture and design collection.

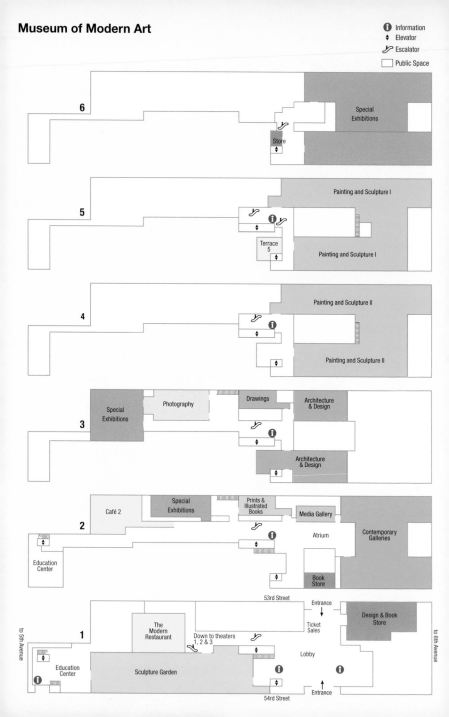

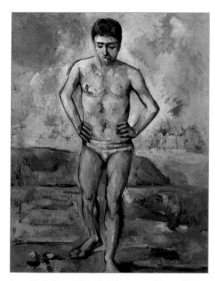

Above: *The Bather*, *c.*1885, by Paul Cézanne, one of the great Post-Impressionists and the painter whom Henri Matisse described as "the father of us all."

Above: *Sleeping Woman*, 1929. Man Ray was a Surrealist pioneer of photographic techniques like solarization.

Below: *La Clownesse assise* (*The Seated Clowness*), 1896, Henri de Toulouse-Lautrec. Diminutive Lautrec is best known as a postermaker and chronicler of the Belle Epoque, and the girls of Paris's fin de siècle Moulin Rouge nightclub in particular.

Above: *Les Demoiselles d'Avignon*, 1907. Pablo Picasso's monumental canvas drew on African masks and Iberian sculpture, and is a landmark in the story of modern art.

Right: Yoko Ono's *Wishing Tree.*

FIFTH AVENUE

Paris has the Champs-Elysées, London has Bond Street, Rome has the Via Veneto, but only New York has Fifth Avenue

There are few streets that evoke the essence of the city as powerfully as Fifth Avenue. It's all here – the audacity of the Empire State Building, the ambition of the Rockefeller Center, and the old-world elegance of the Plaza Hotel.

Fifth Avenue begins at Washington Square, near the crooked streets of Greenwich Village. Rolling up past the Flatiron Building to Madison Square Park – the site of the original Madison Square Garden – the avenue marches past the Empire State Building and the Rockefeller Center, hugs Central Park for 26 scenic blocks, before plunging into "Museum Mile" (see page 228), and some of the city's most important art collections.

Timeline of the city

Continuing past the mansions and embassies of the Upper East Side, Fifth runs a sketchy course through Harlem, bisecting Marcus Garvey Park, before coming to a halt just before the Harlem River. South to north, culturally, socially, and economically, few streets in the world can provide a more varied tour of extremes. It's a timeline of the city.

LEFT: looking down Fifth Avenue.
RIGHT: the view from the Empire State.

EMPIRE STATE BUILDING Ⓐ

Address: 350 Fifth Ave (at 33rd and 34th sts), www.empirestatebuilding.com
Telephone: 212-736 3100
Opening Hours: daily 8am–2am
Entrance Fee: charge
Subway: 34th St/Herald Sq

The world's most famous skyscraper rises like a rocket from the corner of 33rd Street. When it was completed in 1931, this was the tallest structure in the world. Presently the city's tallest building, and set to remain so

Main Attractions
EMPIRE STATE BUILDING
NEW YORK PUBLIC LIBRARY
ROCKEFELLER CENTER
SAKS FIFTH AVENUE
ST PATRICK'S CATHEDRAL
GRAND ARMY PLAZA
PLAZA HOTEL
CENTRAL PARK

Maps and Listings
MAP, PAGE 184
RESTAURANTS, PAGE 192

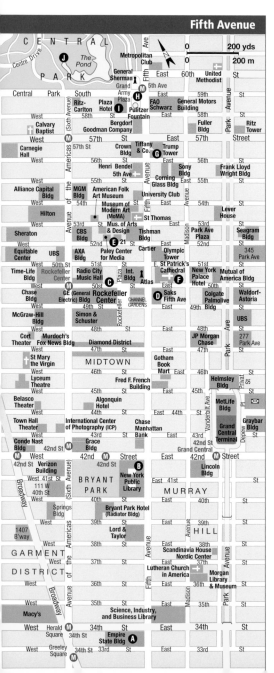

Fifth Avenue

until One World Trade Center is completed – but, at 1,454ft (443 meters) and with 102 stories, the Empire State now stands in height below buildings in Kuala Lumpur, Taipei, and Chicago's Sears Tower. When it comes to the view, however, the Empire State can't be beat. On a clear day you can see for as far as 80 miles (130km), while at night, Manhattan spreads out far below, a floating sea of winking, twinkling lights.

The empire strikes back

If you plan to visit during the day, try to get here as early as possible, as the long lines can take something away from the experience. At the concourse level, enter the marble Art Deco lobby, where you are directed to the high-speed elevator that zips straight up to the 86th-floor observation deck. Outside, there are powerful binoculars to peer through, and a couple of souvenir stands in the covered viewing area.

If this is your first visit to New York, it's a good idea to rent the audio tour – an entertaining and informative overview of the city as it spreads out in front of you. Expect a security check on arrival, which involves a lot of waiting around.

Observation deck

For an additional fee, you can ascend to the smaller observatory way up on the 102nd floor, which is just about the spot where in 1933 Fay Wray (and more recently Naomi Watts, in the 2005 remake) made her tearful final farewells to the "tallest, darkest leading man in Hollywood," a giant ape by the name of King Kong. Movie posters, photos, and other memorabilia from Wray's private collection are on permanent display in the lobby downstairs.

Kong isn't the only one who met his fate up here. Of the 16 people who have jumped off the building, only two were wearing parachutes,

Optimistic design

The Empire State was planned in the optimistic 1920s, but by the time it was completed the United States was in the depths of the Great Depression, and office space was not fetching a premium. In its first year of operation until March 1932, the observation deck took as much as the rent collected on the whole of the rest of the building put together.

The Empire State Building's upper floors are illuminated at night, and special light displays are put on for festivals and holidays, including the Fourth of July, Christmas, and Hanukkah (see the website for a complete schedule).

Illuminated display

both of whom were arrested as soon as they landed. On a happier note, 14 lucky couples are given permission to plight their troth at the top of the building every Valentine's Day.

The **New York Skyride** (www.skyride.com; charge), inside the building, offers a simulated flight above the city (this is not recommended for those who suffer from motion sickness).

The building was first opened on May 1, 1931, with a dazzling display switched on from Washington DC by President Herbert Hoover, and the illuminations have been a feature ever since. The colored floodlights were installed in 1964, and have traditionally signaled events such as Frank Sinatra's 80th birthday; the singer's death was also marked by the crown of the

LEFT: the Empire State Building.
ABOVE: Kong and Fay Wray climb to the 102nd floor in the 1933 movie King Kong.
BELOW: Taxi SUV

Follow that Cab

There are few more recognizable New York icons than the taxicab, they've been here for more than 100 years. Hansom cabs charging exorbitant fares ruled the streets for a time. That was until 1907, when an enterprising businessman named Harry N. Allen released a fleet of 65 French-made gasoline-powered vehicles into the city. The honeymoon period was short, and Allen soon faced the wrath of his drivers, who unionized and argued for better pay. It's a story that would be repeated many times – drivers and cab companies angrily trading demands.

Checker Cabs were the dominant vehicles for the first half of the 20th century, their bright colors and signature checkered stripes easy to spot on a rainy city street. To regulate the industry, the city established a medallion system in 1930s, which limited the number of official cabs. By 1970, it was a requirement that all official cabs be painted yellow. As automotive trends changed, so too did the design of taxis. Checker Cabs made way for Ford Crown Victorias and the somewhat recent addition of mini vans. In late 2013, the city plans to introduce a completely redesigned New York Taxi, the result of a controversial contest where Nissan was eventually named the victor.

ABOVE: the Beaux Arts New York Public Library.
BELOW: the stone lions in front of the New York Public Library are called *Patience* and *Fortitude*.

building being bathed in blue light, for Frank's nickname "Ol' Blue Eyes." After the death of *King Kong* actress Fay Wray, the Empire State stood for 15 minutes in complete darkness.

On Queen Elizabeth II's Golden Jubilee in 2002, the Empire State paid tribute with a display of purple and gold. Mayor Bloomberg said this was also a way of saying thank you for the support Great Britain gave after the September 11, 2001, attacks. In 2011, the Green Building Council granted the building LEED Gold Status after an extensive, environmentally friendly series of renovations.

Around the Empire State

A few yards north, the less glamorous **Science, Industry, and Business Library** (188 Madison Avenue at 34th Street, tel: 917-275 6975) is a valuable addition to the city's library facilities, with a huge stock of research materials including business and science journals, CD-ROMs, and handbooks for personal or professional study. It's a good place to get online if you've left your laptop behind, with computers for public use. Free tours are offered on Thursdays at 2pm.

Five blocks north at Fifth and 39th Street, **Lord & Taylor** is one of New York's best-known department stores; people have been known to line up just to peer into its windows. Lord & Taylor branches in other cities have closed, however, and the future of this flagship store remains uncertain.

New York Public Library Ⓑ

Address: Fifth Ave (at 42nd St), www.nypl.com
Telephone: 212-930 0830
Opening Hours: Mon–Thur 8am–11pm, Fri 8am–8pm, Sat–Sun 10am–6pm
Entrance Fee: free
Subway: 42nd St/Bryant Park
Directly across the street, in warm weather, office workers and tourists can be found lounging in front of

New York's coolest library, under the watchful gaze of two stone lions that flank the marble steps.

Stretching between 40th and 42nd streets, this glorious 1911 Beaux Arts monument is one of the world's finest research facilities, with a vast collection that includes 15 million items and the first book printed in the United States – the *Bay Psalm Book* from 1640 – and the original diaries of Virginia Woolf.

In addition to a fine collection of paintings, which, controversially, the library is in the process of selling off, there is a third space for exhibitions. Topics are varied and have covered everything from Japanese picture books to New York City garbage.

The biggest treasure of all, however, may be the main Reading Room, a vast, gilded gem with windows that overlook **Bryant Park**. Ask inside about joining one of the tours of the library; they take place two times a day (once a day on Sunday).

ROCKEFELLER CENTER ⓒ

Address: Fifth Ave (at 48th to 51st sts), www.rockefellercenter.com
Telephone: 212-632 3975
Opening Hours: daily 8am–midnight

for Top of the Rock, other attractions close earlier
Entrance Fee: charge for tours and Top of the Rock; otherwise free
Subway: 47th–50th St/Rockefeller Center

At 49th Street, Fifth Avenue lives up to its legend, thanks in large part to the **Rockefeller Center**, one of the world's biggest business and entertainment complexes, and a triumph of Art Deco architecture. The Rockefeller Center has been called a "city within a city," and it's got the numbers to prove it. The center's daily population (including visitors) is more than 200,000. If it were a city, that number would place it in the top 100 biggest in the country. It would certainly be the most crowded. It has more than 100,000 telephones, 48,758 windows, and nearly 400 elevators.

Add to this a 2-mile (3km) underground concourse, numerous stores and over 40 places to eat, four subway lines, a post office, foreign consulates, and the world's most famous auction house, Christie's, and you've got quite a little metropolis. Indeed,

I believe in the sacredness of a promise, that a man's word should be as good as his bond; that character – not wealth or power or position – is of supreme worth.

John D. Rockefeller

LEFT: Rockefeller Center was completed in 1933.
BELOW: view from the Top of the Rock.

ABOVE: the viewing deck at Top of the Rock.
BELOW: Paul Manship's gilded statue, *Prometheus Bringing Fire to the World*, is the centerpiece of Rockefeller Plaza.

when Rockefeller first envisaged the complex – as a development to house the city's burgeoning TV and radio industry – he called it "Radio City."

The **Channel Gardens** – so named because they separate La Maison Française on the left and the British Building on the right, just as these countries flank the English Channel – draw visitors into the center of the plaza. This is where the famous Christmas tree, lit with countless bulbs, captivates holiday visitors. The *Today* show is broadcast from a glassed-in studio here, too.

Tours of **NBC Studios** (charge) depart every 15 minutes; tours of the Rockefeller Center (charge) depart hourly (Mon–Sat 10am–5pm, Sun 10am–4pm).

In summer, there are concerts and outdoor movies in the sunken courtyard, while in the winter there's a hugely popular ice-skating rink.

30 Rock

Rockefeller Plaza is dominated by the 70 floors of the soaring 850ft (259-meter) **GE Building**, number 30 Rockefeller Center, or "30

Rock." Formerly known as the RCA Building, it was renamed after the reacquisition by General Electric (GE) of the company, which it had helped to found in 1919. The Rockefeller family retain offices on the 54th and 56th floors. In 2011, the Federal Communications

Commission approved a merger between NBC and the Comcast cable company, ushering in a new era for 30 Rock. It was inevitable that the Tina Fey and Alec Baldwin sitcom that bears the same name as the building would lampoon the move, referring to its new parent company as "Kabletown... with a K."

Saturday Night Live

As the headquarters of NBC, 30 Rock is the home of the comedy show *Saturday Night Live*, Liz Lemon and the folks at *30 Rock*, and of many of the network's New York facilities. The building was also the setting for a famous photograph taken in 1932 during the construction of the center by Charles C. Ebbets called *Lunchtime atop a Skyscraper*. Sitting astride a steel girder with no harnesses, 11 workers casually lunch and chat, 850ft (260 meters) above the city.

Rockefeller Center's best tourist attraction is the **Top of the Rock** (www. topoftherocknyc.com; daily 8am–midnight; charge). Situated 70 floors above ground, the observation deck offers a different perspective

of the city from the Empire State, including terrific sightings of Central Park, and has one major advantage – a clear view of the iconic building itself. The lines for the deck are often shorter, though purists may argue that the experience lacks the class of visiting the Empire State.

Saks, St Pat's, and 21

Back on Fifth Avenue, **Saks Fifth Avenue ❿** (611 Fifth Avenue, www. saksfifthavenue.com, tel: 212-753 4000; Mon–Sat 10am–8pm, Sun noon–7pm) is the supremely elegant flagship department store for Saks shops across America, from Dallas to San Diego. There are numerous great shopping opportunities here, including an enormous women's shoe department that has its own zip code, 10022. On the next corner up is the **International Building**, with Lee Lawrie's monumental bronze figure of Atlas crouching under the weight of the world, over 25ft (8 meters) tall, at its entrance.

Two streets up is another classic dining venue, **21 ❸** (21 West 52

ABOVE: tours of the NBC studios depart every half-hour on weekdays and every 15 minutes on weekends.
BELOW: skating at Rockefeller Center.

Chocolate fans' eyes pop out when they see La Maison du Chocolat, the exquisite French chocolatiers at the foot of the GE Building in Rockefeller Plaza. In the summer months, there's also freshly made ice cream to savor.

ABOVE: St Patrick's Cathedral
BELOW: the Unicef Snowflake.

Telephone: 212-753 2261
Opening Hours: daily 6.30am–8.45pm, first Mass at 7am daily (8am on Sat)
Entrance Fee: free
Subway: 50th St/Rockefeller Center

The site of St Patrick's was purchased in 1810 to build a Jesuit school, and the cornerstone of the church was laid on August 15 – the Feast of the Assumption – 48 years later. Work was suspended during the Civil War, but the first American cardinal, John McCloskey, got construction back underway in 1865, opening the doors in May, 1879. Extensive renovation in 1927–31 included installation of the great organ.

The cathedral is a formidable Midtown landmark, its Gothic facade an intriguing counterpoint to the angular lines and smooth surfaces of the skyscrapers around it. And yet St Pat's is unmistakably New York: where else would one need tickets to attend midnight Mass? Look around the interior, where F. Scott Fitzgerald married his Southern belle, Zelda, before going on to literary fame and domestic

Street, www.21club.com, tel: 212-582 7200; *see page* 192), where every president since FDR has been elegantly entertained. The atmosphere is hushed, the lighting low – and the steak tartare still sets the standard.

St Patrick's Cathedral ❻

Address: Fifth Ave (at 50 and 51st sts), www.saintpatrickscathedral.org

The Corner of Fifth and Christmas

Most New Yorkers have a "seen it once, don't have to see it again" attitude when it comes to Christmas window displays, but even the biggest Scrooge is bound to crack a smile during a snowy December evening walk down Fifth Avenue. It has been a game of one-upmanship for decades, where retailers like Fendi and Louis Vuitton try to out-do the masters of lights, Saks Fifth Avenue. There's still a place for animatronic angels and elves and that place would be Lord and Taylor, where the dioramas retain the quaint handmade qualities of yesteryear. At other stores technology has yielded some fantastic new amusements in the form of lasers and LED screens. Traditionalists point to the Rockefeller Center Christmas Tree as the peak of holiday ornamentation, but the UNICEF Snowflake, a glittering crystal marvel that hangs at 57th Street and Fifth Avenue, has its legion of fans, especially those who donate $500 to have the crystals etched with messages to loved ones. A Fifth Avenue window walk should actually take you as far east as Lexington Avenue and as far west as Sixth Avenue, because it wouldn't be the same without a peak through the glass at Bloomingdale's and Macy's. All in all it encompasses more than 20 blocks of entertainment and you don't ever have to open your wallet or purse.

hell. Alternatively, take a seat and breathe in the sweet smell of incense – the twinkle of candles and gentle hum of voices makes St Pat's a calming spot in the middle of the hustle of the city.

Serious shopping

Beyond St Patrick's, Fifth Avenue returns to more worldly concerns, namely, upscale shopping. **Tiffany & Co.** and **Cartier**, **Gucci**, and **Pucci** are a few that feed into the avenue's élan.

At 57th Street, ladies who lunch totter on stilettos between **Prada**, **Dior**, and the expensive emporia inside the **Trump Tower G**. Now mainly ultra-luxurious condominiums, the tower is worth stopping by for a glimpse of the big-spending opulence synonymous with Manhattan in the 1980s. Viewers of the first series of Donald Trump's TV show *The Apprentice* will recognize its marble atrium and waterfall.

While part of Fifth Avenue has been colonized by chain stores, retail is still a leisurely pursuit at **Henri Bendel** and **Bergdorf Goodman**. Built on the former site of a Cornelius Vanderbilt mansion, Bergdorf is more like a collection of small boutiques than a department store. Exquisite, and expensive.

Grand Army Plaza H on 59th Street punctuates Fifth Avenue and marks the boundary between Midtown and the Upper East Side. It borders the **Plaza Hotel I** (see page 312), a home-away-from-home for Mark Twain. The Plaza has undergone recent renovation, with some rooms now condominiums or retail spaces. Many have been set aside for visitors, however, and the landmark public rooms remain unaffected.

The views of **Central Park J** (see page 194) are worth the price of a cocktail in the Plaza's wood-paneled Oak Bar.

ABOVE: upscale shopping on 57th Street.
BELOW: the Trump Tower.

BEST RESTAURANTS, BARS AND CAFÉS

Restaurants

21
21 W. 52nd St (at 5th and 6th aves)
Tel: 212-582 7200
www.21club.com
L & D Mon–Fri, D only Sat $$$$
122 [p338, D1]
This ex-speakeasy will never be out of style with Manhattan's movers and shakers. Miniature jockeys line the exterior, while other corporate toys hang from the ceiling. A plaque over Table 30 reads "Bogie's Corner." Sip his favorite tipple, Ramos gin fizz, and order the chicken hash.

Adour Alain Ducasse at the St Regis
2 E. 55th St (at 5th and Madison aves)
Tel: 212-753 4500
www.adour-stregis.com
D Tue–Sat $$$$ 123 [p338, D1]
A match made in cuisine heaven: the five-star

hotel marries the five-star French chef at prices to match.

Aquavit
65 E. 55th St (at Park and Madison aves)
Tel: 212-307 7311
www.aquavit.org
L & D Mon–Fri, D only Sat $$$
124 [p338, E1]
Savor sublime, upscale Scandinavian cuisine, and wonder why you hadn't before.

Bice
7 E. 54th St (at 5th and Madison aves)
Tel: 212-688 1999
www.bicenewyork.com
L & D daily $$$ 125 [p338, D1]
Northern Italian cuisine, served in a very elegant, spacious dining room. It's pretty pricey, but apparently not so much for the high-end Euro and business crowd that frequents the restaurant.

La Bonne Soupe
48 W. 55th St (at 5th and 6th

aves)
Tel: 212-586 7650
www.labonnesoupe.com
L & D daily $$ 126 [p338, D1]
An old standby that serves up lots more than just soup – try the crepes and the quiche too. Hands down, the best vinaigrette salad dressing anywhere.

Burger Heaven
20 E. 49th St (at 5th and Madison aves)
Tel: 212-755 2166
http://burgerheaven.com
B, L, & D Mon–Sat, Br & L Sun $$ 127 [p338, D2]
Midtown workers are willing to put up with the hellish noontime crush at this burger joint, which has a long, diner-style menu with plenty of options.

DB Bistro Moderne
55 W. 44th St (at 5th and 6th aves)
Tel: 212-391 2400
www.danielnyc.com

B, L, & D Mon–Fri, Br & D Sat–Sun $$$$ 128 [p338, D1]
A sleek new take on the bistro concept. Chef Daniel Boulud's power-lunch spot is awash in culinary surprises and Art Deco glitz, with a clientele to match.

La Grenouille
3 E. 52nd St (at 5th and Madison aves)
Tel: 212-752 1495
L & D Tue–Sat $$$$ 129 [p338, D1]
The last of the great classical French Midtown establishments, where a quenelle is still a quenelle and the flowers are rarely more beautiful. A classic.

Harry Cipriani
The Sherry-Netherland Hotel, 781 5th Ave (at 59th and 60th sts)
Tel: 212-753 5566
www.cipriani.com
Br, L, & D daily $$$$ 130 [p336, C4]

Posh branch of the famed Venice home of the bellini; high-fashion types always welcome.

Katsuhama
11 E. 47th St (at 5th and Madison aves)
Tel: 212-758 5909
www.katsuhama.com
L & D daily **$$** 131 [p338, D2]
No frills here, but an affordable Japanese spot that specializes in katsu (Japanese cutlets).

Keen's Steakhouse
72 W. 36th St (at 5th and 6th aves)
Tel: 212-947 3636
www.keens.com
L & D Mon–Fri, D only Sat–Sun **$$$** 132 [p338, C3]
A classic steakhouse dating back to 1885, a stone's throw from the Empire State Building.

Kuruma Zushi
7 E. 47th St (at 5th Ave)
Tel: 212-317 2802
www.kurumazushi.com
L & D Mon–Sat **$$$$** 133 [p338, D2]
This was the sushi place before all the sushi places, and it is still fantastic after 35 years.

Má Pêche
15 W. 56th St (at 5th and 6th aves)
Tel: 212-757 5878
www.momofuku.com
B, L, & D Mon–Sat, B & D only Sun **$$$** 134 [p336, B4]
The latest in the innovative line of Momofuku restaurants, with an eclectic menu inspired by the traditions of Asia, France, and the American South (to name a few).

Mangia
50 W. 57th St (at 5th and 6th aves)
Tel: 212-582 5554
www.mangiatogo.com
B, L, & D Mon–Sat **$** 135 [p336, B4]
Follow the office workers and dine on tasty Mediterranean fare and sandwiches at this noisy, crowded eatery on busy 57th Street.

Michael's
24 W. 55nd St (at 5th and 6th aves)
Tel: 212-767 0555
www.michaelsnewyork.com
B, L, & D Mon–Fri, D only Sat **$$$** 136 [p336, B4]
Media and publishing movers and shakers sign deals here; it's open for power breakfasts, too.

Prime Burger
5 E. 51st St (at 5th and Madison aves)
Tel: 212-759 4730
www.primeburger.com
B, L, & D Mon–Fri, B & L Sat. **$** 137 [p338, D1]
This old-school diner-style lunch spot has chairs with individual built-in, tray-style tables. The location is convenient, and the flame-broiled burgers are tasty, but mostly it's just fun to dine in such a nostalgic setting.

Quality Meats
57 W. 58th St (at 5th and 6th aves)
Tel: 212-371 7777
http://qualitymeatsnyc.com
L & D Mon–Fri, D only Sat–Sun **$$$** 138 [p336, B4]
The name of the place really means something here, at a tiptop, high style New American steakhouse.

Sarabeth's
40 Central Park S. (at 5th and 6th aves)
Tel: 212-826 5959
www.sarabeth.com
B, L, & D daily **$$** 140 [p336, B4]
A fancy address for the homey NYC-only chain (Upper Eastside and Upper Westside locations) making excellent baked goods, preserves, soups, and casual food. Best for breakfast, brunch, or lunch.

The Sea Grill
19 W. 49th St (at 5th and 6th aves)
Tel: 212-332 7610
L & D daily **$$$** 139 [p338, D1]
Two places at the Rockefeller Center, with views of skaters or fun-seekers. The first has a good but general menu; the second has excellent fish.

Bars and Cafes

Hale & Hearty Soups
55 W. 56th St (at 5th and 6th aves) 33 [p336, B4]
A chain of good, reliable eateries with a long, frequently changing menu.

King Cole Bar
2 E. 55th St 34 [p336, D1]
Sipping a drink with the gorgeous Maxfield Parrish mural at the St Regis Hotel as a backdrop can't be beaten. Tea, coffee, and snacks, too.

Morrell Wine Bar & Café
1 Rockefeller Plaza 35 [p336, D1]
A noisy, fun crowd spills out onto a sidewalk cafe in summer, and in winter there's a great view of the Christmas tree.

Oak Bar at The Plaza
10 Central Park South (at the Plaza Hotel) 36 [p336, C4]
One of the most elegant of the historic hotel bars, with sumptuous wood paneling, gleaming chandeliers, and a lovely view of Central Park.

'wichcraft
555 5th Ave (at 46th St) 37 [p336, D2]
This sandwich and panini shop is a little more expensive than your average deli, but it's also the most casual outpost of Tom Colicchio's restaurant empire.

Prices for a three-course dinner per person with half a bottle of wine:

$ = under $20
$$ = $20–$45
$$$ = $45–$60
$$$$ = over $60

LEFT: Adour Alain Ducasse. **RIGHT:** DB Bistro Moderne.

CENTRAL PARK

Stretching from Grand Army Plaza to Harlem, Central Park is the playground and meeting place of the metropolis

This 843-acre (340-hectare) park was designed by Frederick Law Olmsted and Calvert Vaux in 1858. Olmsted's aim was to "supply hundreds of thousands of tired workers who have no opportunity to spend summers in the country with a specimen of God's handiwork." The project was known as "Greensward."

Before construction of the park, this area was swampy land, inhabited by poor Irish and German immigrants and a well-established African-American community known as Seneca Village. All were displaced, a cruel irony after Olmsted's pledge of designing it for "tired workers."

Of late, city officials have been establishing "Quiet Zones" and silencing the buskers that used to fill the park with music. Still, there is a good deal of other no-cost entertainment to be found. In summertime, the New York Public Theater stages *Shakespeare in the Park* at the Delacorte Theater. Tickets are free, but getting a pair requires showing up early in the morning and waiting in line at the box office. The New York Philharmonic and the New York Opera give outdoor performances on the Great Lawn, and SummerStage festival brings contemporary acts to an open-air venue at Rumsey Playfield for concerts, many with free admission. In wintertime, the Wollman Rink provides classes and a picturesque venue for ice skating. For details, visit www.centralpark.org.

ABOVE LEFT: a statue of Lewis Carroll's Mad Hatter, from *Alice's Adventures in Wonderland*.

ABOVE: taking a boat on the lake affords serene views of the Majestic apartment building's post-Art Deco twin towers, which stand by the darker, Gothic-style gables of the famous Dakota building. It also provides an afternoon's gentle exercise; rent boats from the Loeb Boathouse, near East 75th Street.

ABOVE: the Bethesda Fountain was designed with a surrounding terrace to be the park's architectural centerpiece. Along with wonderful views of the lake, the fountain is a perfect spot for romantic meetings.

LEFT: near West 72nd Street, across the street from John Lennon's former New York home in the Dakota building, is "Strawberry Fields." This little area is adorned with flowers most of the time, but especially on his birthday, October 9, and the anniversary of his senseless murder, December 8.

RIGHT: The Boathouse is a lakeside restaurant with an outdoor grill and an espresso cafe. Sheep Meadow Café and Ferrara Café are also great spots for refreshment.

LEFT: Hans Christian Andersen takes a seat and prepares to tell a story. Among the statues to delight the kiddies are Mother Goose, Humpty Dumpty, Little Jack Horner, and Little Bo Peep.

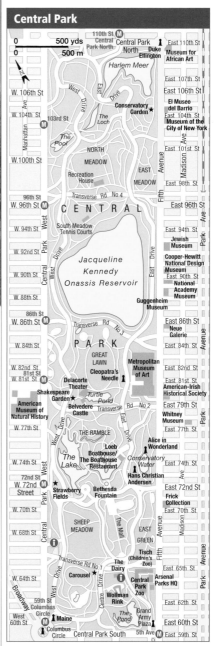

Central Park

0   500 yds
0   500 m

N

110th St

Central Park North

Central Park North

Duke Ellington

East 110th St

Museum for African Art

Harlem Meer

W. 106th St

West Drive

East Drive

East 107th St

East 106th St

El Museo del Barrio

W. 104th St

103rd St

Conservatory Garden ★

East 104th St

Museum of the City of New York

The Loch

East 101st St

W. 100th St

The Pool

NORTH MEADOW

Recreation House

EAST MEADOW

East 98th St

96th St

W. 96th St

Transverse Rd No 4

C E N T R A L

East 96th St

W. 94th St

South Meadow Tennis Courts

East 94th St

Jewish Museum

W. 92nd St

Jacqueline Kennedy Onassis Reservoir

Cooper-Hewitt National Design Museum

W. 90th St

East 90th St

National Academy Museum

W. 88th St

Guggenheim Museum

86th St

W. 86th St

Transverse Rd No. 3

P A R K

East 86th St

Neue Galerie

W. 84th St

GREAT LAWN

East 84th St

W. 82nd St

W. 81st St

Cleopatra's Needle

Metropolitan Museum of Art

East 82nd St

East 81st St

Delacorte Theater

American-Irish Historical Society

Shakespeare Garden ★

Turtle Pond

American Museum of Natural History

Belvedere Castle

Transverse Rd No 2

East 79th St

Whitney Museum

W. 77th St

THE RAMBLE

East 77th St

Alice in Wonderland

W. 74th St

Loeb Boathouse/ The Boathouse Restaurant

Conservatory Water

East 74th St

The Lake

Hans Christian Andersen

East 72nd St

72nd St

W. 72nd Street

Strawberry Fields

Bethesda Fountain

Frick Collection

W. 70th St

East 70th St

SHEEP MEADOW

The Mall

EAST GREEN

W. 68th St

Tisch (Children's Zoo)

Transverse Rd No 1

The Dairy

East 65th St

W. 64th St

Carousel ★

Central Park Zoo

Arsenal

Central Parks HQ

59th St Columbus Circle

Wollman Rink

Centre Drive

Grand Army Plaza

East 62nd St

West 60th St

Maine

The Pond

East 60th St

Columbus Circle

Central Park South

5th Ave

East 59th St

Manhattan Ave

Central Park West

West Drive

East Drive

Fifth Avenue

Madison Avenue

Park Avenue

Broadway

CENTRAL PARK WILDLIFE

The first place many visitors go to see wildlife in Manhattan is the Central Park Zoo, which accommodates scores of exotic creatures in different habitats. The Polar Zone is home to two polar bears, harbor seals, and tufted puffins. The Tropical Zone houses tropical birds as well as lemurs, tamarin monkeys, and innumerable frogs, lizards, snakes, and toads. The Temperate Territory is where California red pandas, Japanese macaques, North American river otters, and mandarin ducks live. Although the present zoo dates only from 1988, the first menagerie was established in 1864. Seventy years later, a "storybook" zoo was created by the Depression-era Works Progress Administration.

It takes a bit more effort, but there's plenty of wildlife to see outside of the walls of the zoo as well. The park is home to fish, reptiles, amphibians, and a handful of mammals including squirrels, raccoons, and woodchucks – not to mention the occasional wayward coyote. There are approximately 230 species of birds that live among the 25,000 trees. If that number seems impressive, consider that from 2009–2011, two men took on the task of mapping all those trees. They mapped 19,933 in total.

ABOVE: a woman walks her dog across the Great Lawn in Central Park after a snowstorm.

ABOVE: some of the zoo's ticket receipts are used to fund the Wildlife Conservation Society's international activities.

BELOW: classic horse-drawn carriages line up along Central Park South between Fifth and Sixth avenues. The vintage buggy rides are available year-round.

Above: the Henry Luce Nature Observatory is housed in Belvedere Castle, which was designed by the park's architect, Frederick Law Olmsted, and constructed in 1872.

Below: on the path to the pond, this bronze bust of Thomas Moore was sculpted in 1879.

Above: the charming gingerbread cottages of Old Dairy Milkhouse were built in 1870, as a milking parlor. The dairy now operates as the park's visitor center, offering guides and park information, in addition to providing a station for the park's rangers. Tue–Sun 10am–5pm.

Left: this little family of life-sized bronze bears are at the entrance to the Pat Hoffman Friedman Playground, on the east side of the park near the Metropolitan Museum.

MIDTOWN EAST

In the mornings, watch the well-dressed masses emerge from Grand Central Terminal and hurry into the shining skyscrapers that surround it, and you might catch a glimpse of the glamorous sheen that still exists well past the Mad Men era

Midtown East covers many of the images Manhattan conjures up when people think of New York. This is where the city's corporate heart beats loudest, where power-lunching, power-shopping, and sidewalk power-phoning is a daily way of life.

Like its counterpart to the west, Midtown East begins above 34th Street, and rises to a bustling climax between 42nd Street and the Queensboro (59th Street) Bridge, beyond which lies the calmer Upper East Side. Stretching east of Fifth Avenue to the East River, it's a compact, energetic microcosm of Manhattan, encompassing steel-and-glass office towers, historic hotels, familiar landmarks like the Chrysler Building, Grand Central Terminal, and the United Nations, and some very exclusive neighborhoods.

HILLS AND BAYS

Along 35th Street is the southern border of **Murray Hill** ⑲, a classy residential area in the shadow of sleek Midtown office buildings, its cross-streets lined by brownstone relics of a more genteel era. A plaque on the south side of 35th Street and

Park Avenue marks the center of an 18th-century farm owned by Robert Murray, "whose wife, Mary Lindley Murray (1726–82), rendered signal service in the Revolutionary War." It was said she cleverly delayed a British advance by inviting the officers to tea, but later, doubt was cast on this story. Close by, on Madison Avenue, the lovely **Church of the Incarnation**, built in 1864, has beautiful stained-glass windows by Tiffany, LaFarge, and Burne-Jones, among others.

Main Attractions
MORGAN LIBRARY & MUSEUM
MADISON AVENUE
GRAND CENTRAL TERMINAL
CHRYSLER BUILDING
UNITED NATIONS
WALDORF-ASTORIA
SONY BUILDING

Maps and Listings
MAP, PAGE 164
SHOPPING, PAGE 209
RESTAURANTS, PAGE 210
ACCOMMODATIONS, PAGE 312

LEFT: the Midtown Manhattan skyline.
RIGHT: the streets of Murray Hill are lined with elegant brownstones.

The Morgan Library has the original manuscript of Charles Dickens's *A Christmas Carol*. On the first Sunday in December each year the library hosts an all-day celebration of the book, with family activities that include storytelling, readings, and dancing.

RIGHT: the West Room of the J.P. Morgan Library.
BELOW: the East Room of the J.P. Morgan Library.

Morgan Library & Museum ⑳

Address: 225 Madison Ave (at 36th St), www.themorgan.org
Telephone: 212-685 0008
Operating Hours: Tue–Thur 10.30am–5pm, Fri 10.30am–9pm, Sat 10am–6pm, Sun 11am–6pm
Entrance Fee: charge (free Fri 7–9pm)
Subway: 33rd St

Also called the Pierpont Morgan Library, this private collection was opened to the public by J.P. Morgan Jr in 1924. It was amassed by his father, Pierpont Morgan, the most powerful banker of his time and an avid collector whose interests ranged from Egyptian to Renaissance art and Chinese porcelain.

The Morgan has been comprehensively renovated and given a new "campus" by brilliant Italian architect Renzo Piano, which integrates with the original historic buildings while doubling the exhibition space. There are artistic, literary, musical, and historical works, including drawings by Rembrandt and Rubens and original scores from Mozart and Beethoven. The history of writing and printing

was one of Morgan's passions, so the library is strong in this area, with 5,000-year-old carved tablets, three Gutenberg Bibles and manuscripts by Charles Dickens, Mark Twain, and other writers.

The new building on Madison Avenue is "crowned" by a beautiful, naturally lit Reading Room, with excellent facilities for 21st-century researchers. You can see the original pillared entrance on 36th Street.

Sniffin Court

From the Morgan, walk east across Park and Lexington avenues, to reach one of the city's tiniest and most charming historic districts. Behind iron gates and opposite a Yeshiva University building, the red-brick row houses of **Sniffen Court** were constructed in Romanesque Revival style at the time of the American Civil War, and were originally stables for Murray Hill's grander residences (now, of course, very expensive and

highly desirable real estate). If you peer through the gates you can make out the horse-relief on the back wall that marks out the former studio of sculptor Malvina Hoffman.

AROUND GRAND CENTRAL

Along the west side of Murray Hill is **Madison Avenue ㉑**. Historically, this has been the spiritual home of the advertising industry, especially the blocks between 42nd and 57th streets. Madison Avenue is one of the city's commercial nerves, where sharp-suited men and women buy their clothes at Brooks Brothers on 44th Street and stop off for cocktails at the Yale Club one block east on Vanderbilt, before running to catch their trains home to leafy suburbs.

Grand Central Terminal ㉒

Address: 42nd St and Lexington Ave, www.grandcentralterminal.com
Telephone: 212-340 2583
Operating Hours: daily 5.30am–2am
Subway: 42nd St/Grand Central

Often incorrectly referred to as "Grand Central Station," the terminal greeted 150,000 people when it opened at 12.01 on the first Sunday in February, 1913. Today, 750,000 people cross the concourse of the opulent building every day – over 1 million pass through daily during the Christmas holidays.

Grand Central has bars, a food court, excellent restaurants, shops, and a branch of the New York Transit Museum to entertain those waiting for a train, as well as the iconic clock as a memorable meeting point.

With entrances at Vanderbilt and 42nd Street, and at Park and Lexington avenues, Grand Central is the hub for Metro-North commuter lines reaching deep into the suburbs of Westchester County and neighboring Connecticut. More than 550 trains depart from here. Grand Central was saved from demolition by the Landmarks Preservation Commission, and so this 1913 Beaux Arts reminder of days when travel was a gracious experience remains almost intact.

Vaulted ceilings

It's also undergone a $200 million restoration to return it to its former glory. Advertising signs were removed, new restaurants and stores

BELOW: Grand Central Terminal prepares for Christmas.

ABOVE: when looking up at the Zodiac ceiling in Grand Central, look for the small black square to see how badly pollution once covered the ceiling.
BELOW: the Grand Concourse of Grand Central Terminal.

opened, including an indoor food hall for last-minute purchases, and the glorious illuminated zodiac on the vaulted ceiling of the main concourse – one of the world's largest spaces – gleams like new.

All apart, that is, from a dark patch above Michael Jordan's The Steak House. This was left untouched, to give an understanding of the extent of the restoration effort.

The magnificent astronomical zodiac ceiling was commissioned by the Vanderbilt family from French artist Paul César Helleu in 1912. The constellations were painted back to front, and the Vanderbilts hastily improvised the explanation that it represents a "God's-eye view."

The four faces of the clock over the information desks are made from opal; the clock has a value estimated by Sotheby's and Christie's at between $10 and $20 million. The flag commemorates the terrorist attacks of September 11, 2001.

Grand tours

Grand Central must be one of few commuter hubs that's a tourist destination, too, and you can spot the out-of-towners pretty easily – they're the ones looking up. Tours are given by the Municipal Art Society every Wednesday at 12.30pm (http://mas.org/tours, tel: 212-453 0050; suggested donation). Self-guided audio tours are also available in the terminal from booths marked "GCT Tour." Before leaving, be sure to see the **Oyster Bar** on the lower level, an architectural and culinary landmark.

Chrysler Building ㉓

Address: 42nd St and Lexington Ave
Subway: 42nd St/Grand Central

One block east on Lexington Avenue, the famed Chrysler Building is one of the jewels of the Manhattan skyline. Erected by William Van Alen for auto tsar Walter Chrysler in 1930, its Art Deco spire rises 1,046ft (319 meters)

into the city air like a stainless-steel rocket ship powered by gargoyles.

The building was designated a New York City landmark on September 12, 1979. Three years later, the stainless-steel arches and triangular windows were illuminated by bright white lights for the first time. This glorious lighting scheme was specified in Van Alen's original plan, but it took the city more than 50 years to implement the scheme.

The Chrysler Building is not open to the public, but visitors are allowed into the lobby. The steel-clad street-level facade is worth seeing up close, while the tower provides classic Manhattan views from any approach in the city.

TOWARD THE UNITED NATIONS AND THE EAST RIVER

Continuing east on 42nd Street, walk on past the crowds and the **Grand Hyatt Hotel** (which adjoins Grand Central, and was built over the old Commodore Hotel), to the former Daily News building, between Third and Second avenues. This Art Deco structure, though no longer

home to the newspaper, looks so much like the headquarters of the fictional *Daily Planet* that they used it in the *Superman* movies. Check out the gigantic globe in the lobby before continuing east toward First Avenue, past the steps leading up to **Tudor City** ㉔, a private compound of Gothic brick high-rises that is positioned at a different street level, and has its own tiny park and play area. The development dates from the 1920s, and was designed to attract middle-class buyers out of the suburbs and back into the city. At the time, land along the East River was filled with slums and slaughterhouses, one reason why all the windows face west, toward the Hudson River.

United Nations ㉕

Address: First Ave and 46th St, www.
un.org/tours
Telephone: 212-963 8687
Operating Hours: guided tours Mon–
Fri 9.45am–4.45pm, audio tours Sat–
Sun 10am–4.15pm
Entrance Fee: charge
Subway: 42nd St/Grand Central

The busy flag-lined entrance of the United Nations is opposite 46th Street. Once inside, the gentle patter of unfamiliar languages reminds you that you are now in international territory. Guided tours depart every 30 minutes from the lobby and last 45 minutes. Audio tours are available in 20 languages. Apart from an occasional exhibition in the lobby, there's not a lot to see unless you take

LEFT: the Chrysler Building today.
BELOW: view of the Chrysler Building in the 1930's.

Building the Chrysler

In a fantastically theatrical gesture, all seven stories of the steel-clad pinnacle were assembled inside the building, then hoisted into place in an hour and a half. Walter Chrysler's automobile business provided inspiration for much of the spectacular detail, but Van Alen may have regretted his choice of client, since his fee was never paid. The Chrysler was the first building to reach above 1,000ft (305 meters), and was the tallest in the world, until the Empire State Building snatched that title the following year.

Unfortunately, visitors are not allowed past the lobby, but stop in to admire the marble, bronze, and hardwoods and the epic murals on urban transportation and human endeavor.

ABOVE: a stained-glass window by Marc Chagall graces the United Nations building.
BELOW: Hugo Chavez, President of Venezuela, addresses the United Nations General Assembly.

the tour, but don't miss the Chagall stained-glass windows or the lower-level gift shop, which sells inexpensive handicrafts from all over the world.

On weekdays, the inexpensive Delegates' Dining Room is often open to the public for lunch: jackets are required for men, and reservations must be made a day in advance (tel: 212-963 7625). The view of the river is almost as interesting as the multilingual eavesdropping.

Historic districts

Back on 42nd Street, the lobby garden of the **Ford Foundation**  – glass-enclosed, all lush trees and flowers – is considered one of the city's most beautiful institutional environments. The building's interior offices look over the small oasis, a clever utilization of a usually uninspiring space. This part of town is also home to three of the city's classiest addresses. **Turtle Bay**, once home to privacy-loving celebrities such as Katharine Hepburn, the conductor Leopold Stokowsky, and author Kurt Vonnegut, is a historic district between 48th and 49th streets where

19th-century brownstones share a garden hidden from the public.

Beekman Place, between First Avenue and the East River, is a two-block enclave of elegant townhouses and apartments set along the river. One of its houses was once the home of famed songwriter Irving Berlin.

Sutton Place is an oft-used synonym for luxury, in books and movies. Starting above 54th Street and stretching north for five blocks, its high-rises are filled with dowagers and poodles. Visual relief is provided by a few still-surviving cul-de-sacs of townhouses, gardens, and promontories offering tantalizing views of the East River.

Nearby is a retail opportunity, the eclectic **Manhattan Art and Antiques Center** ㉗ on Second Avenue between 55th and 56th streets (www.the-maac.com, tel: 212-355 4400). It's a strange cross between a museum of curios and a shopping arcade. Over 100 small stores are housed here in glass-fronted rooms, selling everything from antique clocks and furniture to carved tusks. It's really a place to wander around rather than to shop, unless you have

The United Nations

The name "United Nations" was devised by President Franklin D. Roosevelt and first used in the "Declaration by the United Nations" of January 1, 1942, during World War II, when representatives of 26 nations pledged their governments to continue fighting together. The UN charter was drawn up in 1945 and signed by delegates from 50 countries; in the new millennium, membership had risen to over 190 countries.

Just like a foreign embassy, the United Nations' grounds, which cover 18 acres (7 hectares) along the East River, are not considered a part of the United States, and are outside the jurisdiction of city, state, and federal laws. The UN maintains its own independent police force, fire department, and post office.

a big budget and an even bigger suitcase. On the lower level, you'll find that increasingly rare big-city amenity, public restrooms.

On the way back toward Midtown, another interesting place to call is the **Citigroup Center** ㉘, on 54th Street between Third and Lexington avenues. Its slanted roof makes this a skyline standout, while the indoor atrium lined by shops and cafes makes a pleasant stopping place. Before exiting onto Lexington Avenue, drop by **St Peter's Church**, a modern, angular building, which includes a light and airy chapel. St Peter's is respected for its weekly jazz eucharists (http://saintpeters.org/jazz); it also has frequent concerts.

The **York Theatre** (www.yorktheatre.org), where plays by authors both known and unknown are presented, takes the stage on the church's lower level, and operates a program of community-focused events, such as afternoon films for the elderly.

Walking north, note the landmark **Central Synagogue** ㉙, at the corner of 55th Street. Built in 1872, it adds a note of exotic, Moorish-style grace to an otherwise ordinary block. The synagogue was rebuilt and reopened in September 2001, after being severely damaged by a fire.

Boutiques and galleries

There are boutiques and galleries in both directions on **57th Street**, where the prices on both clothes and paintings get more expensive the closer you walk to Fifth Avenue. Toward Third, expensive gadgets galore are on sale at **Hammacher Schlemmer** (www.hammacher.com), while continuing west on 57th you'll find such fashion fortresses as Turnbull & Asser, Chanel, and Burberry.

Along the way to these stores, be sure to notice the **Fuller Building** (41 East 57th Street, at Madison Avenue), which was built in 1929. There's a handbag store at street level, but the building's (separate) main entrance is embellished by a city skyline motif.

The lobby is another glorious example of Art Deco splendor. The floor mosaics depict the Fuller company's original headquarters when it was located in the Flatiron Building. The Fuller's midsection is home to numerous art galleries; the frequent

LEFT: cabs on Park Avenue.
ABOVE: Tudor City.
BELOW: the distinctive slanted roof of the Citigroup Center.

Skyscrapers

New York has always aimed high, and with landmark new buildings from Norman Foster, Renzo Piano, and Frank Gehry, the city is still reaching for the sky

New York is a vertical city. The first skyscraper was Daniel Burnham's 1902 Flatiron Building, which is 285ft (87 meters) high. Built on a knife-edge lot at Broadway and Fifth Avenue, the Flatiron gained instant élan from its height and classical styling, not to mention a romantic touch from the way it appeared to be sailing up Broadway.

Traditional styles still inspire the tallest buildings, however. Napoleon LeBrun styled the 700ft (210-meter) Metropolitan Life Insurance tower (Madison Avenue at E. 23rd Street) after St Mark's Campanile in Venice. Architect Cass Gilbert built the Woolworth Building, which soars for 792ft (241 meters), but harks back to Gothic styles.

New York's iconic 20th-century skyline was wrought more by politics than art. As buildings rose ever higher, planners feared that city streets were becoming lightless canyons. A 1916 zoning formula capped street-level facades by the width of the street, so towers of unlimited height rose only over a quarter of a building plot. This led to the "setback" feature (step-like recessions near the top of buildings) which is now a New York icon.

The boom and confidence of the 1920s led to the classic era, of which there is no finer example than William Van Alen's famous Chrysler Building. The gleaming spire of the 1,046ft (319-meter) 1930 Art Deco masterpiece tops a pinnacle of stainless-steel automotive motifs and gargoyles. The 1,454ft (443-meter) Empire State Building (Shreve, Lamb, & Harmon) took the "world's tallest" title from the Chrysler in 1931. Raymond Hood's 1934 RCA Building in the Rockefeller Center is more muted Art Deco, softer than the monolithic skyscrapers.

The postwar International style arrived in Mies van der Rohe's 1958 Seagram Building (375 Park Avenue), graceful glass curtain walls rising from an open plaza. Many anonymous 1950s and '60s glass boxes showed the same style with less aplomb. Far above the crowd, the 1,368ft (417-meter) Twin Towers of the World Trade Center (1976) were a New York icon on a par with the Empire State – a status tragically confirmed by the towers' destruction during the terrorist attacks on September 11, 2001.

Recent architectural efforts have again brought imaginative elements to the skyscraper. The triangular panels of the 2006 Hearst Tower, designed by British architect Norman Foster, are integral to the heat, light, and air management system, while Italian Renzo Piano's new tower for *The New York Times* has sunscreen-walls of ceramic tubes. Frank Gehry's Beekman Tower, whose facade suggests rippling water, has become the city's newest avant-garde wonder. In all these awesome structures, New York is always building, always soaring.

LEFT: Beekman Tower.

exhibitions are open to the public. A directory is available from reception.

ABOVE GRAND CENTRAL

The view down Park Avenue stops abruptly at the **MetLife Building** ㉚ (originally known as the Pan-Am Building), which was plonked on top of Grand Central Terminal in the early 1960s. Fortunately, beyond it this part of the avenue still retains some of its original glamour.

The **Waldorf-Astoria** ㉛, between 49th and 50th (see page 314), is one of the city's grand hotels, and has attracted guests of the royal and presidential variety ever since it opened on this site in 1931. The Duke and Duchess of Windsor and Cole Porter were only some of the "permanent residents" who lived in the hotel's exclusive towers. The original Waldorf-Astoria on Fifth Avenue, which had brought a new level of luxury to New York's hotel world in the 1890s, had been torn down to make way for the

Empire State Building. The hotel retains its air of opulent exclusivity, and the high-ceilinged reception area is populated by wealthy guests lounging in overstuffed armchairs.

The domed **St Bartholomew's Church** ㉜ opened its doors on Park Avenue and 50th Street in 1919, and is a fine example of neo-Byzantine architecture. The church has an evocative program of lighting that changes depending on the religious calendar, meaning that a visit around Christmas will reveal a bright, well-lit interior, while during Lent the church is shrouded in darkness.

One block west, on Madison, the fancy **New York Palace Hotel** incorporates as part of its public rooms two of the **Villard Houses**, 19th-century mansions once used as offices by the Archdiocese of New York. Built in 1884 by the architectural firm McKim, Mead, & White, these half-dozen houses were designed to look like one large Italian palazzo. The

ABOVE: Central Synagogue.

DRINK

Mixological lore has it that the Bloody Mary was invented at the King Cole Bar in the St Regis Hotel on E. 55th and Madison. We think it originated at Harry's Bar in Paris, but this is still a peach of a place, with a Maxfield Parrish mural, killer cocktails, and lighting that continues to flatter after too many drinks.

RIGHT: the MetLife
Building was
constructed in 1963, 50
years later than Grand
Central, seen in the
foreground.
BELOW: in the
production studio at
Sony Wonder
Technology Lab.

Picasso for a season

There are lines of limos waiting in front of the **Four Seasons ㉝**, on East 52nd Street between Park and Lexington (see page 210), a restaurant so important that its interior has been declared a historic landmark. Picasso's 22ft (6.7-meter) painted curtain from a 1920 Diaghilev ballet, *Le Tricorne*, hangs inside, and luminaries from the worlds of politics and publishing do likewise.

The restaurant is within the distinctive **Seagram Building**. The tycoon Samuel Bronfman, head of Seagram Distillers, had planned to erect an ordinary office block until his architect daughter introduced him to Mies van der Rohe. The result is one of the most emblematic and influential Modernist constructions of the 1950s.

In the 1980s, some of New York's biggest corporations created public spaces, and contributed significantly to the quality of crowded Midtown life. One of the first was tiny little **Paley Park**, on East 53rd Street between Madison and Fifth avenues,

owner was the journalist and railway magnate Henry Villard, for whom the houses are named.

Almost 100 years later, when two of the mansions were sold to provide a lavish interior for the Palace, New York historians took exception to the sale. Today, the hotel serves afternoon tea beneath a vaulted ceiling designed by Stanford White.

built on the site where the glamorous Stork Club once resided. Slightly raised above street level, the park is an excellent place to stop off and rest from the outside world. Tables and chairs provide ample seating space, and a water feature provides a calming background noise.

Tech wonders

A short walk away, Philip Johnson's mammoth **Sony Building** ㉟ (originally built for at&t), on Madison Avenue between 55th and 56th streets, includes a public arcade squeezed between shops displaying the latest Sony equipment. Drop into the **Sony Wonder Technology Lab** for interactive exhibits and demonstrations of how all this stuff works (www.sonywondertechlab.com, tel: 212-833 8100; closed Sun–Mon).

At 56th Street and Madison is the former **IBM Building**, a sharply angled tower designed in 1983 by Bauhaus-inspired architect Edward Larrabee Barnes. Its entrance is set back away from the street in a hollowed, cut-out part of the building, the empty space seeming to defy the rest of the structure's enormous height and massive weight. The underground concourse often hosts exhibitions of interest to the public.

Alternatively, head for the atrium, previously a bamboo-filled garden but now stripped of much of its greenery to make way for extra seating or artistic and contemplative sculpture. There's casual dining on the mezzanine, where you can kick back and relax before heading back into the adrenaline-pumping Midtown madness outside.

TIP

There's a feast for the eyes as well as the palate at the fabulous Four Seasons restaurant. The most famous piece is the Picasso tapestry, but other artists have included Miró, Jackson Pollock, and Roy Lichtenstein.

SHOPPING

The time-honored shopping along stretches of Fifth Avenue and 57th Street extends into the surrounding neighborhoods, making this one of the premier neighborhoods in the city, and the country, to swipe a credit card.

Accessories

Crouch & Fitzgerald
400 Madison Avenue (at 48th St)
Tel: 212-755 5888
An excellent, old-style supplier of quality bags and briefcases, with in-house monogramming.
Louis Vuitton
One East 57th Street (at 5th Ave)
Tel: 212-758 8877
www.louisvuitton.com
Everyone recognizes the unmistakable logo and design of these popular

designer handbags and luggage.

Antiques

Newel
425 E. 53rd Street (at 1st Ave)
Tel: 212-758 1970
http://newel.com
A family-owned and operated antiques superstore and art gallery, with six floors of treasures. Saturdays are by appointment only.

Books

Bauman's Rare Books
535 Madison Avenue (at 54th and 55th sts)
Tel: 212-751 0011
www.baumanrarebooks.com
A gallery of over 4,000 rare books, including many signed first editions that will make any collector drool.

Gifts

Extraordinary
247 E. 57th Street (at 2nd Ave)
Tel: 212-223 9151
http://extraordinaryny.com
True to its name, this shop features an extraordinary collection of finely crafted, one-of-a-kind gifts.

Home

Baccarat
625 Madison Avenue (at 59th St)
Tel: 212-826 4100.
www.baccarat-us.com
Exquisite crystal and glassware from French masters.
SONY Style
550 Madison Avenue (at 55th St)
Tel: 212-833 8100
http://store.sony.com

A vast showroom of almost all of the electronics giant's products, this is the store that complements the Sony Wonder Technology Lab.

Shoes

Walter Steiger
417 Park Avenue (at 55th St)
Tel: 212-826 7171
www.waltersteiger.com
A comfortable and stylish place to purchase designer shoes for both men and women.

Toys

FAO Schwartz
767 5th Avenue (at 58th St)
Tel: 212-644 9400
www.fao.com
The world's most famous toy store has lost none of its whimsy after nearly 25 years.

BEST RESTAURANTS, BARS AND CAFÉS

Restaurants

Avra Estiatorio
141 E. 48th St (at Lexington and 3rd aves)
Tel: 212-759 8550
http://avrany.com
L & D Mon–Fri, Br & D Sat–Sun
$$$ ⒀ [p338, E2]
This Greek expense-account fave is especially nice in summer, when you can eat on the terrace. Choose grilled fish, a fresh salad, or platters of Mediterranean dips.

BLT Steak
106 E. 57th St (at Park and Lexington aves)
Tel: 212-752 7470
http://bltsteak.com
L & D Mon–Fri, D only Sat–Sun $$$$ ⒁ [p338, E1]
Chef Laurent Tourondel's flagship (others include BLT Fish, BLT Prime) is a luxury steakhouse that's high on posh style, for when the urge to splurge

for fine food hits.

Café Centro
MetLife Bldg, 200 Park Ave (between 45th St and Vanderbilt Ave)
Tel: 212-818 1222
www.patinagroup.com
Br, L, & D Mon–Fri, D only Sat $$ ⒀ [p338, D2]
Attracts a busy office lunch crowd near Grand Central, but it's great for a light dinner and drinks.

Caffé Linda
145 E. 49th St (at Lexington and 3rd aves)
Tel: 646-497 1818
www.caffelinda.com
L & D Mon–Fri, D only Sat–Sun $$ ⒁ [p338, E2]
This cozy little Italian spot may rely on rustic charm, but the straightforward pastas hit the spot on a cold winter's day.

Chin Chin
216 E. 49th St (at 2nd and 3rd aves)
Tel: 212-888 4555

http://chinchinny.com
L & D daily $$$ ⒂ [p338, E2]
Sleek and modern, this fave serves the diplomats and business-meeting crowd carefully prepared, if pricey, upscale Chinese food.

Le Cirque
One Beacon Court
151 E. 58th St (at Lexington and 3rd aves)
Tel: 212-644 0202
www.lecirque.com
L & D Mon–Fri, D only Sat $$$$ ⒃ [p338, E1]
Legendary restaurant relocated to a drop-dead, sleek location, complete with drive-in, drop-off entrance in the courtyard of the new Bloomberg building. Jackets required.

Dawat
210 E. 58th St (between 3rd and 2nd aves)
Tel: 212-355 7555
http://dawatrestaurant.com

L & D Mon–Sat, D only
Sun $$$ ⒄ [p338, E1]
The cuisine of the Subcontinent goes haute amid elegant surroundings at what is arguably the finest Indian eatery in New York City.

Felidia
243 E. 58th St (at 2nd and 3rd aves)
Tel: 212-758 1479
www.felidia-nyc.com
L & D Mon–Fri, D only Sat–Sun $$$ ⒅ [p338, E1]
Italian-American star chef Lidia Bastianich's crown jewel, with a classic menu of pastas, grilled fish, and roasted meats.

Four Seasons
99 E. 52nd St (between Lexington and Park aves)
Tel: 212-754 9494
www.fourseasonsrestaurant.com
L & D Mon–Fri, D only
Sat $$$$ ⒆ [p338, E1]

Since it opened in 1959, the Four Seasons in the landmark Seagram Building has had a clientele that rivals any Who's Who listing. The decor is priceless and the seasonal classics served in the elegant pool room or the grill room are impeccable.

Gilt
The Palace Hotel
455 Madison Ave (at 50th and 51st sts)
www.giltnewyork.com
212-891 8100
D Tue–Sat **$$$$** 150 [p338, D1]
The celebrated restaurant in the Plaza Hotel has an amazing wine list, elegant surroundings, and lovely tasting menus borrowing from European traditions.

La Mangeoire
1008 2nd Ave (at 53rd and 54th sts)
http://lamangeoire.com

Tel: 212-759 7086
L & D Mon–Fri, D only Sat, Br & D Sun **$$** 151 [p338, E2]
Superbly reliable, in the same location for over 30 years, this traditional French restaurant has the friendly feel of a country inn, but in the heart of NY. Great value.

The Palm
837 2nd Ave (between 44th and 45th sts)
www.thepalm.com
Tel: 212-687 2953 plus branches
L & D Mon–Fri, D only Sat **$$$$** 152 [p338, E2]
Huge steaks and lobsters in a narrow space filled with regulars.

Le Périgord
405 E. 52nd St (east of 1st Ave)
www.leperigord.com
Tel: 212-755 6244
L & D Mon–Fri, D only Sat–Sun **$$$$** 153 [p338, E2]
French classic serving a well-heeled Sutton Place clientele for years.

Pershing Square
90 E. 42nd St (at Park Ave)
www.pershingsquare.com
Tel: 212-286 9600
B, L, & D daily **$$$** 154 [p338, D2]
A step away from Grand Central, with crowd-pleasing American fare.

P.J. Clarke's
915 3rd Ave (at 55th St)
http://pjclarkes.com
Tel: 212-317 1616
L & D daily **$$** 155 [p338, E1]
Many think Clarke's has the best hamburgers on the East Side. Lately the historic saloon, dating from the late 1800s and popular in Sinatra's time, has enjoyed a renaissance. A bonus: the kitchen is open until 3am.

Rosa Mexicano
1063 1st Ave (at 58th St)

Tel: 212-753 7407
http://rosamexicano.com
D daily **$$$** [off map]
The Rosa is famous for tableside guacamole, as well as an excellent and imaginative modern Mexican menu.

San Martin
143 E. 49th St (at Lexington and 3rd aves)
www.sanmartinrestaurantny.com
Tel: 212-832 0888
L & D daily **$$$** 156 [p338, E2]
Tasty Italian cuisine in a warm, attractive room.

Shun Lee Palace
155 E. 55th St (at Lexington and 3rd aves)
http://shunleepalace.lanteck.net
Tel: 212-371 8844
L & D daily **$$$** 157 [p338, E2]
A classic Chinese dining room. A bit more expensive than most, but also better than most.

Smith & Wollensky
797 3rd Ave (at 49th St)
http://smithandwollensky.com
Tel: 212-753 1530
L & D daily **$$$** 158 [p338, E2]
This NY institution is usually packed with a boisterous crowd of stockbrokers and Midtown executives. For a less expensive food option, try the adjacent Wollensky's Grill.

Tao
42 E. 58th St (at Madison and Park aves)
www.taorestaurant.com
Tel: 212-888 2288
L & D Mon–Fri, D only Sat–Sun **$$$** 159 [p338, E1]
A gigantically bold spot that features a towering Buddha in the main dining room. Fight past a noisy bar scene for the privilege of ordering from the delectable but pricey pan-Asian menu.

Prices for a three-course dinner per person with half a bottle of wine:

$ = under $20
$$ = $20–$45
$$$ = $45–$60
$$$$ = over $60

Water Club
East River (at 30th St)
www.thewaterclub.com
Tel: 212-683 3333
L & D Tue–Sat, Br & D Sun **$$$** 160 [p338, D4]
A floating restaurant on the East River with good fish and great views: booking essential. The Crow's Nest up above is less pricey (May–Sept only), as is the Sunday brunch.

Bars and Cafes

Campbell Apartment
Grand Central Terminal 38 [p338, D2]
An elegant hideaway popular with the after-work, before-train crowd or for an after-dinner drink.

Le Colonial
149 E. 57th St (between Lexington and 3rd aves) 39 [p338, E1]
A romantic meeting spot, with Vietnamese food.

Juan Valdez Café
140 E. 57th St 40 [p338, E1]
Colombian coffee and great pastries. Good before or after shopping.

Monkey Bar
Hotel Elysée (between Madison and Park aves) 41 [p338, D1]
Noisy but stylish, thanks to Graydon Carter of Vanity Fair fame. Think banana daiquiris.

Sakagura
211 E. 43rd St (at 2nd and 3rd aves) 42 [p338, D3]
One of the finest selections of sake in the city, with small bites to match.

LEFT: the pool room at the Four Seasons.
ABOVE: P.G. Clarke's.

UPPER EAST SIDE

Opulence is in the air here. Old-money New Yorkers glide from Millionaires' Row to Museum Mile before a session of retail therapy at Barneys or Bloomies

T he Upper East Side's romance with wealth began in the late 1800s, when the Four Hundred – so called because a social arbiter decreed that in all of New York there were only 400 families that mattered – moved into Fifth Avenue, in order to cultivate roots alongside Central Park.

The homes they built were the most luxurious the city had seen – mansions and townhouses furnished like European palaces and filled with priceless art. Since then, the Carnegies, the Fricks, and the Astors have moved to greener pastures, but the Upper East Side has never lost its taste for the good life, and even the areas east of Lexington Avenue, formerly fairly affordable, are now highly desirable.

An air of wealth

The scent of wealth is, unsurprisingly, most intoxicating on the stretch of **Fifth Avenue** ❶ facing the park, known to old-time New Yorkers as **Millionaires' Row**. At the corner of 60th Street is J.P. Morgan's stately **Metropolitan Club** ❷, founded in 1892 after one of the financier's nouveau riche buddies was denied membership of the Union Club. The

enormous **Temple Emanu-El** ❸ cuts a brooding figure at the corner of 65th Street, where 2,500 worshippers can gather under its soaring roof, making this cavernous, echoing temple one of the largest reform synagogues in the world.

In the East 70s are a number of splendid old-style mansions. These include the **Harkness House** (1 East 75th Street), home to the Commonwealth Fund; the chateau-style **James B. Duke House** (1 East 78th Street), which houses the New

Main Attractions
FRICK COLLECTION
METROPOLITAN MUSEUM OF ART
GUGGENHEIM MUSEUM
COOPER-HEWITT NATIONAL DESIGN MUSEUM
JEWISH MUSEUM
WHITNEY MUSEUM OF AMERICAN ART
PARK AVENUE
ROOSEVELT ISLAND

Maps and Listings
MAP, PAGE 214
SHOPPING, PAGE 221
RESTAURANTS, PAGE 222
ACCOMMODATIONS, PAGE 315

LEFT: the Metropolitan Museum of Art.
RIGHT: the view over the Upper East Side and Central Park.

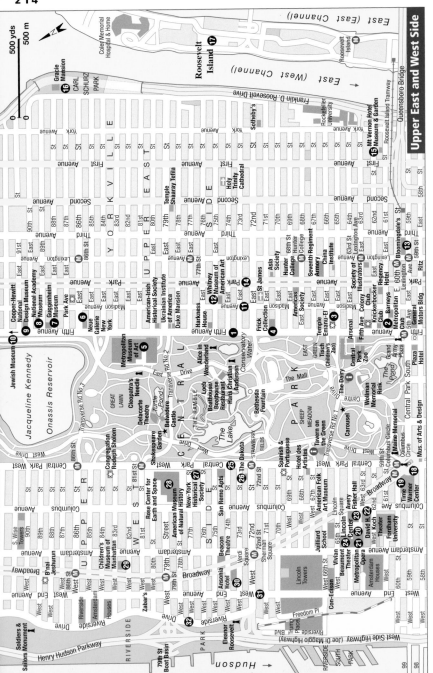

Upper East and West Side

500 yds
500 m
0
0

Hudson

RIVERSIDE SOUTH

RIVERSIDE PARK

Henry Hudson Parkway

Soldiers & Sailors Monument

79th St Boat Basin

Eleanor Roosevelt

West Side Highway (Joe di Maggio Hwy)

West End Avenue

Riverside Drive

Amsterdam Houses

Con-Edison

Freedom Pl

Lincoln Towers

Zabar's

Ansonia Hotel

30
31
32

Verdi

Sherman Square

Beacon Theatre

Fordham University

Juilliard School

Amsterdam Avenue

Columbus Avenue

Broadway

Vivian Beaumont Theater
Metropolitan Opera
David H. Koch Theater
Avery Fisher Hall
Lincoln Center

21 20
22
23

Fordham University

B'nai Jeshurun

S. Wise Towers

Children's Museum of Manhattan
26

American Museum of Natural History
Rose Center for Earth and Space
28

New-York Historical Society
27

San Remo Apts
25

The Dakota
20

Hotel des Artistes

Spanish & Portuguese

Tavern on the Green

American Folk Art Museum

CENTRAL PARK WEST

UPPER WEST SIDE

Congregation Rodeph Sholom

Shakespeare Garden

Belvedere Castle
Delacorte Theatre

Turtle Pond

GREAT LAWN

THE RAMBLE

The Lake

STRAWBERRY FIELDS

Loeb Boathouse
Boathouse Restaurant

Hans Christian Andersen

Bethesda Fountain

SHEEP MEADOW

The Mall

Carousel

Wollman Memorial Rink

Maine Memorial

Columbus Circle

Mus. of Arts & Design
18

Time Warner Center
19

Central Park West

Central Park South

Plaza Hotel

The Dairy

Central Park Zoo

GREEN Tisch (Children's Zoo)

The Pond

Arsenal

Grand Army Plaza

General Motors Bldg

Ritz

Fifth Ave
Metropolitan Club
Knickerbocker Club
Colony Club

Barneys
Regency Hotel

Lexington Ave

Bloomingdale's
13

CENTRAL PARK

Alice in Wonderland

Conservatory Water

Cleopatra's Needle

Transverse Rd No 2

East Drive

Transverse Rd No 3

West Drive

Metropolitan Museum of Art
5

Jacqueline Kennedy Onassis Reservoir

Jewish Museum
10

Cooper-Hewitt National Design Museum
9

National Academy Museum
8

Guggenheim Museum
7

Neue Galerie New York
6

Harkness House

American-Irish Historical Society
Ukrainian Institute of America
Duke Mansion

Frick Collection
4

Whitney Museum of American Art
12

Asia Society
11

St James
14

Seventh Regiment Armory

Hunter College
Hunter College
M College

China Institute

Society of Illustrators

Temple Emanu-El
3

UPPER EAST SIDE

Holy Trinity Cathedral

Temple Shaaray Tefila

YORKVILLE

Fifth Avenue

Madison Avenue

Park Avenue

Lexington Avenue

Third Avenue

Second Avenue

First Avenue

York Avenue

Gracie Mansion
16

CARL SCHURZ PARK

Franklin D. Roosevelt Drive

Sotheby's

Rockefeller University

Roosevelt Island Tramway

Mt Vernon Hotel Museum & Garden
15

Queensboro Bridge

Roosevelt Island
17

Coler Memorial Hospital & Home

East (East Channel)

East (West Channel)

1
2

York University Institute of Fine Arts; and the **Payne Whitney House** (972 Fifth Avenue), a fabulous Renaissance-style palazzo that now serves as the cultural center of the French Embassy.

International relations are the order of the day on the Upper East Side: the Fletcher-Sinclair mansion at 79th and Fifth is the **Ukrainian Institute**, with the **American-Irish Historical Society** farther up at No. 991 (the corner of 80th Street). Between 68th and 69th streets, the classic McKim, Mead, & White

building at 680 Park Avenue is now home to the **Americas Society**, while the Georgian-style house at No. 686 is the **Italian Cultural Institute**.

Frick Collection ❹

Address: 1 E. 70th St (at 5th and Madison aves), www.frick.org
Telephone: 212-288 0700
Opening Hours: Tue–Sat 10am–6pm, Sun 11am–5pm
Entrance Fee: charge
Subway: 68th St/Hunter College

At the corner of Fifth Avenue and 70th Street, this grand art collection is showcased in the former home of steel magnate Henry Clay Frick, whose passion for art was surpassed only by his ruthlessness in business. It consists mostly of works by great European masters from the 16th to the 19th century – Vermeer, Velázquez, Goya, Constable, and more. The gallery is also one of the city's more successful marriages between art and setting, with a tranquil garden court, and soft furnishings to luxuriate in when art-lovers' feet are tired from standing in front of the paintings. The Frick's annual

LEFT: the Garden Court at the heart of the Frick mansion.
BELOW: the Frick mansion.

concert season showcases young classical musicians (tickets must be booked in advance).

MUSEUM MILE

Between 82nd and 104th streets are nine cultural treasures so lavish that this stretch of Fifth Avenue has become known as **Museum Mile** (see page 228).

Metropolitan Museum of Art ❺

Address: 1000 Fifth Ave (at 81st and 82nd sts), www.metmuseum.org
Telephone: 212-535 7710
Opening Hours: Tue–Thur, Sun 9.30am–5.30pm, Fri, Sat 9.30am–9pm
Entrance Fee: charge (recommended)
Subway: 86th St

Opened on its present site in 1880, the Met is a sprawling Gothic behemoth with the largest art collection in the US. The permanent collection is truly impressive, and the newer galleries will show off its exhibits to even better advantage (see page 224).

At 86th Street is the **Neue Galerie New York ❻** (1048 Fifth Avenue,

ABOVE: the *Comtesse d'Haussonville*, by Ingres, from the Frick.
BELOW: the impressive entrance hall of the Metropolitan Museum of Art.

www.neuegalerie.org, tel: 212-628 6200; Thur–Mon 11am–6pm; charge), with Austrian and German art, including pieces by Gustav Klimt. The museum recently started a First Fridays program – they are now open with free admission on the first Friday of each month from 6–8pm. They also have a fantastic book store and a design shop with jewelry, flatware, and stunning items for the home.

Guggenheim Museum ❼

Address: 1071 Fifth Ave (at 89th St), www.guggenheim.org
Telephone: 212-423 3500
Opening Hours: Mon–Wed and Fri, Sun 10am–5.45pm, Sat 10am–7.45pm; closed Thur
Entrance Fee: charge, pay what you wish Sat 5.45pm–7.45pm
Subway: 86th St

Founded in 1937, the Solomon R. Guggenheim Museum – its full name – was relatively new among the city's leading art repositories, but this was no disadvantage. Newcomer though it was, the Guggenheim shared top billing on the cultural marquee thanks largely to Frank

Lloyd Wright's fabulous building, which opened in 1959 to mixed critical reviews but much New York buzz.

The treasures inside are based on Solomon and Peggy Guggenheim's personal collections, showcasing Expressionism, Cubism, and the general trend toward abstraction. Artists given due attention include Klee and Kandinsky, Mondrian and Modigliani, Picasso of course, and later painters like Jackson Pollock and Roy Lichtenstein. Visiting exhibits have run the gamut from the Spanish masters to 20th-century motorcycle design. The Guggenheim really is a New York masterpiece, and one museum not to miss.

Also on Museum Mile at 89th Street is the **National Academy Museum and School of Fine Arts** ❽ (1083 Fifth Avenue, www.nationalacademy.org, tel: 212-369 4880; Wed–Sun 11am–6pm; charge), with a collection of over 5,000 19th–21st-century American artworks. Next comes the **Cooper-Hewitt National Design Museum** ❾ (2 East 91st Street at Fifth Ave, www.cooper-hewitt.org, tel: 212-849 8400) in the landmark Andrew Carnegie mansion. The exhibits, with displays on the history and process of design and an onsite master's program for students, are closed for renovation until 2013, but you can still visit the mansion's marvelous garden.

Jewish Museum ❿

Address: 1109 Fifth Ave (at 92nd St), www.jewishmuseum.org
Telephone: 212-423 3200
Opening Hours: Fri–Tue 11am–5.45pm, Thur 11am–8pm, closes Fri at 4pm in winter
Entrance Fee: charge
Subway: 96th St

One of the world's largest centers of Jewish culture contains a vast collection of historical and contemporary Jewish art, as well as the National Jewish Archive of Broadcasting. In observance of the Sabbath the museum is free on Saturdays, and all electronic exhibits are closed.

At the very top of the "Mile" is the **Museum of the City of New York** at 103rd Street and **El Museo del Barrio** at 104th Street, the city's museum of Latino and Caribbean culture.

ABOVE: the National Academy Museum and School of Fine Arts.
BELOW: the Guggenheim.

EAT

A special place to stop for coffee and a snack on Museum Mile is the Neue Galerie's Café Sabarsky – an evocation of the great cafes of pre-1914 Vienna, with Art Nouveau decor and sinful pastries.

BELOW: runners crossing the 59th street Queensboro Bridge during the New york City Marathon.

EAST SIDE AMBIENCE

Geographically, Fifth Avenue is only one block away from **Madison Avenue** ⑪, but in spirit they're worlds apart. Wave goodbye to the prim and proper salons of the Four Hundred, because Madison Avenue is the land of ritz and glitz – a slick marketplace custom-crafted for the hyperactive, top-of-the-line discriminating consumer. It's a little bit mellower in the pleasant low-90s neighborhood of **Carnegie Hill** than it is in the 60s, but if you cross over from the top of Museum Mile you'll still find plenty of upscale boutiques, gourmet delicatessens, little chi-chi stores, and art galleries worth exploring.

Whitney Museum of American Art ⑫

Address: 945 Madison Ave (at 75th St), www.whitney.org
Telephone: 212-570 3676
Opening Hours: Wed, Thur, Sat, Sun 11am–6pm, Fri 1–9pm
Entrance Fee: charge; pay what you wish Fri 6–9pm
Subway: 77th St

In addition to displaying challenging American art, Marcel Breuer's angular, cantilevered structure is a work of art in its own right, second only to the Guggenheim among the Upper East Side's most striking architectural expressions.

The Whitney collection was founded in 1930 by Gertrude Vanderbilt Whitney, whose tastes were for American Realists like Edward Hopper and George Bellows. Since then the museum's policy has been to acquire pieces that represent the full range of 20th-century American art, with works by Georgia O'Keeffe, Willem de Kooning, Jackson Pollock, and Jasper Johns. Every other year it mounts the Whitney Biennial, a survey of provocative new American art. The space lends itself well to innovative installation art that is bound to shock, inspire, or befuddle you. The Whitney is also planning a Meatpacking District location in the future.

Barneys and Bloomies

From the Whitney to 59th Street, Madison is a bacchanalian feast of conspicuous consumption. The

New York Road Runners

The city's biggest running club, with more than 40,000 members, has its office at 9 East 91st Street, just off Fifth Avenue. Its signature event, sponsored by ING, is the New York Marathon on the first Sunday in November, but that's just one of dozens of races, from 5km to half-marathon distance, it organizes throughout the year. One of the club's most unusual races is September's "Fifth Avenue Mile," which starts from the Met Museum. Some of the world's best runners use the events for training, but they're also open to the public. Even if your jogging speed isn't much faster than a waddle, you can still sign up for a race at www.nyrr.org. It's a fantastic way to meet New Yorkers, to see Central Park and to tour some of the boroughs.

names on the storefronts are a roster of the fashion elite: Ralph Lauren, Yves Saint Laurent, Kenzo, Giorgio Armani, Prada, Calvin Klein.

Most of these megastar stores are more for browsing than serious buying, except for those accompanied by a huge bankroll. A quintessentially New York shopping scene is **Barneys New York** on 61st Street, one of the movers and shakers of Manhattan's retail world. In addition to the best designs, there's a chic lower-level restaurant in which weary wallet-wielders can refresh and revive. Barneys CO-OP, Barneys's smaller sister store, is currently springing up in carefully chosen locations around the city.

Serious shoppers may head straight for one of the city's retail queens: **Bloomingdale's** ⑬ on 59th Street – an institution that dyed-in-the-wool New Yorkers could not live without. Bloomies is almost always crowded – oppressively so at holiday or sale times – but if you only go to one big store, this should be it. Bloomingdale's is so popular, there's now a branch in SoHo. As a reward for the kids afterwards, make a stop at **Dylan's Candy Bar**, a sweet dream come true just

behind Bloomie's, owned by Ralph Lauren's daughter, Dylan.

Park Avenue style

Skipping east to **Park Avenue** ⑭, the scene changes dramatically. Compared to the flashy indulgence of Madison Avenue, Park seems like a highly trafficked Parisian boulevard. A highlight is the **Regency Hotel**, a favorite for power breakfasts among big-wheel media types, and where the elegant library bar serves a jolly decent afternoon tea. Another is the **Colony Club** at 62nd Street, which has a stately red-brick facade, appropriate to the stately society women who make up its members' list.

There are several cultural sites: the museum at the **Society of Illustrators** (128 East 63rd Street between Park and Lexington aves, www.societyillustrators.org, tel: 212-838 2560; Tue 10am–8pm, Wed–Fri 10am–5pm, Sat noon–4pm; free) and the **China Institute** (125 East 65th Street, www.chinainstitute.org, tel: 212-744 8181; daily 10am–5pm, and until 8pm on Tue and Thur; charge). Their exhibitions cover, respectively, the history of illustration and Chinese art.

ABOVE: Bloomingdale's.
BELOW: a Dylan's Candy Bar mural made from jelly beans.

ABOVE: the Roosevelt Island Tram crosses over the East River.
BELOW: the distinctive Seventh Regiment Armory.

Continuing north, it's near-impossible to miss the **Seventh Regiment Armory** at Park and 66th. Built in the 1870s to resemble a medieval castle, the Armory now serves as an exhibition hall for art shows.

At 70th Street, the **Asia Society** (725 Park Ave, http://asiasociety.org, tel: 212-288 6400; Tue–Sun 11am–6pm, until 9pm Fri, except in summer; charge) houses the Rockefellers' collection of Asian art. There are also performances, movies, and other events related to Asian culture.

Yorkville and farther east

East of Park Avenue, the Upper East Side slips in the prestige department, but makes up for it with a dash of self-indulgence. Once dominated by Eastern European immigrants, much of the area is now gentrified, but remnants of the old German and Czech quarters survive in **Yorkville**, between 79th and 98th streets.

Between First and York avenues, the **Mount Vernon Hotel Museum and Garden**  (421 East 61st Street,

www.mvhm.org, tel: 212-838 6878; Tue–Sun 11am–4pm; charge) is one of the few 18th-century buildings still standing proud in Manhattan. Furnished with period antiques, it's a marvel of survival, as it nestles under the Queensboro Bridge. **Sotheby's**,

TIP

Roosevelt Island's subway station is preferred by commuters, but the most enjoyable way to get there is on the Roosevelt Island Tramway, which leaves from the corner of Second Ave and 60th St. On the way, you get a wonderful view of all the great towers of the Upper East Side.

the high-stakes auction house, is 10 blocks away, at York Avenue and 72nd Street.

At 88th Street and East End Avenue, within **Carl Schurz Park**, is **Gracie Mansion** ⑯, another survivor from the 18th century and the official residence of mayors of New York, though Mayor Bloomberg chose not to hang his hat here. It was built by Scots-born Archibald Gracie as a summer home, and was first used in 1942 by Mayor Fiorello LaGuardia. Tours are usually held on Wednesdays and must be reserved (www.nyc.gov/html/om/html/gracie. html, tel: 212-570 4751).

Hitch a ride on the **Roosevelt Island Tramway** at Second Avenue and 60th Street: the views are unique and lovely, especially at sunset.

ROOSEVELT ISLAND ⑰

Across the water by cable-supported tram, Roosevelt Island is a 147-acre (60-hectare) respite from urban living. This tiny (2-mile/3km), tranquil, cigar-shaped island contains one main street, one church, one supermarket, a few restaurants, and one of the city's more recent subway extensions.

This "annexation" made Roosevelt a highly desirable residential neighborhood – witness the sleek apartments of **Manhattan Park**. Amenities include an indoor pool, playgrounds, and five small parks. From the walkways edging the shoreline there are panoramic views of the East Side, and at the north end you can admire a stone lighthouse from 1872. Madison Avenue seems a long way away.

ABOVE: kids on a cold day in Carl Schurz Park.

SHOPPING

It's no surprise that a neighborhood traditionally known for its wealth is full of shops that cater to the wealthy. While there's no shortage of high-end megastores, as covered in the previous two chapters, there is also an eclectic mix of smaller choices.

Beauty

Bond No. 9
680 Madison Avenue (at 61st St) and 897 Madison Ave (at 73rd St)
Tel: 212-794 4480 and 212-838 2780
www.bondno9.com
So much more fun than the perfume counters at the department stores, these scent specialists will let you sample in comfortable and stylish surroundings.
Ricky's
1425 2nd Ave (at 74th St)

Tel: 212-988 2291
www.rickysnyc.com
Part of a citywide chain, this enormous collection of beauty products has fantastic selections and bargains, and four locations on the Upper East Side.

Clothing

Agnès B
1063 Madison Avenue (at 80th and 81st sts)
Tel: 212-570 9333
http://usa.agnesb.com
Fashionable casualwear that is expensive, but won't make you faint.
BCBG Max Azria
770 Madison Avenue (at 66th St) and 1290 Third Avenue (at 74th St)
Tel: 212-717 4225 and 212-991 2056
http://bcbgmaxazriagroup.com
Two outlets of the French chain that is

"bon chic, bon genre." In other words, it's all good.
DKNY
655 Madison Avenue (at 60th St)
Tel: 212-223 3569
www.dkny.com
Donna Karan's first New York store is still the place to browse her latest lines.
INA
208 E 73rd Street (at 2nd and 3rd aves)
Tel: 212-249 0014
www.inanyc.com
A designer consignment store with locations throughout the city. The Uptown version specializes in women's apparel.

Gifts

Dempsey & Carroll
1049 Lexington Avenue (at 74th and 75th sts)
Tel: 212-570 4800
www.dempseyandcarroll.com
Very expensive and very

beautiful stationery, for those who still appreciate the art of letter writing.

Shoes

Camper
635 Madison Avenue (at 59th St)
Tel: 212-339 8675
www.camper.com
In Europe, Camper is synonymous with hip, comfortable, affordable shoes. This is its New York flagship store.

Toys

Jan's Hobby Shop
1435 Lexington Avenue (at 94th St)
Tel: 212-987 4765
For the kid (or adult) who loves models, remote-control vehicles, and kits that reward the patient tinkerer. Grab a model boat and cast it off on the boat pond in Central Park.

BEST RESTAURANTS, BARS AND CAFÉS

Restaurants

L'Absinthe
227 E. 67th St (at 2nd and 3rd aves)
Tel: 212-794 4950
www.labsinthe.com
L & D daily, D only Sat–Sun July–Aug $$$ 161 [p336, D4]
The etched mirrors, polished brass, and French waiters in white aprons are as authentic as the classic brasserie fare.

Beyoglu
1431 3rd Ave (at 80th and 81st sts)
Tel: 212-650 0850
L & D daily $$ 162 [p336, D2]
This casual Turkish eatery serves a meze-style menu including tasty kebabs and dips like roe-studded tarama and garlicky hummus.

Café Sabarsky
1048 5th Ave (at 86th St)
Tel: 212-288 0665
www.cafesabarsky.com
B, L, & D Wed–Mon $$$ 163 [p336, D1]
This Viennese-style restaurant's Museum Mile location makes it handy. Have eggs at brunch; *spätzle* and goulash for lunch and dinner.

Candle 79
154 E. 79th St (at Lexington and 3rd aves)
Tel: 212-537 7179
www.candle79.com
L & D Mon–Fri, Br & D Sat–Sun $$$ 164 [p336, D2]
There are plenty of places to "veg out" in New York, but here's one that is elegant and fits the stylish neighborhood, with sophisticated vegetarian and vegan dishes featuring great organic ingredients.

Daniel
60 E. 65th St (at Park Ave)
Tel: 212-288 0033
www.danielnyc.com
D Mon–Sat $$$$ 165 [p336, C4]
A great chef, Daniel Boulud, presides over this most expensive food kingdom, but gourmets will gladly spend for the unique quality and service he delivers.

Demarchelier
50 E. 86th St (at Madison Ave)
Tel: 212-249 6300
www.demarchelierrestaurant.com
L & D daily $$$ 166 [p336, D1]
Upper East Side bistro with a sense of style and a moderately priced all-day prix-fixe menu.

E.J.'s Luncheonette
1271 3rd Ave (at 73rd St)
Tel: 212-472 0600
http://ejsluncheonette.com
B, L, & D daily $ 167 [p336, D3]
Anybody longing for a 1950s-style chrome interior will feel they've come home here. Cash only is accepted.

Fig & Olive
808 Lexington Ave (at 62nd and 63rd sts)
Tel: 212-207 4555
www.figandolive.com
L & D Mon–Fri, Br & D Sat–Sun $$$ 168 [p336, C4]
Conveniently located for shopping, with a Mediterranean menu, and a raw bar, too.

Girasole
151 E. 82nd St (at Lexington and 3rd aves)
Tel: 212-772 6690
http://girasolerestaurantnyc.com
L & D daily $$$$ 169 [p336, D2]
Feel like a pampered Upper East Side regular at this long-established Italian comfort zone.

Heidelberg
1648 2nd Ave (at 85th and 86th sts)
Tel: 212-628 2332
www.heidelbergrestaurant.com
L & D Mon–Sat, Br & D Sun $$ 170 [p336, E2]

Yorkville's last tribute to Germantown. The *wiener schnitzel* and dumplings are the real thing for lovers of tasty, traditional German fare.

Hospoda
321 E. 73rd St (at 1st and 2nd aves)
Tel: 212-861 1038
www.hospodanyc.com
D Mon–Sat **$$$** 171 [p336, D3]
The latest in the gastropub world has a Bohemian twist. Czech beer and Austrian wine is paired with sumptuous Eastern Europe dishes.

JoJo
160 E. 64th St (at Lexington and 3rd aves)
Tel: 212-223 5656
http://jean-georges.com
L & D Mon–Fri, Br & D Sat–Sun **$$$$** 172 [p336, C4]
The rich emerald and burgundy colors, luxurious fabrics, and warm-hued tiles are as inviting as the menu. One of Manhattan's best French food extravaganzas.

Kings' Carriage House
251 E. 82nd St (at 2nd and 3rd aves)
Tel: 212-734 5490
www.kingscarriagehouse.com
L & D Mon–Sat, Br & D Sun **$$$** 173 [p336, E2]
Cozy two-story Colonial carriage house turned into a restaurant with pre-arranged seating. A different dining experience.

Maya
1191 1st Ave (at 64th and 65th sts)
Tel: 212-585 1818
www.richardsandoval.com
D daily **$$$** 174 [p336, D4]
Acapulco native Richard Sandoval brings his upscale Mexican classics to this bright and colorful dining room.

Nica
354 E. 84th St (at 1st and 2nd aves)
Tel: 212-472 5040
D daily **$$$** 175 [p336, E2]
This cozy place serves Sicilian classics ranging from spaghetti carbonara to braised lamb shank and grilled veal chops.

Pascalou
1308 Madison Ave (at 92nd and 93rd sts)
Tel: 212-534 7522
L & D daily **$$** 176 [p336, D1]
Delicious and excellent value for this expensive area, especially the prix-fixe early dinner.

Pio Pio
1746 1st Ave (at 90th and 91st sts)
Tel: 212-426 5800
www.piopio.com
L & D daily **$** 177 [p336, E1]
For fall-off-the-bone rotisserie chicken done the Peruvian way, there is nowhere better in town than this mini-chain with four locations in Manhattan. Cash only, unless you use American Express.

Sfoglia
135 E. 92nd St (at Lexington Ave)
Tel: 212-831 1402
www.sfogliarestaurant.com
L & D Tue–Sat, D only Sun–Mon **$$$** 178 [p336, E1]
Rustic but hugely popular little northern Italian that serves up such delectable dishes as *fusilli* in *vin santo* cream sauce. Book long in advance for dinner, or go for lunch instead.

Sushi of Gari
402 E. 78th St (at 1st Ave)
Tel: 212-517 5340
www.sushiofgari.com
D daily **$$$** 179 [p336, E3]

The fish at this small Japanese restaurant is as fresh as can be, and the preparations continue to amaze fans.

Il Vagabondo
351 E. 62nd St (at 1st and 2nd aves)
Tel: 212-832 9221
www.ilvagabondo.com
L & D Mon–Fri, D only Sat–Sun **$$$** 180 [p336, D4]
Complete with its own indoor *bocce* (Italian-style bowls) court, not to mention more than decent Italian food.

Vivolo
140 E. 74th St (at Park and Lexington aves)
Tel: 212-737 3533
www.vivolonyc.com
L & D Mon–Sat **$$$** 181 [p336, D3]
Charming Italian in an 1875 townhouse that's been serving East Siders for years in a hard-to-please district.

Bars and Cafes

Café Carlyle
35 E. 76th St 43 [p336, D2]

Prices for a three-course dinner per person with half a bottle of wine:
$ = under $20
$$ = $20–$45
$$$ = $45–$60
$$$$ = over $60

Café Carlyle showcases classic New York style with cabaret entertainment and big band music. Woody Allen occasionally shows up to play the clarinet.

Sant Ambroeus
1000 Madison Ave (at 77th and 78th sts) 44 [p336, D2]
Elegant espressos to marzipan and more – all is heavenly here.

Serendipity 3
225 E. 60th St, around the corner from Bloomies 45 [p336, C/D4]
Dessert delirium is the specialty here, but light fare for lunch and dinner is also available, and the shop up front is good for kids and grans alike.

LEFT: Café Sabarsky. **RIGHT:** lamb chop at Daniel.

THE METROPOLITAN MUSEUM

The *grande dame* of American museums displays many of the oldest treasures and most important moments in the history of art

The Metropolitan Museum of Art is a palatial gallery with a collection of paintings, sculpture, drawings, furnishings, and decorative arts spanning 10,000 years of human creativity. Featuring exemplary works from major European artists such as Bruegel the Elder to Botticelli and from Van Gogh to Velázquez and Vermeer, nearly every civilization is represented. Exhibits feature art objects from Archeulian flints found in Egypt dating to the Lower Paleolithic period (300,000–75,000 BC), right up to 21st-century designs from couturier Alexander McQueen.

The Met has five cafes and bars, ranging from the airy cafeteria to the more formal Petrie Court Café, which offers waiter service. In the summer and fall, you can grab a Martini or some wine and a sandwich on the roof garden, where views of Central Park are unsurpassed. The museum's online gallery has excellent study resources, an art timeline, and podcasts.

ABOVE: the Metropolitan moved to its Fifth Avenue location in 1880, although the facade was remodeled in 1926. In total, the Met houses a collection of more than 2 million pieces.

BELOW: the Met's collection began in 1870, and one of Central Park's architects, Calvert Vaux, along with Jacob Wrey Mold, designed the museum's first permanent home. The Cloisters, a branch dedicated to medieval art, is in Fort Tryon Park.

ABOVE: the Metropolitan has an amazing collection of textiles, including this tunic, which depicts two serpents confronting each other.

The Essentials

Address: 1000 Fifth Avenue at 82nd Street; www.metmuseum.org
Tel: 212-535 7710
Opening Hours: Tue–Thur and Sun 9.30am–5.30pm, Fri, Sat 9.30am–9pm
Entrance Fee: charge (recommended)
Subway: 86th St

GREEK AND ROMAN GALLERIES

The Greek and Roman galleries opened in 2007 and were built specifically to house and display the Metropolitan's art c.900 BC to the early 4th century ad. The collection is a monumental showcase that describes the parallel developments of Greek art in the Hellenistic period and the arts of southern Italy and Etruria, culminating in the rich and varied world of the Roman Empire.

The museum's Greek and Roman pieces have not been seen together since 1949. Many of the thousands of works that are now displayed in the spacious galleries have not been on view to the public since their creation, which was up to 3,000 years ago. The galleries bring under one roof the very foundations of Western artistic civilization.

ABOVE: the museum has a large collection of Cycladic art, including this female marble figure, which dates from c.2500 BC and is attributed to the Bastis Master.

BELOW: this 18th-century chest of drawers was made in Philadelphia, and is part of the Metropolitan's American Decorative Arts collection.

RIGHT: the Iris and B. Gerald Cantor Roof Garden provides a summertime setting for large sculptures, with Central Park and the Upper West Side as backdrops.

RIGHT: the André Mertens Galleries display the Metropolitan's handsome collection of musical instruments, which includes early flutes, Baroque organs, and electric guitars, in addition to this fine Flemish virginal, which dates from the 16th century.

ABOVE: *Young Woman with a Water Jug*, 1660, was painted by the Dutch Master, Johannes Vermeer.

ABOVE: *Madame X* (Madame Pierre Gautreau), by John Singer Sargent, painted in 1883–4.

ABOVE: among the works of artists on display in the American Paintings and Sculpture Gallery is *The Lighthouse at Two Lights*, by Edward Hopper, 1929.

RIGHT: the Met's rich decorative arts collections include medieval works in stained glass, lamps from Tiffany, and wall hangings from William Morris of the English Arts and Crafts movement.

Metropolitan Museum of Art

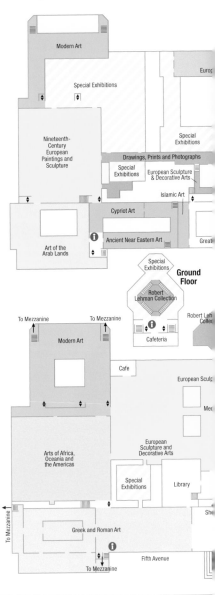

Modern Art

Special Exhibitions

Europ

Nineteenth-Century European Paintings and Sculpture

Special Exhibitions

Special Exhibitions

Drawings, Prints and Photographs

European Sculpture & Decorative Arts

Islamic Art

Cypriot Art

Art of the Arab Lands

Ancient Near Eastern Art

Great

Special Exhibitions

Ground Floor

Robert Lehman Collection

To Mezzanine

To Mezzanine

Robert Leh Collec

Modern Art

Cafeteria

Cafe

European Sculp

Med

European Sculpture and Decorative Arts

Arts of Africa, Oceania and the Americas

Special Exhibitions

Library

To Mezzanine

She

Greek and Roman Art

Fifth Avenue

To Mezzanine

Information
Elevator
Escalator

Second Floor

To third floor
The American Wing

ings

To third floor

Musical Instruments

uropean Paintings

Japanese Art

Shop

To third floor

Chinese Art   Chinese Art

Asian Art | Arts of Korea | Arts of Korea   Asian Art

ny

South Asian Art

ue

Southeast Asian Art

To third floor

To third floor   To third floor

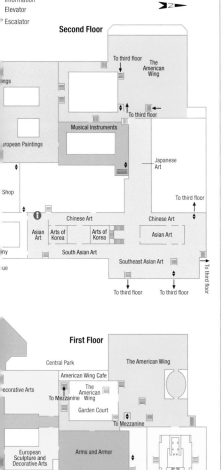

First Floor

Central Park

The American Wing

American Wing Cafe

ecorative Arts

The American Wing
To Mezzanine

Garden Court

To Mezzanine

European Sculpture and Decorative Arts

Arms and Armor

Temple of Dendur

Shop

Grace Rainey Rodgers Auditorium

Egyptian Art

Egyptian Art

Fifth Avenue

nce

ABOVE: *The Great Wave at Kanagawa*, by Katsushika Hokusai, is a paper print made between 1830 and 1832. The artist said of this period in his life, "Nothing I did before the age of 70 was worthy of attention."

ABOVE: a relief of Nebhepetre Mentuhotep II from the Egyptian Middle Kingdom, Dynasty 11, created between 2051–2000 BC. Painted limestone.

LEFT: the Met's collection of Islamic arts includes Anatolian, Ottoman, and Turkoman rugs, with decorative as well as devotional pieces on display. After eight years of construction, the museum will open a new 19,000-sq-ft (1,765-sq-meter) gallery for the collection in late 2011.

MUSEUM MILE

Some of America's finest cultural treasures are housed in fabulous museums that line the east side of Central Park

Museum Mile is a cultural parade of some of the US's finest examples of art, culture, and history, housed in nine, mainly opulent, galleries along Fifth Avenue, from 82nd Street and the Metropolitan Museum of Art, all the way north to the Latin American cultural museum, El Museo del Barrio, at 104th Street.

A newcomer to the auspicious mile (which is now, technically, more than a mile), the Museum for African Art, is due to open its latest incarnation by the end of 2012 between 109th and 110th streets, the first museum to be built on the mile since 1959. The Neue Galerie features German art and cultural exhibits. The Solomon R. Guggenheim Museum, housed in the remarkable spiral Frank Lloyd Wright building, hosts exhibitions on a grand scale. The Jewish Museum has art and culture from its own perspective at 92nd Street.

The National Academy Museum and School of Fine Arts tutored John Singer Sargent and Thomas Eakins, among other talents, while a branch of the Smithsonian, the Cooper-Hewitt National Design Museum, showcases highly decorative arts in a Beaux Arts mansion.

ABOVE: *Pershing Square Bridge*, 1993, by Bascove, can be seen in the Museum of the City of New York.

ABOVE: the Neue Galerie is devoted to early Austrian and German art, including works by Gustav Klimt. There are also cultural exhibits on show.

LEFT: Frank Lloyd Wright's architectural showpiece is the Solomon R. Guggenheim Museum on Fifth Avenue.

MUSEUM MILE FESTIVAL

From 6 to 9pm on the second Tuesday in June each year, the Museum Mile Festival signals that Fifth Avenue is closed to road traffic from the Metropolitan Museum at 82nd Street, for an entire mile north.

Musicians, street performers, and food stalls line the length of the route, and all of the museums are open to the public for free in what is the city's biggest and most culturally diverse block party.

Special temporary exhibits are often mounted to coincide with the festival, and art activities with kids in mind are held in the street. Live music is performed, some for dancing, some for background listening, and some for contemplation, ranging from jazz to string quartets to Broadway show tunes.

The event has been a highly popular fixture in the New York cultural calendar since the festival's inception in the late 1970s, and regularly attracts a high-spirited crowd of more than 50,000 art-lovers, fun-seekers, and aficionados.

BELOW: *Goldfish Vendor*, 1928, by Reuven Rubin, from *Culture and Continuity: The Jewish Journey* at the Jewish Museum.

BELOW: *First Night Game, Yankee Stadium, May 28, 1946,* by Paolo Corvino, from the Museum of the City of New York. In addition to exhibits, the museum owns an 1851 double-decker fire truck, and organizes excellent walking tours of the city.

RIGHT: the Cooper-Hewitt National Design Museum's international collection includes decorative arts, product design, textiles, and wallpapers, and is housed in this exquisite mansion on the edge of Central Park. The library has more than 70,000 books, and there is an archive of drawings and photographs.

UPPER WEST SIDE

More laidback than its counterpart across the park, the land of ballet and dinosaur bones is also an underrated place to dine and shop

The highlights of the Upper West Side tend to be around Broadway, Columbus and Amsterdam avenues, a sort of 24-hour circus squeezed between the calm of Riverside Drive and Central Park West. The entrance to all this is **Columbus Circle** 🔞, with its hustling bustle of cars, pedestrians, and skateboarders, and the Time Warner Center, whose asymmetric glass towers loom over and almost dwarf the stately statue of Christopher Columbus.

High-flyers

The southern part of the neighborhood has moved up in the world in recent years, due in great part to the Time Warner Center, but also to the growth of residential apartment towers in the far west, home to prosperous young hedge-funders and their starter families.

On the south side of Columbus Circle, look for the striking concrete-and-glass building which is the new home of the **Museum of Arts and Design** (www.madmuseum.org, tel: 212-299 7777; Tue–Sun 11am–6pm, Thur–Fri until 9pm; charge).

The museum opened in 2008, with double its previous space. On the north side is the gleaming **Trump International Hotel and Tower** (see page 315). The hotel is across from the gateway to Central Park, which is usually thronged with people playing music, eating lunch, passing through, or just plain hanging out. Vendors crowd the sidewalks, and pedicab drivers troll for passengers.

The **Time Warner Center** 🔟 has made space for dozens of new stores aimed squarely at affluent shoppers,

Main Attractions
COLUMBUS CIRCLE
TIME WARNER CENTER
LINCOLN CENTER
METROPOLITAN OPERA
AVERY FISHER HALL
AMERICAN MUSEUM OF NATURAL HISTORY
RIVERSIDE PARK

Maps and Listings
MAP, PAGE 214
SHOPPING, PAGE 239
RESTAURANTS, PAGE 240
ACCOMMODATIONS, PAGE 315

LEFT: the view from the Time Warner Center over Columbus Circle.
RIGHT: the Trump International Hotel and Tower, with its gleaming globe.

ABOVE: outside the Time Warner Center.
BELOW: the San Remo Apartments and Central Park West in wintertime.

and some very pricey restaurants, including an eatery that is currently New York's most expensive, **Masa**. The center does have less expensive options, including a branch of the organic produce chain Whole Foods, where you can pick up something to eat in the food court or as a picnic in Central Park.

CNN is on the third floor of the Time Warner Center, and you can peek through the windows at the studio. On the north side of the complex at the corner of 60th Street and Broadway is the entrance to the home of **Jazz at Lincoln Center** (www.jalc. org, tel: 212-258 9800), a world-class concert venue (see page 242).

Following Columbus

After soaking up culture at Lincoln Center, cross **Columbus Avenue** for the **American** Folk **Art Museum** (2 Lincoln Square, www.folkartmu-seum.org, tel: 212-595 9533; Tue–Sat noon–7.30pm, Sun noon–7.30pm; charge). This was a secondary branch of the main museum (formerly on West 53rd Street), but due to budget-ary issues, it is now the sole branch and home to traditional art from the 18th and 19th centuries. The collec-tion has some beautiful and striking pieces of art and textiles that would be equally at home in a gallery at the MoMA, including a lovely collection of Amish quilts and a more recent addition – a patchwork-quilt memorial to the victims of the attack on the World Trade Center. The museum also has a great little gift shop.

THE BROADWAY CULTURE TOUR

If culture is high on your list, try this route through the Upper West Side. From Columbus Circle, Broadway swerves west toward Columbus Avenue and nicks the corner of Lincoln Center, flanked on one side by the Juilliard School and on the other by **Fordham University**. Even to be accepted at the **Juilliard School** is an honor, as the highly selective enrollment and small classes draw some of the most talented students in America. Trumpeter Miles Davis was an alumnus, and for a while lived a few blocks north on West 77th Street.

Lincoln Center ⑳

Address: Columbus Ave (between 62nd and 65th sts), www.lincol-ncenter.org
Telephone: various box offices, see following paragraph
Opening Hours: tours daily 10.30am–4.30pm

Entrance Fee: charge
Subway: 66th St/Lincoln Center

Construction of the **Lincoln Center for the Performing Arts** (see page 242) began in 1959 as part of a massive redevelopment plan to clean up the slums that occupied the site. Now, the center is one of the city's most popular venues, with attendance running at about 5 million people a year.

Around Lincoln Center

The black marble fountain in the middle of the plaza is surrounded by the glass-and-white-marble facades of the center's three main structures. The **Metropolitan Opera** ㉑ (www.metoperafamily.org, tel: 212-362 6000) is directly in front, with two large murals by Marc Chagall behind the glass wall – *Le Triomphe de la Musique* to the left, *Les Sources de la Musique* to the right. The Met is home to the Metropolitan Opera Company from September to April, and the American Ballet Theater from May to July. Although marvelous, its productions and performers carry a hefty price tag, but the tiny

TIP

There are few places in Manhattan where the difference between an express and local train makes as big a difference. Hop on a D or A train at Columbus Circle and the next stop will be 125th Street. Choose a B or C and 125th will be your 8th stop.

BELOW: a ballet performance at the Lincoln Center.

TIP

If dioramas are not enough, the American Museum of Natural History is willing to try to bring you closer to the real thing. The museum runs a tour division (www.amnhexpeditions. org), with lecturer-led journeys to see the solar eclipse from Machu Picchu, to explore the geologic wonders of Iceland, or to dig for dinosaur bones in Colorado.

Gallery Met just off the main foyer has a collection of paintings which you can see free of charge.

To the left of the central fountain, the **David H. Koch Theater** (http://davidhkochtheater.com, tel: 212-870 5500) is shared by the New York City Opera and the New York City Ballet – both more adventurous than the Met, and less expensive. The third side of the main plaza is occupied by **Avery Fisher Hall** (tel: 212-875 5030), home of the New York Philharmonic and the Mostly Mozart summer concert series.

Two secondary courtyards flank the Metropolitan Opera. On the right, the **Vivian Beaumont Theater** (tel: 212-362 7600) is fronted by a shady plaza and reflecting pool, around which office workers gather for lunch. The oxidized bronze sculpture in the center of the pool is by Henry Moore. A spindly steel sculpture by Alexander Calder is near the entrance to the **Library of the Performing Arts**. The Bandshell in **Damrosch Park** is used for free concerts in summer. These are usually around lunchtime,

but there are occasional performances in the early evenings too. Over the last few years the Lincoln Center complex has been gradually transformed, with new street-level entrances for many venues and a major overhaul of **Alice Tully Hall**, used for chamber music. Most visible is the new two-story building at 65th Street that houses the Elinor Bunin Monroe Film Center. On its roof, an Illumination Garden invites visitors to relax in a slightly incongruous, but lovely, grassy enclave. The entire complex is more stunning than ever.

CENTRAL PARK WEST

Central Park West takes over from Eighth Avenue, branches off Columbus Circle and heads up into the West Side's most affluent residential section. The apartment houses overlooking the park are among the most lavish in the city – like the famous twin towers of the **San Remo Apartments**, built in 1931 – and the cross streets, especially 74th, 75th, and 76th, are lined with equally splendid brownstones. At the corner

BELOW: Lincoln Center and the Metropolitan Opera building.

dedicated to his memory, is across the street a few steps into Central Park (see page 194).

These days, foreign students buy Lennon merchandise from the surrounding stands, and visitors converse on memorial benches bordering Strawberry Fields' *Imagine* mosaic.

From 72nd Street, it's a short walk Uptown, past the somber facades of the Universalist Church and the **New-York Historical Society** ㉗ (170 Central Park West, www.nyhistory.org, tel: 212-873 3400; Tue–Sun until at least 5pm; charge), New York's oldest museum, with permanent exhibitions on the city's history, to the 79th Street entrance of the American Museum of Natural History, the *grande dame* of Manhattan museums, which sprawls over several blocks of the city.

of West 67th Street, the **Hotel des Artistes** has numbered Valentino, Isadora Duncan, Noel Coward, and Norman Rockwell among its tenants, and was once home to the **Café des Artistes**, an exquisite hideaway on the first floor with the perfect ambience for a rendezvous – unfortunately, it closed in 2009.

The most famous apartment building on this stretch is **The Dakota** ㉖, built in 1884 by Henry Hardenbergh, who also designed the Plaza Hotel. At the time, people joked that it was so far outside the city, "it might as well be in the Dakota Territory," which explains the Indian's head above the entrance.

Imagine

Urban streets caught up with The Dakota soon enough, and over the years the building has attracted tenants like Boris Karloff, Leonard Bernstein, and Lauren Bacall, and was the setting for the 1968 movie *Rosemary's Baby*. Most famously, John Lennon lived at The Dakota and was shot outside it in 1980. **Strawberry Fields**, a touching knoll

American Museum of Natural History ㉘

Address: 79th St (at Central Park West), www.amnh.org
Telephone: 212-769 5100
Opening Hours: daily 10am–5.45pm
Entrance Fee: charge
Subway: 81st St

LEFT: dinosaurs grace the halls of the American Museum of Natural History.
BELOW: exhibits from the American Museum of Natural History.

TIP

On the first Friday of each month, the American Museum of Natural History hosts a "Starry Nights" series of jazz concerts in the unique setting of the giant glass shell of the Rose Center for Earth and Space.

Guarded by an equestrian statue of Theodore Roosevelt, the museum's main entrance is one of many additions built around the original structure (see page 246). The original facade – a stately Romanesque arcade with two towers – was built in the late 1800s, and can be seen from 77th Street. The front steps have become a regrouping point, where families and school groups study guidebooks and maps.

For children, a visit to the museum is a must, but with 45 exhibition halls housed in 25 buildings, there's plenty for grown-ups to see, too. Some of the exhibits are more successful than others, but choice is the main problem here.

Highlights include a 34-ton (31,000kg) meteorite, the largest blue sapphire in the world, and a full-sized model of a blue whale. The world's tallest dinosaur – the 50ft (15-meter) Barosaurus – is in the Theodore Roosevelt Rotunda.

The museum also includes a gigantic screen **Imax Theater**, in addition to the **Rose Center for Earth and Space**, which houses the **Hayden Planetarium**.

BELOW: a cycle path.

From October to May the **Butterfly Conservatory** provides a popular opportunity to see some rare and beautiful tropical butterflies as they flutter around a temporary enclosure erected inside the building.

Don't even think about doing the whole museum in one shot, and expect to spend some of your time trying to find your way around, despite having a floor plan.

Classic and organic

Head back over to Columbus Avenue for some high-grade browsing. Shopping along this Uptown stretch can be a pleasant, almost small-town activity in comparison with the Midtown mayhem of Macy's and other places. Trees line the sidewalks, while dogwalkers spilling over from Central Park contribute to a gentler pace.

The Uptown branch of **Kiehl's** (154 Columbus Avenue), a generations-old natural cosmetics and perfume apothecary, is worth visiting. New editions to the classic range include lip-glosses and SPF-rated

Life in the Bike Lane

Organizations like Transportation Alternatives (www.transalt.org), a non-profit seeking to "reclaim New York's streets from the automobile," have found friends in the Bloomberg Administration. Since 2006, the number of bike lanes in the city has doubled, with more than 400 miles (644km) now available to the hundreds of thousands of urban cyclists. The organization will tell you to forget the cab or the 2 or 3 train, the quickest way up the West Side is by bicycle on the Waterfront Greenway along the Hudson River. It's true. You can easily pedal from Houston Street to 72nd street in 15 minutes, with the added bonus of spectacular river views. Locals know this, of course, and every morning the Greenway is like a miniature highway of joggers and cyclists – some in business suits racing to meetings.

With the addition of bike lanes on Columbus Avenue and 77th, 78th, 90th, and 91st streets, not to mention Riverside and Central parks, negotiating the Upper West Side on two wheels has never been easier. Don't worry about bringing your own ride. Many shops, including Toga Bikes at West End Avenue and 64th Street (http://togabikes.com, tel: 212-799 9625), offer rentals for reasonable prices.

face cream, all in traditionally simple packaging. Hair-accessory headquarters **Thérapie New York** is found at 309 Columbus, with children's clothes and toys as well as organic shampoos.

There are far too many clothes stores to list by name, but those that deserve special mention are north of 68th Street. There's outrageous fashion at **Betsey Johnson** (248 Columbus), upscale women's wear at **Eileen Fisher** (341 Columbus), and equally upscale men's wear at **Frank Stella** (440 Columbus).

Columbus's proximity to Central Park – the Uptown dog-walker's playground – is recognized at various pet stores. There's also a wide selection of funky vintage wear (and wares) at a flea market every Sunday between 76th and 77th streets (www.greenfleamarkets. com). Here, locals like to browse before or after brunch with friends or family.

THE FAR WEST

Skipping west to **Amsterdam Avenue**, the scene is dressed down but still trendy: restaurants, boutiques, and bars with a twentysomething clientele dominate, though there are a few remaining Latino-flavored grocer's stores and traditional neighborhood shops like **West Side Kids** at 84th Street, with its unusually intelligent toy inventory.

At 80th and Broadway, **Zabar's** (www.zabars.com) is the gourmet store against which gourmet stores are measured. Even if you're not in the mood for buying, it's worth elbowing your way to the counter for a free taste of all the goodies; visiting the store is worthwhile for the smells alone.

At 212 West 83rd Street, the amusing **Children's Museum of Manhattan** ㉙ (www.cmom.org, tel: 212-721 1223; Tue–Sun 10am–5pm, Sat until 7pm; charge) is a brightly colored multilevel kiddy kingdom

ABOVE: the lavish interior of the Beacon Theatre.

Kids' stores on Columbus are good value. Kidville is a "boutique" and hair salon with fire trucks, airplane, and car-shaped seats to entice the under-5s in for a haircut.

with interactive exhibits and special events. The noise level is high, so arrive very calm or come equipped with earplugs.

And at West 89th Street, just off Amsterdam Avenue, spare a thought for the Claremont Riding Academy, the last surviving riding stables in Manhattan, which after 115 years in business closed in April, 2007.

Off-Off-Broadway

In recent years, new meaning has been added to the term "Off-Broadway," with an Upper West Side scene that includes performances and literary readings at **Symphony Space**, on Broadway between 94th and 95th streets, and the **Beacon Theatre**, 2124 Broadway at 74th Street, a popular music venue where you might catch James Taylor (either one) one night and a gospel group the next.

Shopping continues on Broadway with the appearance of **Barneys CO-OP** at 2151, the "neighborhood-sized" and more laidback

relation of the upscale department store that is popping up at desirable locations throughout the city. Thrift-store fans with an aversion to actual thrift stores can find cute and kooky things at **Urban Outfitters** (at both 72nd and 100th streets and Broadway).

Occupying the entire block between 73rd and 74th streets is the **Ansonia Hotel** ⑩, and while it's a little worn around the edges, this is still the *grande dame* of West Side apartment buildings, with a resident list that over the years included Enrico Caruso, Igor Stravinsky, Arturo Toscanini, and Theodore Dreiser.

The hotel was particularly popular with singers and musicians because its thick internal walls allowed them to practice without disturbing the neighbors. Although retailers now dominate the first floor, the Ansonia's mansard roof, towers, and fabulous terracotta detailing still add up to a Beaux Arts fantasy that captures the gaze and won't let go.

BELOW: alfresco dining at the 79th Street Boat Basin.

Down by the Riverside

A tour of the far west of New York finishes nicely by taking 72nd Street to **West End Avenue ⬤**, then on to Riverside Drive. North of 72nd Street, West End Avenue is affluent and strictly residential; a great place to live, but not a particularly fascinating place for visitors. Humphrey Bogart lived for a while in Pomander Walk, an English-style mews situated between 94th and 95th streets, West End Avenue, and busy Broadway.

South of 72nd Street, a mini-city of high-rise apartments has altered the Hudson River skyline on Riverside Boulevard, not to be confused with **Riverside Drive ⬤**, which winds along the edge of Frederick Law Olmsted's **Riverside Park**. The 72nd Street entrance has a bronze sculpture of Eleanor Roosevelt, one of only four statues of real-life women gracing New York's parks.

This is a picturesque corner of Manhattan, with sweeping views of the Hudson River. In warm weather, Manhattanites come to the **79th Street Boat Basin** for drinks and burgers.

LEFT: taking religion to the streets.

SHOPPING

Many of the stores located here can be found in other neighborhoods, but that only speaks to their quality. Upper West Siders have a knack for bringing quality closer to home, a pocket of Manhattan they love dearly.

Books

Westsider Rare & Used Books
2246 Broadway (at 80th St)
Tel: 212-362 0706
http://westsiderbooks.com
The neighborhood's best used-book store also carries rare records. Browsers and collectors will rejoice.

Clothing

Club Monaco
2376 Broadway (at 87th St)
Tel: 212-579 2587
www.clubmonaco.com
As chains go, Club Monaco stands above most, with excellent selection and customer service and versatile, affordable fashion. Locations throughout the city.
Loehmann's
2101 Broadway (at 73rd St)
Tel: 212-882 9900
www.loehmanns.com
A giant warehouse with deep discounts on top designers, proving that not every chic dress in New York needs to be priced over $100.
Mint
448 Columbus Avenue (at 81st and 82nd sts)
Tel: 212-362 6250.
http://shopmint.com
A cute boutique with fun and affordable clothes for women.

Food

Jacques Torres
285 Amsterdam Avenue (at 73rd and 74th sts)
Tel: 212-787 3256
www.mrchocolate.com
The Uptown outlet of a beloved chocolatier where you can get chocolate by the pound or fresh (and strong!) hot chocolate.

Home

Jonathan Adler
304 Columbus Avenue (at 74th St)
Tel: 212-787 0017
www.jonathanadler.com
Playful – but not too wild – stripes and prints decorate Adler's attractive line of products for the home.

Mall

Time Warner Center
Columbus Circle
Tel: 212-823 6300
www.shopsatcolumbuscircle.com
Rather than listing all the excellent stores in the bottom levels of the neighborhood's most recognizable shopping complex, why not visit and browse them all? Grab a bite to eat at Whole Foods if you're in a rush.

Shoes

West NYC
147 W. 72nd St
(at Amsterdam and Columbus aves)
Tel: 212-787 8595
www.westnyc.com
Designer sneakers and apparel popular with the skateboard and hip-hop set.

BEST RESTAURANTS, BARS, AND CAFES

Restaurants

A Voce
10 Columbus Circle (3rd Floor)
Tel: 212-823 2523
www.avocerestaurant.com
Open: L & D Mon–Sat, Br & D Sun $$$ 182 [p336, B3]
Italian country cuisine. The veal *agnolotti* with a soffritto sauce is outstanding, as are the rustic potato wedges. They have a sister restaurant just north of Madison Square Park.

Artie's Deli
2290 Broadway (at 82nd and 83rd sts)
Tel: 212-579 5959
www.arties83rd.com
Open: B, L, & D daily $$ 183 [p336, B1]
Hang out among the hanging salamis in this gentrified, kid-friendly deli.

Bar Boulud
1900 Broadway (at 63rd and 64th sts)
Tel: 212-595 0303
www.danielnyc.com
Open: L & D Mon–Fri, Br & D Sat–Sun $$$ 184 [p336, B3]
Daniel Boulud's wine-and-charcuterie restaurant, across from the Lincoln Center, is a great place to get a lardon salad or a plate of pâté before a show.

Barney Greengrass
541 Amsterdam Ave (near 86th and 87th sts)
Tel: 212-724 4707
www.barneygreengrass.com
Open: B & L Tue–Sun $$ [off map]
This old-school smoked-fish spot is the real deal – it has been open for more than 100 years. Barney serves up some of the best sturgeon, white fish, and Nova on the Upper West Side.

Café Frida
368 Columbus Ave (at 77th and 78th sts)
Tel: 212-712 2929
www.cafefrida.com
Open: L & D Mon–Sat, Br & D Sun $$$ 185 [p336, B1]
Rich Mexican cuisine at a bar-restaurant behind the Museum of Natural History.

Café Luxembourg
200 W. 70th St (at Amsterdam and West End aves)
Tel: 212-873 7411
www.cafeluxembourg.com
Open: B, L, & D Mon–Fri, Br & D Sat–Sun $$$ 186 [p336, B2]
This classic French bistro is within walking distance of Lincoln Center. With a lovely Art Deco dining room, this is a long-running success.

Calle Ocho
45 W. 81st St (at Columbus Ave and Central Park West)
Tel: 212-873 5025
http://calleochonyc.com
Open: D Mon–Fri, Br & D Sat–Sun $$ 187 [p336, C1]
Regular young professionals dine well on innovative versions of classic Cuban and Latin dishes, washed down with what many claim are New York's best mojitos.

Dovetail
103 W. 77th St (at Columbus Ave)
Tel: 212-362 3800
http://dovetailnyc.com
Open: D daily, L Fri, Br Sat–Sun $$$$ 188 [p336, C1]
Heralded as the best restaurant to hit the Upper West Side in ages, this place behind the American Museum of Natural History serves New American cuisine.

Gennaro
665 Amsterdam Ave (at 92nd and 93rd sts)
Tel: 212-665 5348
www.gennaronyc.com
Open: D daily $ [off map]
Upper West Siders love the casual vibe and hearty Italian dishes (gnocchi, braised lamb) here almost as much as they love the surprisingly low prices.

Isabella's
359 Columbus Ave (at 76th and 77th sts)
Tel: 212-724 2100
www.isabellas.com
Open: L & D Mon–Fri, Br & D Sat–Sun $$ 189 [p336, B1]
Crowded at brunch for all the right reasons: great food and a great location on a Columbus Avenue corner; outdoor tables when possible.

Jean-Georges
1 Central Park W. (at 60th and 61st sts)
Tel: 212-299 3900
http://jean-georges.com
Open: L & D Mon–Sat $$$$ 190 [p336, B3]
Jean-Georges Vongerichten's ultra-chic culinary masterpiece is well worth the price. For the ultimate, try the seven-course tasting menu; for the experience of just being here, order the prix-fixe lunch at a fraction of the cost.

Kefi
505 Columbus Ave (at 84th and 85th sts)
Tel: 212-873 0200
www.kefirestaurant.com
Open: L & D Mon–Fri, Br & D Sat–Sun $$ 191 [p336, C1]
Spectacular Greek dishes at shockingly good prices; it's very popular and for good reason.

Land
450 Amsterdam Ave (at 81st

LEFT: Ouest has stylish food to match its clientele.

and 82nd sts)
Tel: 212-501 8121
www.landthaikitchen.com
Open: D only Mon–Fri, L & D
Sat–Sun $–$$ [p336, B1]
Called the best Thai on
the Upper West Side, and
now with an Upper East
Side branch, too.

Ocean Grill
384 Columbus Ave (at 78th and
79th sts)
Tel: 212-579 2300
www.oceangrill.com
Open: L & D daily $$$
[p336, B1]
Excellent West Side fish
house, but the volume of
noise can detract from
the culinary experience –
best at lunchtime.

Ouest
2315 Broadway (at 83rd and
84th sts)
Tel: 212-580 8700
http://ouestny.com
Open: D daily, Br Sun $$$$
[off map]
This smart eatery is a
place to be "scene." The
clubby atmosphere says it
all, but its food should not
be missed or dismissed.

Picholine
35 W. 64th St (at Broadway and
Central Park West)
Tel: 212-724 8585
www.picholinenyc.com
Open: D daily $$$$ [p336,
B3]
Draped in lavender, this
longtime favorite is one
of the city's most elegant
dining rooms, serving
some of the neighbor-
hood's most inventive
French cuisine.

Porter House New York
10 Columbus Circle (at Broad-
way and 60th St)
Tel: 212-823 9500
www.porterhousenewyork.com
Open: L & D daily $$$$
[p336, B3]
The fourth floor of the
Time Warner Center is as

special as the food pre-
pared here by Michael
Lomonaco, former chef at
Windows on the World.
Expect the best aged beef
at prices called "reasona-
ble" – at least compared
to TWC's neighboring
Masa, NY's priciest tab.

Rack and Soul
258 W. 109th St (at Broadway)
Tel: 212-222 4800
www.rackandsoul.com
Open: L & D daily $$ [off map]
A menu rich in fried
chicken, fried catfish, and
baby back ribs complete
with biscuits and honey is
sinfully delicious. Go for it!

Saigon Grill
620 Amsterdam Ave (at 90th
and 91st sts)
Tel: 212-875 9072
Open: L & D daily $ [off map]
The Vietnamese dishes
are carefully prepared –
consider crispy spring
rolls served with mint
and lettuce wrappers,
pork chops marinated in
lemongrass, or shrimp
and scallops fried and
tossed with a tangy-
sweet glaze. Takeout too.

Shake Shack
366 Columbus Ave (at 77th and
78th sts)
Tel: 646-747 8770
http://shakeshack.com
Open: L & D daily $–$$
[p336, B1]
Down the block from the
Natural History Museum;
kids and adults alike
feast on burgers, fries,
and milkshakes.

Telepan
72 W. 69th St (at Columbus Ave
and Central Park W.)
Tel: 212-580 4300
http://telepan-ny.com
Open: D daily, L Wed–Fri, and Br
Sat–Sun $$$$ [p336, B2]
A real purist, the chef
here uses only the fresh-
est locally grown ingredi-

ents, in a New American
cuisine with the silly
name "haute barnyard."

Bars and Cafes

Alice's Tea Cup
102 W. 73rd St (between
Columbus and Amsterdam
aves) [p336, B2]
A whimsical place for
light lunch, tea, and intimate conversations.

Boat Basin Café
79th St on the Hudson River
[p336, B1]
Hands-down the most
popular Upper West Side
outdoor eating and drink-
ing spot, with a boister-
ous Thursday-night bar
scene. Open Apr–Oct.

Bin 71
Columbus Ave at 71st St
[p336, B2]
An intimate modern Ital-
ian wine bar frequented by
Upper West Side regulars.

Bouchon Bakery
10 Columbus Cirlce (in the Time
Warner Building) [p336, B3]
Affordable bistro/bou-
langerier. Takeout also
available.

Gray's Papaya
2090 Broadway (at 72nd St)
[p336, B2]
A two hot-dog dinner with
a fruit-juice chaser.
Stand-up only. Whaddya
expect for three bucks?

Hudson Bar
Hudson Hotel, W. 58th St off 8th
Ave [p336, A3]
Very sleek and chic bar in
a Philippe Starck-
designed hotel.

O'Neal's
49 W. 64th St (opposite Lincoln
Center) [p336, B3]
A fixture in the Lincoln
Center area for drinks
and food.

Popover Café
551 Amsterdam Ave (between
86th and 87th sts) [p336,
B3]
A great place for break-
fast or brunch.

RIGHT: Oysters Rockefeller originated in New Orleans.

LINCOLN CENTER

Lincoln Center for the Performing Arts is a massive cultural village, with companies from opera to jazz and two dozen excellent performance venues

A meeting place, an outdoor space in which to relax, a plaza with sculptures, and a mini-metropolis of concert venues: Lincoln Center is all of these and more. New York City's capital of culture covers more than 16 acres (6 hectares) and includes a community of 11 institutes that teach, commission, and showcase almost all forms of musical and theatrical art.

Permanent home to both the Philharmonic and the Metropolitan Opera, the center is also a place of study, encompassing the Juilliard School, the School of American Ballet, and both the Film and Chamber Music societies. On just about any night of the week, something exciting and innovative will be happening here.

ABOVE: under the directorship of Wynton Marsalis, Jazz at Lincoln Center's home is the Frederick P. Rose Hall in the Time Warner Center. The hall encompasses three performance spaces and the Irene Diamond Education Center.

ABOVE: Lincoln Plaza is the epicenter of culture in New York.

RIGHT: at the core of the Juilliard Jazz Orchestra are 18 musicians following a two-year jazz studies program.

ABOVE: the Director of Conducting and Orchestral Studies at the Juilliard School, James DePriest, is also the permanent conductor of the Tokyo Metropolitan Symphony Orchestra.

The Essentials

Address: Columbus Aves, between 62nd and 65th sts; www.lincolncenter.org
Tel: 212-721 6500
Opening Hours: tours daily 10.30am–4.30pm
Entrance Fee: charge for performances
Subway: 66th St/ Lincoln Center

THE METROPOLITAN OPERA

The first performance of the Metropolitan Opera was of Charles Gounod's *Faust*, which took place on October 22, 1883. Tenor Enrico Caruso and conductor Arturo Toscanini graced the stage of the opera house's first premises, on 39th Street and Broadway.

The Met's new home opened in 1966 with the world premiere of Samuel Barber's *Antony and Cleopatra*. The company is committed to bringing opera to a wider audience. Initiatives include reduced-price tickets, live high-definition broadcasts to theaters in the US and in Europe, streaming internet transmissions, and satellite radio broadcasts.

For anyone with shaky Italian or German, there are simultaneous translations to individual screens at every seat in the opera house.

ABOVE: Robert McFerrin made history as the first black male soloist in the Metropolitan Opera's history when he sang in the 1995 production of *Aida*.

LEFT: soprano Renée Fleming as Tatiana in Tchaikovsky's opera *Eugene Onegin*.

ABOVE: tickets for Lincoln Center performances go on sale up to a year in advance, and can be booked from the website. The entire outdoor space of Lincoln Plaza is now covered by free broadband Wi-Fi internet access. Be careful if using your laptop by the fountains, though.

ABOVE: classical and modern architectural styles blend to make the airy plaza a relaxing place to be.

LEFT: a popular public space both day and night, the computer-controlled fountains in the plaza are adjusted according to the wind, in order to prevent visitors sitting nearby from being drenched with water.

IMPROVEMENTS TO LINCOLN CENTER

Since 1959, when President Dwight D. Eisenhower broke ground for the new Lincoln Square Urban Renewal Project, this cultural village within New York has continued to grow and mature. Ongoing improvements occur regularly; the most recent ones include a new book store for Juilliard, modernization to the Alice Tully Hall and Peter J. Sharp Theater, stunning new entrances for most venues, and an extensive renovation of the north and central plazas where the two-story Elinor Bunin Monroe Film Center was built, complete with a rooftop Illumination Lawn. Many of the plans were completed in time for the center's 50th anniversary in 2009.

ABOVE: dancers and performers can frequently be seen entering and exiting the hall if you're looking for an autograph.

ABOVE: Lincoln Center and the Juilliard School are known for their dance troupes. The New York City Ballet is made up of 92 young dancers who perform mainly contemporary works, most commissioned especially for the company. George Balanchine was the co-founding director.

RIGHT: *Reclining Figure*, a two-piece bronze sculpture, was commissioned for Lincoln Center Plaza in 1963 from English artist Sir Henry Moore, and unveiled in 1965.

RIGHT: Alexander Calder's sculpture *Le Guichet (The Ticket Window)* stands in front of Avery Fisher Hall, and was presented to the center in 1965.

THE AMERICAN MUSEUM OF NATURAL HISTORY

From whales in the depths of the oceans to fragments of far-distant worlds, AMNH makes natural history fun. There's live music, too

The American Museum of Natural History on the Upper West Side has one of the most popular collections in New York City. It's also one of the United States' largest, and takes days to explore. The museum has many features other than its 45 permanent exhibition halls. These include a monthly lecture series – on everything from birds to wine – several traveling exhibitions, an IMAX theater and state-of-the-art planetarium, monthly music events and the recent Mystery at the Museum, a game where visitors hunt for clues and explore lesser-seen corners of the museum. The bones still bring the crowds, though, and they're as awe-inspiring now as they were when paleontologist – and Indiana Jones inspiration – Roy Chapman Andrews was director over 75 years ago.

ABOVE: in addition to this prehistoric creature, the museum's collection includes a 50ft (15-meter) Barosaurus skeleton, said to be the world's highest free-standing mount dinosaur.

ABOVE: a dramatic, full-size model of a blue whale dominates the Milstein Family Hall of Ocean Life. Marine ecosystems, including coral reefs, are depicted, along with dioramas and exhibits on vertebrates and invertebrates.

The Essentials

Address: 79th Street and Central Park West; www.amnh.org
Telephone: 212-769 5100
Opening Hours: daily 10am–5.45pm
Entrance Fee: charge; audioguides also available
Subway: 81st St

ABOVE: the museum's dioramas of habitats depict the environs, habits, and behavior of innumerable species of animals, reptiles, insects, and aquatic life. Kids love the elephants in particular.

ROCKING THE ROSE CENTER

Some may say it's a stretch to call any museum cool, but the Rose Center at AMNH is doing its best to engender a new reputation. Director Neil deGrasse Tyson is a jocular fixture on television, appearing in as many science documentaries as late-night talk staples such as *The Daily Show*. After the success of *SonicVision*, a digitally animated music show produced in conjunction with MTV, the Rose

Center introduced *One Step Beyond*, a monthly Friday night concert and dance party. Popular DJs spin records, indie bands take the stage, and cocktails flow past midnight. You won't find such a scene across the park at the Met, that's for sure.

ABOVE: the 77th Street entrance to the museum, which consists of 25 buildings and 46 exhibition halls.

ABOVE: the Rose Center for Earth and Space includes a spiral walking tour of the growth of the universe, vividly demonstrating the concepts of cosmic scale.

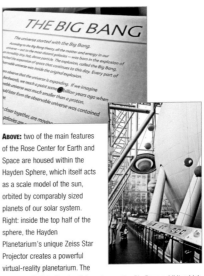

ABOVE: two of the main features of the Rose Center for Earth and Space are housed within the Hayden Sphere, which itself acts as a scale model of the sun, orbited by comparably sized planets of our solar system. Right: inside the top half of the sphere, the Hayden Planetarium's unique Zeiss Star Projector creates a powerful virtual-reality planetarium. The bottom half of the Hayden Sphere houses the Big Bang exhibit, which takes visitors on a multisensory re-creation of the Big Bang and recreates the beginnings of the universe.

ABOVE: vivid representations of animals from all seven continents inform, educate, and delight visitors. This diorama in the Akeley Hall of African Mammals, called Water Hole, features giraffes and antelope.

ABOVE: the museum has nearly 1 million fossil specimens, and more than 600 of them are on view. Most displays are of actual fossils, as opposed to the more commonly seen casts.

RIGHT: in addition to displaying one of the world's largest hunks of space rock – the 34-ton (31,000kg) Cape York meteorite – the Arthur Ross Hall of Meteorites has moon rocks and interactive exhibits, with computer animations of the formation, journeys, and final impact of these gigantic cosmic tourists.

American Museum of Natural History

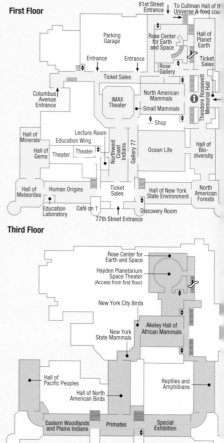

First Floor

81st Street Entrance

To Cullman Hall of the Universe & food court

Parking Garage

Rose Center for Earth and Space

Hall of Planet Earth

Entrance

Entrance

Rose Gallery

Ticket Sales

Ticket Sales

Columbus Avenue Entrance

IMAX Theater

North American Mammals

Small Mammals

Shop

Theodore Roosevelt Memorial Hall

Hall of Minerals

Lecture Room

Education Wing

Hall of Gems

Theater

Theater

Northwest Coast Indians

Gallery 77

Ocean Life

Hall of Bio-diversity

Hall of Meteorites

Human Origins

Ticket Sales

Hall of New York State Environment

North American Forests

Education Laboratory

Café on 1

77th Street Entrance

Discovery Room

Third Floor

Rose Center for Earth and Space

Hayden Planetarium Space Theater (Access from first floor)

New York City Birds

New York State Mammals

Akeley Hall of African Mammals

Hall of Pacific Peoples

Hall of North American Birds

Reptiles and Amphibians

Eastern Woodlands and Plains Indians

Primates

Special Exhibition

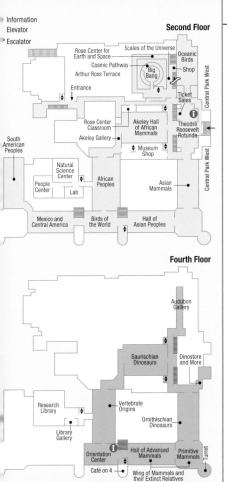

Second Floor

- Information
- Elevator
- Escalator

Rose Center for Earth and Space
Cosmic Pathway
Arthur Ross Terrace
Scales of the Universe
Big Bang
Oceanic Birds
Shop
Entrance
Ticket Sales
Rose Center Classroom
Akeley Hall of African Mammals
Theodre Roosevelt Rotunda
Akeley Gallery
Museum Shop
South American Peoples
Natural Science Center
People Center
Lab
African Peoples
Asian Mammals
Mexico and Central America
Birds of the World
Hall of Asian Peoples
Central Park West
Central Park West

Fourth Floor

Audubon Gallery
Saurischian Dinosaurs
Dinostore and More
Research Library
Vertebrate Origins
Ornithischian Dinosaurs
Library Gallery
Orientation Center
Hall of Advanced Mammals
Primitive Mammals
Café on 4
Wing of Mammals and their Extinct Relatives
Turret

HUMAN ORIGINS

The museum's Anne and Bernard Spitzer Hall of Human Origins exhibits remains and artifacts from our ancestor's progression to humanity and the birth of civilization. Using fossil records, carbon dating, and the latest gene technology, mankind's development from a threatened hunter-gatherer to a dexterous toolmaker and gregarious mass communicator is traced and described.

The oldest human finds, the 93,000-year-old remains of a woman and child buried near Nazareth in Israel, give clues to the progress of civilization at that time, significantly from the very fact that they were buried, depicting a formal ritual.

ABOVE AND BELOW: exhibits tell the histories of man and civilization, drawing from cultures all over the world, including these rarities from Asia.

BELOW LEFT: the Hall of Human Origins presents human evolution from our earliest ancestors, through the rise to Homo erectus and the development of tools, hunting, and farming.

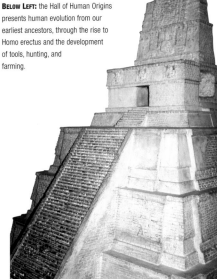

HARLEM AND THE HEIGHTS

Harlem is in the wake of a renaissance, with new museums and celebrated dining. The leafy quiet of Morningside, Hamilton, and Washington Heights have been rediscovered

An Alabama-born, African-American professor recalled being an 18-year-old in Europe in the late 1950s. He was asked repeatedly about Harlem, a place he'd never been in his life. His inquisitors didn't want to hear this. The man was black; he lived in the United States; therefore he had to be from Harlem. What they didn't know was that the only thing he "knew" was based on the same stereotypes shared by the Europeans, that Harlem was full of naughty nightlife, devilish dancing, mind-blowing music, dangerous dudes, and wicked women.

Harlem heritage

That heritage is palpable up and down the neighborhood's avenues. But there was, and is, much more to Harlem. As well as the area's well-documented attractions, urban pioneers driven out of the rest of Manhattan by rising prices have discovered Harlem's handsome buildings – even ex-president Bill Clinton has an office on 125th Street. These are now being restored to their former elegance, and real-estate prices are climbing. Harlem is recapturing some of its classy heyday.

In the early 1900s, black people began moving into homes on

135th Street, west of Lenox Avenue. From then on, Harlem became a place where Americans of African descent made their presence felt. Poet Langston Hughes (see page 256) and writer Zora Neale Hurston, along with musicians Duke Ellington, Billie Holiday, and Ella Fitzgerald, all launched their careers here in the 1920s and '30s, during what was termed the Harlem Renaissance.

Later, Harlem, or more precisely, a restaurant called Sherman's Barbeque at 151st Street and Amsterdam

Main Attractions
APOLLO THEATER
STUDIO MUSEUM
SCHOMBURG CENTER
EL MUSEO DEL BARRIO
MUSEUM OF THE CITY OF
  NEW YORK
COLUMBIA UNIVERSITY
THE CLOISTERS
DYCKMAN FARMHOUSE MUSEUM

Maps and Listings

LEFT: the world famous Apollo Theater.
RIGHT: the succinctly named Harlem Deli.

TIP

Harlem hasn't been this good in years. Try Shrine at 2271 Adam Clayton Powell Jr Blvd for Afrobeat, soul, and funk, and the top-notch, refurbished Lenox Lounge on Lenox Avenue for great jazz and drinks.

Avenue, was where music producer Phil Spector's all-girl singing group The Ronettes brought The Beatles in 1964. More headlines were made in the mid-1970s when Cuba's Fidel Castro took up residence in Harlem's Hotel Teresa, where he brought in live chickens and made his own food for fear he might be poisoned while attending UN functions in Midtown.

New attractions

Two cultural institutions have continued Harlem's post-millennium renaissance. **The Gatehouse** (150 Convent Avenue at 135th Street; www.harlemstage.org, tel: 212-281 9240) opened in 2006 in a renovated building, and showcases new theater and dance groups and musicians. And in 2012, a long-anticipated permanent home for the **Museum for African Art** will open (see page 256).

Geographically, the area is divided into Central Harlem (which includes 125th Street), East Harlem (sometimes called Spanish Harlem), and West Harlem, encompassing Morningside and Hamilton Heights. The most enjoyable way to see this part of the city is to take an organized tour.

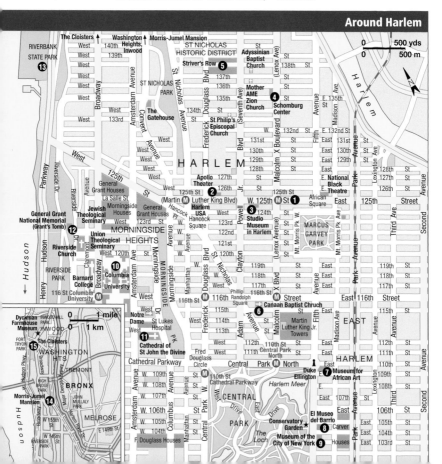

Around Harlem

125TH STREET ❶

A good place to begin is Harlem's famous main drag. It's Fifth Avenue and Times Square compressed into one river-to-river street, a street where every north–south Manhattan subway stops and several north–south buses cross over. A main shopping area, it's vibrant with throngs of people, street vendors, and music blasting from record stores. Officially, 125th Street is now known as **Martin Luther King Boulevard**, and it's home to many of Harlem's foremost attractions.

Apollo Theater ❷

Address: 253 W. 125th St (at Frederick Douglass Blvd), www.apollotheater.com
Telephone: 212-531 5305
Opening Hours: box office Mon–Fri 10am–6pm, Sat noon–5pm
Subway: 125th St

This is where the presence of singers Billie Holiday, Mahalia Jackson, Dinah Washington, and Ella Fitzgerald can still be felt, especially during the Apollo's weekly Amateur Night (every Wednesday). Other music stars whose careers have been launched at the Apollo include Stevie Wonder and Marvin Gaye.

The experience of seeing rising young talent, while at the same time being a part of the highly responsive, and sometimes harshly critical Apollo audience, is not to be missed. The legendary James Brown lay in state here in December 2006, before his funeral in Georgia. Thousands of fans filed past his onstage coffin, as tracks from the singer's *Live at the Apollo* were broadcast to the crowds outside. For information on Apollo tours, tel: 212-531 5337.

There's more nightlife at the old-style **Showman's Bar** at No. 375, a jazz club that still hosts live acts, and at the **Cotton Club**, which moved to No. 656. The **Lenox Lounge** at 288 Lenox Avenue, home to Billie, Miles, and Coltrane, offers a great night in its famous, refurbished Zebra Room.

Studio Museum in Harlem ❸

Address: 144 W. 125th St (near Adam Clayton Powell Jr Blvd), www.studiomuseum.org
Telephone: 212-864 4500

TIP

The Greater Harlem Chamber of Commerce is at 200A West 136th Street, tel: 212-862 7200. Visit http://harlemdiscover.com to discover what's going on whatever month you're visiting.

BELOW: the Amateur Night Show Off Quarter Finals at the Apollo Theater.

The Harlem Gospel Choirs

While many are sleeping off a raucous night, or sipping mimosas to nurse a hangover, early morning singing is filling the churches uptown

In Harlem, Sunday means church and church means gospel. Originating from hymns and the negro spirituals sung during the days of slavery, gospel music is an essential part of the African-American, primarily Baptist, church service. It is also profoundly moving and entertaining. Sunday church services are drawing crowds you might find at the Beacon Theater or Radio City Music Hall on a Friday night, and entrance fees are much more competitive (ie free).

An early morning subway ride to 125th Street will put you right in the thick of things. You can easily walk south to Mount Neboh Baptist Church (http://mountneboh.org, tel: 212-866 7880) on 114th Street and Adam Clayton Powell Jr Blvd. This is where soul singer Freddie Jackson first found his voice, and the choir continues to entrance audiences. Or you can venture north to Abyssinian Baptist Church (www.abyssinian.org, tel: 212-862 7474) at 132 Odell Clark Place (formerly 138th St) and Adam Clayton Powell Jr Blvd. Noted religious thinker Reverend Calvin Butts leads a congregation that has been meeting for over 200 years. On 125th Street itself, neighboring the Studio Museum, is The Greater Refuge Temple (www.greaterrefugetemple.org, tel: 212-866 1700), a Pentecostal church housed in a former movie theater. The atmosphere is still theatrical, with a guitar, organ, drums, and more than 50 singers filling the room with spirit.

There are a few things to remember. Not all the churches can accommodate every new visitor. Lines to enter fill up early, and seating is given first to members of the congregation. You should always contact churches in advance if you plan on visiting with a large group and to confirm that there will indeed be a gospel performance that day. It goes without saying that you should never forget that these are places of worship and should be treated as such. Gentlemen should remove hats, cell phones should be silenced, and the utmost respect should be shown to the local parishioners.

To take some of the guesswork out of where and when to visit, you can consult http://harlemonestop.com. You could also sign onto a tour with Harlem Spirituals – New York Visions (www.harlemspirituals.com; tel: 212-391 0900) whose Harlem Gospel Tours take in historic sites and a gospel service, or another bus service that will pick you up in Midtown and ferry you northward to the music and worship.

Many Harlem eateries, such as the legendary Sylvia's (www.sylviasrestaurant.com, tel: 212-996 0660), host Gospel brunches for those who prefer their songs with a side of bacon.

LEFT: a congregation offers up thanks as they pray during Mass.

ABOVE: the Abyssinian Baptist Church.
BELOW: poet Langston Hughes, whose ashes are interred at the Schomburg Center.

Opening Hours: Thur–Fri noon–9pm, Sat 10am–6pm, Sun noon–6pm
Entrance Fee: charge, free Sun
Subway: 125th St

This dynamic museum hosts changing exhibitions in addition to a permanent collection of contemporary work by artists of the African diaspora. There are extensive archives, including those of James Van Der Zee, who photographed Harlem's jazzy dancing days of the 1920–40s. The Studio Museum also holds workshops and shows films. A short distance away, at 2031 Fifth Avenue, the **National Black Theatre** is an innovative performing arts complex that hosts music, dance, and drama performances.

From 125th Street, walk up one of the neighborhood's north–south streets, like **Malcolm X Boulevard** (also called Lenox Avenue) or **Adam Clayton Powell Jr Boulevard** (also Seventh Avenue). Malcolm X Boulevard is probably Central Harlem's best-known street after 125th Street.

Schomburg Center ❹

Address: 515 Malcolm X Blvd (at 135th St), www.nypl.org/research/sc
Telephone: 212-491 2200
Opening Hours: Tue–Thur noon–8pm, Fri–Sat 10am–6pm
Entrance Fee: free
Subway: 135th St

The landmarks along Malcolm X Boulevard include this Center for Research in Black Culture. Here lie, interred beneath the foyer, the ashes of the acclaimed poet Langston Hughes. There is no more fitting spot than this library, a goldmine of books, records, films, and photos about black Americans in general and Harlem in particular, and where Alex Haley did much of the research for his book, later a TV epic, *Roots*.

From the Schomburg it's a short distance to the **St Nicholas Historic District**, rows of 19th-century townhouses situated between 137th and 139th streets, known as **Striver's Row ❺** in honor of the professionals who moved here in the 1920s.

Along the side streets are evidence of the regeneration achieved by this new era of Harlem professionals.

On a Sunday morning in Central Harlem, don't miss the opportunity to attend services at a local church.

ABOVE: the Apollo Theater exhibition at the Museum of the City of New York.

Jazz poet Langston Hughes's works made him a light of the Harlem Renaissance of the 1920s and '30s. His earthy sketches of black life were controversial: "I knew only the people I had grown up with," he wrote, "and they weren't people whose shoes were always shined, who had been to Harvard, or who had heard Bach."

The fervor of the singing and the response of the congregations are stirring; it's a spiritual experience that is hard to replicate elsewhere.

Sunday gospel

To judge by the diversity of the congregation who show up at **Canaan Baptist Church** ❻ on 116th Street every Sunday, visitors from all over the world have made this discovery already, as non-New Yorkers are as much in evidence as Harlemites.

Harlem's churches have long played a significant role in its political, economic, and cultural life. In addition to the Canaan, the **Abyssinian Baptist Church**, the **St Philip's Episcopal Church**, and the **Mother AME Zion Church** have all been influential since the early 1900s.

Gospel tours are conducted by **Harlem Spirituals-New York Visions** (www.harlemspirituals.com; tel: 212-391 0900). Evening jazz tours can be arranged, too.

EAST HARLEM

Traditionally, this was considered Spanish Harlem, its residents having close ties with Puerto Rico. But East Harlem also includes a strong Haitian presence, as well as the remnants of an old Italian section along First and Pleasant avenues, above 114th Street. Frank Sinatra enjoyed the pizzas at **Patsy's**, 2287 First Avenue (between 117th and 118th streets, www.thepatsyspizza.com) so much that it's said he used to have stacks of them flown across the country to his mansion in California. Patsy's still does a mean pizza today; the secret is a coal-fired oven.

Three other East Harlem attractions are part of the famous "Museum Mile" (see page 228) that begins on the Upper East Side and, with a stately march of cultural awareness, continues north into Harlem.

The **Museum for African Art** ❼ (www.africanart.org), which has had a nomadic existence since it opened in 1984, has finally found a permanent home on Fifth Avenue between 109th and 110th Street. It is the first new museum to be built along Museum Mile since the Guggenheim, in 1959. Celebrating and showcasing the cultural life and heritage of Africa, there is a tower of luxury condos built above, facing Central Park, while the museum itself has a shimmering glass wall on one side, and a soaring wall of wood from Ghana on the other. It is scheduled to open in mid-2012.

El Museo del Barrio ❽

Address: 1230 Fifth Ave (at 104th Street), www.elmuseo.org
Telephone: 212-831 7272
Opening Hours: Tue, Thur–Sat 11am–6pm, Wed 11am–9pm, Sun 1pm–5pm
Entrance Fee: charge
Subway: 103rd St

New York's leading Latino cultural institute was originally founded by Puerto Rican educators and artists, but now covers the artistic impact of the Caribbean, too. Festivals and workshops held throughout the year are designed to involve the immediate community as well as visitors in projects that usually relate to its four special exhibitions. The museum's permanent collection of paintings and sculpture is particularly strong on works from the 1960s and '70s.

Museum of the City of New York ❾

Address: 1220 Fifth Ave (at 103rd Street), www.mcny.org
Telephone: 212-534 1672
Opening Hours: daily 10am–6pm
Entrance Fee: charge
Subway: 103rd St

Founded in 1923 and originally housed in Gracie Mansion, now the mayor's home, the museum has amassed a collection of over 1 million artifacts and artworks related to the city's ever-changing character and phenomenal growth. Antiquated fire trucks, antique toys, elegant bedroom furniture that once belonged to the Rockefellers – this is no dry and dusty slog through history, but a museum as vibrant and exciting as the city it chronicles.

ABOVE: the external wall of El Museo del Barrio.
BELOW: Columbia University.

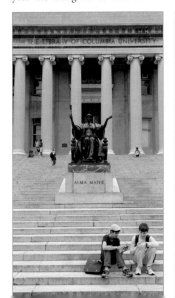

Ivy on the Hudson

NYU students share their campus with their fellow West Villagers. At Columbia, they have their own private swatch of the city, a quad that may not compete with the grassy stretches of their Ivy League peers, but is still unique in Manhattan.

There are more than two dozen buildings in the quad alone, and dozens more in the surrounding Morningside Heights neighborhood making up Columbia, Barnard, and Teacher's College. The Low Memorial Library is the jewel in the crown of the campus. A granite domed structure evoking classical Greek architecture, it sits within a series of lawns, its steps and plaza doubling as a meeting place and as a venue to watch outdoor concerts and theater. The library is flanked to the east and west by St Paul's Chapel and Earl Hall, which serve as spiritual and religious anchors.

Uris Hall, home to the lauded business school, is to the north, and the Joseph Pulitzer-funded Journalism Hall, where countless media giants have studied, is to the south. The enormous Butler Library, part of one of the 10 biggest academic collections in the country, dominates the far southern end.

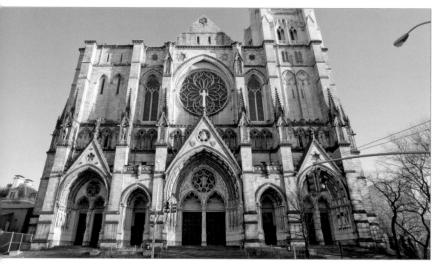

ABOVE: St John the Divine.

WEST HARLEM TO WASHINGTON HEIGHTS

West Harlem extends from around Amsterdam Avenue to Riverside Drive, taking in the Convent Avenue and Sugar Hill areas, along with Hamilton and Morningside Heights. Many of Harlem's white residents live in this district, which encompasses **Columbia University** and **Barnard College**, as well as the Jewish Theological and Union Theological seminaries. All these are located on or near upper Broadway.

At 112th Street and Amsterdam Avenue, the impressive **Cathedral of St John the Divine** is home to the city's largest Episcopal congregation; it is said to be the world's second-largest Gothic cathedral. At Riverside Drive and 120th Street, the non-denominational **Riverside Church** has the world's largest bell carillon atop its 22-story tower. Both churches host special religious and cultural events throughout the year.

Grant's Tomb

Address: Riverside Drive (at 122nd Street), www.nps.gov/gegr

Telephone: 212-666 1640
Opening Hours: daily 9am–5pm
Entrance Fee: free
Subway: 116th St

Officially the General Grant National Memorial, this granite mausoleum is the final resting place of Civil War general and former president Ulysses S. Grant and his wife, Julia; it was dedicated in 1897 as a national-park site, and is said to be inspired by Les Invalides in Paris, which contains Napoleon's tomb.

Parks and historic homes

Farther north on Riverside Drive, Manhattan's only state park opened in 1993 on the 28-acre (11-hectare) site of a former sewage-treatment plant alongside the Hudson between 137th and 145th streets. Today, the swimming pools, skating rink, and spectacular views of **Riverbank State Park** are enjoyed by an estimated 3 million people every year.

West and North Harlem have many other historical attractions. Around 160th Street is the **Jumel Terrace Historic District**, built up in the 1880s and 1890s. **Jumel Terrace** itself is a street of 20 beautifully presented row houses; the famous singer and activist Paul Robeson had a home nearby, on **Sylvan Terrace** on 161st.

Morris-Jumel Mansion ⑭

Address: 65 Jumel Terrace (at 162nd Street), www.morrisjumel.org
Telephone: 212-923 8008
Opening Hours: Wed–Sun 10am–4pm
Entrance Fee: charge
Subway: 163rd St

Built in 1765, this lovely Palladian-style mansion served as George Washington's headquarters during the American Revolution, and was visited by Queen Elizabeth II during the American Bicentennial of 1976.

Cultural complex

Audubon Terrace, back on Broadway between West 155th and 156th streets, is lined by stately neoclassical structures built as cultural institutions between 1905 and 1923. Admission to both of them is free: the **American Academy and Institute of Arts and Letters** (www.

artsandletters.org, tel: 212-368 5900), whose members have included luminaries from Mark Twain to Toni Morrison; and the **Hispanic Society of America** (www.hispanic society.org, tel: 212-926 2234), with a superb collection including El Greco

SHOP

One-stop shopping awaits at Harlem USA (www.harlem-usa.com), a huge complex at 300 125th Street. As well as several chain stores, there's a gym and the multi-screen Magic Johnson movie theater.

ABOVE: the interior of Grant's Tomb.
BELOW: Grant's Tomb.

SHOPPING

While few make the trek up to Harlem just to shop, there are definitely some unique stores worth checking out.

Books

Hue-Man Bookstore
2319 Frederick Douglas Boulevard (at 124th and 125th sts)
Tel: 212-665 7400
http://huemanbookstore.com
The country's largest book store dedicated to African-American literature stocks a wide range of genres from children's fiction to local history. It hosts a packed programme of author readings and signings, plus open-mic nights.

Clothing

Goliath
175 E. 105th Street (at 3rd and Lexington aves)
Tel: 212-360 7683
www.goliathny.com
An emporium of sneakers and urban attire for men and women that's frequented by rappers.
Swing
1960 Adam Clayton Powell Jr Boulevard (at 118th St)
Tel: 212-222 5802
http://swing-nyc.com
Selling itself as a "concept shop," this little boutique has an eclectic collection of art, housewares, and beauty products alongside clothes for women and children.

ABOVE: The Cloisters.
BELOW: the famous unicorn tapestry at The Cloisters.

EAT

Eat well and do good: the New Leaf Restaurant & Bar (http://newleaf restaurant.com), nestled in the wooded approach to The Cloisters, serves New American food in a rustic setting. A portion of the profits goes toward the upkeep of Fort Tryon Park.

and Goya. The Hispanic Society was renovated in early 2010; additions included new decorative arts galleries and early 20th-century masterworks by Spanish artists such as Sorolla.

Once mainly Irish, today far-northern **Washington Heights** is pleasantly ethnically mixed, as Dominicans, Puerto Ricans, Haitians, and others claim it for their own. New York's largest Jewish educational institution, **Yeshiva University**, has a campus on 185th Street. The tiny **Bennett Park**, between 183rd and 185th streets, was named after a Scottish immigrant and holds the honor of being the highest point on the island at a whopping 265 feet (81 meters) above sea level.

On West 192nd Street, Frederick Law Olmsted's son designed lovely **Fort Tryon Park** (67 acres/27 hectares), a hilly patch of lawns and gardens with meandering paths, unobstructed views of the Hudson River, and perfect spots for shady picnics. This is not the park for a game of softball or to watch a concert. It's for relaxation and contemplation, a reminder of a New York when there

were quiet getaways. It is no wonder that here you will find The Cloisters, a stately and serene branch of the Metropolitan Museum of Art.

The Cloisters ⓱

Address: Fort Tryon Park, www.met museum.org

Telephone: 212-923 3700
Opening Hours: Tue–Sun Mar–Oct 9.30am–5.15pm, Nov–Feb 9am–4.45pm
Entrance Fee: charge
Subway: 190th St

The Cloisters is an inspiring spot, built to showcase the Metropolitan's collection of medieval art. French and Spanish monastic cloisters, a 12th-century chapterhouse, and Gothic and Romanesque chapels were shipped from Europe and reassembled on this site, stone by stone. The prize of the collection is the six hand-woven 15th-century Unicorn Tapestries. Visiting is as much about exploring the building and its grounds as it is about the art. Your admission to the Met will get you access to The Cloisters on the same day, and both are covered by the CityPass.

In Inwood

The parks don't end there. Further north, in **Inwood**, the wild and woolly Inwood Hill Park is home to nature trails and bald eagles. It reaches as far as the Spuyten Duyvil Creek, which separates Manhattan from the Bronx and connects the Hudson to the Harlem River Canal. While you are in the area, stop by the pretty **Dyckman Farmhouse Museum** (http://dyckmanfarmhouse.org, tel: 212-304 9422; Fri–Sun 11am–5pm; charge). A Dutch-Colonial cottage from 1785, it was restored in 1915.

ABOVE: Amy Ruth's restaurant.

RESTAURANTS

Amy Ruth's
113 W. 116th St (at Lenox and 7th aves)
Tel: 212-280-8779
www.amyruthsharlem.com
B, L, & D Tue–Sun, L & D only Mon **$**
The restaurant attracts political, sports, and entertainment luminaries, but the big pull is the Southern food.

Dinosaur Bar-B-Que
700 125th St (at 12th Ave)
Tel: 212-694 1777
www.dinosaurbarbque.com
L & D daily
$$–$$$

This import from upstate is a candidate for the best barbecue in the city. Blues acts on the weekend.

Londel's Supper Club
2620 Frederick Douglass Blvd (at W. 138th and W. 140th sts)
Tel: 212-234 6114
www.londelsrestaurant.com
L & D Tue–Sat, Br Sun
$$–$$$
Weekend jazz nights are a big attraction at this friendly soul-food haven with a most welcoming owner presiding.

Melba's
300 W. 114th St (at Frederick Douglass Blvd)
Tel: 212-864 7777
www.melbasrestaurant.com
D Tue–Fri, Br & D Sat–Sun
$$–$$$
Start with one of the luscious rum cocktails, then move on to ribs or select one of the other yummy soul-food items on Melba's menu.

Miss Maude's Spoonbread Too
547 Lenox Ave (at 137th and 138th sts)
Tel: 212-690 3100
www.spoonbreadinc.com/miss_maudes.htm
L and D daily **$**
One of Harlem's most inviting restaurants. Most diners come for the fried chicken, Southern-style.

Sylvia's
328 Lenox Ave (at 126th and 127th sts)
Tel: 212-996 0660
www.sylviasrestaurant.com
B, L, & D Mon–Sat, Br & D Sun
$$
Soul food, Harlem-style. It's a good idea to book. Gospel brunch on Sundays.

Prices for a three-course dinner per person with half a bottle of wine:

$ = under $20
$$ = $20–$45
$$$ = $45–$60
$$$$ = over $60

THE OUTER BOROUGHS

Some come for the art and music, while others have lived here their entire lives. For 6.5 million New Yorkers, the boroughs of Brooklyn, Queens, the Bronx, and Staten Island are home

New York City

Staten Island, Queens, Brooklyn, the Bronx: these are places some visitors to Manhattan simply don't go to, except maybe to see the zoo or a ballgame, or to take the ferry.

But they're really missing out. The Outer Boroughs offer parks, cafes and gourmet restaurants, museums, and history. Cool bars buzz around Williamsburg in Brooklyn; woodlands and the Verrazano-Narrows Bridge beckon on Staten Island; New York's oldest – and thriving – movie studios are in Queens; and the home of Edgar Allen Poe engages the mind in the Bronx. There are architectural sites of Old New York. As well as the zoo, botanical gardens, and Yankee Stadium, of course.

Being so overlooked, these attractions – all less than an hour from Broadway, and accessible by public transportation – have the added plus of being (with few exceptions) uncluttered by other out-of-towners.

Neighborhoods

The key word in the Outer Boroughs is "neighborhood." Neighborhoods change, overlap, and can be a bazaar of ethnic delight. Stroll through Middle Eastern stores selling frankincense and myrrh, order pasta in Italian, and have *kasha* served in Yiddish.

Some new neighbors are artists and young professionals in search of affordable rents. As the prices of Manhattan soar, a new generation has turned to former industrial zones, like Long Island City in Queens and Williamsburg in Brooklyn, to live. Co-ops flourish where warehouses once thrived. Burned-out buildings become galleries or restaurants. Then

Main Attractions
BROOKLYN ACADEMY OF MUSIC
BROOKLYN MUSEUM OF ART
PROSPECT PARK
RED HOOK AND WILLIAMSBURG
CONEY ISLAND
FLUSHING MEADOWS CORONA PARK
MUSEUM OF THE MOVING IMAGE
STATEN ISLAND
HISTORIC RICHMOND TOWN
EDGAR ALLAN POE COTTAGE

Maps and Listings
MAP, PAGE 264
SHOPPING, PAGE 278
RESTAURANTS, PAGE 286

LEFT: the New York City Marathon starts on Staten Island's Verrazano-Narrows Bridge.
RIGHT: the Enid A. Haupt Conservatory in the Bronx's New York Botanical Garden.

ABOVE: cruise to Brooklyn from Lower Manhattan by water taxi.

real-estate values skyrocket, and the artists turn their sights elsewhere.

Amid the new is the older side of the boroughs: the avenues, parks, and palazzi built as grand civic projects in the late 19th century. Architects like Frederick Law Olmsted and Calvert Vaux found open space here unavailable in Midtown. With sweeping gestures, they decked the boroughs with buildings inspired by the domes and gables of Parisian boulevards.

Despite this grandeur, however, one thing "the boroughs" lack is Manhattan's easy grid system. Off the parkways, they are a maze of

streets and expressways. With a little attention, though, it's easy to uncover neighborhoods that can be explored at a comfortable pace on foot – places where the boroughs really breathe.

BROOKLYN ❶

The over 70 sq miles (180 sq km) at the southeast tip of Long Island encompass the second-most populous borough of New York City, Brooklyn. More than 2.4 million people live here, which would make it the fourth-largest metropolis in the United States if it weren't a part of New York City. Just a 20-minute

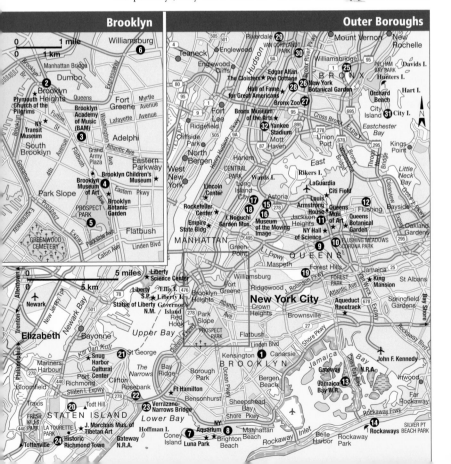

ride on the subway from the heart of Manhattan will take you out to Williamsburg or Prospect Park.

Another scenic way to escape from Manhattan is via the **Brooklyn Bridge**. A stroll across the walkway leads to **Fulton Ferry Landing**, where cobblestoned streets are coming back to life after lying dormant for decades. It was here that the borough inaugurated its first mass transit, to Wall Street. In 1814 Robert Fulton's steam ferry, the *Nassau*, replaced the East River's earlier rowboats, sailboats, and vessels powered by horses on treadmills. Ferries remained the main way to cross until the Brooklyn Bridge opened in 1883.

DUMBO

Brooklyn's modern-day renaissance began in now-classic New York style – following the trail of artists. When Soho got too expensive, they moved over the water to lofts in **DUMBO** (for **D**own **U**nder the **M**anhattan **B**ridge **O**verpass), now a thriving neighborhood that includes the innovative cultural hubs **St Ann's Warehouse** (38 Water Street, www. stannswarehouse.org, tel: 718-254 8779) and Galapagos (16 Main Street,

http://galapagosartspace.com, tel: 718-222 8500).

Young families followed – so many that recently revitalized **Brooklyn Bridge Park** incorporated into its design a "destination playground," a carrousel, open grass fields, and a rock beach on the East River where the Brooklyn Bridge Park Conservancy holds ecology classes for curious minds of all ages. The conservancy has been doing all it can to attract people to the glorious new spaces, and it's working. Outdoor movies are always big draws, as was the swimming pool that floated in the East River for a summer. In autumn, there are fall foliage tours; in the winter, ice-skating. Construction continues with new piers containing sporting fields, lawns, and river access, opening in the near future.

When dumbo became too expensive, the artists moved to Williamsburg, and when they were priced out of Williamsburg, they colonized Red Hook and just about every other corner of the metropolis

ABOVE: DUMBO flea market.
BELOW LEFT: Brooklyn Bridge as seen from Dumbo.
BELOW: ice cream on sale by Brooklyn Bridge.

ABOVE: elegant
Brooklyn Heights.
RIGHT: Brooklyn street
scene.
BELOW: the
neighborhood of DUMBO
stands for Down Under
(the) Manhattan Bridge
Overpass.

where the cost of studio space wasn't extortionate and like-minded creative types were likely to follow.

Wherever artists went, they left behind a series of neighborhood revivals when they moved on. For instance, you can listen to chamber music, jazz, and avant-garde music at **Bargemusic** (Fulton Ferry Landing, Brooklyn, www.bargemusic.org, tel: 718-624 4061), a converted old coffee barge that's moored at the end of Old Fulton Street.

It's on the other side of the Fulton Ferry Landing from the **River Café** (see page 287), considered one of the city's most romantic restaurants. Around the bend to the east is the old **Brooklyn Navy Yard** (now an industrial park, not open to visitors), where ships like the USS *Missouri* were built during World War II.

Brooklyn Heights ❷

Directly inland from the Fulton Ferry, the property has always been

hot. **In Brooklyn Heights**, where streets are lined with narrow row houses, brownstones change hands for sums in the million dollars.

Along the river edge of the Heights is the **Brooklyn Heights Promenade**, a walkway that overlooks the East River and the Brooklyn

Bridge, and offers a movie-star view of the Manhattan skyline. A stroll along here and through the Heights can be extremely pleasant. Each block is iced with wrought-iron flourishes, stained-glass windows, stone busts, and fancy trims. On the corner of **Willow Street** and **Middagh** is the oldest wooden house in the district, dating to 1824.

Before the Civil War, **Plymouth Church of the Pilgrims** (www.plymouthchurch.org, tel: 718-624 4743; tours available by appointment on weekdays, without an appointment after Sunday morning service), on **Orange Street** between Henry and Hicks, served as a stop on the Underground Railroad, while Henry Ward Beecher (Harriet Beecher Stowe's brother) preached abolitionism to the congregation.

Many streets in the Heights, like Middagh and Hicks, take their names from the neighborhood's early gentry. Five, however, are named after flora – **Pineapple**, **Cranberry**, **Orange**, **Poplar**, and **Willow** streets.

The **Brooklyn Historical Society** (128 Pierrepont Street, www.brooklynhistory.org, tel: 718-222 4111; Wed–Fri, Sun noon–5pm, Sat 10am–5pm; charge) is in a landmark building. Browse and enjoy its rich mix of "Old Ebbett's Field" baseball memorabilia, maritime artifacts, and Coney Island exhibitionism. A block away is **St Ann and the Holy Trinity** church. Dating to the 1840s, it has the oldest stained-glass windows made in the US.

On the southern slope of Brooklyn Heights is the **Civic Center**, with its Greek Revival **Borough Hall** (209 Joralemon Street, www.visitbrooklyn.org, tel: 718-802 3820). From here, it's a short walk down Boerum Place to the fun **New York Transit Museum** (Boerum Place and Schermerhorn Street, www.mta.info/mta/museum, tel: 718-694 1600; Tue–Fri 10am–4pm, Sat–Sun 11am–4pm; charge). In a classic 1930s-era subway station, the museum has exhibits on the city's transportation systems, along with vintage subway cars and buses.

Keep walking south past State Street and turn right on **Atlantic Avenue**. Between Court and Henry streets, stores bulge with imported spices, dried fruits, olives, and halvah.

TIP

Brooklyn's East River waterfront has been undergoing the same upscale transition as the Hudson River in Manhattan. Oh-so-cool Red Hook (and the city's only Ikea) is hard to reach by subway or bus, but it's easy by water taxi. Go to www.nywatertaxi.com.

BELOW: the Brooklyn Heights Promenade provides amazing views of Manhattan.

TIP

The free HOB Connection bus (www. heartofbrooklyn.org; first Sat of the month 5pm–11pm) leaves from the Brooklyn Museum every 30 minutes and makes stops at restaurants and art and entertainment venues throughout Prospect Heights, a great way to see the borough at its liveliest.

Some bakeries cook their filo pastries in coal-burning ovens. This Middle Eastern bazaar shares the sidewalk with a number of antiques shops. These have plenty of interesting stock (Victorian, Art Deco, 1930s, 1940s), and are usually open on weekends, if not every day.

Fort Greene

On the other side of Brooklyn's not terribly attractive downtown is another cache of worthwhile sights. From Brooklyn Heights, walk east on Atlantic Avenue, and turn left on Flatbush Avenue.

At Flatbush and Hanson Place, one block down, you'll find the **Brooklyn Flea Market** housed in One Hanson Place, a former bank. The schedule and location of the market change frequently, so check the website (www.brooklynflea.com) before setting out.

Just a few blocks down, you'll find **Junior's** (www.juniorscheesecake.com), home to Brooklyn's original claim to cheesecake fame, and BAM, the Brooklyn Academy of Music.

RIGHT: One Hanson Place.
BELOW: the famous Brooklyn Flea Market.

Brooklyn Academy of Music (BAM) ❸

Address: Peter Jay Sharp Building, 30 Lafayette Ave, www.bam.org
Telephone: 718-636 4100
Opening Hours: Box office phone Mon–Fri 10am–6pm, Sat noon–6pm
Entrance Fee: charge
Subway: Atlantic Ave, Nevins St, Fulton St

At the corner of Lafayette Avenue and Ashland Place is this innovative school and performance space for music, film and the performing arts. Its spectrum has included multimedia maestro Laurie Anderson, Martha Clarke's performance art, and the music of minimalist composer Philip Glass. Home to the experimental **Next Wave Festival** since 1982, it includes the beautifully restored **BAM Harvey Theater** (formerly known as the Majestic Theater), the **lively BAM Café**, and four screening rooms, known as the **BAM Rose Cinemas**. Just around the corner is a massive new shopping mall, **Atlantic Terminal**.

Prospect Heights and Park Slope

Follow Flatbush Avenue in the other direction from Fort Greene, and you'll make your way on the road that separates **Park Slope**, to your right, and **Prospect Heights**, to your left. Here you'll find, at Grand Army Plaza, the entrance to Brooklyn's green lung, Prospect Park. The neighborhood of Park Slope runs along Prospect Park's western border, and is filled with Victorian row houses, many of which have been divided up into apartments. It has become a popular neighborhood for Manhattan defectors and young families. Seventh Avenue, wall-to-wall with stores and restaurants, is two blocks west of the park.

Make a left from Grand Army Plaza onto Eastern Parkway, and you'll see a number of cultural attractions lining the boulevard.

Brooklyn Museum of Art ❹

Address: 200 Eastern Parkway, www.brooklynmuseum.org
Telephone: 718-638 5000
Opening Hours: Wed, Fri–Sun 11am–6pm (first Sat of each month until 11pm), Thur 11am–10pm
Entrance Fee: charge
Subway: Eastern Parkway/Brooklyn Museum

This marvelous museum – the second-largest in New York after the Metropolitan – has an Egyptian collection considered by many the best outside of Cairo and London.

Wonderfully eclectic, the Brooklyn museum displays an array of world-class exhibits, including 28 period rooms and an unusual outdoor sculpture garden of New York

ABOVE: Grand Army Plaza and the Soldiers' and Sailors' Memorial Arch.
BELOW: the Brooklyn Academy of Music now features dance, film, and theater, in addition to music.

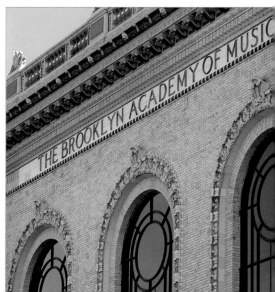

building ornaments. There are many other highlights in addition to its celebrated Egyptian relics. A global museum, it has lovely artifacts from Polynesia, Africa, and Southeast Asia, Japanese ceramics, and an *Art in the Americas* section with highlights from ancient Peruvian textiles to modern bowls from New Mexico's Pueblos.

American art

The kaleidoscope of American art continues with Colonial decorative art, including a reconstructed 1675 Dutch interior from Brooklyn itself, and a comprehensive display of 18th- and 19th-century American paintings with contemporary masterpieces by artists such as Georgia O'Keeffe. Lastly, there's an impressive stock of European – especially French and 19th-century – art, including sculptures by Rodin and major paintings by Degas, Cézanne, Monet, and Matisse, and a photography collection that is excellent.

Grand Army Plaza

Beside the museum is the **Brooklyn Botanic Garden** (1000 Washington Avenue, www.bbg.org, tel: 718-623 7200; Tue–Fri 8am–6pm, Sat–Sun 10am–6pm; charge), covering 52 acres (21 hectares). The Japanese gardens alone are worth a visit, especially

when the cherry trees bloom in spring, but it's pleasant in any month.

The huge traffic circle at the western end of the Parkway is **Grand Army Plaza**, where the **Soldiers' and Sailors' Memorial Arch** – a Civil War memorial designed by John H. Duncan, architect of Grant's Tomb, with sculptures by Frederick MacMonnies – provides a formal entrance to the 585 acres (237 hectares) that make up **Prospect Park** ❺. The park, plaza, and boulevards were all designed by Frederick Law Olmsted and Calvert Vaux, and are considered to be their best work, even better perhaps than Central Park.

Prospect Park

Grand Army Plaza is their most literal tribute to Paris – an Arc de Triomphe at the focal point of the borough. Roam dreamily through the romantic park: the **Long Meadow**, the **Ravine, and Nethermead**. For details, check www.prospectpark.org, tel: 718-965 8951. At the **Children's Corner** (near Prospect Park Subway), as well as an antique carrousel, there is the **Lefferts Historic House** (tel:

718-789 2822; Apr–Nov Thur–Sun, Dec and Feb–Mar Sat–Sun; free), a two-story Dutch farmhouse built in 1777–83. Interactive exhibits portray African and Native American life in 19th-century Flatbush.

Williamsburg

North of the Manhattan Bridge, up the East River, there's another connection to Manhattan, the **Williamsburg Bridge**, which is, naturally, also the entryway to **Williamsburg** ❻. At the foot of the bridge is the **Peter Luger Steakhouse** (see page 287). Across Broadway, the lovely, Renaissance-style **Williamsburg Savings Bank** building was constructed in 1875, while north up Driggs Avenue, the onion-domed Russian Orthodox **Cathedral of the Transfiguration** (228 N. 12th Street, www.roct.org, tel: 718-387 1064), dating from 1922, demonstrates the area's ties to Eastern Europe. This part of Brooklyn is hopping right now. **Bedford Avenue** is the main drag, with clothes stores and cafes neighboring happily.

One block west is **Berry Street**, another place with hip restaurants,

Barnum's Circus (later the Barnum & Bailey Circus) opened in Brooklyn in 1871. "The Greatest Show on Earth" was an instant success. By taking the circus on tour (in 65 railcars), the show was playing to 20,000 people a day by 1874.

BELOW: John Singer Sargent's 1889 painting *An Out-of-Doors Study.*

TIP

Queens was the home of Louis Armstrong, Dizzy Gillespie, Count Basie, Billie Holiday, Ella Fitzgerald, and John Coltrane. Queens Jazz Trail tours can be booked through Flushing Town Hall, tel: 718-463 7700.

cafes for people-watching, and some intriguing street-corner galleries and eclectic stores. Williamsburg has a vibrant arts community, and some of the outdoor murals and graffiti are of a high quality. The center for all this creativity is the **Williamsburg Art & Historical Center** (135 Broadway at Bedford, www.wahcenter.net, tel: 718-486 7372).

Crown Heights and East Brooklyn

East of central Brooklyn in **Crown Heights**, Hasidic Jews and immigrants from the West Indies are building communities that are worlds apart, but only a few doorsteps away. Also here is **Brooklyn Children's Museum** (145 Brooklyn Avenue, at St Mark's Avenue, www.brooklynkids.org, tel: 718-735 4400; Tue–Fri 11am–5pm, Sat–Sun 10am–5pm; charge). Founded in 1899, this is the oldest children's museum in America and very much a hands-on learning experience, with thousands of interesting artifacts to wonder at – and almost as many buttons and knobs to twiddle. Child-powered vehicles, too.

Even farther east is **Brownsville**. Before World War II, this was a mainly Jewish slum, where local legend locates the headquarters for Murder Inc. – the notorious 1930s gangster ring – in a candy store on Livonia Avenue. (For a Brownsville classic book, check out *A Walker in the City* by Alfred Kazin.)

Coney Island ⓥ

On the coast to the south is Coney Island, which is not actually an island, but a peninsula. The famous name of Coney Island really belongs to what was once New York's premier vacation center, and urbanites have been escaping here ever since the summers of the 1840s. Get a **Nathan's Famous** hot dog at the enormous stand on Surf and Stillwell. The grills, first fired up in 1916, can sizzle more than 1,500 dogs an hour on a hot summer's day.

Tempt fate aboard the **Cyclone**, the granddaddy of roller coasters, with 2,640ft (805 meters) of steel-and-wood track and cars speeding at 68mph (109kph). Along with **Deno's Wonderwheel** (www.wonderwheel.com), a giant Ferris wheel surrounded by quaint rides for young children, this is all that remains of the old Coney Island amusements. 2009 saw the arrival of some boisterous new neighbors, the **Scream Zone** and **Luna Park** (www.lunaparknyc.com). Their 19 brand new rides, a combination of whimsical retro designs and stomach-churning modern engineering, are categorized as Mild Thrill, Moderate Thrill, and High Thrill.

For a number of years, it seemed that the age of the amusement park was over in Coney Island, but it is back with a vengeance, and it has been part of the revitalization of the entire neighborhood. The 2001 arrival of the minor league **Brooklyn Cyclones** (www.brooklyncyclones.com) baseball team, which plays at nearby MCU Park, certainly helped kickstart the revival. The boardwalk,

BELOW: shopping on Bedford Avenue.

once a seedy stretch of planks, is now a (mostly) pleasant place to stroll, cycle and watch the seagulls swooping over the ocean.

The popular **New York Aquarium** (www.nyaquarium.com, tel: 718-265 3474; daily 10am until at least 4.30pm, depending on season;

charge) is located just behind the beach, at West 8th Street and Surf Avenue. With an outdoor theater where frisky and lovable sea lions perform, this metropolitan home for ocean life is one of the borough's best-known attractions.

Farther east on the boardwalk is **Brighton Beach ⓽**, which for years was an enclave of elderly Jews, made famous by playwright Neil Simon. But in the 1970s a new wave of migrants, mainly Russians and Ukrainians, began moving into the area, which soon became known as "Little Odessa." Today Russian restaurants, book stores, markets, and other businesses have infused the neighborhood with vitality. Dance the night away at one of the exuberant nightspots on **Brighton Beach Avenue**.

QUEENS ⓽

Visitors taking taxis from JFK International Airport into Manhattan pass as swiftly as traffic allows through

ABOVE: Nathan's Famous hot dogs are a Coney Island tradition.
LEFT: the big wheel at Coney Island's Astroland Amusement Park.
BELOW: after that Nathan's hot dog, why not finish with some cotton candy?

ABOVE AND RIGHT:
images of jazz legend
Louis "Satchmo"
Armstrong's home.

Queens, but the borough is more than just a point of arrival. Named for Queen Catherine of Braganza, wife of Charles II of England, it is a diverse community, with one of the largest Greek neighborhoods outside of Athens, and immigrants from all around the world.

The area between **Northern Boulevard** and **Grand Central Parkway**, once a swamp and later the "Corona Garbage Dump," ended up as the glamorous grounds for the 1939 and 1964 World's Fairs. Now known as **Flushing Meadows-Corona Park ❿**, it is an expanse of 1,255 acres (508 hectares) that includes museums, sports facilities, and botanical gardens. On display in what was the 1939 and 1964 World's Fair's New York City Building – now the **Queens Museum of Art** (www.queensmuseum.org, tel: 718-592 9700; Wed–Sun noon–6pm; charge) – is the **Panorama of the City of New York**, a scale replica of the city in meticulous detail.

The **New York Hall of Science** (www.nyscience.org; tel: 718-699 0005; daily Apr-Aug, Tue–Sun Sept–Mar, opening hours dependent on season; charge), near the park's 111th Street entrance, is well known for its hands-on exhibits and rocket ships in the outdoor Rocket Park. The park also has a theater, a zoo, an indoor skating rink (in the same building as the Museum of Art), and an antique carrousel.

Close by are two nationally recognizable sports arenas, the **USTA Billie Jean King National Tennis Center**, open to public players but also home of the US Open every September; and the new **Citi Field**, which became home of the Mets in 2009 (http://newyork.mets.mlb.com). Also in the neighborhood, the 38-acre (15-hectare) **Queens Botanical Garden** (43–50 Main Street, www.queensbotanical.org, tel: 718-886 3800; Tue–Sun 8am–6pm, until 4.30pm in winter; free) has the largest rose garden in the northeast, and is a good spot for weddings.

Louis Armstrong House ⓫

Address: 34–56 107th St (at 34th and 37th aves), Corona, www.satchmo.net
Telephone: 718-478 8274
Opening Hours: Tue–Fri 10am–5pm, Sat–Sun noon–5pm
Entrance Fee: charge
Subway: 103rd St/Corona Plaza

Louis and Lucille Armstrong came to live in this modest house in 1943, a year after they were married, and stayed here for the rest of their lives, despite Louis being one of the world's most famous faces. Louis died in his sleep here in 1971, and Lucille stayed on until her own death in 1983.

Lucille had much more to do with the decoration of the house than Louis did – he was often on tour – but "Satchmo's" den has been restored to look exactly as it did in his lifetime. Also part of the museum are the **Louis Armstrong Archives** (Queens College, 65–30 Kissena Boulevard, www.louisarmstrong house.org/about/contact.htm; weekdays by appointment; free), the first stop for hundreds of jazz researchers from all over the world.

Flushing and its Little Asia

East of the park, **Flushing** ⓬ is packed with history, and perked up by "**Little Asia**," with one of the biggest Hindu temples in North America, on **Bowne Street**.

The **Quaker Meeting House**, built in 1696, is the oldest place of worship in New York City. A good place to learn about the area is the **Queens Historical Society** (143–135 37th Avenue, www.queenshistorical society.org, tel: 718-939 0647; Tue, Sat–Sun 2.30–4.30pm).

Most people assume the largest stretches of land in Queens belong to **JFK** and **LaGuardia** airports. These sprawling terminals with their long runways are huge, but an even more impressive acreage remains undeveloped – nearly a quarter of the borough of Queens is kept as parkland, under preservation orders.

South of the JFK runways, **Jamaica Bay Wildlife Refuge** ⓭ (Cross Bay Boulevard, www.nps.gov/gate, tel: 718-318 4340; free) gives a home to more than 300 species of birds, as well as scores of small creatures like raccoons, chipmunks, and turtles.

Long Island City in QNS (as residents like to define their area), promotes itself as the eastern counterpoint to Chelsea, with more light, more space, and less glamour. But glamour does come its way: both The Sopranos and Sex and the City were made at LIC's Silvercup Studios.

BELOW: the Queens building called 5 Pointz, a labor of love by local writer Meres.

the biggest municipal beach in the country, easy to reach by subway from Midtown Manhattan. To the east is **Far Rockaway**; to the west is **Neponsit**, where old mansions echo the bygone splendor of Rockaway days when wealthy New Yorkers vacationed here. Sadly, **Belle Harbor** was the site of the tragic incident on November 13, 2001, when American Airlines Flight 587 crashed shortly after take-off from JFK, killing 260 people, including some residents and rescue workers from 9/11.

ABOVE: nearly one quarter of Queens is reserved for parkland.
BELOW: the Museum of the Moving Image is a fun, stylish ride through aspects of modern visual culture.

Trail maps, available from National Park Rangers at the visitor center, guide hikers and strollers to some beautiful routes through luscious groves of red cedar and Japanese pine trees. Workshops about birds are also available year-round. The birds of Jamaica Bay avoid tangling with passing jet-powered flyers thanks to an innovative program using falcons to encourage them away from the danger areas.

Big beach

Along the southernmost strip of Queens, **The Rockaways** 🄮 form

Astoria and movieland

On the other side of Queens, facing Manhattan across the East River, **Astoria** 🄯 is a modest section of small apartment buildings and semi-detached homes. Traditionally a Greek enclave, Astoria has lately attracted migrants from across the world. Along main drags like **Steinway Street** and **Broadway** are Greek delis, Italian bakeries, Asian markets, and restaurants. And despite the movie stars working nearby, the side streets remain pretty quiet.

Astoria has also regained its old status as the center of New York's

Museum of the Moving Image

The Museum of the Moving Image was the first institute in the US devoted to exploring the art, history, technique, and technology of film, television, and video. It is part of the Kaufman Astoria Studios complex, which was Paramount Pictures' East Coast facility in the 1920s. Along with nearby Silvercup Studios, this is the largest and busiest production facility between London and Hollywood, favored by such luminaries as Woody Allen and Martin Scorsese.

The museum has a pleasing feel, with plenty of early film and TV equipment. The permanent *Behind the Screen* exhibition features interactive workstations where you can select sound effects for famous movies, or insert your own dialogue into classic scenes. There is also a gallery devoted to temporary exhibitions, which has hosted a diverse range of themes, including the first video games exhibition in 1989.

The more than 400 yearly film screenings are held most Friday evenings and weekend afternoons. In 2011, the museum completed a $68 million expansion that added another state-of-the-art theater, a screening room, two ampitheaters, and a learning center, not to mention a new shop, lobby, and cafe.

Moving Image

film industry. The motion-picture business here dates back to the 1920s, when the Marx Brothers and Gloria Swanson were among those working at what was then the Famous Players-Lasky Studios. The **Kaufman Astoria Studios** (www.kaufmanastoria.com) now occupy the old site. Films and commercials are rolling again, here and at **Silvercup Studios** (www.silvercupstudios.com) in nearby Long Island City.

Museum of the Moving Image ⓰

Address: 35th Ave (at 37th St), Astoria, www.movingimage.us
Telephone: 718-784 0077
Opening Hours: Tue–Thur 10.30am–5pm, Fri 10.30am–8pm, Sat–Sun 10.30am–7pm
Entrance Fee: charge
Subway: Steinway St

This museum evokes the glory days of early New York filmmaking, when Astoria's studios were known as "Hollywood on the Hudson." It also has fascinating and fun exhibits that demonstrate how movies are made and the possibilities of new technologies, and hosts regular film screenings (Fri–Sun) in some of the city's most enjoyable movie theaters.

Long Island City ⓱

West of Astoria, Long Island City also has much to offer visitors. An aging industrial section, it was discovered in the 1980s by the arts community. From 2002–4, MoMA qns was relocated here, while it awaited the completion of its improved premises in Manhattan. **P.S.1 Contemporary Art Center** (22–25 Jackson Avenue, at 46th Avenue, http://momaps1.org, tel: 718-784 2084; closed Thur–Mon noon–6pm; charge) is an exuberant exhibition space attached to the Museum of Modern Art that's dedicated to showing the work of emerging artists, and one of the city's most exciting venues.

Sculpture parks

A lovely, leafy landmark is **the Isamu Noguchi Garden Museum ⓲** (9-01 Vernon Boulevard at 33rd Road,

ABOVE: Jacob Riis Park on The Rockaways are the country's biggest municipal beach.
BELOW: geese strut their stuff at Jamaica Bay Wildlife Refuge.

a converted factory building, while others encircle a garden of the artist's design. The overall effect is one of harmony and serenity, a far cry from Manhattan's screaming streets.

Just up Vernon Boulevard, more outdoor art can be enjoyed in the 4½-acre (2-hectare) **Socrates Sculpture Park** (www.socratessculpturepark.org, tel: 718-956 1819; free). Started by artists, this grass expanse has been made an official city park. The view across to Manhattan, through giant sculptures, is delightful.

Garden suburb

A neighborhood worth exploring is **Forest Hills** ⑲. Best known for the West Side Tennis Club (www.foresthillstennis.com, tel: 718-268 2300), once host to the US Open, this part of Queens was inspired by

ABOVE: innovative P.S.1, affiliated with the Museum of Modern Art, has its premises in an old schoolhouse.

www.noguchi.org, tel: 718-204 7088; closed Wed–Fri 10am–5pm, Sat–Sun 11am–6pm; charge). Almost 250 works by the Japanese sculptor are displayed in 13 galleries created from

SHOPPING

Shopping

A trip to the outer boroughs will reveal ethnic enclaves and plenty of box-stores, but also a variety of world-class shops that would be at home in Manhattan.

Art

Pierogi
177 North 9th Street (at Bedford and Driggs aves), Brooklyn
Tel: 718-599 2144
www.pierogi2000.com
This artist-run gallery has been a vital part of the art scene since 1994 when Williamsburg saw its mass migration of creative talent.

Books

Book Court
163 Court Street (at Pacific and Dean sts), Brooklyn

Tel: 212-875 3677
www.bookcourt.org
There are numerous signings from celebrity authors at Brooklyn's beloved book store.

Clothing

Beacon's Closet
88 N. 11th Street (at Wythe Ave) and 92 5th Avenue (at Warren St), Brooklyn
Tel: 718-486 0816 and 718-230 1630
www.beaconscloset.com
Vintage fashion in Williamsburg and Park Slope.
Built by Wendy
46 N. 6th Street (at Kent Ave), Brooklyn
Tel: 718-384 2882
www.builtbywendy.com
Wendy Mullin, the master of denim and designer T-shirts favored by young celebrities, has expanded to cover all

avenues of women's fashion. The outlet store is in Williamsburg, and the flagship in Little Italy.
Ethereal Boutique
47-38 Vernon Blvd (at 48th Ave), Queens
Tel: 718-482 8884
www.etherealnyc.com
Manhattan style with a Long Island City address, this little shop has a unique and eclectic selection of clothing, much of it inspired by the owner's world travels.

Department Stores

Everything Goes
140 and 208 Bay Street and 17 Brook Street (near Victory Blvd), Staten Island
Tel: 718-273 7139
www.etgstores.com
Not so much a department store as a collection of funky and fun shops found within easy walking distance of the Staten

Island ferry, including a vintage clothing outlet, a book store, a gallery, and a furniture retailer.

Food

Arthur Avenue
Arthur Avenue (at E. 187th St), the Bronx
www.arthuravenuebronx.com
Rather than visit a single store, walk down Arthur Avenue in the Belmont neighborhood of the Bronx for your pick of Italian delicacies.

Home

The Brooklyn Kitchen
100 Frost Street (at Leonard St and Manhattan Ave), Brooklyn
Tel: 718-389 2982
www.thebrooklynkitchen.com
An overflowing cornucopia of food products for the discerning cook, with all the necessary equipment to go along with it.

the English "Garden Suburb" movement. Planning began in 1906 with a low-cost housing endowment, but in 1923, the project only half completed, residents took over management and began vetting newcomers. The mock-Tudor district turned fashionable, and styled itself "lawn-tennis capital of the western hemisphere."

For a change of pace, a day at the races can be fun. Events at **Aqueduct Racetrack** (www.nyra.com, 110-00 Rockaway Boulevard; tel: 718-641 4700), include the Wood Memorial and the Gotham Stakes.

STATEN ISLAND 20

Once upon a time in New York, there was an island with roads paved by oyster shells, where yachts swayed by resort hotels, European-style finishing schools were founded, and where Americans first played tennis.

Could this be Staten Island, the least-known borough? To most New Yorkers, this is just the place where the famous ferry goes. As the poet Edna St Vincent Millay wrote: "We were very tired, we were very merry – we had gone back and forth all night on the ferry." Yes,

come for the ride, but try to reserve some time for Staten Island itself.

The ferry lands at **St George** 21, where part of the extensive ferry collection is shown at the **St George Ferry Terminal** (1 Bay Street). Two blocks away is the **Staten Island Museum** (http://statenislandmuseum.org, tel: 718-727 1135; daily noon–5pm, opens at 10am on Sat; charge), in a dignified 1918 building at 75 Stuyvesant Place.

Snug Harbor Cultural Center (1000 Richmond Terrace, www. snugharbor.org, tel: 718-448 2500; Tue–Fri 8am–6pm, Sat–Sun 10am–6pm, closes at 4.30 in winter) is a short bus ride from St George. The handsome visitor center first opened in 1831 as a home for retired seamen. Now its 83 acres (34 hectares) of wetlands and woodlands are a Smithsonian affiliate. Within the center's grounds is the **Staten Island Botanical Garden** (free), with an orchid collection and Chinese Scholar's Garden (charge). Here, too, is the fun **Staten Island Children's Museum** (http://statenislandkids.org, tel: 718-273 2060; Tue–Sun; charge), an interactive experience for kids.

ABOVE: a day at Aqueduct Racetrack can be fun.
BELOW: an artist's impression of the planned Fresh Kills Park.

Fresh Kills Park

Formerly the site of an immense landfill that made Staten Island the target of far too many jokes, Fresh Kills is on track to be the biggest park built in the city in over 100 years, with 2,200 acres (890 hectares) available for development. Work has only just begun on the island's western coast and may continue for the next 30 years, but visitors can look forward to nature trails through wetlands and woods, with memorials, sports fields, waterfront access, art installations, and just about everything that makes the type of park that any city in the world would envy. And one day those jokes will be a distant memory.

ABOVE: Staten Island ferry passengers.
RIGHT: the Verrazano-Narrows Bridge as seen from the ferry.

TIP

On Sundays, a special shuttle bus runs to the Isamu Noguchi Garden Museum from the Upper East Side in Manhattan. It picks up at Park Avenue and 70th St (by the Asia Society), and runs at 30 minutes past each hour, 12.30pm– 3.30pm. Buses return from the garden on the hour, 1pm–5pm.

Rosebank ㉒

East of the ferry is Rosebank, home to Staten Island's first Italian-American community. The **Garibaldi-Meucci Museum** (420 Tompkins Avenue, www.garibaldi meuccimuseum.org, tel: 718-442 1608; Wed–Sat 1pm–5pm; charge), commemorates Antonio Meucci, who invented a type of telephone years before Alexander Graham Bell. Exhibits focus on this and his other inventions, and his friendship with Italian hero Giuseppe Garibaldi, who stayed here on his 1850 visit to New York. This simple house was Meucci's home until his death in 1889.

A bus or taxi ride away, the **Alice Austen House Museum** (2 Hylan Boulevard, www.aliceausten.org, tel: 718-816 4506; Mar–Dec Thur–Sun noon–5pm; charge) is a 1690s cottage surrounded by a pretty garden that was the home of a pioneering woman photographer from 1866 to 1945.

Verrazano-Narrows Bridge ㉓ features in many of the island's easterly views. When built in 1964, it was the longest suspension bridge in the world. The Verrazano connects Staten Island to Brooklyn and brought great change to the island. The traffic that poured across its magnificent span brought Staten Island's fastest, least controlled construction boom. Now, laws are in place to prevent this from happening again.

Taking to the Staten hills

Because a glacier ridge runs through the middle of the island, Staten's six hills – **Fort, Ward, Grymes, Emerson, Todt,** and **Lighthouse** – are the highest points in New York City. Handsome mansions with breathtaking views stand on the ridge of Todt Hill, the highest point on the eastern seaboard south of Maine. Take a taxi up **Signal Hill**, a narrow hairpin lane. Along the way, alpine homes peek out of the cliff, half-hidden by rocks and trees. At the top, beyond the wonderful views from the ridge, is the core of the island. Called the **Greenbelt** (www.

Bronx Bombers or the Amazin's?

New York is very much a baseball town, and from April through October eyes are fixed on two very important diamonds

New York-based baseball-lovers are literally divided into two groups – Yankee fans and Mets fans. It's not the most congenial of competitions, either. The Yankees, regarded by their fans as the primary hometown team, are proud of their endless winning streaks and an incredible 27 World Series titles; the Mets, who see themselves as the inheritors of the Brooklyn Dodgers mantle, a team that moved to LA in 1958, have a less glowing record with only two World Series titles to their name, but just as much pride. Fans spar often, in offices and bars around the city.

But both had reason to be proud in 2009: at the beginning of the baseball season, both of New York City's major league teams opened new stadiums. In 2008, the old stadiums had been broken down, and seats sold to fans.

It was the first time in America that two teams opened new stadiums in the same town at the same time. Both fields are open-air, and have natural grass; both are right across from the old stadiums, and therefore still reached by most attendants by subway.

Citi Field replaced the Mets' previous stadium, Shea, in Flushing, Queens. The architecture of the new building makes a lot of references to the Dodgers, including a rotunda named for Jackie Robinson, the first modern-day African-American major league baseball player. Yankee Stadium, which had opened in 1923, was replaced by a new site of the same name at 161st Street in the Bronx. The architects also managed to keep some aspects of the old stadium that fans were sentimental about,

such as the view of the elevated subway line from the bleachers.

As members of separate leagues – American League for the Yankees and National League for the Mets – the teams had merely a cordial rivalry for many years, meeting only during exhibition games. The 1990s brought inter-league play, and things have gotten far more heated. Every year since 1999, they face off six times during the regular season, split between three-game stretches at each ballpark. They call them "Subway Series," a reference to the legendary World Series of yesteryear when the Yankees would play the New York Giants or New York Dodgers and a subway fare was the only travel expense for fans of the "away" team. It's been over 50 years since the Giants and Dodgers slipped away to California, and the only true Subway Series since occurred in 2000. The Yankees won, as they so often do.

The rivalry will continue for years to come, but the acrimony will always be a bit tempered. There are bigger enemies out there. Ask a Yankee fan what team they hate the most and you will always get the same answer: the Boston Red Sox. Ask a Mets fan the same question and they're likely to say the Philadelphia Phillies... or perhaps the Yankees.

RIGHT: the Mets' Johan Santana pitches.

BELOW: demonstrating 18th-century skills in Staten Island's Historic Richmond Town.

sigreenbelt.org, tel: 718-667 3450, for information on walking trails), this enormous expanse of meadows and woodland has been preserved by a civic plan that tightly controls or prohibits development. **High Rock Park** is a 90-acre (36-hectare) open space.

On **Lighthouse Hill** is an idyllic corner imported from the Himalayas, the **Jacques Marchais Museum of Tibetan Art** (338 Lighthouse Avenue, www.tibetanmuseum.org, tel: 718-987 3500; Wed–Sun 1pm–5pm; charge.

Historic Richmond Town ㉔

Address: 441 Clarke Ave, www.historicrichmondtown.org
Telephone: 718-351 1611
Opening Hours: Wed–Sun 1pm–5pm
Entrance Fee: charge
Bus: Bus S74 from Staten Island Ferry Terminal

Less than a mile from Lighthouse Hill on Richmond Road is a restored 17th- and 18th-century village, showing 300 years of life on Staten Island. On a 100-acre (40-hectare) site, more than 15 buildings have been restored. The former County Clerk's and Surrogate's office, from 1848, was the first part of

Richmond to be brought back to life. Staff in period garb conduct tours, and old-fashioned skills are demonstrated in this local "living museum."

THE BRONX ㉕

In 1641, a Scandinavian, Jonas Bronck, bought 500 acres (200 hectares) of the New World from Native Americans. After building his home on virgin land, he and his family found the area remote and lonely, so they threw parties for friends.

The Indian land was called Keskeskeck (or Rananchqua, the native Siwanou name), but the name was changed, the story goes, by Manhattanites asking their neighbors, "Where are you going on Saturday night?" and being answered, "Why, to the Bronck's."

The tale is certainly questionable, but the Bronx *had* been virgin forest, and *did* begin with Jonas's farm. Idyllic woods seem unimaginable in today's Bronx, but a part of its original hemlock forest remains untouched in the 250-acre (100-hectare) **New York Botanical Garden ㉖** 200th Street and Kazimiroff Boulevard, www.ny

bg.org, tel: 718-817 8700; Tue–Sun 10am–6pm, until 5pm in winter; charge).

The **Enid A. Haupt Conservatory,** constructed in 1902, is the botanical garden's grandest structure, a veritable crystal palace with a central Palm Court and connecting greenhouses. There are plenty of outdoor gardens to explore, which are particularly wonderful in the springtime, such as the Everett Children's Adventure Garden, which has kid-size topiaries and mazes.

Bronx Zoo ㉗

Address: Bronx River Parkway (at Fordham Rd), www.bronxzoo.com
Telephone: 718-220 5100
Opening Hours: daily 10am–4.30pm
Entrance Fee: charge
Subway: East Tremont Ave/West Farms Square

This 265-acre (107-hectare) park is the country's largest urban zoo – and shares **Bronx Park** with the Botanical Garden. Popular exhibits include the **African Plains,** the **Baboon Reserve, the Aquatic Bird House,** and the **Butterfly Garden.** There's a **Children's Zoo,** a monorail ride through **Wild Asia,** and a 40-acre (16-hectare) complex with moats to keep the big cats away from their prey – that would be you. The **Congo Gorilla Forest** has acres of forest, bamboo thickets, and families of lowland gorillas, while Madagascar! has lemurs galore.

Along the Grand Concourse

The zoo is at the geographic heart of the Bronx, but its architectural and nostalgic heart may be the **Grand Concourse.** This Champs-Elysées-inspired boulevard began as a "speedway" through rural hills. As the borough became more industrialized, it achieved a classy role as the Park Avenue of the Bronx, stretching as it does for more than 4 miles (6km).

On the Grand Concourse, at 165th Street, is the recently **expanded Bronx Museum of the Arts** (www. bronxmuseum.org, tel: 718-681

ABOVE: Wave Hill in the fall.

TIP

Don't miss the Jacques Marchais Museum of Tibetan Art. Built in the style of a Himalayan mountain temple and surrounded by tranquil gardens, the museum was the vision of a Victorian-era actress who wanted to bring Tibetan culture to New York. It's open Wed–Sun 1–5pm.

ABOVE: New York Botanical Garden.
BELOW: monkey madness at the Bronx Zoo, the country's largest urban zoo.

6000; Thur–Sun 11am–6pm, until 8pm on Fri; charge, free Fri), which hosts exhibitions reflecting the multicultural nature of the Bronx.

Edgar Allan Poe Cottage ㉘

Address: 2640 Grand Concourse (at Kingsbridge Rd), www.bronxhistorical society.org
Telephone: 718-881 8900
Opening Hours: Sat 10am–4pm, Sun 1–5pm
Entrance Fee: charge
Subway: Kingsbridge Rd

At the north end of the Grand Concourse, writer Edgar Allan Poe's cottage sits humbly among the high-rise apartment blocks on Kingsbridge Road. Poe moved here in 1846, hoping the then-country air would be good for his consumptive young wife and cousin, Virginia. But she died at an early age, leaving Poe destitute; the haunting poem *Annabel Lee* was a reflection of his distress. The cottage has been a museum since 1917, run by the Bronx Historical Society.

The West and North Bronx

Farther up is **Riverdale** ㉙. It's hard to believe this is the Bronx, as the curvy roads wind through hills lined with mansions. A drive down Sycamore Avenue to Independence Avenue leads to **Wave Hill** (www.wavehill.org, tel: 718-549 3200; Tue–Sun 9am–5.30pm, until 4.30 in winter; charge, free Tue and Sat mornings). This once-private estate, now a city-owned environmental center, has greenhouses and gardens overlooking the Hudson. It's a pretty spot, and the site of outdoor concerts and dance performances.

East of Riverdale, **Van Cortlandt Park** ㉚ stretches from West 240th to West 263rd streets, and includes stables, tennis courts, and acres of playing fields. The **Van Cortlandt House Museum** (Broadway at W. 246th Street; www.vancortlandthouse.org, tel: 718-543 3344; Tue–Sun; charge), overlooks the park's lake. Built in 1748 by Frederick Van Cortlandt, a wealthy merchant, it is filled with some of the family's original furnishings and possessions.

On the park's east side, **Woodlawn Cemetery** (Webster Avenue, www.thewoodlawncemetery.org, tel: 718-920 0500) is permanent home to about 300,000 New Yorkers. Herman Melville, Duke Ellington, and five former mayors are just a handful of the celebrities at rest in the elaborate mausoleums. Over 400 acres (162 hectares) of trees, hills, and streams have made this a place for strolling since it opened in 1863.

Farther east is **Orchard Beach**, a summer destination with nature trails, riding stables, and a golf course. On the way, the road passes Co-Op City, a sprawling 1960s housing development that looms over the horizon like a massive urban beehive.

The road ends at **City Island** ㉛, a little slice of New England. Accessible by car, bus, or boat, this 230-acre (93-hectare) island off the Bronx coast has remained quietly detached from the rest of the city. The boatyards along **City Island Avenue** yielded masterworks like *Intrepid*, twice winner of the America's Cup race. Today, the street has fishing-gear emporia and

craft shops, along with galleries and seafood restaurants. Be sure to see stately **Grace Church**.

The South Bronx

The opposite end of the borough – in location and reputation – is the **South Bronx**. Its best-known landmark is the baseball stadium with the nickname The House That Ruth Built, though actually, this is the house built for Ruth; its shortened right field was originally designed to make Babe Ruth's home-run slugging a little easier.

More World Series championship flags and American League pennants have flown over **Yankee Stadium** ㉜ http://newyork.yankees.mlb.com, tel: 718-293 4300) than any other baseball field in the US.

Since Babe Ruth, other stars of the field have included Joe DiMaggio, Lou Gehrig, Mickey Mantle, and Derek Jeter. But, just like Shea Stadium, it too was replaced by a new stadium in 2009. As a result, tickets are more expensive. Fortunately, the team is justifying the extra fees – they won the World Series in 2009, too.

BELOW: lighthouse, City Island.
BELOW: City Island is a slice of New England tucked away in the Bronx.

BEST RESTAURANTS, BARS AND CAFÉS

Restaurants

Blue Ribbon
280 5th Ave (between 1st and Garfield Pl), Park Slope, Brooklyn
Tel: 718-840 0404
www.blueribbonrestaurants.com
D daily **$$$**
With reservations for only parties of five or more, it means there's usually a wait for this excellent New American menu.

Bohemian Hall and Beer Garden
29-19 24th Ave, Astoria, Queens
Tel: 718-274 4925
www.bohemianhall.com
D only Mon, Wed–Fri, L & D Sat–Sun **$$**
Reasonably priced goulash and kielbasa, washed down with plenty of beer: something they've been doing here for almost 100 years.

Chef's Table at Brook-

lyn Fare
200 Schermerhorn Street (at Hoyt and Bond sts), Boerum Hill, Brooklyn
Tel: 718-248 0050
www.brooklynfare.com
D only Tue–Sat **$$$$**
To some, this is the finest restaurant outside of Manhattan, with a prix-fixe dinner featuring 25–30 small plates. Bring your appetite and wallet. Reservations must be made six weeks in advance by phone on Monday mornings at 10.30am, sharp. You can also shop at their wonderful grocery store.

DiFara
1424 Ave J (at E 15th St), Midwood, Brooklyn
Tel: 718-258 1367
www.difara.com
L & D Wed–Sun **$**
A perennial contender for the best pizza in all of New York. Cash only.

Dominicks
2335 Arthur Ave (at Crescent Ave and 186th St), the Bronx
Tel: 718-733 2807
L & D Wed–Mon **$$**
A family-style Italian eatery where there is no menu. Just sit down and let the waiter guide you. What it lacks in decor it makes up for in portions and down-home deliciousness.

Fette Sau
354 Metropolitan Ave (at Havemeyer and Roebling sts), Williamsburg, Brooklyn
Tel: 718-963 3404
www.fettesaubbq.com
D only Mon–Fri, L & D Sat–Sun **$$**
The German name, which translates as "fat pig," may confuse some. Yes there are sausages, but mostly this is mouthwatering Southern barbecue with a rotating menu depending on what

meats have been smoking for the last day.

The Good Fork
391 Van Brunt St (at Coffey and Van Dyke sts), Brooklyn
Tel: 718-643 6636 www.goodfork.com
D only Tue–Sun **$$**
Hip Red Hook has a waterfront winner here when it comes to good and reasonably priced food. There's also a warm, comforting room.

Grimaldi's
19 Old Fulton St (at Front and Water sts)
Tel: 718-858 4300
www.grimaldisnyc.com
L & D daily **$**
One of Brooklyn's original pizza spots, Grimaldi's still has lines around the block for their thin-crust, coal-fired pizzas.

The Grocery
288 Smith St (between Sackett and Union sts), Carroll Gds, Brooklyn

Tel: 718-596 3335
http://thegroceryrestaurant.com
D only Tue–Wed, L & D Thur–
Sat $$$
Local four-star, one-room
phenomenon serving
New American cuisine. It
offers a weekday vegetar-
ian tasting menu.
Joe's Shanghai
136-21 37th Ave (at 138th St),
Flushing, Queens
Tel: 718-539 3838
www.joeshanghairestaurants.com
L & D daily $$
The Queens outlet of the
Chinese juggernaut
known for its addictive
and tongue-scalding
soup dumplings.
Noodle Pudding
38 Henry St (at Middagh and
Cranberry sts), Brooklyn
Tel: 718-625 3737
D Tue–Sun $
Come for the warm
atmosphere, practically-
giving-it-way wine list,
and great pasta dishes.
**Peter Luger Steak-
house**
178 Broadway (at Driggs Ave),
Williamsburg, Brooklyn
Tel: 718-387 7400
www.peterluger.com
L & D daily $$$$

Brooklyn's oldest restau-
rant still holds the grand
title of "King of all Steak
Places." Book months in
advance and bring plenty
of cash. No credit cards!
River Café
1 Water St (at Fulton Ferry),
Brooklyn
Tel: 718-522 5200
www.rivercafe.com
L & D Mon–Sat, Br & D Sun
$$$$
The unsurpassed loca-
tion and views of Man-
hattan from under the
Brooklyn Bridge, plus
excellent haute cuisine,
make this a magical spot.
Bookings can be difficult,
so start early.
Roberto
603 Crescent Ave (at Adams Pl
and Hughes Ave), The Bronx
Tel: 718-733 9503
www.roberto089.com
L & D Mon–Fri, D only Sat $$$
A rustic favorite in a neig-
borhood of Italian restau-
rants. They also own Zero
Otto Nove, a well-loved
pizzeria and trattoria
around the corner.
Sripraphai
6413 39th Ave (at 64th St),
Woodside, Queens
Tel: 718-899 9599
http://sripraphairestaurant.com
L & D Thur–Tue $
Regarded as the best
Thai food in the region.
Stone Park Café
324 5th Ave (at 3rd St),
Brooklyn
Tel: 718-369 0082
http://www.stoneparkcafe.com
D only Mon, L & D Tue–Fri, Br &
D Sat–Sun $$$
Comfortable, casual New
American food that s a
big hit with the Park
Slope crowd.
La Superior
295 Berry St (at S. 2nd and S.
3rd sts), Williamsburg, Brooklyn
Tel: 718-388 5988

www.lasuperiornyc.com
L & D daily $$
It may have a haughty
name, but reasonable-
prices and fresh and fast
food are what distinguish
this Mexican eatery.
Taverna Kyclades
33-07 Ditmas Blvd (at 33rd and
35th sts), Astoria, Queens
Tel: 718-545 8666
www.tavernakyclades.com
L & D daily $$
Unencumbered, afforda-
ble Greek fare in a Greek
neighborhood.
Thakali Kitchen
74-14 37th Ave (at 74th St),
Jackson Heights, Queens
Tel: 718-898 5088
http://thakalikitchen.com
L & D daily $$
One of the city's few Nep-
alese restaurants, featur-
ing authentic and unique
dishes prepared by immi-
grants from the Himala-
yan kingdom. Vegetarian
options are available.
Tournesol
50-12 Vernon Blvd, Long Island
City, Queens
http://tournesolnyc.com
Tel: 718-472 4355
D only Mon, L & D Tue–Fri, Br &
D Sat–Sun $$
A charming bistro just
across the East River.
Hearty French food and a
great brunch.
Trattoria Romana
1476 Hylan Blvd (at Benton
Ave), Staten Island
Tel: 718-980 3113
www.trattoriaromana.com
L & D daily $$
A wood-burning stove
that roasts everything
from pizzas to pigs is the
centerpiece at this
Staten Island Italian star.
Water's Edge
44th Dr and East River (at Ver-
non Blvd), Queens
Tel: 718-482 0033
www.watersedgenyc.com
L & D Mon–Fri, D only Sat $$$$
From a Long Island City

location with great view,
this romantic spot serves
delicious food with an
emphasis on fresh fish. A
free ferry service is avail-
able from Manhattan.

Bars and Cafes

Almondine
85 Water St
Located in Brooklyn's
trendy DUMBO, this is a
great place to dip into hot
coffee, pastries, or sand-
wiches while touring gal-
leries. Also in Park Slope.
Athens Café
32-07 30th Avenue (at 32nd
and 33rd sts)
This lively sidewalk cafe
in Astoria, Queens, is
good for pastries, coffee,
and people-watching.
Bronx Ale House
216 West 238th St
(at Broadway)
Serves spectacular craft
beers and microbrews.
Char No. 4
196 Smith St (at Baltic and War-
ren sts)
Serves Brooklynites over
100 selections of whis-
key and hearty food to
match.
**Danny Brown's Wine
Bar & Kitchen**
104-02 Metropolitan Ave (at
71st Dr)
This is the place in
Queens to get great wine
by the bottle or glass.
Mile End
97a Hoyt St (at Atlantic Ave and
Pacific St)
This place is Brooklyn's
newest Jewish deli, by
way of Montreal.

LEFT: River Café. **ABOVE:** hot dog stand.

EXCURSIONS

A trip outside of the city presents a variety of distractions, from visiting vineyards and perusing art galleries, to hiking in the mountains or braving the frosty Atlantic

Beyond the boroughs, in what is commonly known as the tri-state area of New York, Connecticut, and New Jersey, is where much of the city's workforce lives. They settle down here for the grassy lawns, garages, and school systems. Even though Manhattanites gently tease these suburbanites – aka the "bridge-and-tunnel" crowd – they also envy them a bit. Why else would cityfolk escape to quieter shores on the weekends? As big and wonderful as New York City is, there are things that you just can't find there. For those, you hop a train or rent a car and go on an adventure. The best times to venture out into these wilds are May, September, and October, when the crowds are thinner and the days bright, warm, and pleasant.

LONG ISLAND

It's home to Brooklyn and Queens, two international airports, another domestic one, a professional hockey team, a national seashore and nearly 8 million people. It's the biggest island in the contiguous United States. It's technically in New York State, but it's a singular place, tethered to the

mainland by a handful of bridges and tunnels and proud of its own slang, accent, and cuisine. Long Island ice tea, anyone?

The Hamptons

Some would have you believe that everyone in Manhattan owns a house in the Hamptons, and come summertime they all scoot off on the weekends for beachside parties at the mansions of Billy Joel, Jerry Seinfeld, and Martha Stewart. For a select group of the wealthy, this may

PRECEDING PAGES: Hasidic Jewish families in Williamsburg. **LEFT:** Bear Mountain Bridge in the Hudson River Valley. **RIGHT:** the view from Montauk Point Lighthouse on Long Island.

TIP

Arrive in the Hamptons by train or bus and you'll have to rely on your feet or taxis. The ambitious start-up Hamptons Free Ride (http://hamptons freeride.com, tel: 646-504 3733) in East Hampton is dedicated to providing a less tiring, more affordable option. They offer free rides to and from the beach aboard their advertisement-plastered electric vehicles. Time will tell if their business model is truly sustainable.

be true, but the majority of New Yorkers only pop in for an occasional visit or weekly house rental.

Most know that the Hamptons are located on the southern shores of Long Island, but their exact borders can be a bone of contention. The most liberal interpretation has them stretching from the relatively humble hamlet of **Westhampton**, 80 miles (129km) west of the city, all the way to **Montauk**, 50 more miles to the east at the island's tip, and from the sandy Atlantic coast to the northern bays near preppy **Sag Harbor**. The towns of **Southampton ❶** and **East Hampton ❷**, and the hamlets and villages contained within the center of each, make up what everyone would agree is the heart of the region, and this is where you'll find the majority of inns, restaurants, and high-end shopping that distract visitors when they're not sunbathing.

Locals have a love-hate relationship with summer denizens. On one hand, visitors provide a well-needed jolt to the local economy. On the other, they transform these sleepy places into raucous playgrounds for

the privileged. The debate is somewhat pointless. With white sand beaches this alluring, it would be impossible to keep them away. The beaches are the natural attraction, of course, and **Coopers Beach** in Southampton Village is among the best patches of sand and celebrities, while **Hither Hills** showcases the windswept beauty and seaside wildlife of Montauk. Historical and cultural attractions are lower on the totem pole, but a visit to the **Pollock Krasner House & Study Center ❸** (830 Springs-Fireplace Road, http://sb.cc.stonybrook.edu/pkhouse, tel: 631-324-4929; June–Aug Thur–Sun 1pm–5pm, May, Sep–Oct by appointment; charge) in East Hampton is a must for any student of art history. This is where, from 1946–52, Jackson Pollock created many of his masterpieces.

The easiest way to get to any major town in Long Island is to catch a **Long Island Railroad** (aka LIRR, www.mta.info/lirr, tel: dial 511 in New York City) train out of Penn Station. The Hamptons are serviced by the Montauk Branch, and

BELOW: Shinnecock Bay in the Hamptons.

each of the seven Hampton stations is within a few miles of the nearest beach. There are only three or four departures daily and trains can be packed on weekends, so plan ahead and arrive early. Many New Yorkers, especially young ones, choose to ride the **Hampton Jitney** (www.hamptonjitney.com, tel: 212-362 8400) instead. It's a bus – albeit a comfortable one deemed worthy by picky Upper East Siders – that stops along Lexington Avenue between 80th and 40th streets, runs out to Queens, and then moves onto the Hamptons. The advantage: it departs daily, at least

once an hour. The disadvantage: it costs more than the train and is subject to traffic jams.

To the west

Not part of the Hamptons, but closer to Manhattan is **Jones Beach State Park ❹** (www.nysparks.com/parks/10/details.aspx, tel: 516-785 1600), where the city comes to swim and see outdoor concerts. It's definitely not the best beach around and crowds can be suffocating, but it's a quick drive from Manhattan. Further east is **Fire Island ❺**, a skinny – and buggy – barrier island, with a

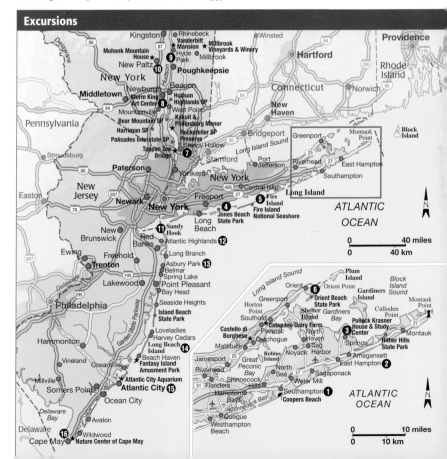

Excursions

TIP

Car rental rates in Manhattan are staggeringly high. If venturing beyond the reaches of public transportation, consider taking a train or bus to a suburban rental location with lower prices. Many companies, including Enterprise (www.enterprise.com), are willing to pick customers up at stations and bring them to their lots.

BELOW: Thomas Cole (1801–48), painter of the Hudson River School, c.1845.

well-established gay community and New York's only national seashore (www.nps.gov/fiis, tel: 631-687 4750). Most of the island is without roads, which means you must arrive by ferry and groceries and luggage must be transported along boardwalks with little red wagons. It's charming, to be sure, but accommodations are few and far between.

The North Fork

The shape of Long Island is a bit like the forked tongue of a lizard. Its eastern end is split between two pointed peninsulas separated by a bay. The South Fork is where the Hamptons bask in the sun. The North Fork is a more rural getaway, where farmers still work the land and vintners ply the rich soil.

Agricultural businesses, such as **Catapano Dairy Farm** (33705 North Road, Peconic, www.catapanodairy-farm.com, tel: 631-765 8042; daily 10am–5pm), are often open to the public and sell fresh produce on site. Catapano is along Route 48, one of only two thoroughfares on the North Fork. The scenic drives along it and

Route 25 will yield numerous farm-stands and the fork's main attraction: vineyards.

One of the most important winemaking states in the country, New York has growing regions in the Hudson Valley and the Finger Lakes, but Long Island is where the state's most diverse wine varieties are produced. Merlots get the primary praise, but there are Cabernets, Syrahs, Chardonnays, sparkling wines and more to sample. With more than 40 vineyards in all, **Castello di Borghese** (17150 County Rte 48, http://castellodiborghese.com, tel: 631-734-5111; May–Dec daily, Jan–Apr Thur–Mon, from at least 11.30am–5pm) in Cutchogue claims the title of the oldest and, arguably, the best. Consult the **Long Island Wine Council** (www.liwines.com, tel: 631-722 2220) for listings and general information.

There are beaches here too, situated along the Long Island Sound, with views of Connecticut to the north. The beach at **Orient Beach State Park** ❻ (http://nysparks.state. ny.us/parks/106/details.aspx, tel:

Hudson River Valley School

There was no campus. There were no scheduled classes. The studying was done outdoors. This "school" was actually an art movement, made up of 19th-century American landscape painters. Thomas Cole is generally acknowledged as the movement's father, and when his romantic paintings of a trip to the Hudson River and the Catskills caught the eye of wealthy patron Daniel Wadsworth, the style began to dominate the New York City art scene.

Key figures in the movement included Frederic Church, Asher Durand, Albert Bierstadt, and Sanford Gifford. Inspired by European masters, such as J.M.W. Turner and John Constable, these painters would set out into the wilderness to capture billowing clouds, raging waterfalls, and towering mountains in oil. Then they'd bring their exaggerated depictions back to the city, where enthusiastic collectors would snatch them up. The large scale and epic nature of the paintings drew huge crowds to exhibitions.

These days, you can view many of the masterpieces at the Albany Institute of Art (www.albanyinstitute.org) and the Wadsworth Atheneum (www.thewadsworth.org) in Hartford, Connecticut.

631-323 2440) rings a rare maritime forest at the tip of the fork, and is a gorgeous place for a walk. Most of the area's accommodations and restaurants are split between the towns of **Southhold** and **Greenport**, both accessible by public transportation. For train service, use LIRR's **Ronkonkoma Branch**. The Hampton Jitney offers bus service to the North Fork as well, but not as frequently as it does to its namesake. Taxis are harder to find and the area isn't exactly walkable, though it is a cyclist's dream. Your best bet is to drive or, if you're spending the day sampling wine, have someone else drive for you. **North Fork Wine Tours** (www.northforkwinetours. com, tel: 631-723 0505; charge) has some popular shuttle options.

HUDSON VALLEY

Travel north of Long Island and past the Tappan Zee Bridge, which spans the Hudson River between Nyack and Tarrytown, and the urban sprawl will be behind you. More wine awaits, as well as art, nature, cuisine, and some of the country's most historically important homes.

History and hiking

Washington Irving's Headless Horseman haunted **Sleepy Hollow ❼**. The cute little town of the same name, along Route 9 North on the southeastern banks of the Hudson, will remind you of that early and often, especially during the Halloween season. At the **Old Dutch Church and Burying Ground** (www.odcfriends.org, tel: 914-631 4497) you can read gravestones marked with names familiar from Irving's tales, as well as visit New York's oldest church. Pair it with a trip to **Kykuit** (www.hudson-valley.org, tel: 914-631 8200; May–Oct Wed–Mon from 9am; charge), former home to four generations of Rockefellers with stunning gardens, art and architecture on display. A living-history museum, **Philipsburg Manor** (www.hudsonvalley.org, tel: 914-631 8200; Apr–Oct Wed–Mon 10am–5pm; charge) is Kykuit's neighbor and an intriguing window

LEFT: the Fire Island Lighthouse.
ABOVE: cars are not allowed on Fire Island, so visitors must bring supplies in via backpack or wagon.

EAT

The Hudson Valley's Blue Hill at Stone Barns (630 Bedford Road, Pocantico Hills, www. bluehillfarm.com; tel: 914-366 9600; D daily, L Sun) harvests ingredients at their local farm and is better than almost all the restaurants in the city.

into 18th-century America. Stretch your legs at nearby **Rockefeller State Park Preserve** (http://nys-parks.state.ny.us/parks/59/details.aspx, tel: 914-631 1470), where immaculate carriage roads are perfect for a stroll or jog, or even a horseback ride.

On the opposite bank of the river, the cliffs of **Palisades Interstate Park** serve up some grueling climbs for cyclists, while **Harriman State Park** (http://nysparks.state.ny.us/parks/145/details.aspx, tel: 845-786 2701) has lakes and hiking in the closest patch of significant forest to the city. The **Appalachian Trail** snakes through Harriman and into **Bear Mountain State Park**, before crossing the Hudson at the Bear Mountain Bridge and entering **Clarence J. Fahnestock Memorial State Park** (http://nysparks.state.ny.us/parks/133/details.aspx, tel: 845-225 7207), where a popular campground is a draw for high-rise dwellers.

Art and wine

Fahnestock connects to the **Hudson Highlands State Park** in charming **Cold Spring**, where you can look back west across the river and see the **United States Military Academy at West Point** (www.westpoint-tours.com, tel: 845-446 4724; daily; charge), which can be visited on a guided tour. You will see the cliffs of Storm King State Park. Just beyond the park is **Storm King Art Center ⑧** (Old Pleasantville Road, Mountainville, www.stormking.org, tel: 845-534 3115; Apr–Nov Wed–Sun 10am–5pm) where art, not nature trails, are the lure. Explore acres of grassy fields and lightly forested areas decorated with modern sculptures, some as big as small buildings.

North of Storm King, post-industrial Newburgh is a rare raggedy town on the picturesque river, but back east across the Newburgh-Beacon Bridge is even more modern art, housed inside at the **Dia: Beacon** (www.diabeacon.org, tel: 845-440 0100; Thur–Mon from at least 11am–4pm; charge). Be warned, this tends to be modern art in its most contentious form, focusing on shapes and large installations.

BELOW: Shelter Island.

Shelter Island

Wedged between the forks of Long Island is a friendly and isolated community with families who can trace their local routes back hundreds of years, to when the Quakers came here to avoid persecution. Shelter Island's Mashomack Preserve, run by the Nature Conservancy, covers more than 2,000 acres (800 hectares), including large swathes of protected wetlands. A network of hiking and birding trails provides access to forests, beaches, and saltwater marshes. There are only two ways to get here: from the North (www.northferry.com) and South (www.southferry.com) forks, and only by ferry. Of course, you'll have to get out to the ends of Long Island first.

The core of the **Hudson Valley Wine Country** (www.hudsonvalleywinecountry.org) is north of Newburgh and Beacon. **Millbrook Vineyards & Winery** (26 Wing Road, Millbrook, www.millbrookwine.com, tel: 845-677 8383; daily, noon–5pm) is one of the most visited, but over a dozen other producers are nearby, and over a dozen more are further up and down the river. **Little Wine Bus** (http://thelittlewinebus.com, tel: 917-414 7947) organizes weekend trips out of Midtown Manhattan for those who don't have a designated driver.

Mansions

Traveling to the eastern banks of the Hudson is easy by commuter rail. The **Hudson Line** on Metro-North Rail (www.mta.info, tel: in Manhattan dial 511) out of Grand Central Terminal runs right along the river and makes frequent stops until reaching Poughkeepsie north of Beacon. Out of Penn Station, the **Port Jervis Line** of New Jersey Transit (www.njtransit.com, tel: 973-275-5555) makes a few stops in New York State west of the Hudson.

To get further north, **Greyhound** (www.greyhound.com, tel: 800-231 2222) has various bus routes and **Amtrak** (www.amtrak.com, tel: 800-872 7245) trains stop a few times on their way to Albany, but a car is definitely your best bet. On the east side of the Hudson, be sure to visit **Hyde Park ⑨**, home to the **Culinary Institute of America** and its associated restaurants (www.ciachef.edu, tel: 845-471-6608), as well as the **Presidential Library of Franklin Delano Roosevelt** (4079 Albany Post Road, www.fdrlibrary.marist.edu, tel: 800-337 8474; daily 9am–5pm). This is also where the Vanderbilts lived, and the **Vanderbilt Mansion** (4079 Albany Post Road, www.nps.gov/vama/index.htm, tel: 845-229 9115; charge) is perhaps the most notable of the many gilded-age estates that line the water. Upriver, Rhinebeck is a pretty country getaway beloved by harried office workers and the site of September's **Hudson Valley Wine &**

ABOVE: the United States Military Academy at West Point.

ABOVE: Mark Di Suvero's sculpture-
Mother Peace at Storm King Art Center.
BELOW: the 18th-century Philipsburg Manor in Sleepy Hollow.

Food Fest (www.hudsonvalleywine fest.com).

On the west side of the Hudson, **New Paltz** ⑩ brims with galleries and shops, and is the last major town before the gateway to the **Catskill Mountains**. And the breathtaking – and breathtakingly expensive – Mohonk **Mountain House** (1000 Mountain Rest Road, www.mohonk. com, tel: 845-255 1000) with its spa, golf course, and acres of sprawling grounds and nature trails is the grand gatekeeper.

THE JERSEY SHORE

While the Hudson Valley has always attracted praise for its bucolic beauty, New Jersey has been battling a bad reputation for decades. Television shows like *The Real Housewives of New Jersey* and *The Jersey Shore* have done little to rehabilitate that reputation, but a visit to the Garden State's beach towns – or "Down the Shore" – is sure to change a few minds with the coastline's diverse natural beauty.

Without a car

As the seagull flies, it's barely 15 miles (24km) from the northern tip of the Jersey Shore at **Sandy Hook** ⑪ to Downtown Manhattan. However, driving between the two can take upwards of two hours. In the summer, the **Seastreak Ferry** (www. seastreak.com, tel: 800-262 8743) makes the trip in a third of the time, with the bonus of gorgeous views. The ferry lands at **Fort Hancock** in Sandy Hook, part of the Gateway National Recreation Area (www.nps. gov/gate, tel: 732-872 5970). Explore the grounds, where more than 100 former military buildings still stand, as well as the country's oldest surviving lighthouse. A museum explains the history, while the interiors of some former officers' homes are often open to the public.

Atlantic Highlands ⑫, the only other Jersey Shore town accessible by ferry, is to the south, and has stately Victorian homes and parks with paths for walkers, runners, and cyclists, including the seaside Henry

Hudson Trail. To reach points further south, a ride on along **North Jersey Coast Line** (www.njtransit.com, tel: 973-275 5555) train from Penn Station is the simple choice. It will bring you to **Long Branch**, once a favorite resort of 19th-century commanders-in-chief who worshipped at the currently under renovation **Church of the Presidents** (1260 Ocean Ave, www.churchofthepresidents.org, tel: 732-223 0874). Two train stops later and you'll be in **Asbury Park ⑬**. Made famous by Bruce Springsteen, the town has seen better days – and worse ones – but people still come for shows at **The Stone Pony** (913 Ocean Ave, www.stoneponyonline.com, tel: 732-502 0600), where "The Boss" cut his teeth over 35 years ago. It's a rite of passage for any New Jersey band to play this legendary room.

The train continues through **Belmar**, where college students and 20-somethings sleep shoulder-to-shoulder in summer-share houses and party into the night, much to the chagrin of the more buttoned-up and affluent neighboring communities of **Spring Lake** and **Sea Girt**. The last stop is at Bay Head, just after **Point Pleasant**, a family-friendly town with a bustling boardwalk and a very popular beach.

Peninsulas and islands

To visit the nicest shore towns you'll need a car. The **Garden State Parkway**, which runs 173 miles (278km) along coastal New Jersey, was built in 1952 to offer residents better beach access and a leafy, truck- and advertisement-free route north-to-south. 60 years later, it's clogged with cars on summer weekends, and if your vehicle isn't equipped with an E-Z Pass, you'll need to carry plenty of quarters to feed the occasional toll plazas. Still, it's by far the best way to get to places like Barnegat Peninsula, home to **Seaside Heights**, the hard-partying community portrayed in *The Jersey Shore* television show. For all the negative attention it receives – some of it deserved – Seaside Heights

Jersey Shore locals refer to two types of visitors: Bennies and Shoobies. A Benny is rabble-rouser from up north, particularly the urban communities of Bayonne, Elizabeth, Newark, or New York. A Shooby is a day-tripper, typically from the regions near Philadelphia, the type of person who brings his lunch in a shoebox and doesn't contribute to the local economy.

BELOW: the beach at Long Branch.

is often forgotten as the entryway to **Island Beach State Park** (www.nj.gov/dep/parksandforests/parks/island.html, tel: 732-793 0506), a pristine 10-mile (16km) stretch of beach and dunes enjoyed by swimmers, walkers and surfers.

At the southern tip of the park and peninsula, it's less than 1,000ft (300 meters) across Barnegat Bay to **Long Beach Island** and its iconic red and white **Barnegat Lighthouse** (www.state.nj.us/dep/parksandforests/parks/barnlig.html, tel: 609-494 2016), but unless you have a boat, you'll have to drive back to the Parkway and loop around to get there. A skinny barrier island, it is commonly referred to as LBI, and families come here to escape the boardwalks and all-night parties. There are nightclubs on the island, as well as mini-golf and the **Fantasy Island** amusement park (320 Seventh Street, Beach Haven, www.fantasyislandpark.com, tel: 609-492 4000), but they are sprinkled sparsely throughout the 18-mile (29km) length. The northern half

of the island – where towns wear colorful names like **Loveladies** and **Harvey Cedars** – has very little commercial development. It consists almost exclusively of sprawling beach- and bay-side seasonal homes for the rich. The southern half, anchored by **Beach Haven**, is where most day-trippers come, and with miles of beach access, it's usually easy to find a private stretch of sand. The beaches are considered public land but, as with many shore towns, there is a small charge during peak season. Don't be surprised if a teenager checking and selling "beach badges" approaches you.

Blackjack and B&Bs

The most famous Jersey Shore town is also its most contradictory one. **Atlantic City** , the skyline of which can be seen to the south of LBI on a clear day, is both a glittering home to gambling and entertainment and a sad display of urban decay. Casinos like the Borgata, the Tropicana, Caesars, Harrahs, and the Trump Taj Mahal can compete

BELOW: the poker room at the Taj Casino.
RIGHT: boardwalk casinos in Atlantic City.

with those in Las Vegas, but if you step off the immense and instantly recognizable boardwalk and stroll a few blocks, you will find dilapidated streets that haven't aged well since being immortalized on the *Monopoly* game board. Come for cards and dice, boxing matches, and the **Atlantic City Aquarium** (800 North New Hampshire Avenue, www.oceanlife center.com, tel: 609-348 2880; daily 10am–5pm), but not for sightseeing. Weekend train service from Penn Station aboard the **Atlantic City Express** (www.acestrain.com, tel: 877-326 7428) is available for the first time in years, while Greyhound offers daily bus service on the **Lucky Streak** (www.luckystreakbus.com, tel: 800-231 2222), a wiser choice than the offers of free transport aboard sketchy shuttle buses you might see advertised on utility poles.

South of Atlantic City, the island town of **Avalon** is a quaint community with high sand dunes. It was also the setting of an eponymous 1990 film directed by Barry Levinson. If you're looking for a cocktail, it's a little difficult to find in **Wildwood**, where the boardwalk is packed with amusements geared toward families, but alcohol is only starting to be served near the beach after a 100-year ban. The town's reputation for good clean fun goes back to the days when Dick Clark's *American Bandstand* visited for a summer, doo-wop bands performed outside, and Bill Haley and the Comets debuted the immortal "Rock Around the Clock."

Driving down the Parkway, you're bound to see bumper stickers reading "Exit 0." These cars will belong to fans of **Cape May ⓰**, the southernmost point in the state, where brightly colored Victorian homes sit along tree-lined streets and the pace of life is leisurely. For the B&B experience on the shore, Cape May has no peers. It is also an ornithologist's delight, with enthusiasts flocking to the **Nature Center of Cape May** (1600 Delaware Ave, tel: 609-898 8848) to spot shore and seabirds.

ABOVE: shoppers on Washington Street Victorian Mall in Cape May.
BELOW: the Old Victorian Bed & Breakfast Inn at Cape May.

INSIGHT GUIDES **TRAVEL TIPS**
NEW YORK CITY

TRANSPORTATION

GETTING THERE AND GETTING AROUND

From the song *On the Town* comes the saying: "The Bronx is up and the Battery's down – New York's geography makes it easy to get around," which pretty much sums things up. The layout of Manhattan couldn't be simpler, with a grid of numbered streets through most of the island that makes it near-impossible to get lost. Compactness also makes most of Manhattan easy – and inviting – to explore on foot. After a while, when the feet get weary, you're never far from a subway station, a bus, or a bright yellow taxi.

GETTING THERE

By Air

Airports

New York's two major airports, **John F. Kennedy International** (**JFK**) and **LaGuardia** (**LGA**), are both in Queens, east of Manhattan on Long Island, respectively 15 and 8 miles (24 and 13km) from Midtown. Driving time to/ from Kennedy is estimated at 90 minutes, but heavy traffic can often double this, so leave lots of time if you're catching a flight. LaGuardia is used for shorter US domestic and some Canadian

routes, and does not have any intercontinental flights.

New York's third airport, **Newark Liberty International** (**EWR**), is used by a growing number of international flights. It's really in New Jersey but, although a little bit farther from Manhattan than JFK, it's often quicker to reach. It's also newer, cleaner, and less chaotic than Kennedy.

Between the three, you will have access to just about every major airline in the world, or at least a connecting partner. Domestic coach fares can range from $100–750, while international fares are generally $500 and up, and include applicable taxes. You will not need to pay any

BELOW: hailing a cab.

additional arrival or departure taxes at the airport.

Airport to City Transportation

AirTrain is an airport rail system that connects **JFK** and **Newark** airports with the subway and rail networks. Howard Beach (A train) and Sutphin Boulevard (E, J, and Z train) subway stops and Long Island Railroad's Jamaica Station connect to jfk (www.airtrainjfk. com, tel: 718-244 4444), and a special airport rail station connects to Newark (www.airtrain newark.com, tel: 973-961 6000). At each airport, AirTrain runs every few minutes and takes about 10 minutes from each terminal. The trip between AirTrain JFK and Midtown Manhattan takes 20 minutes by LIRR and about 45 minutes by subway. It's 25 minutes from AirTrain Newark to Penn Station.

The reasonably priced New York Airport Service (www.nyair-portservice.com, tel: 212-875 8200) buses run between both LaGuardia and JFK airports and Manhattan. Pick-up and drop-off points include: Port Authority Bus Terminal, Penn Station, and Grand Central Terminal, with a transfer service available to or from Midtown hotels. Buses from JFK run 6.15am–11.00pm.

From LaGuardia, the **M60** bus to upper Manhattan subway stations operates 5am–1am, while the **Q33** bus runs to 74th St subway stop in Jackson Heights, Queens, from which various trains run to Manhattan. For exact schedules check www.mta.info or dial 877-690-5114 or 511 in New York City.

Newark Liberty Airport Express (www.coachusa.com, tel: 908-354 3330) operates express buses daily between Newark airport and Manhattan, stopping along 42nd St. Buses run 4am–1am.

There are several **minibus** services from all three airports to Manhattan. A big plus is that they take you door to door, direct to hotels or private addresses, but this can be slow, with many stops. **Super Shuttle** (www.super shuttle.com, tel: 212-258 3826) offers a frequent service. It can be booked online, at airport ground transportation centers, or from courtesy phones at the airports.

The **cheapest routes** from JFK to the city are by AirTrain, or by MTA bus to one of several subway stations in Queens. If you have a group of 3 or 4, a taxi can be an affordable and easy option.

Each airport has a busy taxi stand, and you rarely have to wait more than a few minutes. From LaGuardia to Manhattan, drivers will charge the metered rate, which will generally be in the $30 range, excluding a tip. A trip from JFK to Manhattan is a flat rate of $45, excluding a tip. At Newark, the taxi stand determines your rate depending on the exact destination. Expect to pay around $50, plus the tunnel tolls and tip, to get to Midtown.

Don't forget to leave plenty of time getting to and from the airports if traveling by road; the traffic can be very bad, especially during rush hours on business days, and on holidays.

By Rail

Trains arrive and depart from two railroad hubs in Manhattan:

Grand Central Terminal at Park Ave and 42nd St (lines to the northern suburbs, upstate New York and Connecticut), **and Pennsylvania Station** at Seventh Ave and 33rd St (for Long Island, New Jersey, and destinations serviced by Amtrak). City buses stop outside each terminal, and each has a subway station. Amtrak information: www.amtrak.com, tel: 212-630 6400, or (toll-free) 800-872 7245.

By Road

Driving

From the south, the **New Jersey Turnpike** leads into lower Manhattan via the Holland (Canal Street) or Lincoln (Midtown) tunnels and offers access farther north via the George Washington Bridge. From the north, the **New York State Thruway** and Interstate 95 connect with Henry Hudson Parkway or the Bruckner Expressway toward northern Manhattan. Driving in from the Long Island airports, access is via either the **Midtown Tunnel** or the **Triborough Bridge**, and down Manhattan's FDR (East River) Drive.

On a Bus

The busy **Port Authority Bus Terminal** (8th Ave, at 40th and 42nd sts) sits atop two subway lines and is used by long-distance companies (including **Greyhound**, www.greyhound, tel: 1-800-231 2222) and local commuter lines. City buses stop outside. A modern terminal with stores and other facilities, it nevertheless tends to attract more than its share of shady individuals; though well-policed, and cleaner than in years past, it's not a place to trust strangers or to leave bags unguarded.

Upstarts MegaBus (http://us.megabus.com, 877-462-6342) and BoltBus (www.boltbus.com, tel: 877-265-8287) provide transit between almost 20 cities in northeastern US and Canada on comfortable coaches equipped

with Wi-Fi and electrical outlets. If you book early for off-peak travel, rates can be as low as a few dollars. Most buses pick up and drop off at locations within a couple blocks of Penn Station.

By Sea

Stretching along the Hudson from 46th to 54th streets in Manhattan (at 12th Ave), the **Manhattan Cruise Terminal** (www.nycruise.com, tel: 212-246 5450) has customs facilities and good bus connections to Midtown. There is also a **Brooklyn Cruise Terminal** (www.nycruise.com, tel: 718-246 2794) and a port at Cape Liberty (www.cruiseliberty.com, 201-823 3737) in Bayonne, NJ, just 15 minutes from Newark Airport.

GETTING AROUND

On Arrival

Orientation

Generally, avenues in Manhattan run north to south; streets east to west. North of Houston Street, streets are numbered, which makes orientating oneself very easy. Below Houston navigating can be tricky, but as long as you know the general location of some major stretches of pavement – Broome, Canal, Chambers, Worth and Fulton on the horizontal; Hudson, Broadway, Lafayette, Bowery and Allen on the vertical – you'll never go astray more than a few blocks. Even-numbered streets tend to have one-way eastbound traffic; odd-numbered streets, westbound. There are very few exceptions. Most avenues are one-way, north or south, the major exception being Park Avenue, which is wide enough for two-way traffic.

Buses do not stop on Park Avenue but they do on most other avenues, as well as on major cross-streets (most two-way): Houston, 14th, 23rd, 34th, 42nd,

57th, 66th, 86th, 116th, 125th, and a few others. Subway trains crosstown at 14th and 42nd sts, but there is no north–south line east of Lexington Ave (until the long-gestating Second Avenue Subway arrives) or west of Eighth Ave and Broadway above 59th St.

Public Transportation

Subways and Buses

Subways and buses run 24 hours a day throughout the city, although they are less frequent after midnight. There are many subway routes, identified by letters or numbers; some share the same tracks, so be careful to get the right train. Detailed directions between any two addresses – including both train and bus options – are available online at www.hopstop.com.

The standard single fare for a subway or local bus journey (no matter how far you travel) is currently $2.50 if you buy a SingleRide ticket, or $2.25 if you buy a $10 or $20 MetroCard. You can add as much money as you want to a **MetroCard**, and for every $10 spent, a 7 percent bonus is added. Discounted unlimited-ride cards are also available, valid for seven or 30 days. SingleRide tickets are found only at station vending machines, but MetroCards and passes can also be bought at some newsstands and hotels.

Vending machines are located at all stations and accept cash and credit or debit cards. They have easy-to-follow touch-screen instructions and dispense new MetroCards or add money to your existing card.

Transfers between subways and buses are free. Buses do accept cash in the form of coins, but you will need exact change and you will not receive reduced rates. Express buses, which operate during rush hour on weekdays, charge $5.50. Of course, fares are always subject to change.

For general **bus and subway** information, check www.mta.info or tel: 718-330 1234 or 511 in New York City. Every station should include a subway map, but only a select few are wheelchair-accessible.

PATH (Port Authority Trans-Hudson) trains run under the river between Manhattan and Hoboken, Jersey City, and Newark in New Jersey. The Downtown line leaves from the World Financial Center. The Midtown line stops along 6th Avenue at 33rd, 23rd, 14th, and 9th streets and at the corner of Christopher and Hudson streets. It's a slightly cheaper and sometimes quicker alternative to the 1 or F trains and it accepts MetroCards, though not unlimited ones. For more information check www.panynj.gov, tel: 800-234 7284.

Private Transportation

Bicycling

Riding a bike in New York is easier and safer than ever, with the number of bike lanes doubling in the last two years. Bike-only greenways along the Hudson and East rivers make north–south travel a breeze and, except for in Midtown, there are lanes almost every 10 blocks to make crossing the island less death-defying. For an interactive map of bike lanes visit www.nycbikemaps.com. Remember to wear a helmet, stay off sidewalks and highways, and obey all traffic signs and signals. Just because it's safer, doesn't mean there still aren't plenty of dangers.

If you don't bring your own wheels, you can rent some, either from the ubiquitous vendors in Central Park or from a local bike shop. Waterfront Bicycle Shop in the West Village (391 West Street, www.bikeshopny.com, tel: 212-414 2453) has affordable options right next to the Hudson River Greenway. In the near future, for the cost of a multi-day rental, you will be able to join the new bike-sharing program (www.nycitybike share.com), which will give you unlimited access to bikes throughout the city. For more on the program, as well as additional maps and safety tips, visit the Department of Transportation at www.nyc.gov/html/dot.

Car Services

You can hail a yellow cab, but you can't book one. For that, you'll need a car service. These can range from limousines and town cars to shuttle vans and sedans. You may be solicited by drivers of "gypsy cabs," usually nondescript black cars used by local car services, but you would be wise to call a trusted service. A few reliable ones include luxury-minded **Allstate** (www.allstatelimo.com, tel: 212-333 3333), Downtown's **Delancey** (http://delanceynyc. com, tel: 212-228 3301), and air-

BELOW: subways operate 24 hours a day.

ABOVE: bike lane.

port specialists **Dial 7** (www.dial7.com, tel: 212-777 7777).

Driving in New York

Driving around Manhattan is not fun. Visitors arriving by car would do well to leave their vehicle parked in a garage and use public transportation, as traffic and scarce parking space make driving in the city a nightmare.

CAR RENTAL

Alamo, www.alamo.com:
US 1-800-327 9633
International 1-800-522 9696
Avis, www.avis.com:
US 1-800-331 1212
International 1-800-331 1084
Budget, www.budget.com:
US 1-800-527 0700
International 1-800-527 0700
Dollar, www.dollar.com:
US 1-800-800 4000
International 1-800-800 6000
Enterprise, www.enterprise.com:
US 1-800-325 8007
International 1-800-325 8007
Hertz, www.hertz.com:
US 1-800-654 3131
International 1-800-654 3001
National, www.nationalcar.com:
US 1-800-227 7368
International 1-800-227 3876
Thrifty, www.thrifty.com:
US 1-800-847 4389
International 1-918-669 2168

If you must drive, remember certain rules of the city: the speed limit is 30mph (50kmh) unless otherwise indicated; the use of seat belts is mandatory; the speed limit on most highways in New York is 55mph (90kmh) and is strictly enforced – look out for signs, as on some major highways this has now been raised to 65mph (105kmh). Right turns are prohibited at red lights throughout the city.

Parking

While street parking is at least possible in some areas outside of Midtown, a garage or parking lot is the safer (though far more expensive) choice. You can find garages and lock-in discounted rates at www.nyc.bestparking.com and www.iconparkingsystems.com. If you happen to find a parking spot on the street, obey posted parking regulations, which may include parking only on one side of the street on alternate days, or call **311** for more information. Never park next to a fire hydrant and don't leave your car over the time limit, or it may be towed away.

Buying Gas

Service stations are few and far between (11th and 12th avenues on the West Side are good hunting grounds). They are often open in the evening and on Sundays.

Breakdowns

Your car rental company should have its own emergency numbers in case of breakdown. Otherwise, the **Automobile Club of New York** (ACNY), a branch of the American Automobile Association (AAA, www.ny.aaa.com), will help members and foreign visitors affiliated with other recognized automobile associations. In case of a breakdown, or for other problems along the way, call their Emergency Road Service (tel: 800-222 4357) or wait until a police car comes along.

Car Rental

Since New York City has the highest car rental and parking rates in the US, we don't recommend you rent a car unless you plan to leave the city a few times. If you do need a car, you'll find it's generally cheaper to rent at the airport than in Manhattan, and cheaper still to rent a car outside of New York City, where prices are more competitive. It's a good idea to make car rental reservations online before you leave home. (A curious twist is that weekend rentals in Manhattan are more expensive than weekday rates, since most New Yorkers do not own cars and rent when they go away for weekends.)

You will need a major credit card to rent a car, plus your driver's license. The minimum age for renting a car is 21, but some companies will not rent to drivers under 25, or when they do will impose a high, additional fee.

Taxis

Taxis, all metered, cruise the streets and must be hailed, although there are official taxi stands at places like Grand Central and Penn Station. Hail with an outstretched arm, from near an intersection if possible, so they can see you and have ample space to pull over. If the number on the roof is lit, it means the taxi is available. Be sure to flag down an official, yellow cab, not an unlicensed "gypsy" cab. Flat fares to and from the airports can usually be negotiated, but bridge and tunnel tolls, and the tip, of course, will be extra.

One fare covers all passengers up to four (five in a few of the larger cabs). The meter starts at $2.50 and increases by 40¢ every fifth-of-a-mile (or 40¢ for waiting time). There is a 50¢ surcharge from 8pm–6am and a $1 surcharge for peak hours (4–8pm weekdays). Taxis are now able to accept credit cards. A list of your rights as a passenger should be posted in the vehicle and can be read at http://www.nyc.gov/html/tlc/html/passenger/taxicab_rights.shtml. A lawsuit is currently underway to require all new taxis to be wheelchair-accessible by 2014.

24-hour hotline: telephone 212-692 8294 or 311 in New York City.

ACCOMMODATIONS

SOME THINGS TO CONSIDER BEFORE YOU BOOK THE ROOM

Choosing a Hotel

The old adage that New York has more of everything is only a slight exaggeration when it comes to hotel accommodations. The following list is hardly exhaustive, but represents a sample of hotels in Manhattan in the budget-to-luxury range, plus a few inexpensive places of distinction, and alternatives. A good percentage of accommodations, especially chains, are located in Midtown, for the obvious advantage that most attractions are only a short taxi or subway ride away. Still, the city has good options in every neighborhood, and the listings touch on some unique ones in each corner of Manhattan. Be aware that, with the exception of "Luxury," these categories are not hard and fast. When making reservations, ask about special weekend or corporate rates and package deals. Better prices are often available via the hotels' websites, especially if you pay upfront. It's always a good idea to book by credit card to secure a guaranteed late arrival. In addition to regular hotels, we've included a few "suite hotels," and bed and breakfast services. The former are basically apartments, available from a few nights up to a month; the latter are modeled on those in the UK and Europe. Make room reservations as far in advance as possible, and remember that the prices listed here are for low season, and rates go up over holidays and peak travel times. In New York, the low season is January–March, as well as July–August.

BELOW: hotel porters usually expect a tip.

TRANSPORTATION

ACCOMMODATIONS

ACTIVITIES

A – Z

LOWER MANHATTAN/SOHO AND TRIBECA/EAST VILLAGE AND THE LOWER EAST SIDE/GREENWICH VILLAGE

Cooper Square Hotel
25 Cooper Square (on Bowery between East 5th and East 6th sts)
Tel: 212-475 5700, 888-251 7979
www.thecoopersquarehotel.com
① [p340, C3]
A hot hotel in a trendy part of town, the Cooper Square is a shiny new build. It has 145 rooms and a new bar and restaurant called The Trilby, named after its signature scotch-based cocktail. $$$$

Crosby Street Hotel
79 Crosby St (at Spring and Prince sts)
Tel: 212-226 6400
www.firmdale.com
② [p340, B4]
This sleek hotel has a spectacular location in the middle of SoHo. While the standard rooms may be small, the ones on upper floors have spectacular views. $$$$

Gansevoort Meatpacking NYC
18 Ninth Ave (at 13th St)
Tel: 212-206 6700, 877-426 7386
www.hotelgansevoort.com
③ [p338, A1]
The Meatpacking District's first luxury hotel has a huge rooftop bar and swimming pool, as well as breathtaking views of the Downtown skyline and sunsets. Bedrooms are fashionably appointed. $$$$

Mercer Hotel
147 Mercer St (at Prince St)
Tel: 212-966 6060, 888-918 6060
www.mercerhotel.com
④ [p340, B3]
In the heart of SoHo, a converted 1890s land-

ABOVE: room at The Standard.

mark with 75 rooms featuring high loft ceilings, arched windows, and spacious bath facilities. Owner Andre Balazs also has Chateau Marmont in LA, plus hotels in Miami, and the clientele here is similarly stylish. There is a second-floor roof garden, a library bar with 24-hour food and drink service, and the highly regarded Mercer Kitchen restaurant. $$$$

Soho Grand Hotel
310 West Broadway (at Grand St)
Tel: 212-965 3000, 800-965 3000
www.sohogrand.com
⑤ [p340, B4]
A sophisticated yet totally comfortable 18-story hotel, with industrial-chic decor and stunning views. The service is excellent, and the lobby and bar are the rendezvous of choice for media types and music stars. As befits a place owned by the heir to the Hartz Mountain pet empire, pets are welcome. Exercise, groom-

ing, and feeding services are available. $$$$

The Standard Hotel
848 Washington St (at 13th St)
Tel: 212-645 4646, 877-550 4646
www.standardhotels.com
⑥ [p338, A1]
The High Line passes under the elevated Standard Hotel, where rooms are decked out with leather furniture, glass tables, and a fully modern sheen. In the winter, there is an ice rink. Year-round it has one of the Meatpacking District's most popular bars and restaurants, The Standard Grill. $$$$

Tribeca Grand
2 Avenue of the Americas (at Walker St)
Tel: 212-519 6600, 800-519 6600
www.tribecagrand.com
⑦ [p340, B1]
Cool, subtle, and modern, the Tribeca is the sister hotel to the Soho Grand, and has similar amenities. The guest rooms are welcoming and calm, while the Church Lounge is a meet-

ing place, a cocktail bar, and a place for brunch. Wi-Fi, iPods, and Bose sound systems are just some of the tech toys in the guest rooms. $$$$

Abingdon Guest House
21 Eighth Ave (at West 12th and Jane sts)
Tel: 212-243 5384
www.abingdonhouse.com
⑧ [p340, B1]
It's romance on a shoestring at this nine-room hostelry between the West Village and the Meatpacking District. Accommodation is spread between two townhouses, and each of the tiny rooms is individually decorated: some have four-posters,

PRICE CATEGORIES

Price categories are for a double room for one night in the low season. Be aware that rates can almost double over holidays:

$$$$ = over $375
$$$ = $275–$375
$$ = $175–$275
$ = under $175

ABOVE: penthouse at Hotel on Rivington.

some fireplaces. The rooms facing Eighth Avenue can be a little noisy, so ask for the Garden Room in the back. No smoking. **$$**

Blue Moon Hotel
100 Orchard St (at Delancey St)
Tel: 212-533-9080
www.bluemoon-nyc.com
🄌 [p342, D1]
Once a run-down tenement building, now a modern hotel with a historic feel in a neighborhood famous for housing immigrants. Rooms are named after stars of the Vaudeville era such as Al Jolson and Fanny Brice, and are twice the size of an average New York hotel room. **$$**

The Hotel on Rivington
107 Rivington St (at Essex and Ludlow sts)
Tel: 212-475 2600
www.hotelonrivington.com
🄉 [p340, C4]
This high-design, high-

end hotel towers above other buildings, making for spectacular views from the floor-to-ceiling windows of the large guest rooms. The hipster neighborhood means the hotel – and its bar and restaurant – draw the young and fashionable rather than business clients. **$$**

The Maritime Hotel
363 West 16th St (at 9th Ave)
Tel: 212-242 4300
www.themaritimehotel.com
🄊 [p338, B1]
Located at the north end of the Meatpacking District, the hotel draws in the fashion crowd, and its outdoor cafes are a nightlife destination in warm weather. Its porthole windows and austere 1960s design make this an original – or an eyesore. **$$**

The Millennium Hilton
55 Church St (at Fulton St)

Tel: 212-693 2001, 800-445 8667
www1.hilton.com
🄓 [p342, B2]
Adjacent to Wall St and its "canyons" of financial movers and shakers, this Hilton hotel affords the opportunity to be near Hudson River breezes – after being pampered by the large selection of in-house services. Rooms at the front of the hotel overlook the 9/11 Memorial and One World Financial Center. **$$**

Washington Square Hotel
103 Waverly Place (at northwest corner of Washington Square Park)
Tel: 212-777 9515, 800-222 0418
www.washingtonsquarehotel.com
🄕 [p340, B2]
Once a seedy hotel where musicians and writers penned classics (Papa John of the Mamas and the Papas wrote California Dreamin' here in the 1960s), Washington Square has been renovated, but hasn't lost its Greenwich Village charm. **$$**

Best Western Seaport Inn
33 Peck Slip (at Front St)
Tel: 212-766 6600, 800-468 3569
www.seaportinn.com
🄔 [p342, B3]
A block from South Street Seaport, this

19th-century warehouse has 72 rooms featuring Federal-era antiques and amenities like DVD players and mini-fridges. Some rooms have Jacuzzis and/or terraces with views of Brooklyn Bridge. **$**

Holiday Inn Downtown/Soho
138 Lafayette St (at Howard St)
Tel: 212-966 8898, 888-465 4329
www.holidayinn.com
🄖 [p340, B4]
In a renovated historic building, this hotel right on the edge of Chinatown is much nicer than you might expect from an international chain hotel group. **$**

The Jane
113 Jane Street (at West St)
Tel: 212-924 6700
www.thejanenyc.com
🄗 [p340, A1]
This inexpensive far West Village spot looks out over the Hudson River and also has rooms with shared bathrooms, and some with bunk beds. **$**

The Larchmont
27 West 11th Street (at 5th and 6th aves)
Tel: 212-989-9333
www.larchmonthotel.com
🄘 [p340, C2]
Located on a picturesque street of upscale 19th-century townhouses in Greenwich Village, this small, basic hotel is a find – if you don't mind sharing a bathroom. **$**

UNION SQUARE AND CHELSEA

Gramercy Park Hotel
2 Lexington Ave (at 21st St)
Tel: 212-920 3300, 866-784 1300
www.gramercyparkhotel.com
🄙 [p340, D1]
The now very fashionable

(thanks to Ian Schrager) Gramercy has an impressive and sumptuous Baroque-inspired decor by New York artist Julian Schnabel. A drawback: the rooms can be dark,

and the public bar off the lobby can be very crowded at night. A plus: guests are allowed to use exclusive Gramercy Park across the road. In 2009, Danny Meyer opened

trendy restaurant Maialino in the hotel. **$$$$**

Inn at Irving Place
56 Irving Place (at 17th St)
Tel: 212-533 4600, 800-685 1447
www.innatirving.com

⑲ [340 D2]
A pair of graceful townhouses transformed into a facsimile of a country inn, with a cozy fireplace-lit tea salon, and 12 elegant rooms and suites featuring four-poster beds. A two-block walk from Gramercy Park and a short distance from Union Square. There's a nice little restaurant on the Inn's lower level that serves a fantastic afternoon tea. **$$$$**

The Roger Williams Hotel
131 Madison Ave (at 31st St)
Tel: 212-448 7000, 888-448 7788
www.therogernewyork.com
⑳ [p338, C3/4]
The Roger Williams has exchanged its sleek, stark style for a warmer approach, using bold colors and natural wood. The lobby has a soaring atrium, while the bedrooms are home-from-home cozy, with lots of space, thick bathrobes, down comforters, and CD players. The pent-

houses have lovely balconies with views of the Empire State Building. **$$$$**

W New York Union Square
201 Park Ave South (at 17th St)
Tel: 212-253 9119, 877-946 8357
www.whotels.com
㉑ [p340, C1/2]
Bordering the Flatiron District, this stylish hotel has one foot in Gramercy Park and the other in a Downtown "attitude." Everything here is top-of-the-line, including the under-bar lounge and Olives restaurant. **$$$**

Ace Hotel
20 West 29th St (at Broadway and 5th Ave)
Tel: 212-679 2222
㉒ [p338, C4]
www.acehotel.com
Small but stylish rooms in the former Breslin Hotel, with the fabulous new Breslin Bar on the ground floor. "Cheap Rooms" are sometimes available for less than $200. **$$**

BELOW: W New York Union Square.

Affinia Shelburne
303 Lexington Ave (at 37th St)
Tel: 212-689 5200, 866-246 2203
www.affinia.com
㉓ [p338, D3]
Affordable prices for large or small suites with kitchen facilities in a pleasant hotel – with the added bonus of a rooftop bar and garden. Good value for families. **$$**

Chelsea Pines Inn
317 West 14th St (at 8th Ave)
Tel: 212-929 1023, 888-546 2700
www.chelseapinesinn.com
㉔ [p338, B1]
A bright and friendly guesthouse, with breakfast served in the solarium or garden. Popular with the gay community. **$$**

Jolly Madison Towers Hotel
22 East 38th St (at Madison Ave)
Tel: 212-802 0600
www.jollymadison.com
㉕ [p338, D3]
Renovated with a European flair, this large hotel offers special rates throughout the year, making it an affordable option compared to other hotels of its standing nearby. **$$**

Morgans
237 Madison Ave (at 37th St)
Tel: 212-686 0300, 800-697 1791
www.morganshotel.com
㉖ [p338, D3]
The original brainchild of Ian Schrager and the late Steve Rubell, and surprisingly for New York, still one of the most fashionable temporary addresses in Manhattan; an ultra-modern enclave for hip movie stars and other millionaires. The decor's original stark, dramatic grays have been

replaced by warmer tones, but there's still a minimalist ambience. Service is known to be extraordinary. **$$**

Gershwin Hotel
7 East 27th St (at 5th Ave)
Tel: 212-545 8000
www.gershwinhotel.com
㉗ [p338, C4]
An artsy hotel just north of Madison Square Park inspired by Andy Warhol and aimed at the young, fashionable, and cash-strapped. One floor provides housing for struggling models, many rooms have bunk beds, and there are good packages for families and weekend stays. Temporary art exhibits in the lobby. **$**

Hampton Inn Chelsea
108 West 24th St (at 6th Ave)
Tel: 212-414 1000
www.hershahotels.com
㉘ [p338, B4]
Hi-tech decor sets the tone at this Chelsea spot situated at the doorstep of the gallery scene. Great location for shopping on nearby Avenue of the Americas. **$**

Ramada Inn Eastside
161 Lexington Ave (at 30th St)
Tel: 212-545 1800, 800-567 7720
www.applecorehotels.com
㉙ [p338, D4]
A friendly, cozy, 1900s hotel. Conveniently located for Downtown and Midtown. **$**

PRICE CATEGORIES

Price categories are for a double room for one night in the low season. Be aware that rates can almost double over holidays:

$$$$ = over $375
$$$ = $275–$375
$$ = $175–$275
$ = under $175

MIDTOWN WEST AND MIDTOWN EAST

Algonquin Hotel
59 West 44th St (at 5th and 6th aves)
Tel: 212-840 6800, 888-304 2047
www.algonquinhotel.com
⑳ [p338, C2]
Once a haven for New York's literary Round Table set, and still an all-time favorite, the Algonquin retains its low-key, oak-paneled charm. Clubby and Victorian in demeanor, civilized in its treatment of guests, it's near theaters and is less expensive than its rivals. Its website offers a best-rate guarantee. **$$$$**

Millennium UN Plaza Hotel
United Nations Plaza (44th St and 1st Ave)
Tel: 212-758 1234, 866-866 8086
www.millennium-hotels.com
㉛ [p338, E3]
The clientele here is as you might expect, and some appreciate the busy atmosphere as UN representatives bustle through the heroically

proportioned lobby. Benefits to non-ambassadorial guests include rooms with views of the East River, a fitness center, a tennis court, and a swimming pool. **$$$$**

Peninsula New York
700 Fifth Ave (at 55th St)
Tel: 212-956 2888
www.peninsula.com
㉜ [p336, B4]
One of the city's most lavish hotels, where richly appointed rooms go for about $500 (slightly less with corporate rates). The hotel's health club and spa are truly luxurious. It's also in a prime location on Fifth Avenue and has a wonderful rooftop bar. **$$$$**

The Plaza
Fifth Ave (at Central Park South)
Tel: 212-759 3000, 800-850 0909
www.fairmont.com/thePlaza
㉝ [p336, B/C4]
Edwardian-style splendor top to toe. The high ceilings are decorated

with murals and the service is close to old-world elegance. The Oak Bar and the Oak Room are traditional favorites as pre- and post-theater spots. Sadly, many floors are now condos (the penthouse sold for $56 million – NY's largest condo deal at the time), but there are still some hotel rooms, and suites, that are open to the public. Fortunately, most of the hotel's iconic rooms, like the ballroom and the Palm Court, have been refurbished and retain their original elegance. **$$$$**

St Regis
2 East 55th St (at 5th Ave)
Tel: 212-753 4500, 800-759 7550
www.stregis.com
㉞ [p336, D1]
A grand Edwardian wedding cake of a building, filigreed and charmingly muraled (by the likes of Maxfield Parrish). The St Regis is a magnet for somewhat older, moneyed guests who appre-

ciate the ambience of a more regal age. The location doesn't hurt; nor does the Alain Ducasse-helmed restaurant. **$$$$**

The Sherry-Netherland
781 Fifth Ave (at 59th St)
Tel: 212-355 2800, 877-743 7710
www.sherrynetherland.com
㉟ [p336, C4]
An old-fashioned luxury hotel with such a faithful club of visitors that reservations must be made well in advance. Grandly expansive spaces, both public and in the 40 rooms and suites (the rest of the building is private apartments), with royal treatment to match. **$$$$**

Hotel Iroquois
49 West 44th St (at 5th and 6th aves)
Tel: 212-840 3080, 800-332 7220
www.iroquoisny.com
㊱ [p338, C/D2]
Built in the early 1900s, this once-shabby hotel has received a facelift and now offers upscale but good-value accommodations on the same block as more expensive hotels. **$$$**

InterContinental The Barclay
111 East 48th St (at Lexington Ave)
Tel: 212-755 5900, 800-496 7621
www.intercontinentalnybarclay.com
㊲ [p338, D2]
Opened in the 1920s as The Barclay, this hotel blends executive-class efficiency with majestic spaces and a full range of pampering services. Includes two fine restaurants, a clothier, and a gift shop. **$$$**

BELOW: rooftop bar at the Peninsula.

TRANSPORTATION

ACCOMMODATIONS

ACTIVITIES

A – Z

New York Palace
455 Madison Ave (at 50th St)
Tel: 212-888 7000, 800-804-7035
www.newyorkpalace.com
 [p338, D1]
A grandiose monument to lavish pomp and excess and appointed in a style that can only be called postmodern Rococo, the Palace has a regime of flawlessly detailed service to make the average guest feel like an imperial pasha. The hotel's Gilt restaurant has two Michelin stars. **$$$**

Omni Berkshire Place
21 East 52nd St (at Madison Ave)
Tel: 212-754 5000, 800-843 6664
www.omnihotels.com
[p338, D1]
Although it's been acquired by the Omni chain, the Berkshire retains its old-fashioned grace and attention to personal service. Known by some guests as "a junior Plaza," it's comfortable and comforting, a tastefully appointed oasis of calm in the heart of the Midtown bustle. **$$$**

Le Parker Meridien
119 West 56th St (at 6th Ave)
Tel: 212-245 5000, 800-543 4300
www.parkermeridien.com
[p336, B4]
Part of the internationally known French chain: modern, airy, with an excellent restaurant, Norma's (known for its great breakfast), a bar with one of the city's best burgers, health facilities that include a swimming pool, and a barbershop. **$$$**

Renaissance New York
714 Seventh Avenue (at W. 48th St)

Tel: 212-765 7676, 800-228 9290
www.renaissancehotels.com
[p338, C1]
One of the stars of Times Square, with 300-plus rooms, most of them featuring large-screen TVs, oversized bathtubs, and other ample comforts. Convenient for theaters, restaurants, and Midtown businesses. **$$$**

The Royalton
44 West 44th St (at 5th and 6th aves)
Tel: 212-869 4400, 800-691 1791
www.royaltonhotel.com
[p338, C2]
Another chic and ultramodern creation from Ian Schrager of Studio 54 fame. Every line and appointment – from the lobby to the lavatories – is as boldly, coldly futuristic as the set of a sci-fi film, complete with video and stereo gadgetry. Still, the Royalton bends over backwards to provide the scurrying, "can-do" pampering expected by its clientele. Handy for the theater district. **$$$**

The Westin New York
270 West 43rd St (at 8th Ave)
Tel: 212-201 2700, 866-837 4183
www.westinny.com
[p338, C2]
With its multicolored-mirrored exterior, this 45-story hotel near Times Square is one of the more popular hotels in the neighborhood. **$$$**

Dylan Hotel
52 East 41st St (at Madison Ave)
Tel: 212-338 0500
www.dylanhotel.com
[p338, D2/3]
A small, sleek, upscale boutique hotel at reasonable prices, centrally

ABOVE: New York Palace.

located blocks away from Grand Central Terminal. Housed in a 1903 Beaux Arts building once home to a chemists' society. **$$**

Hilton New York
1335 Avenue of the Americas (at 53rd St)
Tel: 212-586 7000, 800-445 8667
www.newyorktowers.hilton.com
[p336, B4]
A typical Hilton: huge, modern, impersonal, but consistent, and with the service expected. **$$**

Hotel Edison
228 West 47th St (at Broadway)
Tel: 212-840 5000, 800-637-7070
www.edisonhotelnyc.com
[p338, C1]
Hotels in the bottom price ranges hardly ever really stand out, but the Edison is an exception. Though the Art Deco lobby can be chaotic, the rooms in this huge hotel are quite comfortable, pleasantly if simply decorated, and quiet. May be the best deal in NYC. **$$**

Hotel Pennsylvania
401 Seventh Ave (at 33rd St)
Tel: 212-736 5000, 800-223 8585
www.hotelpenn.com
[p338, B/C3]

This vast hotel is across from Madison Square Garden and Penn Station and near the Javits Center. Its range of packages makes it good value for few frills, and nothing can take away its history. Built in 1919 by the Pennsylvania Railroad, the Café Rouge Ballroom played host to many of the Big Band era's greats, including Count Basie, Duke Ellington, and the Glenn Miller Orchestra – who immortalized the hotel and its phone number in the 1938 hit *Pennsylvania 6-5000*. It has had the same phone number ever since. **$$**

Hudson Hotel
356 West 58th St (at Columbus Ave)
Tel: 212-554 6000, 800-697 1791
www.hudsonhotel.com

PRICE CATEGORIES

Price categories are for a double room for one night in the low season. Be aware that rates can almost double over holidays.

$$$$ = over $375
$$$ = $275–$375
$$ = $175–$275
$ = under $175

48 [p336, A3]
Another Ian Schrager invention, but a little less expensive than the Royalton, since rooms are smaller. Trendy and stylish, it's a favorite due to its location (not far from the Time Warner Center). The restaurant, Cafeteria, is a magnet for hot nightlife. **$$**

The Mansfield
12 West 44th St (at 5th Ave)
Tel: 212-277 8700, 800-255 5167
www.mansfieldhotel.com

49 [p338, D2]
Less expensive than the Algonquin and the Royalton hotels, which are located on the same street, this intimate, elegant boutique-style hotel mixes old-world style (the building dates from 1903) with modern details. Rooms are small, but the quality and the service is high. The Mansfield is one of those places that happy, satisfied guests return to on subsequent visits to New York City. **$$**

The Paramount
235 West 46th St (at Broadway and 8th Ave)
Tel: 212-764 5500, 877-692 0803
www.nycparamount.com

50 [p338, C1]
A fashion statement in the heart of Times Square. The rooms and public spaces, designed by Philippe Starck, dazzle and amaze: amenities include beds with headboards made of reproductions of famous paintings, a fitness club, and the intimate Library Bar. Rooms are small but well equipped. **$$**

W New York
541 Lexington Ave (at 49th St)
Tel: 212-755 1200, 877-946 8357

www.whotels.com
51 [p338, E2]
The flagship of a chain of sybaritic hotels-as-spas, W's interior was designed by David Rockwell and features Zen-like rooms where grass grows on the windowsills and quilts are inscribed with New Age-y aphorisms. There's a juice bar, a spa with good fitness facilities, and a trend-setting cocktail lounge Whiskey Blue. **$$**

The Waldorf=Astoria
50th St and Park Ave
Tel: 212-355 3000, 800-925 3673
www.waldorfastoria.com

52 [p338, D2]
The most famous hotel in the city during its heyday in the 1930s and 1940s, with a pre-war panache that's been restored to something like its early glory. The look of the lobby and public spaces combines H.G. Wells's heroic concept of the future with Cecil B. DeMille's view of Cleopatra's Egypt; the combination never fails to lift the spirits. Tiny rooms have an old-world charm, and the connected Waldorf Towers is luxurious. **$$**

Comfort Inn Convention Center
442 West 36th St (at 10th Ave)
Tel: 212-714 6699, 877-424 6423
www.comfortinn.com

53 [p3386, B2]
Very far west, but good access to public transportation and the Jacob Javits Center. Perfect for conventioneers. **$**

Comfort Inn Manhattan
42 West 35th St (at 5th and 6th aves)

Tel: 212-947 0200, 877-424 6423

54 [p338, C3]
www.comfortinn.com
Near Macy's and other shopping. **$**

Comfort Inn Times Square
129 West 46th St (at 6th and 7th aves)
Tel: 212-221 2600, 877-424 6423
www.comfortinn.com

55 [p338, C1]
Located in the heart of the Theater District and extremely reasonably priced. Rooms are fairly small, but a well-situated location makes up for it. **$**

The Hotel at Times Square
59 West 46th St (at 5th and 6th aves)
Tel: 212-719 2300, 800-567 7720
www.applecorehotels.com

56 [p338, D2]
Reasonably priced lodging geared for the business traveler. Located between Fifth and Sixth avenues, it has a business center, a conference room, and an 80-seat meeting room. Budget to moderate rooms available. **$**

The New York Manhattan Hotel
6 West 32nd St (at Broadway and 5th Ave)
Tel: 212-643 7100, 800-567 7720
www.applecorehotels.com

57 [p338, C3]
Smaller rooms for singles; larger rooms for families, complimentary Continental breakfast; some rooms with microfridges. In a convenient location to all Midtown attractions. **$**

The Pod Hotel
230 East 51st St (at 2nd Ave)
Tel: 212-355 0300, 800-742 5945

www.thepodhotel.com
58 [p338, E2]
The former Pickwick Arms hotel has been gutted and re-baptized The Pod. With teeny tiny rooms and hipster decor, it's perfect for budget-conscious young people looking for a modern hotel experience. All rooms have iPod docks, Wi-Fi, and flat-screen TVs. **$**

La Quinta Manhattan
17 West 32nd St (at Broadway and 5th Ave)
Tel: 212-736 1600, 800-567 7720
www.applecorehotels.com

59 [p338, C3]
Like others in the Apple Core Hotels group, rates at this 182-room hotel, a short walk from Macy's and Madison Square Garden, are extremely reasonable, especially considering that the comfortable rooms come with data ports, Wi-Fi, and voicemail. There's also a lobby cafe with entertainment, a restaurant with room service, and – rare in this price category – an open-air rooftop bar where music and snacks can be enjoyed in summer, along with views of the Empire State Building. **$**

Wellington Hotel
871 Seventh Ave (at 55th St)
Tel: 212-247 3900, 1-800-652 1212
www.wellingtonhotel.com

60 [p336, B4]
The location is great for Central Park, Lincoln Center, and Carnegie Hall. A reliable standby for reasonable rates. Some rooms have kitchenettes, and there are two restaurants, including Molyvos, as well as valet parking. **$**

UPPER EAST SIDE AND UPPER WEST SIDE

The Carlyle
35 East 76th St (at Madison Ave)
Tel: 212-744 1600, 888-767 3966
www.thecarlyle.com
61 [p336, D2]
Posh, reserved, and serene, The Carlyle remains one of the city's most acclaimed luxury hotels. The appointments are exquisite, the furnishings antique, and the service tends to be on the formal side. Home of Café Carlyle (Woody Allen plays clarinet here) and Bemelmans Bar, two of the city's most enduring and upscale evening spots. The Carlyle is a favorite with royalty. $$$$

The Franklin
164 East 87th St (at Lexington Ave)
Tel: 212-369 1000, 800-607 4009
www.franklinhotel.com
62 [p336, e1]
Once a bargain for the Upper East Side, this boutique hotel has been upgraded and is now much more expensive, but be on the lookout for special rates. The atmosphere is charming, the breakfast delicious, the bath products are Bulgari, and the robes are Frette. Plasma TV screens, Wi-Fi access, and in-room movies from a library of classics. $$$$

Mandarin Oriental
80 Columbus Circle (at 60th St)
Tel: 212-805 8800, 866-801 8880
www.mandarinoriental.com/new-york
63 [p336, B3]
One of the city's newer

ABOVE: parlor of the Royal Suite, the Waldorf.

luxury hotels, tucked into the aerie of the Time Warner Center at Columbus Circle. Spectacular views of Central Park and the city skyline, hushed surroundings, and the latest of everything make this a sought-after spot for high-end visitors to NY. Try the Thai yoga massage in the spa. $$$$

The Mark
Madison Ave at 77th St
Tel: 212-744-4300
www.themarkhotel.com
64 [p336, D2]
The refurbished new star of the Upper East Side, with elegant, arty furnishings, giant one-bedroom suites, and a restaurant from Jean-Georges Vongerichten. $$$$

The Pierre
2 East 61st St (at 5th Ave)
Tel: 212-838 8000
www.tajhotels.com/pierre
65 [p336, C4]
Justly renowned as one of New York's finest hotels, with a fabulous pedigree that goes back to its opening in the early 1930s. (It's now

run by the Taj Hotels luxury chain.) The hotel was renovated in 2009, and the location on Fifth Avenue is perfect for those intent on business or Midtown shopping; there is a lovely view of Central Park. Rooms are large and elegant, service is top-flight, and dining in the Café Pierre or having afternoon tea in the beautiful Rotunda are among the city's most civilized experiences. $$$$

The Surrey
20 East 76th St (at Madison and 5th aves)
Tel: 212-288-3700, 888-419 0052
www.thesurreyhotel.com
66 [p336, D2]
This Beaux Arts gem reopened in November 2009 after a $60 million renovation. Rooms are as elegant as any in this tony neighborhood, and the hotel is home to an impressive art collection as well. Grab a meal at the Café Boulud restaurant, just off the lobby; in the summer, check out the rooftop garden for a

rare experience that is often exclusive to locals with penthouses. $$$$

Trump International Hotel and Tower
1 Central Park West
Tel: 212-299 1000, 888-448 7867
www.trumpintl.com
67 [p336, B3]
Overlooking Central Park with sweeping views provided by floor-to-ceiling windows, the hotel comes complete with a spa, fitness center, and indoor pool. As flashy as its namesake, the hotel houses a celebrated restaurant, Jean-Georges, and has an enormous silver globe sculpture marking its spot at Columbus Circle. $$$$

PRICE CATEGORIES

Price categories are for a double room for one night in the low season. Be aware that rates can almost double over holidays:

$$$$ = over $375
$$$ = $275–$375
$$ = $175–$275
$ = under $175

Beacon Hotel
2130 Broadway (at 75th St)
Tel: 212-787 1100, 800-572 4969
www.beaconhotel.com
🟤 [p336, B1]
This busy and friendly Upper West Side favorite is adjacent to the Beacon Theater, a good venue for live music. Deals are to be had for families who book rooms with foldaway couches. The location is a great launching pad thanks to the West 72nd St and Broadway public transportation hub, with subway and bus connections leading just about anywhere. **$$**

Gracie Inn
502 East 81 St (at York Ave)
Tel: 212-628 1700, 800-404 2252
www.gracieinnhotel.com
🟤 [p336, E3]
Located on a quiet side street not far from Gracie Mansion (the NY mayor's residence), this is a cross between a city townhouse and a country inn. From single-room studios to a penthouse, rates depend on the length of stay. **$$**

Hotel Wales
1295 Madison Ave
(at 92nd St)
Tel: 212-876 6000, 866-925 3746
www.hotelwalesnyc.com
🟤 [p336, E1]
The Wales was once known for its low rates and splendid views of Central Park. Today it costs more, but still offers a great location in the upmarket Carnegie Hill neighborhood, close to Museum Mile and Central Park. You can feast on the best breakfast in NY next door at Sarabeth's Kitchen, or enjoy the light breakfast offered in the hotel's tea salon, also the setting for afternoon teas and chamber music. **$$**

The Lucerne Hotel
201 West 79th St (at Amsterdam Ave)
Tel: 212-875 1000, 800-492 8122
www.thelucernehotel.com
🟤 [p336, B1]
This landmark hotel is a great place to experience the trendy Upper West Side, where bars and restaurants exist

side-by-side with families in brownstones conducting their daily life. The Nice Matin on the corner has become one of the area's better and more popular restaurants. **$$**

Comfort Inn – Central Park West
31 West 71 St (at Central Park West)
Tel: 212-721 4770, 877-424 6423
www.comfortinn.com
🟤 [p336, B2]
A boutique hotel at bargain prices on the Upper West Side. It's less than a block from Central Park. **$**

Days Hotel Broadway
215 West 94th St (at Broadway)
Tel: 212-866 6400, 800-834 2972
www.dayshotelnyc.com
[off map]
Good location by subway; events at Symphony Space are usually interesting. **$**

Hotel Excelsior
45 West 81st St (at Columbus Ave)
Tel: 212-362 9200
www.excelsiorhotelny.com
🟤 [p336, C1]

An old-fashioned hotel dating from the 1920s, located on a pleasant block between Central Park West and Columbus Avenue shopping and just north of the American Museum of Natural History. It's convenient for museums, shopping, and Central Park. **$**

Marrakech Hotel
2688 Broadway
(at 103rd St)
Tel: 212-222 2954
www.marrakechhotelnyc.com
[off map]
This budget hotel (formerly The Malibu) with a Moroccan-themed decor is a bargain for quality, comfort, and style. It's on the upper end of the Upper West Side, but only a quick subway ride from everywhere. **$**

The Milburn
242 West 76th St (at West End Ave)
Tel: 212-362 1006, 800-833 9622
www.milburnhotel.com
🟤 [p336, B1]
The decor is basic and unimaginative, but this hotel is a good deal, with rooms equipped with kitchenettes, televisions, and internet access. There's also a fitness facility downstairs. It's located on a quiet street not far from Lincoln Center. **$**

BELOW: room at the Mandarin Oriental overlooking Central Park.

PRICE CATEGORIES

Price categories are for a double room for one night in the low season. Be aware that rates can almost double over holidays:

$$$$ = over $375
$$$ = $275–$375
$$ = $175–$275
$ = under $175

ACTIVITIES

THE ARTS, FESTIVALS, NIGHTLIFE, SPORTS AND TOURS

It's just possible there may be somebody somewhere who comes to New York to sleep. But it's certainly the least likely place to choose, because in the Big Apple there's something happening 24 hours a day, 365 days a year. A calendar of events is included in the *Official NYC Guide*, which can be downloaded or ordered by phone (www.nycgo. com/official-nyc-guides, tel: 212- 397 8222; free). For week-by-week details, check the local media and freebie listings publications, and the searchable databases at www.nycgo.com.

THE ARTS

Theater

Few Broadway theaters are actually on Broadway. The alternative to Broadway is Off-Broadway, where performances scarcely differ in quality from the former category, although they are performed in smaller spaces.

The vast majority of Off-Broadway theaters, and the more experimental Off-Off-Broadway theaters, are downtown – particularly in the East Village area. Here you'll find the influential **Public Theater**, a complex of several theaters in one building at 425

Lafayette St, www.publictheater. org, tel: 212-539 8500. The **Theater for the New City** at 155 First Ave, www.theaterforthenewcity.net, tel: 212-254 1109, and **La MaMa**, 74A East 4th St, http://lamama.org, tel: 212-475 7710, are both nearby in the neighborhood and also show new work by experimental artists.

Interesting Off-Broadway productions can also be found around Union Square at the **Union Square Theatre**, 100 East 17th St, tel: 800-982 2787 or 212-871 6834; in SoHo at the **HERE Arts Center**, 145 Sixth Ave, http://here.org, tel: 212-352 3101; and in the West Village, at

BELOW: Off-Broadway.

the **Lucille Lortel Theater**, 121 Christopher St, http://lortel.org, tel: 212- 352 3101, and the **Cherry Lane Theater**, 38 Commerce St, www.cherrylanetheatre. org, tel: 212-989 2020. Near Times Square, the group of Off-Broadway theaters on West 42nd St between Ninth and Eleventh avenues are known as **Theater Row**, of which the best-known is **Playwrights Horizons** at 416 West 42nd Street, www.playwrightshorizons.org, tel: 212-564 1235. One block north, **The Westside Theatre**, 407 West 43rd St, http://westsidetheatre.com, tel: 212-239 6200, is home to new dramatic comedy. In Midtown East, **59E59**, at 59 East 59th St, http://59e59.org, tel: 212-753 5959, is a fine venue.

The *New York Times* offers good listings, as do *The New Yorker*, *Time Out New York*, and *New York* magazines; all are worth checking regularly. A useful source for ticket prices, availability, and/or information about current shows is the non-profit Theatre Development Fund's nyc/ On Stage, at www.tdf.org.

Dance

Numerous renowned dance troupes are based in the city, including the Martha Graham Dance Company, Paul Taylor

ABOVE: Apollo Theater.

Dance Company, Alvin Ailey American Dance Theater, and the Dance Theatre of Harlem.

Performance venues vary widely but include:

Ailey Citigroup Theater, 405 West 55th St, www.alvinailey.org. Tel: 212-405 9000.

Brooklyn Academy of Music (BAM), 30 Lafayette Ave, Fort Greene, Brooklyn, www.bam.org. Tel: 718-636 4100.

City Center, 131 West 55th St, www.nycitycenter.org. Tel: 212-581 1212.

Danspace Project, St Mark's Church, Second Ave at East 10th St, http://danspaceproject.org. Tel: 212-674 8112.

The Joyce Theater, 175 Eighth Ave, www.joyce.org. Tel: 212-691 9740.

Merce Cunningham Studio, 55 Bethune St, www.merce.org. Tel: 212-255 840.

New York City Ballet, 20 Lincoln Center, www.nycballet.com. Tel: 212-870 5570.

New York Live Arts, 219 West 19th St, http://newyorklivearts.org. Tel: 212-691 6500.

Wave Hill, 249th St and Independence Ave, Riverdale, the Bronx, http://wavehill.or. Tel: 718-549 3200. Public garden and cultural center that hosts occasional outdoor, site-specific performances.

Magazines with listings, such as the publications mentioned under "Theater," have information about dance performances, as does the Theatre Development Fund, www.tdf.org.

Concert Halls

Lincoln Center for the Performing Arts, on Broadway between 62nd and 66th streets, is the city's pre-eminent cultural center, with more than two dozen indoor and outdoor venues. It's home to America's oldest orchestra, the New York Philharmonic, which gives 200 concerts annually in **Avery Fisher Hall**, as well as touring worldwide.

Nearby is the **Alice Tully Hall** – renovated extensively in 2008 – which houses the Center's Chamber Music Society. The New York City Opera and New York City Ballet perform at different times in the **David H. Koch Theater**.

Also in this complex are the **Metropolitan Opera House**, home of the Metropolitan Opera Company and, in spring, the American Ballet Theater; **Frederick P. Rose Hall**, home of the prestigious **Jazz at Lincoln Center** series; the excellent **Vivian Beaumont Theater**, the **Mitzi E. Newhouse Theater**, and the brand new Elinor Bunin Munroe Film Center, home to the Film Society. **Walter Reade Theater** hosts the New York Film Festival every fall. Here too are the **Juilliard School**, and the **New York Public Library for the Performing Arts**, an excellent reference source for music and the arts. Tours of Lincoln Center are offered daily between 10am and 5pm; for details, see www.lincolncenter.org, tel: 212-875 5000.

New York's oldest joke concerns the tourist who asks how to get to **Carnegie Hall** and is told "practice, practice." It's quicker to take the N or R subway to 57th St and walk to Seventh Ave or catch a crosstown 57th St bus to this century-old hall, where the world's greatest performers have appeared – and still do on a regular basis. For information on how to see them, visit www.carnegiehall.org or call 212-247 7800.

Venues for classical (and other) music also include **Town Hall**, 123 West 43rd St, http://the-townhall-nyc.org, tel: 212-840 2824; **Merkin Concert Hall**, 129 West 67th St, http://kaufman-center.org, tel: 212-501 3330; the **Kaye Playhouse**, 695 Park Ave at 68th St, http://kaye-playhouse.hunter.cuny.edu, tel: 212-772 4448; **Brooklyn Center for the Performing Arts**, Brooklyn College, www.brooklyncenter.com, tel: 718-951 4500; and the **Brooklyn Academy of Music** (BAM), 30 Lafayette Ave, Brooklyn, www.bam.org. Tel: 718-636 4100.

Opera

In addition to the performances of New York City Opera and the Metropolitan Opera at Lincoln Center, opera can be enjoyed at cozier venues, including **DiCapo Opera Theatre** at 184 East 76th St, http://dicapo.com. Tel: 212-288 9438.

Contemporary Music

Apollo Theater, 253 West 125th St, www.apollotheater.org. Tel: 212-531 5300.

Beacon Theatre, Broadway at 74th St, www.beacontheatre.com. Tel: 212-465 6500.

Madison Square Garden, 4 Penn Plaza, Seventh Ave, between 31st and 33rd sts, www.thegarden.com. Tel: 212-465 671.

Radio City Music Hall, 126 Ave of the Americas at 50th St, www.radiocity.com. Tel: 212-247 4777.

Symphony Space, 2537 Broadway, between 94th and 95th sts, www.symphonyspace.org. Tel: 212-864 5400.

Town Hall, 123 West 43rd St, http://the-townhall-nyc.org. Tel: 212-840 2824.

Art Galleries

There are well over 400 art galleries in the Big Apple but note that mot are closed on Mondays. They're spread around various neighborhoods.

In **Midtown** along 57th St between Sixth Ave and Park Ave; on the **Upper East Side** along upper Madison Ave; in **Chelsea** (particularly around West 22nd and West 24th streets near Tenth Ave); in the **Meatpacking District** around 13th and 14th streets between Tenth Avenue and the West Side Highway; and a few remain in **SoHo** (Swiss Institute of Contemporary Art; Deitch Projects).

From the mid-1990s onward, most of Soho's best-known galleries either closed or moved to **Chelsea**, where the big gallery scene is happening these days. Others relocated to the more traditional 57th St or Fifth Ave/ Madison Avenue area (Gagosian, Leo Castelli), while still others fled to Brooklyn's DUMBO, Williamsburg, or Queens.

As with restaurants, stores, and clubs, galleries spring up overnight and disappear just as quickly. Art fans should consult the listings magazines, as well as the art section of the *New York Times* on Friday and Sunday. A free comprehensive monthly, *Gallery Guide*, can be picked up at various arty locations.

It's also worth checking out the following, most of which have some sort of artist participation:
A.I.R. Gallery, 111 Frost St, DUMBO, Brooklyn, www.airgallery. org. Tel: 212-255 6651. A women's art collective.
Artists Space, 38 Greene St, www.artistsspace.org. Tel: 212-226 3970. New trends, new artists, visual screenings, and performance art.
New Museum of Contemporary Art, 235 Bowery, www.newmuseum.org. Tel: 212-219 1222. Video installations, sculpture, and other works in a stunning new building which is guaranteed to make the entire neighborhood reverberate.
Printed Matter, 195 Tenth Avenue, www.printedmatter.org. Tel: 212-925 0325. Books on, by, and for artists.
P.S.1 Contemporary Art Center, 22–25 Jackson Ave, at 46th Ave, Long Island City, Queens, http://momaps1.org. Tel: 718-784 2084. Up-and-coming artists, multimedia installations, and much more. Affiliated with the Museum of Modern Art and always worth checking out.
White Columns, 320 West 13th St (entrance on Horatio St), http://whitecolumns.org. Tel: 212-924 4212.

Multimedia

Performance art, multimedia presentations, and various uncategorizable events are held at spots around the city, including:
Dixon Place, 258 Bowery, http://dixonplace.org. Tel: 212-219 0736.
The Kitchen, 512 West 19th St, http://thekitchen.org. Tel: 212-255 5793.
La MaMa, 74A East 4th St, http://lamama.org. Tel: 212-475 7710.
P.S.122, 150 First Ave, http://ps122.org. Tel: 212-477 5829.
Symphony Space, 2537 Broadway (at 95th St), www.symphonyspace.org. Tel: 212-864 5400.

FESTIVALS

January

Martin Luther King Day Parade.
National Boat Show, Javits Convention Center. www.nybot show.com.
Winter Antiques Show, 7th Regiment Armory, Park Avenue. www.winterantiquesshow.com.

February

Black History Month.
Chinese New Year celebrations in Chinatown (sometimes Jan). http://explorechinatown.com.
Empire State Building Run-Up race. www.nyrr.org.
Westminster Kennel Club Dog Show, Madison Square Garden. www.westminsterkennelclub.org.

March

The Armory Show, Piers 92 and 94. www.thearmoryshow.com.
The Art Show, 7th Regiment Armory, Park Avenue. www.art dealers.org.
Artexpo New York, Pier 94. http://artexponewyork.com.
Big East Basketball Tournament, Madison Square Garden. www.bigeast.org.
New York City Opera (through April), Lincoln Center. www.nyc opera.com.

BELOW: New York has a busy sporting calendar.

The Photography Show, 7th Regiment Armory, Park Avenue. www.aipad.com.
St Patrick's Day Parade, Fifth Avenue. http://nycstpatricks parade.org.
Whitney Biennial exhibition, Whitney Museum (even years). http://whitney.org.

April

Belmont Racetrack opens. http://www.nyra.com.
Cherry Blossom Festival at Brooklyn Botanic Garden (sometimes May). www.bbg.org.
Earth Day Celebrations.
Easter Parade on Fifth Avenue.
Greek Independence Day Parade.
Havana New York Film Festival. www.hffny.com.
Macy's Spring Flower Show. www1.macys.com.
New York International Auto Show, Javits Convention Center. www.autoshowny.com.
New York Mets and **New York Yankees** baseball season begins. http://mlb.mlb.com.
Tribeca Film Festival. www.tribecafilm.com.

May

American Ballet Theater (through July) at Lincoln Center. www.abt.org.
Five Boro Bike Tour, the country's largest recreational cycling event. www.bikenewyork.org.
Fleet Week, ship tours in Manhattan and Staten Island. www.fleetweeknewyork.com.
New York beaches open. www.nycgovparks.org/facilities/beaches.
New York City Ballet (to June) at Lincoln Center. www.nycballet.com.
Ninth Avenue International Food Festival, from 42nd–57th sts. www.ninthavenuefoodfestival.com.
Taste of Tribeca Food Festival. www.tasteoftribeca.com.
Ukrainian Festival, 7th St and Second Avenue.

Washington Square Outdoor Art Exhibit. http://wsoae.org.

June

Central Park SummerStage shows (through Aug), Rumsey Playfield, Central Park. www.summerstage.org.
Free Metropolitan Opera performances in parks of all five boroughs (sometimes later, through Aug). www.metoperafamily.org.
Gay and Lesbian Pride Day Parade, Fifth Avenue. http://nycpride.org.
Mermaid Parade, Coney Island, Brooklyn. www.coneyisland.com.
Midsummer Night Swing dancing at Lincoln Center (through July). www.midsummernight swing.org.
Movies Under the Stars, Bryant Park (through Aug). www.bryant park.org.
Museum Mile Festival. http://museummilefestival.org.
Puerto Rican Day Parade, Fifth Avenue. www.nationalpuertoricandayparade.org.
River-to-River Festival (through July). www.rivertorivernyc.com.
Salute to Israel Parade, Fifth Ave (sometimes earlier). www.salutetoisrael.com.
Shakespeare in the Park, Delacorte Theater (through July). www.shakespeareinthepark.org.

July

Free New York Philharmonic concerts in major parks. Free concerts also at South Street Seaport. http://nyphil.org.
Harlem Week (longer than a week). http://harlemweek.com.
Lincoln Center Festival and Lincoln Center Out of Doors. www.lincolncenterfestival.org.
Macy's Fourth of July Fireworks, East or Hudson rivers. www.macys.com/fireworks.
Mostly Mozart Festival (to Aug) at Lincoln Center. http://mostly mozart.org.
Museum of Modern Art Summergarden concerts. www.moma.org.

Nathan's Hot Dog Eating Contest, Coney Island, Brooklyn. http://nathansfamous.com.
Thunderbird American Indian Midsummer Pow Wow, three-day event at the Queens County Farm Museum. http://queensfarm.org.
Washington Square Music Festival, Greenwich Village. http://washingtonsquaremusicfestival.org.

August

The Hong Kong Dragon Boat Festival, Flushing, Queens. www.hkdbf-ny.org.
The New York International Fringe Festival. http://fringenyc.org.
US Open Tennis Championships, usta National Tennis Center, Queens (through mid-Sept). www.usopen.org.

September

9/11 Commemorations. www.911memorial.org.
Broadway on Broadway, Times Square. Free live concert. www.broadwayonbroadway.com.
Brooklyn Book Festival, Borough Hall Plaza, Brooklyn. www.brooklynbookfestival.org.
Fashion Week. www.mbfashionweek.com.
Feast of San Gennaro Festival, Little Italy. http://sangennaro.org.
German-American Steuben Day Parade, from Alphabet City to Williamsburg, Brooklyn. www.germanparadenyc.org.
Great North River Tugboat Race and Competition, Hudson River. http://workingharbor.com.
Metropolitan Opera (to April), Lincoln Center. www.metoperafamily.org.
New York Film Festival (to Oct), Lincoln Center. http://filmlinc.com.
New York Giants and Jets football season begins (through Dec). www.nfl.com.
New York Philharmonic (to March), Lincoln Center. http://nyphil.org.

ABOVE: Birdland jazz club.

Next Wave Festival (through Dec), Brooklyn Academy of Music (BAM). www.bam.org.
Richmond County Fair, Historic Richmond Town, Staten Island. http://historicrichmondtown.org.
UN General Assembly opens. www.un.org/en/ga.
Washington Square Art Show. http://wsoae.org.
West Indian-American Day Carnival (Labor Day), Eastern Parkway, Brooklyn. www.wiadca.com.

October

American Ballet Theatre (through to Dec), New York City Center. www.abt.org.
Aqueduct Race Track opens, Queens. www.nyra.com.
Atlantic Antic, Brooklyn (sometimes Sep). www.atlanticave.org.
Big Apple Circus (to Jan), Lincoln Center. www.bigapplecircus.org.
CMJ Music Marathon and Film Festival. www.cmj.com.
Columbus Day Parade, Fifth Avenue. www.columbuscitizens.org.
Halloween Parade, Greenwich Village. www.halloween-nyc.com.
Hispanic Day Parade, Fifth Avenue.
New York Comic-Con, Jacob Javits Center. www.newyorkcomiccon.com.
New York Rangers hockey and

New York Knicks basketball starts, Madison Square Garden. www.thegarden.com.
New Yorker Festival. www.newyorker.com/festival.
Open House New York. http://ohny.org.
Pulaski Day Parade, Fifth Avenue. www.pulaskiparade.com.

November

Christmas Holiday Spectacular (to Jan), Radio City Music Hall. www.radiocitychristmas.com.
Lighting of Christmas Tree, Rockefeller Center (sometimes Dec). www.rockefellercenter.com.
Macy's Thanksgiving Day Parade. www.macys.com/parade.
New York City Ballet (through Feb), Lincoln Center. www.nycballet.com.
New York City Marathon, Staten Island to Central Park. www.nycmarathon.org.
New York Comedy Festival. www.nycomedyfestival.com.
The Nutcracker (running to January), New York City Ballet at the Lincoln Center. www.nycballet.com.
Veterans' Day Parade, Fifth Avenue.

December

Lighting of Giant Chanukah Menorah, Central Park.
New Year's Eve Celebration in Times Square. www.timessquarenyc.org.
New Year's Eve Midnight Run, Central Park. www.nyrr.org.

NIGHTLIFE

Clubs appear and disappear in New York even more abruptly than restaurants. While flagship music venues like the Village Vanguard seem eternal, others, especially the ultra-chic dance clubs, are more ephemeral, seeming to rise and fall (or fail) literally overnight. With these clubs, it's even more important to consult up-to-date listings in publications like the *New Yorker*, *New York* magazine, *Time Out New York*, and the *Village Voice*.

The following represent a range of clubs offering various kinds of live and recorded music, and comedy, cabaret acts, and even poetry readings. Because cover charges, reservation policies, and show times vary from club to club and act to act, it's best to call and ask for specific details geared to a specific night.

Jazz

Midtown

Birdland, 315 West 44th St, www.birdlandjazz.com, tel: 212-581 3080. Elegant jazz club and restaurant. Big-name big bands and jazz greats are the norm, along with smaller well-known or up-and-coming groups holding sway from around 8.30pm. There's a second set at 11pm.
Iridium, 1650 Broadway (at 51st St), www.iridiumjazzclub.com, tel: 212-582 2121. Relocated from the Upper West Side, this club/restaurant has presented some of jazz's most gifted denizens. Definitely worth checking out, especially Monday nights, when late guitar legend Les Paul's backing band is often holding court and hosting notable musicians like Marshall Crenshaw and Graham Parker.
Swing 46, 349 West 46th St, www.swing46.com, tel: 212-262 9554. An all-swing jazz and supper club with live bands every night, and dance lessons. George Gee and his 15-piece Make Believe Ballroom Orchestra get the joint jumping whenever they appear. There's a cover charge.

Uptown

Jazz at Lincoln Center, Broadway at 60th St, www.jalc.org, tel: 212-258 9800. The Frederick P. Rose Hall must be the most lavish purpose-built jazz space in the world: as well as two concert halls it contains **Dizzy's Club Coca-Cola**, named for iconic jazzman John Birks "Dizzy" Gillespie, an intimate club combining breath-taking views, great food, and top jazz performers, seven nights a week – from 6pm dinner seatings to jam-packed after-hours sets. Cover charge, with student discounts at late-night sessions.

Smoke, 2751 Broadway (between 105th and 106th streets), http://smokejazz.com, tel: 212-864 6662. Latin jazz, jazz, blues, and soul vocalists at this Uptown haunt; no cover charge for most late-night shows.

Downtown

Blue Note, 131 West 3rd St, www.bluenotejazz.com, tel: 212-475 8592. The West Village is home to the most famous jazz clubs in the world, and first and foremost is the Blue Note, packed virtually every night for years. The reason is simple: the club presents the very best of mainstream jazz and blues, from time-honored greats to more contemporary acts. The line-up has featured such luminaries as the Modern Jazz Quartet, Etta James, Joe Williams, Betty Carter, the Count Basie Orchestra... the list goes on and on. For diehard fans, there's a late-night session that jams until 4am, after the last set.

The Jazz Standard, 116 East 27th St, www.jazzstandard.net, tel: 212-576 2232. Everything from duos to nine-piece bands and beyond in this basement club. There's a popular restaurant, "Blue Smoke," upstairs, but food downstairs, too.

Smalls, 183 West 10th St, http://smallsjazzclub.com, tel: 212-252 5091. The name is apt. This tiny room isn't about fancy food and a big stage, but for innovative, intimate music played until dawn, it's ideal. $20 cover gets you in for the entire night.

Village Vanguard, 178 Seventh Ave South, www.villagevanguard.com, tel: 212-255 4037. Born over 70 years ago in a Greenwich Village basement, this flagship club cut its teeth helping to launch talents like Miles Davis and John Coltrane. In its adulthood, it hardly keeps up with the "vanguard" anymore, but presents the greats and near-greats of what is now the mainstream. It's also a chance to catch acts that rarely tour. The VV is a terrific evening out, but an extremely popular one – call well in advance or book online to avoid disappointment.

Rock, Dance, Blues

Midtown

B.B. King's Blues Club & Grill, 237 West 42nd St, www.bbkingblues.com, tel: 212-997 4144. In the heart of Times Square, the legendary bluesman's New York venture (there are others around the country, including Memphis) packs them in for the best of the biggest names in R&B. This can include the King himself, stroking the only thing that's never let him down – his guitar, Lucille.

Rodeo Bar, 375 Third Ave at East 27th St, www.rodeobar.com, tel: 212-683 6500. A kitschy Southern roadhouse theme; a loose and lanky honky-tonk atmosphere, and live performances by "cowboy rock" bands.

Roseland, 239 West 52nd St, www.roselandballroom.com, tel: 212-247 0200. Historically, a venue for traditional ballroom dancing; lately, also for private parties, special events, and performances by alternative rock bands or DJ-driven dancing to classic R&B. Check the website for schedules.

Terminal 5, 610 West 56th St, www.terminal5nyc.com, tel: 212-582 6600. A huge multilevel venue for rock and pop acts that have just broken big. Near the Hudson River, it has a nice roof-deck bar.

Downtown

Arlene's Grocery, 95 Stanton St, between Ludlow and Orchard, www.arlenesgrocery.net, tel: 212-995 1652. A low-key, casual Lower East Side bar offering rock, folk, punk, and everything in between. Hosts Monday night live-band karaoke.

The Bitter End, 147 Bleecker St, between Thompson and Laguardia, www.bitterend.com, tel: 212-673 7030. A Greenwich Village landmark, the Bitter End books an eclectic mishmash of folk, folk rock, soft rock, blues, some comedy and cabaret... whatever. A classic example of eternal bohemianism, it's popular with young adult tourists and can be mobbed on weekends.

Bowery Ballroom, 6 Delancey St, www.boweryballroom.com, tel: 212-533 2111. A smaller venue to see big-name rock reunions, up-and-coming indie bands and more. Great sightlines, acoustics, and a comfortable downstairs bar.

Irving Plaza, 17 Irving Pl, www.irvingplaza.com, tel: 212-777 6800. A renovated and relaunched hall near Union Square that's been through more than one incarnation; currently features top indie rock bands.

Joe's Pub, 425 Lafayette St, www.joespub.com, tel: 212-539 8778. Singers, performance artists, musicians: there's a mix here, by Joseph Papp's theater.

Le Poisson Rouge, 158 Bleecker St, http://lepoissonrouge.com, 212-505 3474. A new addition to the Downtown music scene, showcasing more avant-garde rock and dance acts.

Mercury Lounge, 217 East Houston St, www.mercuryloungenyc.com, tel: 212-260 4700. Intimate Lower East Side club with excellent acoustics, catering to a more sophisticated alternative music crowd than usual.

S.O.B.'s, 200 Varick St (at Houston St), www.sobs.com, tel: 212-243 4940. Funky, global jazz, lots of Brazilian beat, but runs the gamut of world and dance music.

The Village Underground, 130 West 3rd St, www.thevillageunderground.com, tel: 212-777

7745. For night-time revelers who like all different types of music, this candlelit, intimate venue might be for you. No cover most weekdays.

Webster Hall, 125 East 11th St, www.websterhall.com, tel: 212-353 1600. Discount passes can be had by booking online for this large, always-jam-packed East Village club which attracts a young crowd. Open Wednesdays to Saturdays from 10pm, it offers all-night dance sessions for fans of everything from rock, reggae, and R&B to house, techno, and who knows; theme nights range from "runway parties" to 1960s psychedelia. Recently, it has been welcoming big-name rock and rap acts in its Grand Ballroom.

Out of Town

Izod Center, The Meadowlands, East Rutherford, New Jersey, www.meadowlands.com, tel: 201-935 3900.
Maxwells, 1039 Washington St, Hoboken, New Jersey, www.maxwellsnj.com, tel: 201-653 1703.
Nassau Coliseum, at Veterans Memorial, Uniondale, Long Island, www.nassaucoliseum.com, tel: 516-794 9300.

Comedy and Cabaret

Midtown

Carolines on Broadway, 1626 Broadway (between 49th and 50th sts), www.carolines.com, tel: 212-757 4100. A well-established restaurant and club with a roster of young comic hopefuls along with some of the biggest names in the "biz."
Don't Tell Mama, 343 West 46th St, www.donttellmamanyc.com, tel: 212-757 0788. A merry spot, long favored by a theatrical crowd. In the front there's a piano bar; the back room is non-stop cabaret, with comedians and torch singers. Leave inhibitions behind, and bring cash (no credit cards accepted).

Gotham City Comedy Club, 208 West 23rd St, www.gothamcomedyclub.com, tel: 212-367 9000. A club that runs the stand-up comedy gamut from unknown first-timers to the irrepressible and unmissable legends like Jackie Mason.
The Metropolitan Room, 34 West 22nd St, www.metropolitanroom.com, tel: 212-206 0440. Sophisticated classic cabaret performers, as well as talented newcomers. An elegant yet surprisingly affordable New York night out that has a reasonable cover charge along with the usual two-drink minimum.
Upright Citizens Brigade Theatre, 207 West 26th St, www.ucbtheatre.com, tel: 212-366 9176. Improv comedy at its most bizarre and inventive. This is where television stars like Amy Poehler and many cast members of *Saturday Night Live* got their start – they still take the stage from time to time.

Uptown

Cafe Carlyle, 35 East 76th St, www.thecarlyle.com, tel: 212-744 1600. In the elegant Carlyle Hotel, an upper-crusty institution of sorts for the social set. There's a hefty cover charge and a two-drink minimum. When he's in

BELOW: Sunshine Cinema.

town, Woody Allen sits in with the New Orleans Jazz Band headed by Eddy Davis.
Comic Strip, 1568 Second Ave at 82nd St, www.comicstriplive.com, tel: 212-861 9386. A popular proving ground for young stand-ups, both known and unknown. Open seven days a week, with three shows on Friday and Saturday nights.
Feinstein's at Loews Regency, 540 Park Avenue at 61st St, http://feinsteinsattheregency.com, tel: 212-339 4095. Singer Michael Feinstein is so devoted to cabaret that he opened his own high-end club in the Regency Hotel.
Stand-Up NY, 236 West 78th St, at Broadway, www.standupny.com, tel: 212-595 0850. Small Upper West Side club that has open-mike evenings (5pm–7pm) three times a week.

Downtown

The Comedy Cellar, 117 MacDougal St, www.comedycellar.com, tel: 212-254 3480. A cramped basement where the tables are packed so close that, even if you don't get the jokes, you may make new friends. The show starts at 8pm and usually feature at least one or two comics you've seen on late-night television.
The Duplex, 61 Christopher St, www.theduplex.com, tel: 212-255 5438. A landmark of the gay West Village, attracting a friendly, mixed audience for comedy and cabaret.
Nuyorican Poets Café, 236 East 3rd St (between Aves B and C), www.nuyorican.org, tel: 212-780 9386. From poetry slams and hip-hop to multimedia, comedy, and music, at a cutting-edge East Village landmark.

Movies

Movie theaters are scattered all over town, with blockbusters shown in every neighborhood and foreign films and arthouse offerings mostly downtown. The city's newspapers and magazines carry complete listings, as well as, usually, the performance times.

There are at least a score of venues that are devoted to showing revival, cult, experimental, and genre films which never make the mainstream circuit. The theaters often have a neighborhood feel, and the films are subtitled.

Theaters worth checking out include the **French Institute/Alliance Française**, 22 East 60th St, www.fiaf.org, tel: 212-355 6100, and the **Japan Society**, 333 East 47th St, www.japansociety.org, tel: 212-832 1155, which specialize in screenings from their respective countries. Places such as **Anthology Film Archives**, 32 Second Ave, http://anthologyfilmarchives.org, tel: 212-505 5181; **Cinema Village**, 22 East 12th St, www.cinemavillage.com, tel: 212-924 3363; **Angelika Film Center**, 18 West Houston (at Mercer St), http://angelikafilmcenter.com, tel: 212-995 2570; the **Sunshine Cinema**, 143 East Houston, www.landmarktheatres.com, tel: 212-330 8182, IFC Center, 323 Sixth Ave (at West 3rd St), www.ifccenter.com, tel: 212-924 7771, and the **Film Forum**, 209 West Houston St, www.filmforum.org, tel: 212-727 8110, all show films of an arty nature.

Independent and foreign films are a specialty at the **BAM Rose Cinemas** at the Brooklyn Academy of Music, 30 Lafayette Ave, Brooklyn, www.bam.org, tel: 718-636 4100, and at Lincoln Center, where the Elinor Bunim Monroe Film Center, www.filmlinc.com, tel: 212-875 5456, is home to the Film Society, and the **Walter Reade Theater**, tel: 212-875 5600, hosts the annual New York Film Festival.

Rarely seen movies or obscure directors are also featured at the **Museum of the Moving Image** in Queens, www.movingimage.us, tel: 718-784 0077, and at the **Museum of Modern Art**, tel: 212-708 9480.

In summer **Bryant Park**, behind the Public Library at 42nd St, hosts free outdoor film screenings; check www.bryantpark.org or tel: 212-512 5700 for current programs.

SPORTS

Participant Sports

New York offers a huge array of recreational facilities. May are found in the city's **parks** – including Central Park, where roads are closed to traffic on summer weekends for the benefit of cyclists, joggers, and in-line skaters. For general information call the Department of Parks and Recreation at 311 (within New York City) or 212-639 9675 (from elsewhere) – or visit www.nycgovparks.org.

Tennis can be played in Central Park and various other parks. For permits and other information, visit www.centralparktenniscenter.com or call 212-360 8133. The city's largest public tennis facility is the usta Billy Jean King National Tennis Center in Queens, home of the US Open, www.usta.com, tel: 718-760 6200.

Rowboats can be rented at the Central Park Lake boathouse, www.thecentralparkboathouse.com (and at Prospect Park in Brooklyn, Kissena Park in Queens, and Van Cortland Park in the Bronx), as can bicycles.

Ice skating is available in winter at both Wollman (www.wollmanskatingrink.com, tel: 212-439 6900) and Lasker (www.laskerrink.com, tel: 917-492 3857) rinks in Central Park, Rockefeller Center (www.rockefellercenter.com, tel: 212-332 7654), and Bryant Park (http://citipondatbryantpark.com, tel: 212-661 6640), as well as year-round at Sky Rink, Pier 61 at the Hudson River (www.chelseapiers.com/sr01.htm, tel: 212-336 6100), part of Chelsea Piers.

Basketball courts and **baseball** and **softball** diamonds are located in city parks, as are miles of **jogging** tracks and trails. (The New York Road Runners Club maintains a running center on the Upper East Side, www.nyrr.org, tel: 212-860 4455.)

You'll find public **golf courses** at Pelham Bay Park, Van Cortlandt Park (both in the Bronx), and at Latourette Park in Staten Island, among other parks in the Outer Boroughs.

For numerous sports in one place, try the **Chelsea Piers Sports and Entertainment Complex** (www.chelseapiers.com, tel: 212-336 6666), which stretches along the Hudson River between 17th and 23rd streets. Facilities include a multi-tiered **golf driving range**, **boating**, **bowling**, **horseback riding**, and **in-line skating**; day passes are occasionally available at the sports/fitness center, which has an Olympic-size swimming pool, a running track, and a **rock-climbing wall**.

Spectator Sports

The city is very proud of its teams, the **New York Yankees** and the **New York Mets**, who play **baseball** from April to October at Yankee Stadium in the Bronx (http://newyork.yankees.mlb.com, tel: 718-293 6000) and Citi Field in Flushing (http://newyork.mets.mlb.com, tel: 718-507 8499). Both had new stadiums built in 2009. A pair of new Class-A minor league baseball teams are also attracting enthusiastic local crowds: Mets' affiliate the **Brooklyn Cyclones**, at MCU Park in Coney Island (www.brooklyncyclones.com, tel: 718-449 8497), and the **Staten Island Yankees**, at Richmond County Ballpark at St George (www.siyanks.com, tel: 718-720 9265).

The **New York Knicks** (www.nba.com/knicks, tel: 212-465 6741) play **basketball** between October and May at Madison Square Garden. The **New York Liberty** (www.wnba.com/liberty, tel:

TRANSPORTATION

ABOVE: carriage ride.

212- 564-9622) women's team can currently be seen in summer at the Prudential Center in Newark, NJ. College team schedules are listed in the daily papers.

The **ice hockey** season runs from October to April, with the **New York Rangers** at Madison Square Garden (http://rangers. nhl.com, tel: 212-465 4459) and the **Islanders** playing at Nassau Coliseum on Long Island (http:// islanders.nhl.com, tel: 516-501 6700). Madison Square Garden is also the main site for important events in **boxing** and (indoor) **tennis**, although the US Open is at the **National Tennis Center** in Flushing Meadows-Corona Park, Queens (www.usopen.org, tel: 718-760 6200), in late August and September.

The **football** season starts in September and lasts through December or January, with both the **New York Giants** (www. giants.com, tel: 201-935 8111) and **New York Jets** (www.newyor-kjets.com, tel: 800-469 5387) playing at MetLife Stadium in The Meadowlands, East Rutherford, NJ.

Soccer takes place between March and October, with the New York Red Bulls (www.newyorkred

bulls.com, tel: 877-727 6223) playing matches at Red Bull Arena in Harrison, NJ. **Cricket** matches are held on Saturdays and summer Sundays in Van Cortlandt Park in the Bronx, as well as on Randall's Island in the East River and at various parks in Brooklyn and Staten Island (http://new yorkcricket.com).

The closest thoroughbred **horse racing** is at **Belmont Park** in Elmont, Long Island (Long Island Railroad from Pennsylvania Station), http://nyra.com, tel: 516-488 6000.

TOURS

Sightseeing Tours

Among the dozens of operators offering sighseeing trips around the city, one of the most popular is **Gray Line New York**, www.gray line.com, tel: 800-669 0051, which features double-decker buses with hop-on, hop-off itineraries.

Manhattan is, of course, an island, so there's a big choice of boat tours, including: **Circle Line**, www.circlelinedowntown.com, tel: 212-563 3200, which operates boat trips around Manhattan and harbor cruises from South Street Seaport; **NY Waterway**, www. nywaterway.com, tel: 800-533 3779, featuring harbor cruises and entertainment cruises. **New York Water Taxi**, www.nywater-taxi.com, tel: 212-742 1969, with stops near the 9/11 Memorial, in Brooklyn, and at Yankee Stadium during the baseball season; **Manhattan by Sail**, www.manhattan-bysail.com, tel: 212-619 0907, which cruises near the Statue of Liberty in a beautiful 1929 dou-ble-masted schooner; and **Spirit Cruises**, www.spiritofnewyork. com, tel: 866-483 3866, which offers luxury cruises with dinner and entertainment afloat.

Other interesting or off-the-beaten track options include: **Art Horizons International**,

www.art-horizons.com, tel: 212-969 9410. Visits to galleries, museums, and artists' studio lofts.
Big Onion Walking Tours, www. bigonion.com, tel: 212-439 1090. Historic, ethnic neighbor-hood tours with zing.
Central Park Bicycle Tours, www.centralparkbiketour.com, tel: 212-541 8759. Guided bike tours, including rentals, through the park.
Central Park Carriage Rides, www.centralparkcarriages.com, tel: 212-736 0680.
Central Park Conservancy, www.centralparknyc.org, tel: 212-310 6600. Free walking tours. Also **Urban Park Rangers Tours**, tel: 311 or 212-639 9675.
Elegant Tightwad Shopping Tours, www.theeleganttightwad. com, tel: 800-808 4614. Designer showroom tours, sample sales.
Harlem Heritage Tours, www. harlemheritage.com, tel: 212-280 7888. Walk around the streets with a local resident.
Harlem Spirituals/New York Visions, www.harlemspirituals. com, tel: 212-391 0900. Gospel tours.
Hush Tours, www.hushtours. com, tel: 212-714 3527. Hip-hop tours.
Lower East Side Tenement Museum, www.tenement.org, tel: 212-982 8420, offers walking tours, led by local historians.
Municipal Art Society, www. mas.org, tel: 212-935 3960. Architectural walks.
Museum of Chinese in the Americas, www.mocanyc.org, tel: 212-619 4785; another walking tour of the immigrant experience.
On Location Tours, www.screen-tours.com, tel: 212-209 3370. See the locations of *Sex and the City*, *The Sopranos*, *Gossip Girl*, and various movies that have been filmed in NY.
Radio City Music Hall, www. radiocity.com, tel: 212-465 6080. Go behind the gold curtain to find out who plays the gigantic Wurlitzers.

ACCOMMODATIONS

ACTIVITIES

A – Z

A – Z

AN ALPHABETICAL SUMMARY OF PRACTICAL INFORMATION

A

Admission Fees

Fees to attractions range from about $10–15. A few museums, like the Met or MoMA, cost more. At some public museums, the entry fee is not strictly obligatory, but there is a "suggested donation." On Thursday or Friday evenings, some museums are free.

B

Budgeting for Your Trip

Your biggest expense will be your hotel room. Expect to pay $199 for a room at a budget hotel during the low season; $325 for a moderate establishment; and $525 at a deluxe hotel. It's possible to eat out cheaply in New York, with main courses ranging from $10 at the lower end to $20 at a moderate place and $30 at an expensive venue. The average cost of a beer is $6 and a glass of wine $10 – and remember to tip $1 per drink. A taxi from JFK Airport to Manhattan costs $45, plus tip and tolls. A single bus or subway ride is $2.50 and a 7-day unlimited MetroCard will set you back $29.

C

Children

At museums you'll find strollers, kid-friendly exhibits, and discounts galore. Navigating the stairs in the subway system with strollers and small children can be tricky, so splurge on taxis when possible.

Climate

New York has four distinct seasons, and is at its best during the spring and fall months. Summer temperatures hover in the mid-70s to mid-80s°F (24–29°C), although heatwaves where the mercury rises to 100°F (38°C) may occur, and uncomfortable humidity is often the rule, especially in July and August.

September and October sometimes usher in a balmy, dry "Indian summer" that fills parks and office plazas with sun worshipers. Winter temperatures can drop below 10 or 15°F (−12 or −9°C), with the average for January closer to 32°F (0°C). The average annual rainfall is 44ins (112cm) and the average snowfall is 29ins (74cm). Raincoats and umbrellas are a good idea year-round.

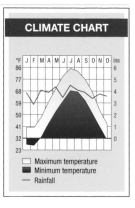

CLIMATE CHART

- ☐ Maximum temperature
- ■ Minimum temperature
- — Rainfall

What to Wear

Except for casual wandering, dress tends to be a little bit more formal compared to other US cities. It's a good idea to ask about proper dress codes for restaurants, clubs, etc.

Crime and Safety

Despite its post 9/11 reputation as "caring, sharing New York," parts of the city are still unsafe, and visitors should not be lulled into any false sense of security. Adopt the typical New Yorker's guise of looking street-smart and aware at all times.

Ostentatious displays of jewelry or wealth invite muggers;

excursions into deserted areas at night (such as Central Park or Battery Park) are equally unwise. Lock your hotel door even when you are inside, and travel to places like Harlem and the Bronx in a group. And even though Times Square has thrown off its seedy mantle, the streets around it attract pickpockets.

The subways are much safer than they were, but when traveling alone at night, stay on alert. Once through the turnstile, stay within sight of the ticket booth. **In emergencies, dial 911 for police, fire, or ambulance.**

Police Precincts

Downtown
1st, 16 Ericsson Place (West Canal St). Tel: 212-334 0611.
5th, 19 Elizabeth St (Chinatown). Tel: 212-334 0711.
6th, 233 West 10th St (Greenwich Village). Tel: 212-741 4811.
7th, 19½ Pitt St (Lower East Side). Tel: 212-477 7311.
9th, 321 East 5th St. Tel: 212-477 7811.
10th, 230 West 20th St. Tel: 212-741 8211.
13th, 230 East 21st St. Tel: 212-477 7411.
Midtown
South, 357 West 35th St. Tel:

212-239 9811.
17th, 167 East 51st St. Tel: 212-826 3211
North, 306 West 54th St. Tel: 212-760 8400.
Uptown
19th, 153 East 67th St. Tel: 212-452 0600.
20th, 120 West 82nd St. Tel: 212-580 6411.
Central Park, Transverse Road at 86th St. Tel: 212-570 4820.
23rd, 162 East 102nd St. Tel: 212-860 6411.
24th, 151 West 100th St. Tel: 212-678 1811.
25th, 120 East 119th St. Tel: 212-860 6511.
26th, 520 West 126th St. Tel: 212-678 1311.
28th, 2271–2289 Eighth Ave (near 123rd St). Tel: 212-678 1611.
30th, 451 West 151st St. Tel: 212-690 8811.
32nd, 250 West 135th St. Tel: 212-690 6311.
33rd, 2207 Amsterdam Ave. Tel: 212-927 3200.
34th, 4295 Broadway. Tel: 212-927 9711.

Customs Regulations

For a breakdown of up-to-date US Customs and Border Protection regulations, visit www.cbp.gov. Tel: 800-232 5378.

BELOW: motorcycle cop.

D

Disabled Travelers

Disabled travelers can obtain information about rights and special facilities from the **Mayor's Office for People with Disabilities**, 100 Gold St, 2nd Floor, New York, NY 10038, www.nyc.gov/html/mopd. Tel: 212-788 2830, TTY: 212-788 2838.

E

Electricity

The US uses a 110-volt current. Electrical adapters are available in hardware and appliance stores and some drugstores.

Embassies and Consulates

Embassies are located in Washington D.C. but most countries have consulates or missions to the United Nations in New York.
Australia: Consulate General, 150 East 42nd Street, www.newyork.consulate.gov.au, tel: 212-351 6500
Canada: 1251 Avenue of the Americas, www.canadainternational.gc.ca/new_york, tel: 212-596 1628
Ireland: 345 Park Avenue, www.consulateofirelandnewyork.org, tel: 212-319 2555
New Zealand: 222 East 41st Street, www.nzembassy.com/usa, tel: 212-832 4038
South Africa: 333 East 38th Street, www.southafrica-newyork.net, tel: 212-213 4880

Emergencies

Telephone Numbers

For all emergencies: police, fire, ambulance, dia **911**.
For non-emergency assistance, dial **311**.

Etiquette

Contrary to popular opinion, New Yorkers are generally a polite bunch, but the one thing you don't want to do is slow them down. Never cut in line, steal a taxi, step into traffic, block a subway door with your arm, or stop on stairs or busy sidewalks. Stand to the right on escalators, so people can pass on the left, and don't stare.

You will see every manner of dress on the streets, but that doesn't mean they are all appropriate for religious buildings. All the usual international practices regarding hats, sunglasses, shoes, and clothing apply to the churches, temples, synagogues, and mosques of New York. If you are unsure what those are, contact the establishment and ask. Always silence cell phones when attending a religious service or any type of performance.

On public transportation, seating preference should be given to the elderly, disabled, and pregnant. If visiting someone's home for dinner, it never hurts to bring a bottle of wine or, perhaps, freshly baked goods as a gift. New Yorkers love to talk, but it's considered tacky to discuss what they pay in rent or what they are paid in salary. Most honking of car horns is considered rude and unnecessary in much of the country, but that would come as news to New York City taxi drivers.

Hold doors, say "thank you," and exercise common courtesy and you will do just fine.

G

Gay and Lesbian

The Gay, Lesbian, Bisexual, and Transgender National Hotline, tel: 888-843 4564 or 212-989 0999, provides information to gay men and women about all aspects of gay life. Locally, GMHC (Gay Men's Health Crisis), 446 West 33rd Street, offers walk-in counseling and a useful hotline, tel: 800-243 7692, and website: www.gmhc.org. The **Lesbian, Gay, Bisexual, and Transgender Community Center**, 208 West 13th St, tel: 212-620 7310, is another helpful local organization. Its website is www.gaycenter.org.

H

Health and Medical Care

Medical services are extremely expensive; always travel with comprehensive travel insurance to cover any emergencies. **New York House Call Physicians**, tel: 646-957 5444, make house calls on a non-emergency basis, for $400 and up. Their website is www.doctorinthefamily.com.

To find a local pharmacy, go to www.cvs.com or www.duanereade.com. Both drugstores have many locations throughout the city, with varying hours. Some are open 24 hours.

Hospitals with Emergency Rooms
Downtown/Midtown
Bellevue Hospital, First Ave and East 27th St, www.nyc.gov/belle

BELOW: hanging out in the West Village.

vue. Tel: 212-562 4141.

Beth Israel Medical Center, First Ave at East 16th St, http://chp-nyc.org. Tel: 212-420 2000.

NYU Langone Medical Center, 550 First Ave at 33rd St, http:// emergency.med.nyu.edu. Tel: 212-263 7300.

St Luke's-Roosevelt Hospital, 59th St at Tenth Ave, http://slred. org. Tel: 212-523 4000.

Uptown

New York-Presbyterian Hospital/Columbia University Medical Center, 630 West 168th St, http://nypemergency.org. Tel: 212-305 6204.

Lenox Hill Hospital, 100 East 77th St at Park Ave, www.lenox-hillhospital.org. Tel: 212-434 3030.

Mount Sinai Hospital, Fifth Ave and East 100th St, www.mountsi-nai.org. Tel: 212-241 6639.

New York-Presbyterian Hospital/Weill Cornell Medical Center, 525 East 68th St, http:// nypemergency.org. Tel: 212-746 0795.

I

Internet

Wi-Fi is available in Union Square and other parts of Manhattan, including at least 10 city parks. More and more hotels provide free Wi-Fi, too. For the latest update check out www.wififreespot.com. Email can be sent from most branches of FedEx copy shops or from branches of the New York Public Library, including the **Science, Industry, and Business Library**, 188 Madison Ave at 34th St, http://www.nypl.org/locations/sibl, tel: 212-592 7000.

Internet cafes are mostly a thing of the past, since Starbucks offers free Wi-Fi and so many people use their phones and laptops to access the internet. Still, you can find them if you look. Check out the **Cybercafe**, 250 West 49th St, www.cyber-cafe.com, tel: 212-333 4109.

L

Left Luggage

Options for luggage storage are limited. Terminal 4 at JFK has a luggage storage service for $4–16 per bag per day, depending on dimensions, tel: 718-751 4020. It's open 24 hours. Other terminals have similar services, but during restricted hours. Penn Station has luggage storage for Amtrak passengers only, located near the 8th Ave entrance, tel: 800-872 7245. In proximity to Penn Station, Port Authority and Grand Central, Schwartz Travel (http://schwartztravel.com, tel: 212-290 2626) has three locations with luggage lockers for $2–10 per bag, per day.

Lost Property

The chances of retrieving lost property are low, but items may have been turned in to the nearest police precinct. To inquire about items left on public transportation (**subway** and **bus**) visit http://lostfound.mtanyct.info or call 212-712 4500. Open Mon, Tue, Fri 8am–3.30pm, Wed, Thur 11am–6.30pm. Or call **311**.

M

Maps

The official **NYC & Co.** provides good maps at its visitors' center (810 Seventh Avenue between 52nd and 53rd streets) and online through its website: www.nycgo.com. Subway and bus maps are available at subway station booths, or from the New York City Transit Authority booth in Grand Central and the Long Island Rail Road information booth in Penn Station, as well as the MTA booth at the **Times Square Visitors' Center**. Maps may also be obtained by calling 718-330

1234 (dial 511 in New York City) or online through the Metropolitan Transit Authority website: www.mta.info.

The *Insight Fleximap to New York City* is laminated and immensely durable. The most detailed street map is a book called *Manhattan Block by Block*, published by Tauranac Maps.

Media

Print

The internationally known *New York Times* isthe paper of choice for most well-informed readers, with its bulky Sunday edition listing virtually everything of consequence. On a daily basis, two tabloids compete for the rest of the audience: the *New York Post*, famed for its garish headlines and downmarket appeal; and the *Daily News*. There are two "commuter" dailies distributed free in the mornings: *AM New York* and *New York Metro*. The best sources of information for what's on in the city are the magazines *New York*, the *New Yorker*, and *Time Out New York*, but there are also two useful free weeklies, the *Village Voice* and the *New York Press*.

Television

The three major networks – all with NY headquarters – are **ABC**, 7 Lincoln Square, tel: 212-456 7000; **CBS**, 51 West 52nd St, tel: 212-975 4321; and **NBC**, 30 Rockefeller Plaza, tel: 212-664 4444. **Fox Broadcasting** has national offices at 1211 Ave of the Americas, tel: 212-852 7111, and **CNN** has moved into offices at the Time Warner Center at Columbus Circle, tel: 212-275 7800.

The **Public Broadcasting System** (**PBS**) can be found on channels 13 and 21 on the VHF band (for those without cable). Other local stations are affiliated with the **Fox** (Channel 5), **UPN** (9), and **WB** (11) networks. These channels broadcast nationally aired shows as well as local programming. In addition, there are half a dozen UHF stations which broadcast in Spanish and other languages.

Cable companies in the city offer over 100 cable and movie channels, although the exact number differs from borough to borough.

Most hotels offer cable in their guest rooms in addition to – for a fee – recent Hollywood movies.

Money

Most ATMs will charge a fee for withdrawing cash. Credit cards are accepted almost everywhere in the city, although not all cards are accepted at all places.

There are numerous outlets for exchanging currency in New York, but a few banks still charge a fee to cash traveler's checks, and a passport must be produced. Dollar traveler's checks are accepted in many hotels, restaurants, and stores in the US, so long as they are accompanied by proper identification, so it's generally easier just to use them as cash rather than change them at a bank.

Travelex, www.travelex.com, tel: 1-800-287 7362; 1578 Broadway at 48th St, tel: 212-265 6063; 1271 Broadway at 32nd St, tel: 212-679 4365; and 30 Vesey St, tel: 212-227 8629. All Travelex offices sell and cash traveler's checks as well as exchange money, as do the many **American Express** offices around town, such as 374 Park Ave, www.amextravelresources. com, tel: 212-421 8240.

Citibank offers exchange facilities at most of its 200 or so branches around the five boroughs. Visit www.citigroup.com or call 800-285 3000.

O

Opening Hours

New Yorkers work long and hard in a city where this is generally seen to be an advantage. Normal business hours are 9am–6pm, but stores, in particular, tend to stay open later. They can get crowded at lunchtime. Many shops also open on Sundays. Banking hours are nominally 9am–5pm but increasingly, banks are opening as early as 8am and staying open until early evening – ATM machines are everywhere.

Port Authority Bus Terminal (Eighth Ave at 42nd St, www. panynj.gov) stays open 24 hrs, tel: 212-564 8484.

Penn Station (Seventh Ave at 32rd St) is open 24 hrs. Long Island Railroad Information: www.

HOW TO SEE A TELEVISION SHOW

With advance planning, it's possible to join the audience of a New York-based TV show. For more details, go to the NYC & Co. Information Center or www. nycgo.com. Here's a selection:

The Daily Show with Jon Stewart and the Colbert Report with Stephen Colbert
These very popular satirical shows have been so overwhelmed by ticket requests that the producers occasionally have to stop offering them to the public. Tickets can only be ordered online at www.thedailyshow.com and www.colbertnation.com. Audience members must be 18 or older. Mon–Thur at Comedy Central Studios, 733 11th Ave; doors open at 5.45pm.

Late Show with David Letterman
Tapings of this popular talk show are Mon–Thur at 5.30pm. Audience members must be 18 or older; proper ID required. Tickets can be applied for online, or by visiting the theater. Standby tick-

ets may be available if you're at the box office by 9.30am on the day of broadcasting. Ed Sullivan Theater, 1697 Broadway, New York, NY 10019. Tel: 212-975 5853. www.lateshowaudience. com.

Late Night with Jimmy Fallon
Tapings Tue–Fri at 5.30pm, and audience members must be at least 16. Reserved tickets are only available by calling 212-664 3056, for a maximum of four. Standby tickets are available on the morning of the show – arrive by 9am at NBC Studios on the 49th Street side of 30 Rockefeller Plaza. More info at www.late-nightwithjimmyfallon.com.

NBC Today Show Through the Window
Tapings of this show are Mon–Fri from 7–10am. An audience is encouraged to watch from the streets outside, but you must get there by dawn. The best place to stand is the southeastern corner. Go to kiosks at 30 Rockefeller Plaza for information.

Saturday Night Live
Tapings of this venerable comedy show are on Saturday, from 11.30pm–1am. Audience members must be 16 or older. A ticket lottery is held each August. Only one email per person will be accepted, for two tickets each. Standby tickets are given out at 7am on the 49th St entrance for the dress rehearsal and the live show, but do not guarantee admission. Email to: www. snltickets@nbcuni.com. NBC Tickets, tel: 212-664 3056; www.nbc.com.

NBC Studio Tour
At least to see the studios of Saturday Night Live and other shows (as long as they're not taping), tag along on the NBC Studio Tour. Attractions include bluescreens to let you "join" presenters on the sets. Tours start at the NBC Experience Store at 30 Rockefeller Plaza, every 15 or 30 minutes, 7 days a week (www. nbc.com/tickets, tel: 212-664 3700; charge).

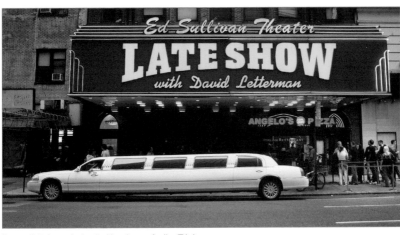

BELOW: tickets can be booked in advance for live TV shows.

mta.info/lirr, tel: 718-217 5477; New Jersey Transit Info: www.njtransit.com, tel: 973-275 5555. **Grand Central Terminal** closes at 1.30am. MetroNorth Information: www.mta.info, tel: 212-532 4900.

P

Postal Services

Manhattan's main post office on Eighth Ave between 31st and 33rd streets is open 24 hours a day for stamps, express mail, and certified mail. To send a letter or postcard internationally will cost approximately $1. To find out where post office branches are located throughout the five boroughs, and to inquire about other mailing rates and methods, call the Postal Service Consumer Hotline: 800-275 8777, or go to www.usps.gov.

R

Religious Services

New York is approximately 70 percent Christian, 11 percent Jewish, 1.5 percent Muslim, 7.4 percent agnostic, with Buddhists, Hindus, and others also represented. Around 6,000 churches, temples, and mosques are scattered throughout the five boroughs. Consult the *Yellow Pages* or ask at the desk of your hotel for the nearest place of worship.

S

Smoking

There is now a no-smoking law in effect in virtually all New York City parks, bars, restaurants, offices, and public buildings. A few hotels still have rooms for smokers; ask when booking.

T

Telephones

International calls, dial: 011 (the international access code), then the country code, city code, and local number.

Most Manhattan numbers have the **212** area code, which has been in existence for dec-

TIPPING

Most New Yorkers in the service industries (restaurants, hotels, transportation) regard tips as a God-given right, not just a pleasant gratuity. The fact is, many people rely on tips to make up for what are often poor hourly salaries. Therefore, unless service is truly horrendous, you can figure on tipping everyone from bellmen and porters (usually $1 a bag; or $2 if only one bag) to hotel doormen ($1 if they hail you a cab), hotel maids ($1–2 a day, left in your room when you check out), restroom attendants (at least 50¢), and room-service waiters (approximately 15 percent of the bill unless already added on). In restaurants, one way to figure out the tip is to double the tax (which adds up to a little more than 16 percent), but the standard restaurant tip is inching closer to 20 percent these days. For parties of six or more, tips are often added to the bill, usually at a rate of 18 percent. In taxis, tip as much as 15 percent of the total fare, with a $1 minimum.

ABOVE: New York's religious community is large and diverse.

ades; newer places might use the **646** or **917** prefix. Brooklyn, Queens, Staten Island, and Bronx numbers are prefixed by **718** (or the newer **347** or **917**). Regardless of the number you are calling from, the area code of the number being called must be used: eg, in a 212 area, if you are calling another 212 number, the 212 prefix must still be used.

Toll-free calls are prefixed by **800**, **888**, **866**, or **877**.

Public phones can be found in various centers. **Telephone dialing cards**, available from newsstands and corner stores, are an inexpensive way to make calls, especially international ones.

Cell phones are ubiquitous. Anyone staying here for more than a few days, or who makes repeated trips to NY, might consider buying a local cell phone: prices are cheap compared to those in many cities.

Useful Numbers

New York has a three-digit number that can be dialed for informa-

tion on a range of services, whether the caller is a New York resident or just a visitor. Calls to **311** are answered by a live operator, 24 hours a day, seven days a week, and information is provided in over 170 languages.

The purpose of a call can be as wide-ranging as tourist destination inquiries, making a complaint about noise or a taxi; finding out about the tax-free shopping weeks held several times a year, or locating lost and found items on public transportation.

Directory help, including toll-free numbers, dial: 555-1212 preceded by the area code you are calling from.

Wrong number refunds, dial: 211.

Time Zone

New York is in the Eastern Standard Time zone (EST). This is five hours behind London, one hour ahead of Chicago, and three hours ahead of California.

PUBLIC HOLIDAYS

As with many other countries in the world, the United States has gradually shifted most of its public holidays to the Monday closest to the actual dates, thereby creating a number of three-day weekends. Holidays that are celebrated no matter what day they fall are:
New Year's Day (January 1).
Independence Day (July 4).
Veterans' Day (November 11).
Christmas Day (December 25).

Other holidays are:
Martin Luther King Jr Day (third Mon in Jan).
President's Day commemorating Lincoln and Washington (third Mon in Feb).
Memorial Day (last Mon in May).
Labor Day (first Mon in Sept).
Columbus Day (second Mon in Oct).
Election Day (first Tue in Nov, every four years for Presidential races).
Thanksgiving (fourth Thur in Nov).

Tourist Information

NYC & Company Visitor Information Center, 810 Seventh Ave (at 52nd and 53rd sts), New York, NY 10019, www.nycgo.com, tel: 212-484 1222, has an abundance of maps, brochures, and information about special hotel packages and discounts at various attractions.

They also publish the *Official NYC Guide*, a listing of activities, hotels, tours, and restaurants. NYC & Co. are able to provide information online, by mail, over the phone, or you can drop by the information center in person (Mon–Fri 8.30am–6pm, Sat–Sun 9am–5pm).

There are also official information kiosks in Harlem

Chinatown, and at the south-western tip of City Hall Park. The website www.nyc.gov is another useful tool for information.

Times Square Visitor Center is at the Embassy Theater, Seventh Ave between 46th and 47th sts, www.timessquarenyc.org, tel: 212-869 1890. It's a source of citywide information, with a ticket counter for shows, email facilities, and ATMs. It's open daily 8am–8pm, with free walking tours.

Greater Harlem Chamber of Commerce, 200A West 136th St, New York, NY 10030, http://greaterharlemchamber. com, tel: 212-862 7200. Information on tours, events, and landmarks in Harlem. There's also an information kiosk at 163 West 125th St.

Bronx Tourism Council, 851 Grand Concourse, Bronx NY 10451, www.ilovethebronx.com, tel: 718-590 2766. Information

CITY WEBSITES

Several boroughs have their own websites, listed here under "Tourist Information." Other websites that provide helpful information include: **www.newyork.citysearch. com** for listings and reviews of current arts and entertainment events, and restaurants and shopping. It's excellent for links to every conceivable aspect of New York City. **www.nyc.gov**, the official site of the City of New York, contains news items, mayoral updates, city agency information, and parking regulations. **www.nycgo.com**, the NYC & Co. Visitor Information site, which also has useful links. **www.nypl.org** is where you'll find everything you ever wanted to know about the New York Public Library. There's also an online information service.

about art, music, and other events.
Brooklyn Tourism and Visitors Center, 209 Joralemon St, Brooklyn, NY 11201, www.visit-brooklyn.org, tel: 718-802 3846. Information on culture, shopping, history, parks, events, and historic sites.

Queens Tourism Council, 90-15 Queens Blvd, Elmhurst, NY 11373, www.discoverqueens. info, tel: 718-592 2082. Provides museum and attraction information and tours.

Council on Arts and Humanities for Staten Island (COAHSI), Snug Harbor Cultural Center, 1000 Richmond Terrace, Staten Island, NY 10301, www.statenislandarts. org, tel: 718-447 3329. Lists cultural events and places of interest.

V

Visas and Passports

Due to increased security, the precise regulations for entry to the United States change often, and vary for citizens of different countries. It's a good

BELOW: tourist information.

idea to check on the current situation before you travel on www.cbp.gov or via a US embassy or consulate in your home country.

Currently, Canadians traveling by air must present a valid passport for entry. Visitors from the UK, Australia, New Zealand, and Ireland qualify for the visa waiver program, and therefore do not need a visa for stays of less than 90 days, as long as they have a valid 10-year machine-readable passport and a return ticket. However, they must apply online for authorization at least 72 hours before traveling at https://esta.cbp. dhs.gov. Citizens of South Africa need a visa. All foreign visitors will have their two index fingers scanned and a digital photograph taken at the port of entry. The process should take only 10–15 seconds.

W

Weights and Measures

The United States uses the Imperial system.

FURTHER READING

Fiction

The Age of Innocence
Edith Wharton
A classic, scathing depiction of New York high society.
Breakfast at Tiffany's
Truman Capote
The charming little novel made famous by the Audrey Hepburn film.
Bright Lights, Big City
Jay McInerney
A tale of fast times and big money in 1980s New York.
Let the Great World Spin
Colum McCann
A dizzying novel revolving around a cast of New York characters in 1974, including the man who walked on a tightrope between the World Trade Center towers.
Time and Again
Jack Finney
A man time travels to 1880s New York and gets a whole new perspective on the city.
Writing New York: A Literary Anthology
edited by Philip Lopate
Observations about life in New York by such literary greats as Henry David Thoreau, Walt Whitman, Maxim Gorky, and F. Scott Fitzgerald. Required reading for city-philes.

Guides

From Abyssinian to Zion, A Guide to Manhattan's Houses of Worship
David W. Dunlop
Listings of churches, temples, synagogues, mosques and all other major religious buildings.
New York: The Movie Lover's Guide
Richard Alleman
A detailed primer on famous film locations in the city.
The WPA Guide to New York City, Federal Writers Project Guide to 1930s New York
Federal Writers Project
The classic guide to New York, compiled during FDR's New Deal.

History and Culture

Gotham: A History of New York to 1898
Mike Wallace and Edwin G. Burrows
Pulitzer Prize-winning narrative about the city's early years; in-depth, with an emphasis on some of its characters.
The Great Bridge
David McCullogh
An exhaustive and thrilling history of the building of the Brooklyn Bridge.
The Island at the Center of the World
Russell Shorto
An account of the city in its early days, when it was called New Amsterdam.
Low Life
Luc Sante
Everything you always wanted to know about the gangs, gangsters, and general riff-raff who thrived at the edge of New York's society in the 19th century.

Lower East Side Memories: A Jewish Place in America
Hasia R. Diner
A cultural history of the Lower East Side and its Jewish community.
Manhattan '45
Jan Morris
A speculative portrait of a thriving city in the wake of World War II.
New York: An Illustrated History
Ric Burns
Coffee-table history, with brilliant photographs.
New York Characters
Gillian Zoe Segal
An exuberant and sympathetic account of 66 New Yorkers, photographed in their distinctive environments.

Memoir

Gone to New York
Ian Frazier
A collection of essays about the city from the 1970s–2000s.
Here is New York
E.B. White
An ode to the city in 1948 from the master stylist and author of Charlotte's Web.
Liar's Poker
Michael Lewis
A portrait of life on Wall Street in the 1980s.
Waterfront, A Journey Around New York
Phillip Lopate
A combination of memoir and cultural history – with a little nature thrown in – centered on the city's waterfront.

NEW YORK CITY STREET ATLAS

The key map shows the area of New York City covered by the atlas section. An index of street names and places of interest shown on the maps can be found on the following pages. For each entry there is a page number and grid reference

Map Legend

	Freeway with Exit
	Freeway (under construction)
	Divided Highway
	Main Road
	Secondary Road
	Minor Road
	Track
	International Boundary
	State/County Boundary
	National Park/Reserve
✈	Airport
†	Church (ruins)
†	Monastery
⌖	Castle (ruins)
∴	Archaeological Site
∩	Cave
★	Place of Interest
⌂	Mansion/Stately Home
☼	Viewpoint
⚑	Beach
	Freeway
	Divided Highway
	Main Roads
	Minor Roads
	Footpath
	Railroad
	Pedestrian Area
	Important Building
	Park
Ⓜ	Subway
🚌	Bus Station
❶	Tourist Information
✉	Post Office
✚	Cathedral/Church
☾	Mosque
✡	Synagogue
⚐	Statue/Monument
∏	Tower

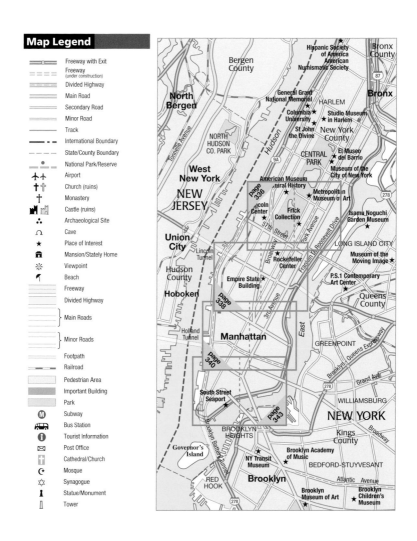

Restaurants ❶

Midtown West
104 Le Bernardin B4
107 Carnegie Deli B4
108 China Grill B4
110 Gallagher's Steakhouse A4
111 Il Gattopardo B4
115 The Modern B4
117 Russian Tea Room B4
119 Trattoria Dell'Arte B4
121 Wondee Siam and Wondee Siam II A4

Fifth Avenue
123 Adour Alain Ducasse at the St Regis B4
126 La Bonne Soupe B4
130 Harry Cipriani C4
134 Má Pêche B4
135 Mangia B4
136 Michael's B4
138 Quality Meats B4
140 Sarabeth's B4

Midtown East
159 Tao E1

Upper East Side
161 L'Absinthe D4
162 Beyoglu D/E2
163 Café Sabarsky D1
164 Candle 79 D2
165 Daniel C4
166 Demarchelier D1
167 E.J.'s Luncheonette D3
168 Fig & Olive C4
169 Girasole D2
170 Heidelberg E2
171 Hospoda D3
172 JoJo C/D4
173 Kings' Carriage House E2
174 Maya D4
175 Nica E2
176 Pascalou D1
177 Pio Pio E1
178 Sfoglia E1
179 Sushi of Gari E3
180 Il Vagabondo D4
181 Vivolo D3

Upper West Side
182 A Voce B3
183 Artie's Deli B1
184 Bar Boulud B3
185 Café Frida B1
186 Café Luxembourg B2
187 Calle Ocho C1
188 Dovetail C1
189 Isabella's B1
190 Jean-Georges B3
191 Kefi C1
192 Land B1
193 Ocean Grill B1
194 Picholine B3
195 Porter House New York B3
196 Shake Shack B1
197 Telepan B2

Bars & Cafés ❶

Midtown West
29 Burger Joint B4

Fifth Avenue
33 Hale & Hearty Soups B4
36 Oak Bar at The Plaza C4

Upper East Side
43 Cafe Carlyle D2
44 Sant Ambroeus D2
45 Serendipity 3 C/D4

Upper West Side
46 Alice's Tea Cup B2
47 Boat Basin Café B1
48 Bin 71 B2
49 Bouchon Bakery B3
50 Hudson A3
51 O'Neal's B3
52 Gray's Papaya B2
53 Stone Rose B3

Jacqueline Kennedy Onassis Reservoir

Transverse Rd No.3

GREAT LAWN

Belvedere Castle
Turtle Pond
Transverse Rd No.2

Alice in Wonderland

Hans Christian Andersen

Conservatory Water

Cleopatra's Needle

Metropolitan Museum of Art

American Irish Historical Society

Ukrainian Institute of America

Harkness House

Lenox Hill Hospital

77th St

Whitney Museum of American Art

Frick Collection

St James

Asia Society

Hunter College

Seventh Regiment Armory

68th St Hunter College

China Institute

Society of Illustrators

63rd St Lexington Ave

Bloomingdale's

59th St

Jewish Museum

Cooper-Hewitt National Design Museum

National Academy Museum

Guggenheim Museum

Neue Galerie New York

Park Ave Synagogue

East 96th St

95th St
94th St
93rd
92nd
91st
90th
89th
88th
87th
86th St
86th
85th
84th
83rd
82nd
81st
80th
79th
78th
77th
76th
75th
74th
73rd
72nd
71st
70th
69th
68th
67th
66th
65th
64th
63rd
62nd
61st

Park Avenue
Madison Avenue
Fifth Avenue
Lexington Avenue
Third Avenue
Second Avenue
First Avenue
York Avenue
East End Avenue
Franklin D. Roosevelt Drive

Holy Trinity Cathedral

JOHN JAY PARK

UPPER EAST SIDE

0   100   200   300   400 yds
0   100   200   300   400 m

Hotels 🏨

Midtown
32 Peninsula New York B4
33 The Plaza B/C4
34 St Regis B4
35 The Sherry-Netherland C4
40 Le Parker Meridien B4
45 Hilton New York B4
48 Hudson Hotel A3
60 Wellington Hotel B4

Upper East and West Side
61 The Carlyle D2
62 The Franklin E1

63 Mandarin Oriental B3
64 The Mark D2
65 The Pierre C4
66 The Surrey D2
67 Trump International Hotel and Tower B3
68 Beacon Hotel B1
69 Gracie Inn E3
70 Hotel Wales E1
71 The Lucerne Hotel B1
72 Comfort Inn – Central Park West B2
73 Hotel Excelsior C1
74 The Milburn B1

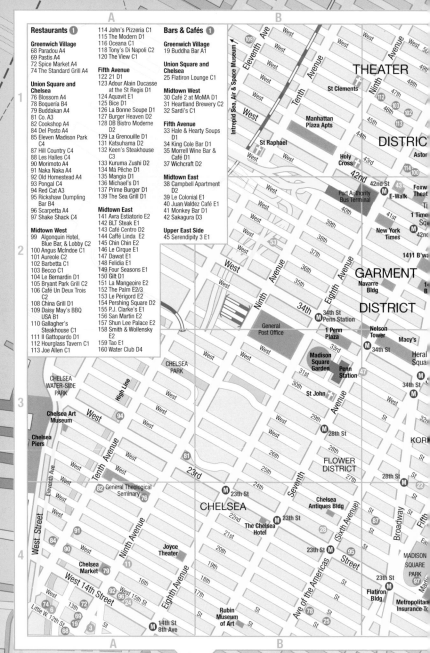

Restaurants 🔴

Greenwich Village
68 Paradou A4
69 Pastis A4
72 Spice Market A4
74 The Standard Grill A4

Union Square and Chelsea
76 Blossom A4
78 Boqueria B4
79 Buddakan A4
81 Co. A3
82 Cookshop A4
84 Del Posto A4
85 Eleven Madison Park C4
87 Hill Country C4
88 Les Halles C4
90 Morimoto A4
91 Naka Naka A4
92 Old Homestead A4
94 Pongal C4
94 Red Cat A3
95 Rickshaw Dumpling Bar B4
96 Scarpetta A4
97 Shake Shack C4

Midtown West
99 Algonquin Hotel, Blue Bar, & Lobby C2
100 Angus McIndoe C1
101 Aureole C2
102 Barbetta C1
103 Becco C1
104 Le Bernardin D1
105 Bryant Park Grill C2
106 Café Un Deux Trois C2
108 China Grill D1
109 Daisy May's BBQ USA B1
110 Gallagher's Steakhouse C1
111 Il Gattopardo D1
112 Hourglass Tavern C1
113 Joe Allen C1
114 John's Pizzeria C1
115 The Modern D1
116 Oceana C1
118 Tony's Di Napoli C2
120 The View C1

Fifth Avenue
122 21 D1
123 Adour Alain Ducasse at the St Regis D1
124 Aquavit E1
125 Bice D1
126 La Bonne Soupe D1
127 Burger Heaven D2
128 DB Bistro Moderne D2
129 La Grenouille D1
131 Katsuhama D2
132 Keen's Steakhouse C3
133 Kuruma Zushi D2
134 Mà Pêche D1
135 Mangia D1
136 Michael's D1
137 Prime Burger D1
139 The Sea Grill D1

Midtown East
141 Avra Estiatorio E2
142 BLT Steak E1
143 Café Centro D2
144 Caffé Linda E2
145 Chin Chin E2
146 Le Cirque E1
147 Dawat E1
148 Felidia E1
149 Four Seasons E1
150 Gilt D1
151 La Mangeoire E2
152 The Palm E2/3
153 Le Périgord E2
154 Pershing Square D2
155 P.J. Clarke's E1
156 San Martin E2
157 Shun Lee Palace E2
158 Smith & Wollensky E2
159 Tao E1
160 Water Club D4

Bars & Cafés 🔴

Greenwich Village
19 Buddha Bar A1

Union Square and Chelsea
25 Flatiron Lounge C1

Midtown West
30 Café 2 at MoMA D1
31 Heartland Brewery C2
32 Sardi's C1

Fifth Avenue
33 Hale & Hearty Soups D1
34 King Cole Bar D1
35 Morrell Wine Bar & Café D1
37 Wichcraft D2

Midtown East
38 Campbell Apartment D2
39 Le Colonial E1
40 Juan Valdez Café E1
41 Monkey Bar D1
42 Sakagura D3

Upper East Side
45 Serendipity 3 E1

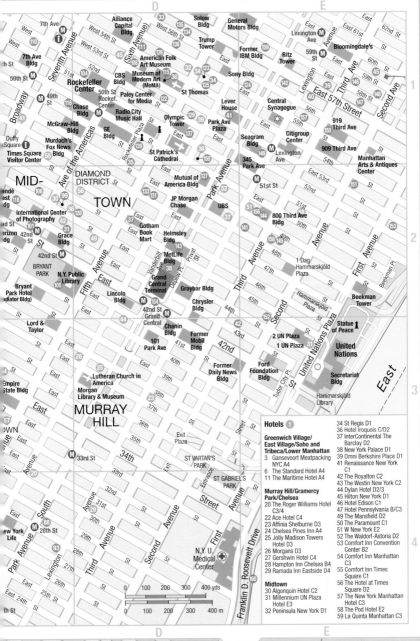

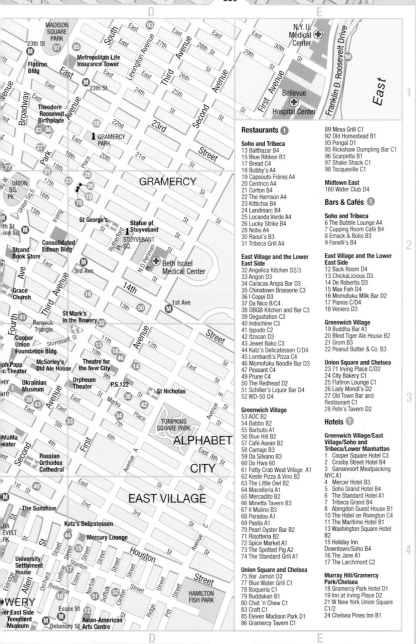

Restaurants

Soho and Tribeca
13 Balthazar B4
15 Blue Ribbon B3
17 Bread C4
18 Bubby's A4
19 Capsouto Frères A4
20 Centrico A4
21 Corton B4
22 The Harrison A4
23 Kittichai B4
24 Landmarc B4
25 Locanda Verde A4
26 Lucky Strike B4
30 Nobu A4
31 Tribeca Grill A4

East Village and the Lower East Side
32 Angelica Kitchen D2/3
33 Angon D3
34 Caracas Arepa Bar D3
35 Chinatown Brasserie C3
36 I Coppi D3
37 Da Nico B/C4
38 DBGB Kitchen and Bar C3
39 Degustation C3
40 Indochine C3
41 Ippudo C2
42 Itzocan D3
43 Jewel Bako C3
44 Katz's Delicatessen C/D4
45 Lombardi's Pizza C4
46 Momofuku Noodle Bar D3
47 Peasant C4
49 Prune C4
50 The Redhead D2
51 Schiller's Liquor Bar D4
52 WD-50 D4

Greenwich Village
53 AOC B2
54 Babbo B2
55 Barbuto A1
56 Blue Hill B2
57 Café Asean B2
58 Camaje B3
59 Da Silvano B3
60 Do Hwa 60
61 Fatty Crab West Village A1
62 Kesté Pizza & Vino B2
63 The Little Owl B2
64 Macelleria A1
65 Mercadito B2
66 Minetta Tavern B3
67 Il Mulino B3
68 Paradou A1
69 Pastis A1
70 Pearl Oyster Bar B2
71 Risotteria B3
72 Spice Market A1
73 The Spotted Pig A2
74 The Standard Grill A1

Union Square and Chelsea
75 Bar Jamón D2
77 Blue Water Grill C1
78 Boqueria C1
79 Buddakan B1
80 Chat 'n Chew C1
83 Craft C1
85 Eleven Madison Park D1
86 Gramercy Tavern C1

89 Mesa Grill C1
92 Old Homestead B1
93 Pongal D1
95 Rickshaw Dumpling Bar C1
96 Scarpetta B1
97 Shake Shack C1
98 Tocqueville C1

Midtown East
160 Water Club D4

Bars & Cafés

Soho and Tribeca
6 The Bubble Lounge A4
7 Cupping Room Café B4
8 Emack & Bolio's B3
9 Fanelli's B4

East Village and the Lower East Side
12 Back Room D4
13 ChickaLicious D3
14 De Robertis D3
15 Max Fish D4
16 Momofuku Milk Bar D2
17 Pianos C/D4
18 Veniero D3

Greenwich Village
19 Buddha Bar A1
20 Blind Tiger Ale House B2
21 Grom B3
22 Peanut Butter & Co. B3

Union Square and Chelsea
23 71 Irving Place C/D2
24 City Bakery C1
25 Flatiron Lounge C1
26 Lady Mendl's D2
27 Old Town Bar and Restaurant C1
28 Pete's Tavern D2

Hotels

Greenwich Village/East Village/Soho and Tribeca/Lower Manhattan
1 Cooper Square Hotel C3
2 Crosby Street Hotel B4
3 Gansevoort Meatpacking NYC A1
4 Mercer Hotel B3
5 Soho Grand Hotel B4
6 The Standard Hotel A1
7 Tribeca Grand B4
8 Abingdon Guest House B1
10 The Hotel on Rivington C4
11 The Maritime Hotel B1
13 Washington Square Hotel B2
15 Holiday Inn Downtown/Soho B4
16 The Jane A1
17 The Larchmont C2

Murray Hill/Gramercy Park/Chelsea
18 Gramercy Park Hotel D1
19 Inn at Irving Place D2
21 W New York Union Square C1/2
24 Chelsea Pines Inn B1

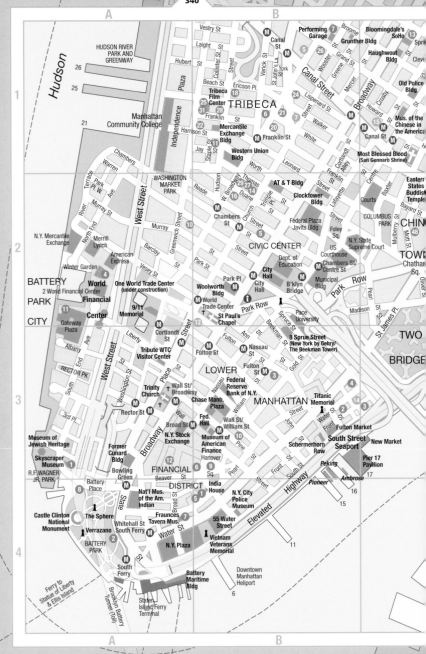

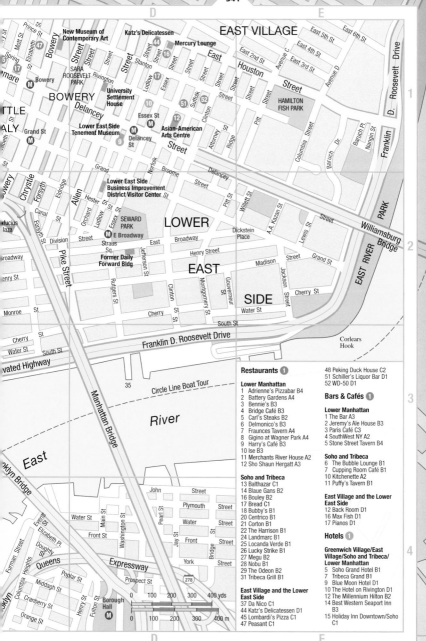

Restaurants ❶

Lower Manhattan
1 Adrienne's Pizzabar B4
2 Battery Gardens A4
3 Bennie's B3
4 Bridge Café B3
5 Carl's Steaks B2
6 Delmonico's B3
7 Fraunces Tavern A4
8 Gigino at Wagner Park A4
9 Harry's Café B3
10 Ise B3
11 Merchants River House A2
12 Sho Shaun Hergatt A3

Soho and Tribeca
13 Balthazar C1
14 Blaue Gans B2
16 Bouley B2
17 Bread C1
18 Bubby's B1
20 Centrico B1
21 Corton B1
22 The Harrison B1
24 Landmarc B1
25 Locanda Verde B1
26 Lucky Strike B1
27 Megu B2
28 Nobu B1
29 The Odeon B2
31 Tribeca Grill B1

East Village and the Lower East Side
37 Da Nico C1
44 Katz's Delicatessen D1
45 Lombardi's Pizza C1
47 Peasant C1

48 Peking Duck House C2
51 Schiller's Liquor Bar D1
52 WD-50 D1

Bars & Cafés ❶

Lower Manhattan
1 The Bar A3
2 Jeremy's Ale House B3
3 Paris Café C3
4 SouthWest NY A2
5 Stone Street Tavern B4

Soho and Tribeca
6 The Bubble Lounge B1
7 Cupping Room Café B1
10 Kitchenette A2
11 Puffy's Tavern B1

East Village and the Lower East Side
12 Back Room D1
16 Max Fish D1
17 Pianos D1

Hotels ❶

Greenwich Village/East Village/Soho and Tribeca/Lower Manhattan
5 Soho Grand Hotel B1
7 Tribeca Grand B1
9 Blue Moon Hotel D1
10 The Hotel on Rivington D1
12 The Millennium Hilton B2
14 Best Western Seaport Inn B3
15 Holiday Inn Downtown/Soho C1

STREET INDEX

ART AND PHOTO CREDITS

Alamy 33, 100, 104, 113, 115, 127B, 140, 207, 220T, 236, 254, 255T, 258, 294, 297, 298T, 301T
Algonquin Hotel 176
Dave Allocca/Rex Features 237
Art Archive 27B
AWL Images 16, 54, 142B, 146, 162, 198, 250, 292, 295L
Cristina Bejarano 155
Karen Blumberg 64
Michael Bodycomb/The Frick Collection 215T&B
Howard Brier 277B
Brooklyn Museum of Art/Central Photo Archives 270BL&BR, 271
Franco Caruzzo 127T
Century 21 84
Children's Museum of the Arts 99T
Collections of the New York Historical Society 102TL
Corbis 9BL, 26L, 28R, 29, 31, 34, 36, 43, 80, 88, 218, 256, 281, 290
Carolyn Contino/BEI/Rex Features 169
Mary Evans Picture Library 28T
Fotolia 8C, 9CL, 10T, 11T&CL, 119B, 132
Fotolibra 284T
Four Seasons 210
The Frick Collection 216T
Getty Images 11CR, 35, 37, 38R, 39, 48, 89, 114T, 134R, 135BR, 165T, 166T, 172B, 174, 253, 255B, 262, 263, 274R
Gramercy Park Hotel 147
Gramercy Tavern 158
greyloch on flickr 219B
H&H Bagels 175
Tony Halliday 82B, 232B
Robert Harding World Imagery 25, 291, 299
Sarah Heiman 269
Hotel on Rivington 310
Daniel Huggard 268B
Hotel Gansevoort 8BL
iStockphoto 1, 6R, 7CL&BL, 40L, 65R, 71BR, 82T, 101, 140T, 157T, 185BL, 190B, 201, 203T, 204B, 206, 213, 219T, 259B, 265L, 295R, 296, 298B, 301B, 302
Britta Jaschinski/APA 5B, 7TR, 20L, 21L&R, 22L, 24T, 51L, 56, 65L, 72T, 73BR, 74, 76B, 77B, 78TR, 87, 98T, 99B, 106, 107, 111, 112TL, 117T, 118B, 119T, 121TL&B, 125, 128, 133T, 134L, 137B, 138T&BL, 142T, 145, 149B, 163, 166B, 168, 170T&B, 171, 183, 185TL, 186T, 187T&B, 188T&B, 189T, 190T, 193, 199, 205TR&B, 211, 216B, 221, 231, 232T, 234, 239, 240, 241, 257T, 264, 265BR, 266BL&R, 269B, 273BR, 274L, 275, 276T&B, 278, 285T, 287, 306, 323, 327, 328, 331, 332

Bernd Jonkmanns/laif/Camerapress 267
Jens Karlsson 102TR
Ozan Kilic 284B
Jason Kuffer 321
Patrick Kwan 123T
Library of Congress 28B, 203B
Maya Lin Studio/MCA 126
Daniel Lobo 222
Lordcolus on flickr 135BL
Paul Lowry 165B
Illustrated London News 30
Mandarin Oriental 316
Merchant's House Museum 112TR&B
The Metropolitan Museum of Art 260T&B
Mockford & Bonetti/APA 4B, 7C&BR, 70, 71T, 204T, 317B
Momos 114B
Morgan Library 200T&B
National Museum of the American Indian 75T
New York City Ballet 233
New York Palace Hotel 313
New York Public Library 26R, 32
Keiko Niwa/Lower East Side Tenement Museum 120, 121TR
Abe Nowitz/APA 6CL, 7TL, 9TR, 12/13, 17L&R, 20R, 55, 57, 71L, 72B, 73T&BL, 75B, 76T, 77T, 78B, 81TL, 83, 94, 95, 97T&B, 98B, 105, 110, 118T, 122, 131, 135T, 136TR&B, 138BR, 139, 141T, 144, 149T, 150, 151, 152T&B, 153B, 154T&B, 156T&B, 157B, 159, 182, 186B, 191T&B, 202B, 205TL, 208T, 217T&B, 220B, 230, 235B, 251, 257B, 259T, 261, 304T&B, 307, 308B, 317T, 318, 325, 333
Richard Nowitz/APA 4T, 6TL, 7CR, 51R, 69, 78TL, 79, 81TR&B, 85, 86T, 123B, 167T&B, 280T&B, 326
PA/EPA 41
Padraic on flickr 277T
Douglas Palmer 268T
Peninsula Hotels 312
Andrea Pistolesi 18
David Poe 50
Mark Read/APA 129, 136TL
River Café 286
Rubin Museum of Art 153T
Thomas Schauer/Daniel 223
Roger Schultz 172T
Sipa Press/Rex Features 41R, 42
Sony 208B
The Standard 309
Starwood Hotels & Resorts 192, 308T, 311
SuperStock 10B, 44/45, 49B, 68, 86B, 124, 141L&BR, 143, 173, 189B, 212, 265T, 270T, 272, 273T, 282, 283, 288/289, 300L
Tips Images 14/15, 62/63, 235T
Tony the Misfit on flickr 273BL

TopFoto 26B, 38L, 137T
David Trawin 285B
Tribeca Film Festival 49R, 103
Tribeca Grand Hotel 102B
Trump Entertainment Resorts 300R
ukanda on flickr 279T
Waldorf-Astoria Hotel 315
Charlie Walker 116
Wellcome Images 279B
Jay Woodworth 266T
Ed Yourdon 19, 22R, 23, 24B, 47, 60/61, 130, 133B, 202T, 238, 319

PHOTO FEATURES

52/53: all images **Alamy** except 52/53T **Universal/Everett/Rex Features**
58/59: Thérèse De Belder/Wafels & Dinges 59BL; Fotolia 58TL, 59TR; iStockphoto 58/59B; Abe Nowitz/APA 58CR; Rickshaw Dumplings 59BR; Ed Yourdon 58BL, 58/59T
90/91: Corbis 90CR; **iStockphoto** 91BR; **Library of Congress** 91BL; **Mockford & Bonetti/APA** 90L, 91BL; **Nowitz/APA** 90/91
92/93: all **Britta Jaschinski/APA**
108/109: Dan Callister/Rex Features 108/109B; **Century 21** 109BR; **Fotolia** 109C; **Kevin Foy/Rex Features** 109TR; **Abe Nowitz/APA** 108BR, 109BL; **Mark Read/APA** 108TL&BL
160/161: Jaschinski/APA 161C; Nowitz/APA 160TL, 160/161, 161BL; TopFoto 160BR, 161BR; Marcus Wilson-Smith/APA 161TR
178/181: All **Museum of Modern Art** except 181BR **Alamy** and 178TL&179BL **Jaschinski/APA**
194/195: All **Ed Yourdon** except 194BL **Mockford & Bonetti/APA** and 195CR **Jaschinski/APA**
196/197: All **Jaschinski/APA** except 196/197 **Getty Images** and 197BR **Ed Yourdon**
224/227: all **Metropolitan Museum of Art** except 224/225 **Jaschinski/APA** and 224BR, 225CR, 226B **Mockford & Bonetti/APA**
228/229: Jewish Museum/John Parnell 229CR; Museum of the City of New York 228/229, 229CL; Nowitz/APA 228BL&BR; Mike Yamashita/Woodfin Camp 229BR
242/245: all **Jaschinski/APA** except 242/243 **Alamy;** 242CR, 243CR, 244/245 **Juillard School** and 245CL&BL **Metropolitan Opera**
246/249: all **American Natural History Museum** except 247TR, CR&BR, 248T&BL **Jaschinski/APA** and 246TL **Mockford & Bonetti/APA**

INDEX

RESTAURANTS

BARS AND CAFES

INSIGHT GUIDE
NEW YORK CITY

Project Editor
Astrid deRidder
Series Manager
Rachel Lawrence
Designer
Tom Smyth
Map Production
**original cartography Berndtson
& Berndtson, updated by Apa**
*Cartography
Production*
**Tynan Dean, Linton Donaldson and
Rebeka Ellam**

Distribution

UK
Dorling Kindersley Ltd
A Penguin Group company
80 Strand, London, WC2R 0RL
customerservice@dk.com
United States
Ingram Publisher Services
1 Ingram Boulevard, PO Box 3006,
La Vergne, TN 37086-1986
customer.service@ingrampublisher
services.com
Australia
Universal Publishers
PO Box 307
St Leonards NSW 1590
sales@universalpublishers.com.au
New Zealand
Brown Knows Publications
11 Artesia Close, Shamrock Park
Auckland, New Zealand 2016
sales@brownknows.co.nz
Worldwide
**Apa Publications GmbH & Co.
Verlag KG (Singapore branch)**
7030 Ang Mo Kio Avenue 5
08-65 Northstar @ AMK
Singapore 569880
apasin@singnet.com.sg

Printing

CTPS-China
© 2012 Apa Publications (UK) Ltd
All Rights Reserved

First Edition 1991
Eighth Edition 2012

ABOUT THIS BOOK

What makes an Insight Guide different? Since our first book pioneered the use of full-color photography used creatively in travel guides in 1970, we have aimed to provide not only reliable information but also the key to a real understanding of a destination and its people.

Now, when the internet can supply inexhaustible (but not always reliable) facts, our books marry text and pictures to provide that more elusive quality: knowledge. To achieve this, they rely on the authority of locally based writers and photographers.

This new edition of *City Guide New York* was commissioned by **Astrid de Ridder** and updated by **Aaron Starmer**, who has spent the last twelve years haunting the streets, parks, and restaurants of New York City. Aaron has written and contributed to numerous guidebooks and is the author of two novels for young people, *DWEEB* and *The Only Ones*.

As well as checking and updating every chapter, Aaron also wrote the feature boxes on the World Trade Center, Washington Square Park and Harlem's Gospel Choirs. He contributed a completely new chapter on day trips and excursions from New York City, covering Long Island, Hudson Valley, and the Jersey Shore.

This edition builds on text of writers who contributed to previous editions, including **John Gattuso**, who wrote the history section, **Sherri Eisenberg**, **Kathy Novak**, **Mimi Tompkins**, **Tom Cavalieri**, **Joanna Potts**, **Divya Symmers**, **Nick Rider**, **David Whelan**, **A. Peter Bailey**, **Michele Abruzzi**, **John Wilcock**, and **John Strausbaugh**.

The principal photographers were **Abe Nowitz** and **Britta Jaschinski**, both regular contributors to Insight Guides. Special thanks also to **Ed Yourdon**. The book was copy-edited by **Pamela Afram**, proofread by **Neil Titman** and the index was compiled by **Penny Phenix**.

SEND US YOUR THOUGHTS

We do our best to ensure the information in our books is as accurate and up-to-date as possible. The books are updated on a regular basis using local contacts, who painstakingly add, amend, and correct as required. However, some details (such as telephone numbers and opening times) are liable to change, and we are ultimately reliant on our readers to put us in the picture.

We welcome your feedback, especially your experience of using the book "on the road". Maybe you recommended a hotel that you liked (or another that you didn't), or you came across a great bar or new attraction that we missed.

We will acknowledge all contributions, and we'll offer an Insight Guide to the best letters received.

Please write to us at:
**Insight Guides
PO Box 7910, London SE1 1WE**
Or email us at:
insight@apaguide.co.uk

THE WORLD OF
INSIGHT GUIDES

Different people need different kinds of travel information.
Some want background facts. Others seek personal
recommendations. With a variety of different products – Insight Guides,
Insight City Guides, Step by Step Guides, Smart Guides,
Insight Fleximaps and our new Great Breaks series –
we offer readers the perfect choice.

Insight Guides will turn your visit into an experience.